Archibald Alexander

Thoughts on Religious Experience' To Which is Added an Appendix

Archibald Alexander

Thoughts on Religious Experience' To Which is Added an Appendix

ISBN/EAN: 9783337719647

Printed in Europe, USA, Canada, Australia, Japan

Cover: Foto ©Lupo / pixelio.de

More available books at **www.hansebooks.com**

THOUGHTS

ON

RELIGIOUS EXPERIENCE.

TO WHICH IS ADDED

AN APPENDIX, CONTAINING "LETTERS TO THE AGED," &c. &c.

BY THE

Rev. ARCHIBALD ALEXANDER, D. D.

Professor of Pastoral and Polemic Theology in the Princeton Theological Seminary.

PHILADELPHIA:
PRESBYTERIAN BOARD OF PUBLICATION,
NO. 821 CHESTNUT STREET.

Entered according to Act of Congress in the year 1841 by
A. W. MITCHELL, M. D.
in the Office of the Clerk of the District Court for the Eastern District
of Pennsylvania.

Entered according to Act of Congress in the year 1868 by
THE TRUSTEES OF THE
PRESBYTERIAN BOARD OF PUBLICATION,
in the Office of the Clerk of the District Court for the Eastern District
of Pennsylvania.

CONTENTS.

CHAPTER I.
Early religious impressions.—Different results.—Classes of persons least impressed.—Examples of ineffectual impressions.   13

CHAPTER II.
Piety in children.—Comparatively few renewed in infancy and childhood.—Soul awakened in different ways.—Legal conviction not a necessary part of true religion.—Progress of conviction.   22

CHAPTER III.
The new birth an event of great importance.—The evidences of the new birth.—Diversities of experience in Converts.—Examples.—Causes of diversity.   35

CHAPTER IV.
Causes of diversity in experience continued.—Effect of temperament.—Melancholy.—Advice to the friends of persons thus affected.—Subject continued.—Illustrative cases.—Causes of melancholy and insanity.   48

CHAPTER V.
Effect of sympathy illustrated.—Cautions in relation to this subject.—A singular case in illustration.   69

CHAPTER VI.
Erroneous views of regeneration.—The correct view.—The operation of faith.—Exercises of mind, as illustrated in President Edwards's Narrative.—The operations of faith still further explained.   79

CHAPTER VII.
Considerations on dreams, visions, &c.—Remarkable conversion of a blind infidel from hearing the Bible read.   102

CHAPTER VIII.
Religious Conversation.—Stress laid by some on the knowledge of the time and place of conversion.—Religious experience of Halyburton.   120

CHAPTER IX.
Christian experience of R—— C——.—Narrative of Sir Richard Hill's experience.   134

CHAPTER X.
Imperfect sanctification.—The spiritual warfare.   156

CONTENTS.

CHAPTER XI.
Narrative of G—— A—— S——, an Episcopal Clergyman.
Narrative of a young Officer in the Army. . . . 167

CHAPTER XII.
The spiritual conflict.—Various exhibitions of it.—Evil thoughts.
A case in illustration. 177

CHAPTER XIII.
Growth in grace.—Signs of it.—Practical directions how to
grow in grace.—Hindrances to it. 191

CHAPTER XIV.
Backsliding.—The Backslider restored. . . . 205

CHAPTER XV.
The rich man and the poor.—The various trials of believers. 215

CHAPTER XVI.
Death-bed of the Believer. 225

CHAPTER XVII.
Death-bed exercises of Andrew Rivet. . . . 234

CHAPTER XVIII.
Death-bed exercises and speeches of Rev. Thomas Halyburton. 250

CHAPTER XIX.
Dying Experience of Mr. John Janeway, the Rev. Edward Payson, and Rev. Samuel Finley, D. D. . . . 259

CHAPTER XX.
Remarks on death-bed Exercises, with several illustrative examples. 271

CHAPTER XXI.
Death-bed exercises of Mr. Baxter, and the Rev. Thomas Scott, D. D. 282

CHAPTER XXII.
Preparation for death.—The state of the soul after death. 294

PRAYER for one who feels that he is approaching the borders of another world. 307

APPENDIX.
Letters to the Aged. 313
Counsels of the Aged to the Young. 343
Counsels to Christian Mothers. 374
Letter to a Mourning Afflicted Widow. . . . 387
Letter to a Bereaved Widower. 392

PREFACE.

THERE are two kinds of religious knowledge, which though intimately connected as cause and effect, may nevertheless be distinguished. These are the knowledge of the truth as it is revealed in the Holy Scriptures, and the impression which that truth makes on the human mind when rightly apprehended. The first may be compared to the inscription or image on a seal; the other to the impression made by the seal on the wax. When that impression is clearly and distinctly made, we can understand, by contemplating it, the true inscription on the seal more satisfactorily, than by a direct view of the seal itself. Thus it is found, that nothing tends more to confirm and elucidate the truths contained in the word, than an inward experience of their efficacy on the heart. It cannot, therefore, be uninteresting to the Christian, to have these effects, as they consist in the various views and affections of the mind, traced out, and exhibited in their connexion with the truth, and in their relation to each other. There is, however one manifest disadvantage, under which we must labour, in acquiring this kind of knowledge, whether by our own experience, or that of others; which is, that we are obliged to follow a fallible guide; and the pathway to this knowledge is very intricate, and the light which shines upon it, often obscure. All investigations of the exercises of the human mind are attended with difficulty; and never more so, than when we attempt to ascertain the religious or spiritual state of our hearts If, indeed, the impression of the truth were perfect, there would exist little or no difficulty, but when it is a mere outline and the lineaments obscure, it becomes extremely difficult to determine whether it be the genuine impress of the truth: especially as in this case, there will be much darkness and confusion in the mind, and much that is of a nature directly opposite to the effects of the engrafted word. There is, moreover, so great a variety in the constitution of human minds, so much diversity in the strength of the natural passions, and so wide a difference in the temperament of Christians, and so many different degrees of piety, that the study of this department of religious truth is exceedingly difficult. In many cases the most experienced and skil ful casuist will feel himself at a loss; or may utterly mistake, in regard to the true nature of a case submitted to his consideration. The complete knowledge of the deceitful heart of man, is a prerogative of the omniscient God. "I the Lord search the hearts and try the reins of the children of men." But we are not on this account forbidden to search into this subject; so far is this from being true, that we are repeatedly exhorted to examine ourselves, in relation to this very point; and Paul expresses astonishment, that the Corinthian Christians should have made so little progress in self-knowledge. "Examine yourselves," says he, "whether you be in the faith—prove your own selves—know ye not that Jesus Christ is in you, except ye be reprobates?" In judging of religious experience, it is all important to keep steadily in view the system of divine truth, contained in the Holy Scriptures; otherwise, our experience, as is too often the case, will degenerate into enthusiasm. Many ardent professors, seem too readily to take it for granted, that all religious feelings must be good. They therefore take no care to discriminate between the genuine and the spurious, the pure gold and the tinsel. Their only concern is about the ardour of their feelings; not considering, that if they are spurious, the more intense they are, the further will they lead them astray. In our day, there is nothing more necessary than to distinguish carefully between true and false experiences, in religion; to "try the spirits whether they are of God." And in making this discrimination, there is no other test but the infallible word of God; let every thought, motive, impulse and emotion, be brought to this touchstone. "To the law and the testimony; if they speak not according to these, it is because there is no light in them."

If genuine religious experience is nothing but the impression of divine truth on the mind, by the energy of the Holy Spirit, then it is evident that a knowledge of the truth is essential to genuine piety; error never can, under any circumstances, produce the effects of truth. This is now generally acknowledged. But it is not so clearly understood by all, that any defect in our knowledge of the truth, must, just so far as the error extends, mar the symmetry of the impression produced. The error, in this case, is of course not supposed to relate to fundamental truths, for then there can be no genuine piety; but where a true impression is made, it may be rendered very defective, for want of a complete knowledge of the whole system of revealed truth; or its beauty marred by the existence of some errors mingled with the truth, which may be well illustrated by returning again to the seal. Suppose that some part of the image inscribed on it has been defaced, or that some of the letters have been obliterated, it is evident, that when the impression is made on the wax, there will be a corresponding deficiency or deformity, although in the main the impress may be correct. There is reason to believe, therefore, that all ignorance of revealed truth, or error respecting it, must be attended with a corresponding defect in the religious exercises of the person. This consideration teaches us the importance of truth, and the duty of increasing daily in the knowledge of our Lord and Saviour Jesus Christ. This is the true and only method of growing in grace. There may be much correct theoretical knowledge, I admit, where there is no impression corresponding with it on the heart; but still, all good impressions on the heart, are from the truth, and from the truth alone. Hence we find, that those denominations of Christians which receive the system of evangelical truth, only in part, have a defective experience; and their Christian character, as a body, is so far defective; and even where true piety exists, we often find a sad mixture of enthusiasm, self-righteousness, or superstition. And even where the theory of doctrinal truth is complete, yet if there be an error respecting the terms of Christian communion, by narrowing the entrance into Christ's fold to a degree which his word does not authorize this single error, whatever professions may be made to the contrary with the lips, always generates a narrow spirit of bigotry, which greatly obstructs the free exercise of that brotherly love which Christ made the badge of discipleship.

If these things be so, then let all Christians use unceasing diligence in acquiring a correct knowledge of the truth as it is in Jesus; and let them pray without ceasing for the influence of the Holy Spirit, to render the truth effectual in the sanctification of the whole man, soul, body, and spirit. "SANCTIFY THEM THROUGH THY TRUTH, THY WORD IS TRUTH," was a prayer offered up by Christ, in behalf of all whom the Father had given him.

ADVERTISEMENT.

THE following thoughts on Religious Experience, were, for the most part, published in successive numbers, in the "Watchman of the South," and thence transferred to several other papers, belonging to different denominations; so that they have been pretty widely circulated through the religious community. They were commenced without any view to their being collected into a volume; and, indeed, without any plan or purpose, in regard to the extent to which the subject would be pursued. They were generally written hastily, in such fragments of time as could be spared from the daily duties of an arduous profession, and in a state of health far from being perfect. This is the only apology which the author has to offer, for the imperfections which will doubtless be found in them. For although he has cursorily revised them since the call was made for their re-publication, in this form, yet he has made no alteration of any consequence. He is thank ful to God, that they have been made useful to a single soul; and that they may be rendered still more so, is his humble prayer. He would, however, inform the reader that one third or one fourth of this volume, principally the latter part, has never before been published.

ADDENDUM TO P. 21 —Since the above was published, an aged friend, who recognized the person spoken of, informed me that this lady, after some time spent in gayety, resumed her profession of religion, and until her decease exhibited good evidence of genuine piety.

ADDENDUM TO P. 119.—Some time after the above account was published, the Rev. Robert Steel, D. D., informed the author that, owing to his ignorance of certain circumstances, he had not done justice to Mr. Inglis, in his account of his latter days. He has since learned that what he took for penuriousness, arose from anxious desire to save as much money from his scanty income, as would enable him to liquidate some debts which he had contracted before he was struck with blindness. The author feels assured that his readers will be gratified with this explanation, as it is a gracious promise to such saints as live many years, "that they shall still bring forth fruit in old age." Psa. xcii. 14.

A. A.

RELIGIOUS EXPERIENCE.

CHAPTER I.

Early religious impressions—Different results—Classes of persons least impressed—Examples of ineffectual impressions.

THERE is no necessity for any other proof of native depravity, than the aversion, which children early manifest to religious instruction and to spiritual exercises. From this cause it proceeds, that many children, who have the opportunity of a good religious education, learn scarcely any thing of the most important truths of Christianity. If they are compelled to commit the catechism to memory, they are wont to do this without ever thinking of the doctrines contained in the words which they recite; so that, when the attention is at any time awakened to the subject of religion, as a personal concern, they feel themselves to be completely ignorant of the system of divine truth taught in the Bible. Yet even to these, the truths committed to memory are now of great utility. They are like a treasure which has been hidden, but is now discovered. Of two persons under conviction of sin, one of whom has had sound religious instruction, and the other none, the former will have an unspeakable advantage over the latter in many respects.

Many children, and especially those who have pious parents, who speak to them of the importance of salvation, are the subjects of occasional religious impressions, of different kinds. Sometimes they are alarmed by hearing an awakening sermon, or by the sudden death of a companion of their own age; or, again, they are tenderly affected, even to tears, from a consideration of the goodness and forbearance of God, or from a representation of the love and sufferings of Christ. There are also seasons of transporting joy, which some experience, especially after being tenderly affected with a sense of ingratitude to God for his wonderful goodness, in sparing them and bestowing so many blessings upon them. These transient emotions of joy cannot always be easily accounted for, but they are commonly preceded or accompanied by a hope, or persuasion, that God is reconciled and will receive them. In some cases it would be thought that these juvenile exercises were indications of a change of heart, did they not pass away like the morning cloud, or early dew, so as even to be obliterated from the mind which experienced them. Some undertake to account for these religious impressions, merely from the susceptible principle of human nature, in connection with the external instructions of the word, and some striking dispensations of Providence; but the cause assigned is not adequate, because the same circumstances often exist, when no such effects follow. Others ascribe them to the evil spirit, who is ever seeking to deceive and delude unwary souls, by inspiring them with a false persuasion of their good estate, while they are in the gall of bitterness and bonds of iniquity. While I would not deny that Satan may take advantage of these transient exercises to induce a false hope, I cannot be persuaded that he produces these impressions; for often the persons, before experiencing them, were as careless and stupid as he could wish them to be; and because the tendency of these impressions is salutary. The youth, thus affected, becomes more tender in conscience, forsakes known sin before indulged, has recourse to prayer, and feels strong desires after eternal happiness. These are not what Satan would effect, if he could; unless we could suppose that he was operating against himself, which our Saviour has taught us to be impossible. I am of opinion, therefore, that these transient impressions should be ascribed to the common operations of the Spirit of God, and may have some inexplicable connection with the future conversion and salvation of the person. There is a common practical error in the minds of many Christians in regard to this matter. They seem to think that nothing has any relation to the conversion of the sinner, but that which immediately preceded this event; and the Christian is ready to say, I was awakened under such a sermon, and never had rest until I found it in Christ; making nothing of all previous instructions and impressions. So, when a revival occurs under the awakening discourses of some evangelist, people are ready to think that he only is the successful preacher whose labours God owns and blesses; whereas, he does but bring forward to maturity, feelings and convictions, which have been long secretly forming and growing within the soul, but so imperceptibly, that the person himself was little sensible of any change. It may be justly and scripturally compared to a growing crop: after the seed is sown it vegetates, we know not how, and then it receives daily the sun's influence, and from time to time, refreshing showers; but about the time of earing, after a long drought, there comes a plentiful shower, by means of which, nutriment is afforded for the formation of the full corn in the ear. No one will dispute the importance and efficacy of this last shower in maturing the grain; but had there been no cultivation and no showers long before, this had never produced any effect.

Whether those who are never converted, are the subjects of these religious impressions, as well as those who are afterwards brought to faith in Christ, is a question not easily answered. That they experience dreadful alarms and pungent convictions at times, and also tender drawings, cannot be doubted; but whether those "chosen in Christ" are not, in their natural state, subject to impressions which others never experience, must remain undetermined, since we know so little of the real state of the hearts of most men; but as there is, undoubtedly, a special providence exercised by Christ over those sheep not yet called into the fold, I cannot but think it probable that they are often influenced by the Holy Spirit in a peculiar manner, to guard them against fatal errors and destructive habits, and to prepare them, by degrees, to receive the truth.

We know very little, however, of what is passing in the minds of thousands around us. The zealous preacher often concludes and laments that there is no impression on the minds of his hearers, when, if the covering of the human heart could be withdrawn, he would be astonished and confounded at the variety and depth of the feelings experienced. Those impressions which manifest themselves by a flow of tears, are not the deepest, but often very superficial; while the most awful distresses of the soul are entirely concealed by a kind of hypocrisy, which men early learn to practise, to hide their feelings of a religious kind from their fellow-creatures. A man may be so much in despair as to be meditating suicide, when his nearest friends know nothing of it. The attempt at immediate effect, and the expectation of it, is one of the errors of the present times; indeed, it is the very watch-word of a certain party. But let us not be misunderstood; we do not mean to say that all men are not under indispensable obligations immediately to obey all the commands of God. Concerning this, there can be no difference of opinion. But the persons to whom we refer seem to think that nothing is done towards the salvation of men, but at the moment of their conversion, and that every good effect must be at once manifest. Perhaps some one may infer that we believe in a gradual regeneration, and that special grace differs from common, only in degree; but such an inference would be utterly false, for there can be no medium between life and death; but we do profess to believe and maintain, that there is a gradual preparation, by common grace, for regeneration, which may be going on from childhood to mature age; and we believe that, as no mortal can tell the precise mo ment when the soul is vivified, and as the principle of spiritual life in its commencement is often very feeble, so it is an undoubted truth, that the development of the new life in the soul may be, and often is, very slow; and not unfrequently that which is called *conversion* is nothing else but a more sensible and vigorous exercise of a principle which has long existed. Just as the seed under ground may have life, and may be struggling to come forth to open day; but it may meet with various obstructions and unfavourable circumstances which retard its growth. At length, however, it makes its way through the earth, and expands its leaves to the light and the air, and begins to drink in from every source that nutriment which it needs. No one supposes, however, that the moment of its appearing above ground is the commencement of its life; but this mistake is often made in the analogous case of the regeneration of the soul. The first clear and lively exercise of faith and repentance is made the date of the origin of spiritual life, whereas it existed in a feeble state, and put forth obscure acts long before. I find, however, that I am anticipating a discussion intended for another part of this work.

At present, I wish only to remark further, that what has been said about early impressions and juvenile exercises of religion is not applicable to all.

There are, alas! many who seem to remain unmoved amidst all the light and means by which most are surrounded in this land; and these, too, are often found in the families of the pious, and do actually pass through more than one revival without partaking of any unusual influence, or experiencing any strong religious feeling. Esau had a title to the birthright, and yet he so despised this peculiar blessing, that he actually sold it for "a mess of pottage." Abraham, too, had his Ishmael, and Jacob a troop of ungodly children. Eli's sons were wicked in the extreme, and Samuel's came not up to what was expected from the children of such a father. Among all David's children we read of none who feared God but Solomon. Those, however, who become extremely wicked have often resisted the strivings of the Spirit; and not unfrequently the most impious blasphemers and atheists have once been much under the influence of religious light and feeling; but quenching the Spirit, have been given up to " believe a lie," and " to work all uncleanness with greediness."

We have said that there are some persons who grow up to manhood without experiencing any religious impressions, except mere momentary thoughts of death, and judgment; and these may be persons of a very amiable disposition and moral deportment, and these very qualities may be, in part, the reason of their carelessness. They commit no gross sins, the remembrance of which wounds the conscience. Being of a calm and contented temper, and fond of taking their ease, they shun religious reflection, and turn away their thoughts from the truth, when it is presented to them from the pulpit. Some persons, of this description, have been awakened and converted, at mature age, and have then confessed, that they lived as much without God as atheists, and seldom, if ever, extended their thoughts to futurity. Of course they utterly neglected secret prayer, and lived in the midst of gospel light, without being in the least affected by it.

There is, moreover, another class, who seem never to feel the force of religious truth. They are such as spend their whole waking hours in the giddy whirl of amusement or company. Full of health and spirits, and sanguine in their hopes of enjoyment from the world, they put away serious reflection as the very bane of pleasure. The very name of religion is hateful to them: and all they ask of religious people is to let them alone, that they may seize the pleasures of life while within their reach. If we may judge from appearances, this class is very large. We find them the majority in many places of fashionable resort. The theatre, the ball-room, and the very streets are full of such. They flutter gaily along, and keep each other in countenance; while they are strangers to all grave reflection, even in regard to the sober concerns of this life. If a pious friend ever gets the opportunity of addressing a word of serious advice to them, their politeness may prevent them from behaving rudely, but no sooner is his back turned, than they laugh him to scorn, and hate and despise him for his pains. They habituate themselves to think that religion is an awkward unseemly thing, and wonder how any person of sense can bear to attend to it. Very often this high reverie of pleasure is short: in such a world as this, events are apt to occur, which dash the cup of sensual delights, while it is at the lips. Death will occasionally intrude even upon this gay circle, and put a speedy end to their unreasonable merriment. O how sad is the spectacle, to see one of the votaries of fashion suddenly cut down, and carried to the grave!—When mortal sickness seizes such persons, they are very apt to be delirious, if not with fever, yet with fright; and their officious but cruel friends make it their chief study, to bar out every idea of religion, and to flatter the poor dying creature with the hope of recovery, until death has actually seized his prey. Such an event produces a shock in the feelings of survivors of the same class, but such is the buoyancy of their feelings, and their forgetfulness of mournful events, that they are soon seen dancing along their slippery path, with as much insane thoughtlessness, as before. Nothing, which ever occurs, tends so much to disturb the career of this multitude, as when one of their number is converted unto God. At first they are astounded, and for a moment pause, but they soon learn to ascribe the change to some natural cause, or to some strange capriciousness of temper, or disappointment in earthly hopes. Very soon you will see them as much estranged from such an one, although before an intimate friend, as if he had never been of the number of their acquaintances. Often his nearest relatives are ashamed of him, and as much as possible, shun his company. How absurd then is it, for any to pretend, that men naturally love God, and only need to know his character to revere it! If there be a truth established beyond all reasonable question, by uniform experience, it is, that lovers of pleasure are the enemies of God.

The class of speculating, money-making, business-doing men, is probably as numerous, and, though more sober in their thoughts, yet as far from God, and as destitute of religion as those already described; but as we find these not commonly among the youth, but middle aged, we shall not attempt to delineate their character, or describe their feelings. I must return to the consideration of early religious impressions which do not terminate in a sound conversion to God. Some five and forty years ago, I was frequently in a family where the parents, though respecters of religion, were not professors. They had a sweet, amiable little daughter, eight or ten years of age, who had all the appearance of eminent piety. She loved the Bible, loved preaching and religious people, was uniform and constant in retiring for devotional exercises, and spoke freely, when asked, of the feelings of her own mind. I think I never had less doubt of any one's piety than of this little girl's. There was no forwardness, nor pertness; nor any assumption of sanctimonious airs. All was simplicity, modesty, and consistency; she was grave but not demure; solemn and tender in her feelings, without affectation. She applied for admission to the communion—and who dare refuse entrance into the fold to such a dear lamb? Here my personal acquaintance ends. But years afterwards, upon inquiry, I found that when she grew up to womanhood, she became gay and careless, and entirely relinquished her religious profession. My Methodist neighbour, I know, if he had the chance to whisper in my ear, would say, "I have no difficulty in accounting for this case; she was a child of God, but fell from grace." But I have never been able to adopt this method of explaining such phenomena. There are few truths of which I have a more unwavering conviction, than that the sheep of Christ, for whom he laid down his life, shall never perish. I do believe, however, that grace may for a season, sink so low in the heart into which it has entered, and be so overborne and buried up, that none but God can perceive its existence. Now, that may have been the fact in regard to this dear child; for her later history is unknown to me. She may, for aught I know, be still alive, and be now a living, consistent member of Christ's Church, and may possibly peruse these lines, though if she should she may not recognize her own early features, taken down from memory after the lapse of so many years. But the picture is not of one person only, but of *many;* differing only in trivial circumstances. [See p. 12.]

I retain a distinct recollection of another case of a still earlier date; and where the history is more complete. An obscure youth, the son of religious parents, in a time of awakening, seemed to have his attention drawn to the concerns of his soul; so that he seriously and diligently attended on all religious meetings. He had the appearance of deep humility; and though free to speak, when interrogated, was in no respect forward or self-sufficient. Indeed, he was scarcely known, or noticed, by the religious people who were in the habit of attending prayer meetings. It happened, that on an inclement evening, very few were present, and none of those who were accustomed to take a part in leading the devotional exercises. The person, at whose house the meeting was held, not wishing to dismiss the few who were present, with a single prayer, asked this youth if he would not attempt to make a prayer. He readily assented, and performed this service with so much fervency, fluency, and propriety of expression, that all who heard it were astonished. From this time he was called upon more frequently than any other, and often in the public congregation; for some people preferred his prayers to any sermons; and I must say, that I never heard any one pray, who seemed to me to have such a *gift of prayer.* The most appropriate passages of Scripture seemed to come to him in rapid succession, as if by inspiration. Now the common cry was, that he ought to be taken from the trade which he was learning, (for he was an apprentice)—

and be put to study. The thing demanded by so many, was not difficult to accomplish. He began a regular course of academical studies, and his progress, though not extraordinary, was respectable. But, alas! how weak is man—how deceitful is the heart! This young man soon began to exhibit evidence too plain, that conceit and self-confidence were taking root and growing very rapidly. He became impatient of opposition, arrogant towards his superiors, and unwilling to yield to reproof administered in the most paternal spirit. When the time came to enter upon trials for the ministry, the Presbytery, to which he applied, refused to receive him under their care. But this solemn rebuff, instead of humbling him, only provoked his indignation, and, as if in despite of them, he turned at once to the study of another profession, in which he might have succeeded had he remained moral and temperate in his habits; but falling into bad company, he became dissipated, and soon came, without any known reformation, to a premature end. Now suppose this man had been permitted to enter the ministry, the probability is, that though his unchristian temper would have done much evil, yet he would have continued in the sacred office to his dying day. "*Let him that thinketh he standeth take heed lest he fall.*"

CHAPTER II.

Piety in children—Comparatively few renewed in infancy and childhood—Soul awakened in different ways—Legal conviction not a necessary part of true religion—Progress of conviction.

It is an interesting question, whether now there are any persons sanctified from the womb. If the communication of grace ever took place, at so early a period of human existence, there is no reason why it should not now sometimes occur. God says to Jere miah, "Before I formed thee in the belly, I knew thee, and before thou camest forth out of the womb, I sanctified thee." And of John the Baptist, Gabriel said to Zacharias, his father, "And he shall be filled with the Holy Ghost, even from his mother's womb." The prophet Samuel also seems to have feared the Lord from his earliest childhood. In later times, cases have often occurred, in which eminently pious persons could not remember the time when they did not love the Saviour and experience godly sorrow for their sins; and, as we believe that infants may be the subjects of regeneration, and cannot be saved without it, why may it not be the fact, that some who are regenerated live to mature age? I know, indeed, that many conceive that infants are naturally free from moral pollution, and, of course, need no regeneration; but this opinion is diametrically opposite to the doctrine of Scripture, and inconsistent with the acknowledged fact, that, as soon as they are capable of moral action, all do go astray, and sin against God. If children were not depraved, they would be naturally inclined to love God, and delight in his holy law; but the reverse is true. Perhaps one reason why so few are regenerated at this early age is, lest some should adopt the opinion that grace came by nature, or that man was not corrupt from his birth. Some have opposed the idea that any are sanctified from their birth, for fear that mere moralists and those religiously educated should indulge the hope that they were born of God, although they have experienced no particular change, in any part of their lives, as far back as memory reaches. But, allowing that some may improperly make this use of the doctrine, it only proves that a sound doctrine may be abused. All the doctrines of grace have been thus abused, and will be, as long as "the heart is deceitful above all things." There is, however, no ground for those who are still impenitent, to comfort themselves with the notion that they were regenerated in early infancy; for piety in a child will be as manifest as in an adult, as soon as such a child comes to the exercise of reason; and in some respects, more so, because there are so few young children who are pious, and because they have more simplicity of character, and are much less liable to play the hypocrite than persons of mature age. Mere decency of external behaviour, with a freedom from gross sins, is no evidence of regeneration; for these things may be found in many whose spirit is proud and self-righteous, and entirely opposite to the religion of Christ: and we know that outward regularity and sobriety may be produced by the restraints of a religious education and good example, where there are found none of the internal characteristics of genuine piety. Suppose then, that, in a certain case, grace has been communicated at so early a period, that its first exercises cannot be remembered, what will be the evidences which we should expect to find of its existence? Surely, we ought not to look for the wisdom, judgment, and stability of adult years, even in a *pious* child. We should expect, if I may say so, a childish piety—a simple, devout, and tender state of heart. As soon as such a child should obtain the first ideas of God, as its Creator, Preserver, and Benefactor, and of Christ, as its Saviour, who shed his blood and laid down his life for us on the cross, it would be piously affected with these truths, and would give manifest proof, that it possessed a susceptibility of emotions and affections of heart, corresponding with the conceptions of truth which it was capable of taking in. Such a child would be liable to sin, as all Christians are, but, when made sensible of faults, it would manifest tenderness of conscience and genuine sorrow, and would be fearful of sinning afterwards. When taught that prayer was both a duty and a privilege, it would take pleasure in drawing nigh to God, and would be conscientious in the discharge of secret duties. A truly pious child would be an affectionate and obedient child to its parents and teachers; kind to brothers and sisters, and indeed, to all other persons; and would take a lively interest in hearing of the conversion of sinners, and the advancement of Christ's kingdom in the world. We ought not to expect from a regenerated child uniform attention to serious subjects, or a freedom from that gaiety and volatility which are characteristic of that tender age; but we should expect to find the natural propensity moderated, and the temper softened and seasoned, by the commingling of pious thoughts and affections with those which naturally flow from the infant mind. When such children are called, in Providence, to leave the world, then commonly their piety breaks out into a flame, and these young saints, under the influence of divine grace, are enabled so to speak of their love to Christ and confidence in him, as astonishes, while it puts to shame aged Christians. Many examples of this kind we have on record, where the evidence of genuine piety was as strong as it well could be. There is a peculiar sweetness, as well as tenderness, in these early buddings of grace. In short, the exercises of grace are the same in a child as in an adult, only modified by the peculiarities in the character and knowledge of a child. Indeed, many adults in years, who are made the subjects of grace, are children in knowledge and understanding, and require the same indulgence, in our judgments of them, as children in years.

To those who cannot fix any commencement of their pious exercises, but who possess every other evidence of a change of heart, I would say, be not discouraged on this account, but rather be thankful that you have been so early placed under the tender care of the great Shepherd, and have thus been restrained from committing many sins, to which your nature, as well as that of others, was inclined. The habitual evidences of piety are the same, at whatever period the work commenced. If you possess these, you are safe; and early piety is probably more steady and consistent when matured by age, than that of later origin, though the change, of course, cannot be so evident to yourselves or others.

If piety may commence at any age, how solicitous should parents be for their children, that God would bestow his grace upon them, even before they know their right hand from their left; and, when about to dedicate them to God, in holy baptism, how earnestly should they pray that they might be baptized with the Holy Ghost—that while their bodies are washed in the emblematical laver of regeneration, their souls may experience the renewing of the Holy Ghost, and the sprinkling of the blood of Jesus. If the sentiments, expressed above, be correct, then may there be such a thing as *baptismal regeneration;* not that the mere external application of water can have any effect to purify the soul; nor that internal grace uniformly or generally, accompanies this external washing, but that God, who works when and by what means he pleases, may regenerate by his SPIRIT, the soul of the infant, while in his sacred name, water is applied to the body. And, what time in infancy is more likely to be the period of spiritual quickening, than the moment when that sacred rite is performed, which is strikingly emblematical of this change? Whether it be proper to say that baptism may be the *means* of regeneration, depends on the sense in which the word *means* is used. If in the sense of presenting motives to the rational mind, as when the word is read or heard, then it is not a *means;* for the child has no knowledge of what is done for it. But, if by *means*, be understood something which is accompanied by the divine efficiency, changing the moral nature of the infant, then, in this sense, baptism may be called the means of regeneration when thus accompanied by divine grace. The reason why it is believed, that regeneration does not usually accompany baptism, is simply because no evidences of spiritual life appear in baptized children, more than in those which remain unbaptized.

The education of children should proceed on the principle that they are in an unregenerate state, until evidences of piety clearly appear, in which case, they should be sedulously cherished and nurtured. These are Christ's lambs—"little ones, who believe in him" whom none should offend or mislead upon the peril of a terrible punishment. But though the religious education of children should proceed on the ground that they are destitute of grace, it ought ever to be used as a means of grace. Every lesson, therefore, should be accompanied with the lifting up of the heart of the instructer to God for a blessing on the means. "Sanctify them through thy truth; thy word is truth."

Although the grace of God may be communicated to a human soul, at any period of its existence, in this world; yet the fact manifestly is, that very few are renewed before the exercise of reason commences; and not many, in early childhood. Most persons, with whom we have been acquainted, grew up without giving any decisive evidence of a change of heart. Though religiously educated, yet they have evinced a want of love to God, and an aversion to spiritual things. Men are very reluctant, it is true, to admit that their hearts are wicked, and at enmity with God. They declare that they are conscious of no such feeling, but still the evidence of a dislike to the spiritual worship of God, they cannot altogether disguise; and this is nothing else but enmity to God. They might easily be convicted of loving the world more than God, the creature more than the Creator; and we know that he, who will be the friend of the world, is the enemy of God. Let the most moral and amiable of mankind, who are in this natural state, be asked such questions as these, Do you take real pleasure in perusing the sacred Scriptures, especially those parts which are most spiritual? Do you take delight in secret prayer, and find your heart drawn out to God, in strong desires? Do you spend much time in contemplating the divine attributes? Are you in the habit of communing with your own hearts, and examining the true temper of your souls? No unregenerate persons can truly answer these, and such like questions, in the affirmative. It is evident, then, that most persons, whom we see around us, and with whom we daily converse, are in the gall of bitterness and bond of iniquity, and, continuing in that state, where Christ is they never can come. And yet, alas! they are at ease in Zion; and seem to have no fear of that wrath which is coming. Their case is not only dangerous, but discouraging. Yet those who are now in a state of grace, yea, those of our race who are now in heaven, were once in the same condition. You, my reader, may now be a member of Christ's body, and heir of his glory; but you can easily look back, and remember the time, when you were as unconcerned about your salvation, as any of the gay, who are now fluttering around you. The same power which arrested you, is able to stop their mad career. Still hope and pray for their conversion. But tell me, how were you brought to turn from your wayward, downward course? This, as it relates to the external means of awakening, would receive a great variety of answers. One would say, "While hearing a particular sermon, I was awakened to see my lost estate, and never found rest or peace until I was enabled to believe in the Lord Jesus Christ." Another would answer, "I was brought to consideration, by the solemn and pointed conversation of a pious friend, who sought my salvation." While a third would answer, "I was led to serious consideration, by having the hand of God laid heavily upon me, in some affliction." In regard to many, the answer would be, that their minds were gradually led to serious consideration, they scarcely know how. Now, in regard to these external means or circumstances, it matters not, whether the attention was arrested, and the conscience awakened, by this or that means, gradually or suddenly. Neither do these things at all assist in determining the nature of the effect produced. All who ever became pious must have begun with serious consideration, whatever means were employed to produce this state of mind. But all who, for a season, become serious, are not certainly converted. There may be solemn impressions and deep awakenings which never terminate in a saving change, but end in some delusion, or the person returns again to his old condition, or rather to one much worse; for it may be laid down as a maxim, that religious impressions opposed, leave the soul in a more hardened state than before; just as iron, heated and then cooled, becomes harder. In general, those impressions which come on gradually, without any unusual means, are more permanent than those which are produced by circumstances of a striking and alarming nature. But even here there is no general rule. The nature of the permanent effects is the only sure criterion. "By their fruits ye shall know them."

That conviction of sin is a necessary part of experimental religion, all will admit; but there is one question respecting this matter, concerning which there may be much doubt; and that is, whether a *law-work*, prior to regeneration, is necessary; or, whether all true and salutary conviction is not the effect of regeneration. I find that a hundred years ago, this was a matter in dispute between the two parties, into which the Presbyterian church was divided, called the old and new side. The Tennents and Blairs insisted much on the necessity of conviction of sin, by the law, prior to regeneration; while Thompson and his associates were of opinion, that no such work was necessary, nor should be insisted on. As far as I know, the opinion of the necessity of legal conviction has generally prevailed in all our modern revivals: and it is usually taken for granted, that the convictions experienced are prior to regeneration. But it would be very difficult to prove from Scripture, or from the nature of the case, that such a preparatory work was necessary. Suppose an individual to be, in some certain moment, regenerated; such a soul would begin to see with new eyes, and his own sins would be among the things first viewed in a new light. He would be convinced, not only of the fact that they were transgressions of the law, but he would also see, that they were intrinsically evil, and deserved the punishment to which they exposed him. It is only such a conviction as this that really prepares a soul to accept of Christ in all his offices; not only as a Saviour from wrath, but from sin. And it can scarcely be believed, that that clear view of the justice of God, in their condemnation, which most persons sensibly experience, is the fruit of a mere legal conviction, on an unregenerate heart. For this view of God's justice is not merely of the fact, that this is his character, but of the divine excellency of his attributes, which is accompanied with admiration of it, and a feeling of acquiescence or submission. This view is sometimes so clear, and the equity and propriety of punishing sin are so manifest, and the feeling of acquiescence so strong, that it has laid the foundation for the very absurd opinion, that the true penitent is made willing to be damned for the glory of God. When such a conviction as this is experienced, the soul is commonly nigh to comfort, although at the moment it is common to entertain the opinion, that there is no salvation for it. It is wonderful, and almost unaccountable, how calm the soul is in the prospect of being for ever lost. An old lady of the Baptist denomination was the first person I ever heard give an account of Christian experience, and I recollect that she said that she was so deeply convinced that she should be lost, that she began to think how she should feel and be exercised in hell; and it occurred to her, that all in that horrid place were employed in blaspheming the name of God. The thought of doing so was rejected with abhorrence, and she felt as if she must and would love him, even there, for his goodness to her; for she saw that she alone was to blame for her destruction, and that He could, in consistence with his character, do nothing else but inflict this punishment on her. Now surely her heart was already changed, although not a ray of comfort had dawned upon her mind. But is there not before this, generally, a rebellious rising against God, and a disposition to find fault with his dealings? It may be so in many cases, but this feeling is far from being as universal as some suppose. As far as the testimony of pious people can be depended on, there are many whose first convictions are of the evil of sin, rather than of its danger, and who feel real compunction of spirit for having committed it, accompanied with a lively sense of their ingratitude. This question, however, is not of any great practical importance; but there are some truly pious persons who are distressed and perplexed, because they never experienced that kind of conviction which they hear others speak of, and the necessity of which is insisted on by some preachers. Certainly that which the reprobate may experience — which is not different from what all the guilty will feel at the day of judgment—cannot be a necessary part of true religion; and yet it does appear to be a common thing for awakened persons to be at first under a mere legal conviction.

Though man, in his natural state, is spiritually dead, that is, entirely destitute of any spark of true holiness, yet is he still a reasonable being, and has a conscience by which he is capable of discerning the difference between good and evil, and of feeling the force of moral obligation. By having his sins brought clearly before his mind, and his conscience awakened from its stupor, he can be made to feel what his true condition is as a transgressor of the holy law of God. This sight and sense of sin, under the influence of the common operations of the Spirit of God, is what is usually styled *conviction of sin*. And there can be no doubt that these views and feelings may be very clear and strong in an unrenewed mind. Indeed, they do not differ in kind from what every sinner will experience at the day of judgment, when his own conscience will condemn him, and he will stand guilty before his judge. But there is nothing in this kind of conviction which has any tendency to change the heart, or to make it better. Some indeed have maintained, with some show of reason, that under mere legal conviction, the sinner grows worse and worse; and certainly he sees his sins to be greater in proportion as the light of truth increases. There is not, therefore, in such convictions, however clear and strong, any approximation to regeneration. It cannot be called a preparatory work to this change, in the sense of disposing the person to receive the grace of God. The only end which it can answer is to show the rational creature his true condition, and to con vince the sinner of his absolute need of a Saviour Under conviction there is frequently a more sensible rising of the enmity of the heart against God and his law; but feelings of this kind do not belong to the essence of conviction. There is also sometimes an awful apprehension of danger; the imagination is filled with strong images of terror, and hell seems almost uncovered to the view of the convinced sinner. But there may be much of this feeling of terror, where there is very little real conviction of sin; and on the other hand, there often is deep and permanent conviction, where the passions and imagination are very little excited.

When the entrance of light is gradual, the first effect of an awakened conscience is, to attempt to rectify what now appears to have been wrong in the conduct. It is very common for the conscience, at first, to be affected with outward acts of transgression, and especially with some one prominent offence. An external reformation is now begun: for this can be effected by mere legal conviction. To this is added an attention to the external duties of religion, such as prayer, reading the Bible, hearing the word, &c. Every thing, however, is done with a legal spirit; that is, with the wish and expectation of making amends for past offences; and if painful penances should be prescribed to the sinner, he will readily submit to them if he may, by this means, make some atonement for his sins. But as the light increases, he begins to see that his heart is wicked; and to be convinced that his very prayers are polluted for want of right motives and affections. He, of course, tries to regulate his thoughts, and to exercise right affections; but here his efforts prove fruitless. It is much easier to reform the life than to bring the corrupt heart into a right state. The case now begins to appear desperate, and the sinner knows not which way to turn for relief, and, to cap the climax of his distress, he comes at length to be conscious of nothing but unyielding hardness of heart. He fears that the conviction which he seemed to have, is gone, and that he is left to total obduracy. In these circumstances he desires to feel keen compunction, and overwhelming terror, for his impression is, that he is entirely without conviction. The truth, however, is, that his convictions are far greater, than if he experienced that sensible distress which he so much courts. In this case, he would not think his heart so incurably bad, because it could entertain some right feeling, but as it is, he sees it to be destitute of every good emotion, and of all tender relentings. He has got down to the core of iniquity, and finds within his breast a heart unsusceptible of any good thing. Does he hear that others have obtained relief by hearing such a preacher, reading such a book, conversing with some experienced Christian? he resorts to the same means, but entirely without effect. The heart seems to become more insensible, in proportion to the excellence of the means enjoyed. Though he declares he has no sensibility of any kind, yet his anxiety increases; and perhaps he determines to give himself up solely to prayer and reading the Bible; and if he perish, to perish seeking for mercy. But however strong such resolutions may be, they are found to be in vain; for now, when he attempts to pray, he finds his mouth as it were shut. He cannot pray. He cannot read. He cannot meditate. What can he do? Nothing. He has come to the end of his legal efforts; and the result has been, the simple, deep conviction that he can do nothing; and if God does not mercifully interpose, he must inevitably perish. During all this process he has some idea of his need of divine help; but until now, he was not entirely cut off from all dependence on his own strength and exertions. He still hoped that, by some kind of effort or feeling, he could prepare himself for the mercy of God. Now he despairs of this, and not only so, but for a season he despairs, it may be, of salvation—gives himself up for lost. I do not say, that this is a necessary feeling, by any means, but I know that it is very natural, and by no means uncommon, in real experience. But conviction having accomplished all that it is capable of effecting, that is, having emptied the creature of self-dependence and self-righteousness, and brought him to the utmost extremity—even to the borders of despair, it is time for God to work. The proverb says, "Man's extremity is God's opportunity:" so it is in this case; and at this time, it may reasonably be supposed, the work of regeneration is wrought; for a new state of feeling is now experienced. Upon calm reflection, God appears to have been just and good in all his dispensations; the blame of its perdition the soul fully takes upon itself; acknowledges its ill-desert, and acquits God. "Against thee, thee only, have I sinned and done this evil in thy sight, that thou mightest be justified when thou speakest, and be clear when thou judgest." The sinner resigns himself into the hands of God; and yet is convinced that if he does perish, he will suffer only what his sins deserve. He does not fully discover the glorious plan according to which God can be just and the justifier of the ungodly who believe in Jesus Christ.

The above is not given as a course of experience which all real Christians can recognize as their own, but as a train of exercises which is very common. And as I do not consider legal conviction as necessary to precede regeneration, but suppose there are cases in which the first serious impressions may be the effect of regeneration, I cannot, of course, consider any particular train of exercises under the law as essential. It has been admitted, however, that legal conviction does in fact take place in most instances, prior to regeneration; and it is not an unreasonable inquiry, why is the sinner thus awakened? What good purpose does it answer? The reply has been already partially given; but it may be remarked, that God deals with man as an accountable, moral agent, and before he rescues him from the ruin into which he is sunk, he would let him see and feel, in some measure, how wretched his condition is; how helpless he is in himself, and how ineffectual are his most strenuous efforts to deliver him from his sin and misery. He is, therefore, permitted to try his own wisdom and strength. And finally, God designs to lead him to the full acknowledgment of his own guilt, and to justify the righteous Judge who condemns him to everlasting torment. Conviction, then, is no part of a sinner's salvation, but the clear practical knowledge of the fact that he cannot save himself, and is entirely dependent on the saving grace of God.

CHAPTER III.

The new birth an event of great importance.—The evidences of the new birth.—Diversities of experience in converts. — Examples.—Causes of diversity.

THERE is no more important event, which occurs in our world, than the new birth of an immortal soul. Heirs to titles and estates, to kingdoms and empires, are frequently born, and such events are blazoned with imposing pomp, and celebrated by poets and orators; but what are all these honours and possessions but the gewgaws of children, when compared with the inheritance and glory to which every child of God is born an heir! But this being a birth from above, and all the blessings and privileges of the young heir, of a hidden and spiritual nature, the world around cannot be expected to take a lively interest in the event. It is with the children of God as with the divine Saviour; "the world knoweth them not, as it knew him not." The night on which He was born, there was a great crowd of the descendants of David, collected from every part of the Holy land, where they were scattered abroad; but none of all these knew that a Saviour was born that night. Yet the angels celebrated the event in a truly celestial hymn, and announced the glad tidings to a company of simple shepherds, who were watching their flocks in the open field. So these celestial inhabitants, the messengers of God, take a lively interest still in events in which a gay and ungodly world feel no concern For "there is joy in the presence of the angels of God over one sinner that repenteth." How they know certainly when a soul is born to God, we need not inquire; for they have faculties and sources of knowledge, unknown to us. We know that "they are all ministering spirits, sent forth to minister for them who shall be heirs of salvation;" but how they carry on their ministry we cannot tell. If the evil spirit can inject evil thoughts into our minds, why may not good spirits suggest pious thoughts, or occasionally make sudden impressions for our warning, or change, by some means, the train of our thoughts? No doubt the devil soon learns the fact, when a sinner is converted unto God; for he has then lost a subject, and, perhaps, no conversion ever takes place, which he does not use every effort to prevent.

But, to return to our subject, the implantation of spiritual life in a soul dead in sin, is an event, the consequences of which will never end. When you plant an acorn, and it grows, you expect not to see the maturity, much less the end of the majestic oak, which will expand its boughs and strike deeply into the earth its roots. The fierce blast of centuries of winters may beat upon it and agitate it; but it resists them all. Yet finally this majestic oak, and all its towering branches, must fall. Trees die with old age, as well as men. But the plants of grace shall ever live. They shall flourish in everlasting verdure. They will bear transplanting to another clime—to another world. They shall bloom and bear fruit in the paradise of God. At such an hour one is born in Zion unto God. Few know it—few care for the event, or consider it of much importance. But, reader, this feeble germ—this incipient bud, will go on to grow and flourish for infinitely more years than there are sands upon the sea-shore. To drop the figure. This renewed soul will be seen and known among the saints in heaven, and assisting in the never-ceasing songs of those who surround the throne of God and the Lamb, millions of ages hereafter. Pure and holy shall it be—"without spot or wrinkle or any such thing." Bright as an angel, and as free from moral taint—but still distinguished from those happy beings, to whom it is equal, by singing a song in which they can never join—in wearing robes made white in the blood of the Lamb; and claiming a nearer kindred to the Son of God, than Gabriel himself. Can that event be of small moment, which lays a foundation for immortal bliss?—for ETERNAL LIFE?

Let us, then, patiently and impartially inquire into some of the circumstances and evidences of the *new birth*. And here I cannot but remark, that among all the preposterous notions which a new and crude theology has poured forth so profusely, in our day, there is none more absurd, than that a dead sinner can beget new life in himself. The very idea of a man's becoming his own father in the spiritual regeneration, is as unreasonable as such a supposition in relation to our first birth. Away with all such soul-destroying, God-dishonouring sentiments. "Which were born not of blood, nor of the will of the flesh, nor of the will of man, but of God"—" Born of the Spirit"—" And you hath HE quickened who were dead in trespasses and sins." But who can trace the work of the Spirit in this wonderful renovation? Can we tell how our bones and sinews were formed in our mothers' wombs? Surely, then, there must be mystery in the second birth. As our Lord said to Nicodemus when discoursing on this very subject: "If I have told you earthly things, and ye believe not, how shall ye believe if I tell you of heavenly things?" " The wind bloweth where it listeth, and thou hearest the sound thereof, but canst not tell whence it cometh, and whither it goeth."

There are, doubtless, great diversities in the appearances of the motions and actings of spiritual life in its incipient stages.

The agent is the same—the deadness of the subject the same—the instrument the same, and the nature of the effect the same, in every case. But still, there are many differing circumstances, which cause a great variety in appearance and expression; such as the degree of vigour in the principle of life communicated I know, indeed, that there are some who entertain the opinion, that the *new creature* as it comes from the hand of God—if I may so speak—is in all respects identical or of equal value. But this is not the fact. There is as much difference in the original vigour of spiritual as of natural life. Now, who does not perceive, what a remarkable difference this will make in all the actings and external exhibitions of this principle? As in nature, some children as soon as born are active and vigorous and healthy, and let all around know quickly that they are alive and have strong feeling too; whereas others come into the world with so feeble a spark of life, that it can hardly be discerned whether they breathe or have any pulsation in their heart and arteries; and when it is ascertained that they live, the principle of vitality is so weak, and surrounded with so many untoward circumstances and symptoms, that there is a small prospect of the infant reaching maturity;—just so it is, in the new birth. Some are brought at once into the clear light of day. They come "out of darkness into the marvellous light" of the gospel. "Old things are" consequently "passed away, and all things are become new." The change is most obvious and remarkable. They are as if introduced into a new world. The Sun of righteousness has risen upon them, without an intervening cloud. Their perception of divine things is so new and so clear, that they feel persuaded that they can convince others, and cause them to see and feel as they do. Indeed, they wonder why they did not always see things in this light, and they do not know why others do not see them as they do. Such persons can no more doubt of their conversion than of their existence. Such a case was that of Saul of Tarsus. Such also was the case of Col. Gardiner. Now this bright day may be clouded over, or it may not. In the case of the two persons mentioned, there does not seem ever to have arisen a passing cloud to create a doubt whether indeed they had been brough.

to enjoy the light of a heavenly day. But many a day which begins with an unclouded sun, is deformed by dark and lowering clouds, and even agitated with tremendous storms, before it closes. So it may be in the spiritual life. Some commence their pilgrimage under the most favourable auspices, and seem to stand so firmly on the mount, that they are ready to say, "I shall never be moved." Yet when their Lord hides his face, they are soon troubled; and may long walk in darkness, and enjoy no light or comfort. And commonly this change is brought about by our own spiritual pride and carelessness.

The opinion commonly entertained, that the most enormous sinners are the subjects of the most pungent convictions of sin, and the most alarming terrors of hell, is not correct. In regard to such, the commencement of a work of grace is sometimes very gradual, and the impressions so apparently slight, that they afford very little ground of sanguine expectations of the result. While, on the other hand, some persons of an unblemished moral character, and who, from the influence of a religious education, have always respected religion, and venerated its ordinances, when brought under conviction, are more terribly alarmed and more overwhelmed with distress, than others whose lives have been stained by gross crimes. The Rev. John Newton, when awakened to some sense of his sinful and dangerous condition, which occurred during a violent and long continued storm at sea, though his judgment was convinced that he was the greatest of sinners, and he doubted whether it was possible for him to be saved; yet seems to have had no very deep feelings or agitating fears. He says, "It was not till after, perhaps, several years, that I had gained some clear views of the infinite righteousness and grace of Christ Jesus my Lord, that I had a deep and strong apprehension of my state by nature and practice; and perhaps till then I could not have borne the sight; so wonderfully does the Lord proportion the discoveries of sin and grace. For he knows our frame, and that if he were to put forth the great ness of his power, a poor sinner would be instantly overwhelmed, and crushed as a moth." And, though from this time there was a sensible change, and his mind was turned towards religion, yet it is evident from the history of his life, as well as his experiences afterwards, that grace existed during several years, in the feeblest state of which we can well conceive. It appeared so much so to himself, that he warns all persons from considering his experience a model for them. "As to myself," says he, "every part of my case has been extraordinary—I have hardly met a single instance resembling it. Few, very few have been rescued from such a dreadful state, and those few that have been thus favoured, have generally passed through the most severe convictions; and, after the Lord has given them peace, their future lives have been usually more zealous, bright, and exemplary than common." Now this is the opinion which I think, is taken up rather from theory than an observation of facts. I think that those persons, who have been most conversant with exercised souls will say that there is no general rule here—that very pungent convictions and deep distress are found as frequently in those who have been preserved from outbreaking transgressions, as in those noted for their immoralities. There seems, indeed, more reason for severe convictions in the latter case; but convictions are not uniformly proportioned to the magnitude of crimes. And in truth, we are incapable of comparing together the heinousness of the sins of different persons. The moral man, as we call him, may be the greater sinner of the two, when weighed in the balances of the sanctuary. I heard a popular preacher once undertake to prove, that moral men and formal professors must, in all cases, be far more wicked than the blaspheming infidel, and gross debauchee. The argument was plausible, but laboured under one essential defect; and I was of opinion, and still am, that such a doctrine is highly dangerous, and calculated to encourage men to go to all lengths in wickedness. Wher I was a very young preacher, I expressed the opinion, in a sermon preached in North Carolina, that the mere moralist and formalist were more out of the way of conviction than the openly profane. When the sermon was ended, a fierce looking man came up to me and said that I had delivered precisely his opinion on one point, and mentioned the above sentiment. I inquired, when he was gone, who he was, and found that he was the most notorious profligate in all the country; and not long afterwards he was apprehended and imprisoned, at the head of a company engaged in felonious acts. This taught me a lesson which I never forgot. Mr. Newton proceeds thus: "Now, as, on the one hand, my convictions were very moderate, and far below what might have been expected from the dreadful review I had to make; so, on the other, my first beginnings in a religious course were as faint as can well be imagined. I never knew that season alluded to, Revelation ii. 4, usually called the time of "first love." And then he relates facts which give sad evidence of a very low state of grace; and, if it had never risen higher, we should certainly have been inclined to believe that he was not a subject of saving grace. But this leads me to remark a fact analogous to what is common in the natural world; that the infant which, when born, barely gives evidence of life, may not only grow to maturity, but in size and strength may far exceed those who commenced life with more activity and vigour; and so in the spiritual life, when the incipient motions and affections are very feeble, the person may eventually become a mature and eminent Christian, as we have no doubt Mr. Newton did. Another instance of a similar kind, if my memory serves me, was the Rev. Mr. Cecil, who had also been, for many years, a profane infidel; but who, in process of time, became one of the most eminent Christians, as well as spiritual ministers of his day. Dr. Thomas Scott, also, was a Socinian, and yet a preacher in the established Church; but the progress of illumination and conviction in his mind was very gradual. His "Force of Truth" is an admirable little work, and furnishes a full illustration of the sentiment which I wish to inculcate: That grace, in the commencement, is often exceedingly faint and feeble, and yet may grow into a state of maturity and comparative perfection.

In the experience of President Edwards, as recorded by himself, we find no account of any deep and distressing convictions of sin at the commencement of his religious course; though, afterwards, perhaps few men ever attained to such humbling views of the depth and turpitude of the depravity of the heart. But his experience differs from that of those mentioned above, in that his first views of divine things were clear and attended with unspeakable delight. "The first instance that I remember of that sort of inward, secret delight in God and divine things, that I have lived much in since, was, on reading those words, 1 Tim. i. 17, 'Now, unto the King eternal, immortal, invisible, the only wise God, be honour and glory, for ever and ever, Amen.' As I read these words, there came into my soul, and was as it were diffused through it, a sense of the glory of the Divine Being; a new sense, quite different from any thing I ever experienced before. Never any words of Scripture seemed to me as those words did. I thought with myself, how excellent a Being that was, and how happy I should be, if I might enjoy that God, and be rapt up to him in heaven, and be as it were swallowed up in him for ever." "From that time I began to have a new kind of apprehensions and ideas of Christ, and the work of redemption, and the glorious way of salvation by him. An inward, sweet sense of these things, at times, came into my heart; and my soul was led away in pleasant views and contemplations of them. After this, my sense of divine things gradually increased, and became more and more lively, and had more of that inward sweetness. The appearance of every thing was altered. There seemed to be, as it were, a calm, sweet cast or appearance of divine glory, in almost every thing. God's excel.ency, his wisdom, his purity, and his love seemed to appear in every thing." The difference between this and many other cases of incipient piety, is very striking. And yet these views and exercises do not come up to the standard which some set up in regard to Christian experience, because they are so abstract, and have such casual reference to Christ, through whom alone God is revealed to man as an object of saving faith. And if there be a fault in the writings of this great and good man on the subject of experimental religion, it is, that they seem to represent renewed persons as at the first, occupied with the contemplation of the attributes of God with delight, without ever thinking of a Mediator. But few men ever attained, as we think, higher degrees of holiness, or had made more accurate observations on the exercises of others. His work on the Affections is too abstract and tedious for common readers; but it is an excellent work, although I think his twelve marks might with great advantage be reduced to half the number, on his own plan. The experimental exercises of religion are sure to take their complexion from the theory of doctrine entertained, or which is inculcated at the time.

The variety which appears in the exercises of real converts does not depend alone on the different degrees of vigour, in the principle of spiritual life, but on many other circumstances; some of which will now be noticed. The benefit of sound doctrinal instruction to the new-born soul has already been mentioned, but demands a more particular consideration. What degree of knowledge is absolutely necessary to the existence of piety cannot be accurately determined by man, but we know that genuine faith may consist with much ignorance and error. Suppose two persons, then, to have received the principle of spiritual life in equal vigour, but let the one be ignorant and the other well instructed; it is easy to see what a difference this will make in the exercises of the two converts; and also in the account which they are able respectively to give to others of the work of grace on their hearts. It is here taken for granted, that nothing but divine truth can be the object of holy affections, or furnish the motives from which true Christians are bound to act; and that faith in all its actings has respect to revealed truth. But that which is unknown can neither be the object of faith or love, and that which is known obscurely, and viewed indistinctly, can never operate with the same effect as that which is clearly understood. Accordingly, our missionaries inform us, that we ought not to expect the same consistency or maturity in the religion of real converts from heathenism, as from religiously educated persons in our own country. It is a lamentable fact that in this land of churches and of Bibles, there are many who know little more of the doctrines of Christianity, than the pagans themselves. The proper inference from the fact stated is, that they are egregiously in error, who think that the religious education of children, is useless, or even injurious; and their opinion is also condemned who maintain that it matters little what men believe provided their lives are upright. All good conduct must proceed from good principles; but good principles cannot exist without a knowledge of the truth. "Truth is in order to holiness;" and between truth and holiness there is an indissoluble connexion. It would be as reasonable to expect a child born into an atmosphere corrupted with pestilential vapour, to grow and be healthy, as that spiritual life should flourish without the nutriment of the pure milk of the word, and without breathing in the wholesome atmosphere of truth. The new man often remains in a dwarfish state, because he is fed upon husks; or, he grows into a distorted shape by means of the errors which are inculcated upon him. It is of unspeakable importance that the young disciple have sound, instructive, and practical preaching to attend on. It is also of consequence that the religious people, with whom he converses, should be discreet, evangelical, and intelligent Christians; and that the books put into his hands should be of the right kind. There is what may be called a sectarian peculiarity in the experimental reli gion of all the members of a religious denomination When it is required, in order that persons be admitted to commuion, that they publicly give a narrative of the exercises of their minds, there will commonly be observed a striking similarity. There is a certain mould into which all seem to be cast. By the way, this requisition is unwise; few persons have humility and discretion enough to be trusted to declare in a public congregation, what the dealings of God with their souls have been. When ignorant, weak, and fanciful persons undertake this, they often bring out such crude and ludicrous things, as greatly tend to bring experimental religion into discredit. The practice seems also to be founded on a false principle, namely, that real Christians are able to tell with certainty whether others have religion, if they hear their experience. Enthusiasts have always laid claim to this discernment of the spirits, and this enthusiasm is widely spread through some large sects; and when they meet with any professing piety, they are always solicitous to hear an account of their conviction, conversion, &c. A free intercourse of this kind among intimate friends, is no doubt, profitable; but a frequent and indiscriminate disclosure of these secret things of the heart, is attended with many evils. Among the chief is, the fostering of spiritual pride, which may often be detected when the person is boasting of his humility. In those social meetings, in which every person is questioned as to the state of his soul, the very sameness of most of the answers ought to render the practice suspicious. Poor, weak, and ignorant persons, often profess to be *happy*, and to be full of the love of God, when they know not what they say. It is wonderful how little you hear of the spiritual conflict in the account which many professors give of their experience. The people know what kind of answers is expected of them, and they come, as near as they can to what is wished; and it is to be feared that many cry "peace," when there is no peace; and say that they are happy, merely because they hear this from the lips of others. Hypocrisy is a fearful evil, and every thing which has a tendency to produce it should be avoided. Among some classes of religious people, all doubting about the goodness and safety of our state is scouted as inconsistent with faith. It is assumed as indubitably true, that every Christian must be assured of his being in a state of grace, and they have no charity for those who are distressed with almost perpetual doubts and fears. This they consider to be the essence of unbelief; for faith, according to them, is a full persuasion that our sins are forgiven. No painful process of self-examination is therefore requisite, for every believer has possession already of all that could be learned from such examination. Among others, doubting, it is to be feared, is too much encouraged; and serious Christians are perplexed with needless scruples originating in the multiplication of the marks of conversion, which sometimes are difficult of application, and, in other cases, are not scriptural, but arbitrary, set up by the preacher who values himself upon his skill in detecting the close hypocrite, whereas he wounds the weak believer, in ten cases, where he awakens the hypocrite in one. I once heard one of these preachers, whose common mode was harsh, and calculated to distress the feeble minded, attempt to preach in a very different style. He seemed to remember that he should not "bruise the broken reed," nor "quench the smoking flax." A person of a contrite spirit heard the discourse with unusual comfort, but at the close the preacher resumed his usual harsh tone, and said, "Now you hypocrites will be snatching at the children's bread." On hearing which, the broken-hearted hearer felt himself addressed, and instantly threw away all the comfort which he had received. And though there might be a hundred hypocrites present, yet not one of them cared any thing about the admonition.

In some places, anxious inquirers are told that, if they will hold on praying and using the means, God is bound to save them; as though a dead, condemned sinner could so pray as to bring God under obligation to him, or could secure the blessings of the covenant of grace, by his selfish, legal striving. These instructions accord very much with the self-righteous spirit which is naturally in us all; and one of two things may be expected to ensue, either that the anxious inquirer will conclude that he has worked out his salvation, and cry peace; or that he should sink into discouragement and charge God foolishly, because He does not hear his prayers, and grant him his desires. There is another extreme, but not so common among us. It is, to tell the unconverted, however anxious, not to pray at all—that their prayers are an abomination to God, and can answer no good purpose, until they are able to pray in faith. The writer happened once to be cast into a congregation where this doctrine was inculcated, at the time of a considerable revival, when many sinners were cut to the heart, and were inquiring, what must we do to be saved? He conversed with some who appeared to be under deep and awful convictions, but they were directed to use no means, but to believe, and they appeared to remain in a state of perfect quiescence, doing nothing, but confessing the justice of their condemnation, and appearing to feel that they were entirely at the disposal of Him, who " has mercy on whom he will have mercy." The theory, however, was not consistently carried out, for while these persons were taught not to pray, they were exhorted to hear the gospel, and were frequently conversed with by their pastor. But this extreme is not so dangerous as the former, which encourages sinners to think that they can do something to recommend themselves to God, by their unbelieving prayers. The fruits of this revival, I have reason to believe, were very precious. Even among the same people and under the same minister, the exercises of the awakened in a revival are very different. In some seasons of this sort, the work appears to be far deeper and more solemn than in others

CHAPTER IV.

Causes of diversity in experience continued.—Effect of temperament.— Melancholy.—Advice to the friends of persons thus affected.—Subjec continued.—Illustrative cases.—Causes of melancholy and insanity.

WE have before shown how the principle of spiritual life is affected in its appearance by two circumstances—the degree of vigour given to it in its commencement, and the degree of knowledge and maturity of judgment which one may possess above another. We now come to another pregnant cause of the great variety which is found in the exercises and comforts of real Christians, and that is the difference of *temperament* which is so familiar, and which so frequently modifies the characters, as well as the feelings of men in other matters. There can be no doubt, I think, that the susceptibility of lively emotion is exceedingly different in men under the same circumstances. Persons of strong affections and ardent temperament, upon an unexpected bereavement of a beloved wife or child, are thrown into an agony of grief which is scarcely tolerable; while those of a cold, phlegmatic temperament, seem to suffer no exquisite anguish from this or any other cause. Not that they possess more fortitude or resignation, for the contrary may be the fact; but their susceptibilities are less acute. And this disparity appears in nothing more remarkably than in the tendency to entertain different degrees of hope or fear in similar circumstances. For, while some will hope whenever there is the smallest ground for a favourable result, others are sure to fear the worst which can possibly happen; and their apprehensions are proportioned to the magnitude of the interest at stake. Now is it wonderful, that men's religious feelings should be affected by the same causes? When two exercised persons speak of their convictions, their sorrows and their hopes, is it not to be expected, that with the same truths before their minds, those of a sanguine temperament will experience more sensible emotions, and, upon the same evidence, entertain more confident hopes than those of a contrary disposition? And, of necessity, the joy of the one will be much more lively than that of the other. Thus, two persons may be found, whose experience may have been very similar as to their conviction of sin, and exercise of faith and repentance; and yet the one will express a strong confidence of having passed from death unto life; while the other is afraid to express a trembling hope. Of these two classes of Christians, the first is the most comfortable, the latter the safest, as being unwilling to be satisfied with any evidence but the strongest. But there is not only a wide difference from this natural cause of the liveliness of the emotions of joy and sorrow, and of the confidence of the hopes entertained, but usually a very different mode of expression. Sanguine persons, from the very impulse of ardent feeling, have a tendency to express things in strong language constantly verging on exaggeration. They are apt to use superlatives and strong emphasis, as wishing to convey a full idea of their feelings, while those of a colder temperament and more timid disposition, fall below the reality, in their descriptions, and are cautious not to convey to others too high an idea of what they have experienced. This diversity, as the cause is permanent, characterizes the religious experience of these respective classes of Christians through their whole pilgrimage, and may be equally manifest on a dying bed. Hence it appears how very uncertain a knowledge of the internal state of the heart we obtain from the words and professions of serious persons. It should also serve to shake the vain confidence of those who imagine that they can decide with certainty whether another is a truly converted person, merely from hearing a narrative of his religious experience, that two persons may employ the same words and phrases to express their feelings, and yet those feelings may be specifically different. Each may say, "I felt the love of God shed abroad in my heart," which in the one case may be the genuine affection described in these words; while in the other it may be a mere transport of natural feeling; a mere selfish persuasion of being a favourite of heaven; or a high state of nervous exhilaration, produced by a physiological cause. Both these persons may be sincere, according to the popular acceptation of that term; that is, both have really experienced a lively emotion, and both mean to express the simple fact; and yet the one is a real Christian, while the other may be in an unregenerate state. Another thing which ought to destroy this foolish persuasion, that we can certainly determine the true spiritual condition of another person by hearing from him a narrative of his experience, is that any words or phrases which can be used by a really pious man, may be learned by a designing hypocrite. What is to hinder such an one from using the very language and imitating the very manner in which true Christians have been heard to relate their experience? What can prevent deceivers from catching up the narrative of godly exercises so abundantly found in religious biography, and applying it to themselves, as though they had experience of these things? While only two classes of Christians have been mentioned, yet in each of these there are many subordinate divisions, to describe all of which would be tedious and not for edification. The reader can readily apply the general principles to every variety of experience, modified by this cause.

In the preceding remarks, the healthy, constitutional temperament has alone been brought into view; but by far the most distressing *cases of conscience*, with which the spiritual physician has to deal, are owing to a morbid temperament. As most people are inclined to conceal their spiritual distresses, few have any conception of the number of persons who are habitually suffering under the frightful malady of melancholy With some, this disease is not permanent, but occasional. They have only periodical paroxysms of deep religious depression; and they may be said to have their compensation, for the dark and cloudy day, by being favoured with one of peculiar brightness, in quick succession. If their gloom was uninterrupted, it would be overwhelming, but after a dark night, rises a lovely morning without the shadow of a cloud. This rapid and great alternation of feeling is found in those who possess what may be called a mercurial temperament. It is connected with a nervous system peculiarly excitable, and exceedingly liable to temporary derangement. A rough east wind is sufficient to blow up clouds which completely obscure the cheerful sunshine of the soul; while the wholesome zephyrs as quickly drive all these gloomy clouds away. Such persons always have a stomach easily disordered, and one ounce of improper food, or one too much of wholesome food, is cause sufficient o derange the nerves and depress the spirits. The want of refreshing sleep, or watchfulness, is another cause of the same effects; and in its turn, is an effect from disordered nerves. But physical causes are not the only ones which produce this painful state of feeling. It is often produced, in a moment, by hearing some unpleasant intelligence, or by the occurrence of some disagreeable event. But, as was hinted, when these people of nervous temperament are relieved from a fit of depression, their sky is uncommonly free from clouds; their hopes are lively, their spirits buoyant, and nothing can trouble them. These alternations of day and night, of sunshine and darkness, must of necessity affect the feelings in regard to all matters, temporal and spiritual; for as in a dark night every object appears black, so when the mind is overcast with gloomy clouds every view must partake of he same aspect. To many persons this description will be unintelligible; but by others, it will be recognized, at once, as a just view of their own case. But when religious melancholy becomes a fixed disease, it may be reckoned among the heaviest calamities to which our suffering nature is subject. It resists all argument and rejects every topic of consolation, from whatever source it may proceed. It feeds upon distress and despair, and is displeased even with the suggestion or offer of relief. The mind thus affected seizes on those ideas and truths which are most awful and terrific. Any doctrine which excludes all hope is congenial to the melancholy spirit, and it seizes on such things with an unnatural avidity, and will not let them go.

There is no subject on which it is more vain and dangerous to theorize than our religious experience. It is therefore of unspeakable importance that ministers of the gospel, who have to deal with diseased consciences, should have had some experience themselves in these matters. This, no doubt, is one reason why some, intended to be "sons of consolation" to others, have been brought through deep waters, and have been buffeted by many storms, before they obtained a settled peace of mind. It is a proper object of inquiry, why, in our day, so little is heard about the spiritual troubles, of which we read so much in the casuistical treatises of writers of a former age. It can scarcely be supposed that the faith of modern Christians is so much stronger than that of believers who lived in other days, that they are enabled easily to triumph over their melancholy fears and despondency. Neither can we suppose that Satan is less busy in casting his fiery darts, and in attempts to drive the children of God to despair. There is reason to fear, that among Christians of the present time, there is less deep, spiritual exercise, than in former days; and as little is said on this subject in public discourses, there may be greater concealment of the troubles of this kind than if these subjects were more frequently discussed. It is observable that all those who have experienced this sore affliction and have been mercifully delivered from it, are very solicitous to administer relief and comfort to others who are still exposed to the peltings of the pitiless storm; and these are the persons who feel the tenderest sympathy with afflicted consciences, and know how to bear with the infirmities and waywardness which accompany a state of religious melancholy. It is also remarkable, that very generally, they who have been recovered from such diseases, attribute no small part of their troubles to a morbid temperament of body, and accordingly, in their counsels to the melancholy, they lay particular stress on the regular, healthy state of the body.

About the close of the seventeenth century, the Rev. Timothy Rogers, a pious and able minister of London, fell into a state of deep melancholy; and such was the distressing darkness of his mind, that he gave up all hope of the mercy of God, and believed himself to be a vessel of wrath, designed for destruction, for the praise of the glorious justice of the Almighty. His sad condition was known to many pious ministers and people throughout the country, who, it is believed, were earnest and incessant in their supplications in his behalf. And these intercessions were not ineffectual; for it pleased God to grant a complete deliverance to his suffering servant. And having received comfort of the Lord, he was exceedingly desirous to be instrumental in administering the same comfort to others, with which he himself had been comforted. He therefore wrote several treatises with this object in view, which are well calculated to be of service to those labouring under spiritual distress. One of these is entitled, "RECOVERY FROM SICKNESS," another "CONSOLATION TO THE AFFLICTED," and a third, "A DISCOURSE ON TROUBLE OF MIND, AND THE DISEASE OF MELANCHOLY." In the "preface" to this last, the author gives directions to the friends of persons labouring under religious melancholy, how to treat them. The substance of these, I will now communicate to the reader. "1. Look upon your distressed friends as under one of the worst distempers to which this miserable life is obnoxious. Melancholy incapacitates them for thought or action: it confounds and disturbs all their thoughts and fills them with vexation and anguish. I verily believe, that when this malign humour is deeply fixed and has spread its deleterious influence over every part, it is as vain to attempt to resist it, by reasoning and rational motives, as to oppose a fever, or the gout, or pleurisy. One of the very worst attendants of this disease is, the want of sleep, by which in other distresses men are relieved and refreshed; but in this disease, either sleep flies far away, or is so disturbed, that the poor sufferer, instead of being refreshed, is like one on the rack. The faculties of the soul are weakened, and all their operations disturbed and clouded; and the poor body languishes and pines away, at the same time. And that which renders this disease more formidable is, its long continuance. It is a long time often before it comes to its height; and usually as tedious in its declension. It is, in every respect, sad and overwhelming; a state of darkness that has no discernible beams of light. It generally begins in the body, and then conveys its venom to the mind. I pretend not to tell you what medicines will cure it, for I know of none. I leave you to advise with such as are skilled in physic, and especially to such doctors as have experienced something of it themselves; for it is impossible to understand the nature of it in any other way than by experience. There is danger, as Mr. Greenham says, 'that the bodily physician will look no further than the body, while the spiritual physician will totally disregard the body, and look only at the mind.'

"2. Treat those who are under this disease with tender compassion. Remember also, that you are liable to the same affliction; for however brisk your spirits and lively your feelings now, you may meet with such reverses, with such long and sharp afflictions, as will sink your spirits. Many, not naturally inclined to melancholy, have, by overwhelming and repeated calamities, been sunk into this dark gulf.

"3. Never use harsh language to your friends when under the disease of melancholy. This will only serve to fret and perplex them the more, but will never benefit them. I know that the counsel of some is, to rebuke and chide them, on all occasions; but I dare confidently say, that such advisers never felt the disease themselves; for if they had, they would know that thus they do but pour oil into the flames, and chafe and exasperate their wounds, instead of healing them. Mr. Dod, by reason of his mild, meek, and merciful spirit, was reckoned one of the fittest persons to deal with those thus afflicted. Never was any person more tender and compassionate as all will be convinced, who will read the accounts of Mr. Peacock and Mrs. Drake, both of whom were greatly relieved by his conversation.

" 4. If you would possess any influence over your friends in this unhappy state of mind, you must be careful not to express any want of confidence in what they relate of their own feelings and distresses. On this point, there is often a great mistake. When they speak of their frightful and distressing apprehensions, it is common for friends to reply, ' that this is all imaginary'—' nothing but fancy,' ' an unfounded whim.' Now the disease is a real one, and their misery is as real as any experienced by man. It is true, their imagination is disordered, but this is merely the effect of a deeper disease. These afflicted persons never can believe that you have any real sympathy with their misery, or feel any compassion for them, unless you believe what they say.

" 5. Do not urge your melancholy friends to do what is out of their power. They are like persons whose bones are broken, and who are incapacitated for action. Their disease is accompanied with perplexing and tormenting thoughts; if you can innocently divert them, you would do them a great kindness; but do not urge them to any thing which requires close and intent thinking; this will only increase the disease. But you will ask, ought we not to urge them to hear the word of God? I answer, if they are so far gone in the disease as to be in continual, unremitting anguish, they are not capable of hearing, on account of the painful disorder of their minds. But if their disorder is not come to such a distressing height, you may kindly and gently persuade them to attend on the preaching of the word; but beware of using a peremptory and violent method. The method pursued by Mr. Dod, with Mrs. Drake, should be imitated. 'The burden which overloaded her soul was so great, that we never durst add any thereunto, but fed her with all encouragements, she being too apt to overcharge herself, and to despair upon any addition of fuel to that fire which was inwardly consuming her. And so, wherever she went to hear, notice was given to the minister officiating, that he had such a hearer, and by this means she received no discouragement from hearing.'

"6. Do not attribute the effects of mere disease to the devil; although I do not deny that he has an agency in producing some diseases; especially, by harassing and disturbing the mind to such a degree, that the body suffers with it. But it is very unwise to ascribe every feeling and every word of the melancholy man to Satan; whereas, many of these are as natural consequences of bodily disease, as the symptoms of a fever, which the poor sufferer can no more avoid, than the sick man can keep himself from sighing and groaning. Many will say to such an one, 'Why do you so pore over your case and thus gratify the devil?' whereas, it is the very nature of the disease to cause such fixed musings. You might as well say to a man in a fever, 'Why are you not well, why will you be sick?' Some, indeed, suppose, that the melancholy hug their disease, and are unwilling to give it up, but you might as well suppose that a man would be pleased with lying on a bed of thorns, or in a fiery furnace. No doubt the devil knows how to work on minds thus diseased, and that by shooting his fiery darts, he endeavours to drive them to utter despair. But if you persuade them that all which they experience is from the devil, you may induce the opinion in them, that they are actually possessed of the evil one; which has been the unhappy condition of some whose minds were disordered. I would not have you to bring a railing accusation, even against the devil, neither must you falsely accuse your friends by saying that they gratify him.

"7. Do not express much surprise or wonder at any thing which melancholy persons say or do. What will not they say, who are in despair of God's mercy? What will not they do, who think themselves lost, for ever? You know that even such a man as Job cursed his day, so that the Lord charged him 'with darkening counsel by words without knowledge.' Do not wonder that they give expression to bitter complaints; the tongue will always be speaking of the aching tooth. Their soul is sore vexed, and although they get no good by complaining, yet they cannot but complain, to find themselves in such a doleful case And they can say with David, 'I am weary with my groaning: all the night make I my bed to swim, I water my couch with my tears;' yet they cannot forbear to groan and weep more, until their very eyes be consumed with grief. Let no sharp words of theirs provoke you to talk sharply to them. Sick people are apt to be peevish, and it would be a great weakness in you, not to bear with them, when you see that a long and sore disease has deprived them of their former good temper.

"8. Do not tell them any frightful stories, nor recount to them the sad disasters which have overtaken others. Their hearts do already meditate terror, and by every alarming thing of which they hear, they are the more terrified, and their disordered imagination is prepared to seize upon every frightful image which is presented. The hearing of sad things always causes them more violent agitations. Yet you must avoid merriment and levity in their presence, for this would lead them to think that you have no sympathy with them, nor concern for them. A mixture of gravity and affableness will best suit them; and, if I might advise, I would counsel parents not to put their children, who are naturally inclined to melancholy, to learning, or to any employment, which requires much study; lest they should at length be preyed upon, by their own thoughts.

"9. Do not, however, think it needless to talk with them. But do not speak as if you thought their disease would be of long continuance; for this is the prospect which appears most gloomy to the melancholy. Rather encourage them to hope for speedy deliverance. Endeavour to revive their spirits by declaring, that God can give them relief in a moment, and that he has often done so with others; that he can quickly heal their disease, and cause his amiable and reconciled face to shine upon them.

"10. It will be useful to tell them of others, who have been in the same state of suffering, and yet have been delivered. It is, indeed, true, that they who are depressed by such a load of grief, are with difficulty persuaded, that any were ever in such a condition as they are. They think themselves to be more wicked than Cain or Judas, and view their own cases to be entirely singular. It will, therefore, be important to relate real cases of deliverance from similar distress and darkness. Several such cases have been known to me, as that of Mr. Rosewell, and also Mr. Porter, both ministers of the gospel. The latter was six years under the pressure of melancholy; yet both these experienced complete deliverance, and afterwards rejoiced in the light of God's countenance. I myself was near two years in great pain of body, and greater pain of soul, and without any prospect of peace or help; and yet God hath recovered me by his sovereign grace and mercy. Mr. Robert Bruce, minister in Edinburgh, was twenty years in terrors of conscience, and yet delivered afterwards. And so, of many others, who after a dark and stormy night, were blessed with the cheerful light of returning day. Mr. Fox, in his book of Martyrs, gives an account of a certain Mr. Glover, who was worn and consumed with inward trouble, for five years, so that he had no comfort in his food, nor in his sleep, nor in any enjoyment of life. He was so perplexed, as if he had been in the deepest pit of hell, and yet this good servant of God, after all these horrid temptations and buffetings of Satan, was delivered from all his trouble, and the effect was such a degree of mortification of sin, that he appeared as one already in heaven.

"11. The next thing which you are to do for your melancholy friends, is to pray for them. As they have not light and composure to pray for themselves, let your eyes weep for them in secret, and there let your souls melt in fervent holy prayers. You know that none but God alone can help them. Mr. Peacock said to Mr. Dod, and his other friends, 'Take not the name of God in vain, by praying for such a reprobate.' Mr. Dod replied, 'If God stir up your friends to pray for you, he will stir up himself to hear their prayers.' You ought to consider that nothing but prayer can do them good. It is an obstinate disease that nothing else will overcome. Those who can cure themselves by resorting to wine and company, were never under this disease.

"12. Not only pray for them yourself, but engage other Christian friends, also, to pray for them. When many good people join their requests together, their cry is more acceptable and prevalent. When the church united in prayer for Peter, in chains, he was soon delivered, and in the very time of their prayers. All believers have, through Christ, a great interest in heaven, and the Father is willing to grant what they unitedly and importunately ask, in the name of his dear Son. I myself have been greatly helped by the prayers of others, and I heartily thank all those especially, who set apart particular days to remember at a throne of grace, my distressed condition. Blessed be God that he did not turn away his mercy from me, nor turn a deaf ear to their supplications!

"13. Put your poor, afflicted friends, in mind, continually, of the sovereign grace of God, in Jesus Christ. Often impress on their minds, that He is merciful and gracious; that as far as the heavens are above the earth, so far are his thoughts above their thoughts; his thoughts of mercy above their self-condemning, guilty thoughts. Teach them as much as you can, to look unto God, by the great Mediator, for grace and strength, and not too much to pore over their own souls, where there is so much darkness and unbelief. And turn away their thoughts from the decrees of God. Show them what great sinners God has pardoned, and encourage them to believe and to hope for mercy. When Mrs. Drake was in her deplorable state of darkness, she would send a description of her case to distinguished ministers, concealing her name, to know whether such a creature, without faith, hope, or love to God or man—hard-hearted, without natural affection, who had resisted and abused all means, could have any hope of going to heaven? Their answer was, that such like, and much worse, might, by the mercy of God, be received into favour, converted and saved; which did much allay her trouble. 'For,' said she, 'the fountain of all my misery hath been, that I sought that in the law, which I should have found in the gospel; and for that in myself, which was only to be found in Christ.' 'From my own experience, I can testify,' says Mr. Rogers, 'that the mild and gentle way of dealing with such is the best.'"

A volume might be written on the subject of religious melancholy, and such a volume is much needed; but it would be difficult to find a person qualified for the undertaking. We have some books written by pious casuists; and the subject is handled in medical treatises on insanity; but, to do it justice, physiological knowledge must be combined with an accurate acquaintance with the experience of Christians. Burton's "Anatomy of Melancholy," is one of the strangest books I ever read. For curious learning and classical quotations, it cannot be surpassed. And there is much originality of remark, and frequent strokes of wit in the work, but very little valuable information on the subject of which it treats. The author seems to have been himself troubled with fits of melancholy, and, enjoying much learned leisure, amused his melancholy hours by searching after and heaping up much learning, out of the common track. The spiritual physician, who has the cure of diseased souls, takes much less pains to inquire minutely and exactly into the maladies of his patients, than is observable in physicians of the body. I have often admired the alacrity and perseverance with which medical students attend upon anatomical and physiological lectures; although often, the exhibitions are extremely repulsive to our natural feelings. The patience and ingenuity, with which the men of this profession make experiments are highly worthy of imitation. Many of our young preachers, when they go forth on their important errand, are poorly qualified to direct the doubting conscience, or to administer safe consolation to those troubled in spirit. And in modern preaching, there is little account made of the various distressing cases of deep affliction under which many serious persons are suffering. If we want counsel on subjects of this kind, we must go back to the old writers; but as there is now small demand for such works, they are fast sinking into oblivion; and their place is not likely to be supplied by any works which the prolific press now pours forth. It is, however, a pleasing circumstance, that the writings of so many of our old English divines have recently been reprinted in London. But still many valuable treatises are destined to oblivion. The only object which I have in view, in introducing this subject, is to inquire, what connexion there is between real experimental religion and melancholy. And I must, in the first place, endeavour to remove a prevalent prejudice, that in all religious persons there is a strong tendency to melancholy. Indeed, there are not a few who confound these two things so completely, that they have no other idea of becoming religious, than sinking into a state of perpetual gloom. Such persons as these are so far removed from all just views of the nature of religion, that I shall not attempt, at present, to correct their errors. There are others, who entertain the opinion, that deep religious impressions tend to produce that state of mind called melancholy;

and not only so, but they suppose that in many cases, insanity is the consequence of highly raised religious affections. The fact cannot be denied, that religion is often the subject which dwells on the minds of both the melancholy and the insane. But, I am of opinion, that we are here in danger of reversing the order of nature, and putting the effect in the place of the cause. Religion does not produce melancholy, but melancholy turns the thoughts to religion. Persons of a melancholy temperament seize on such ideas as are most awful, and which furnish the greatest opportunity of indulging in despondency and despair. Sometimes, however, it is not religion which occupies the minds and thoughts of the melancholy, but their own health, which they imagine, without reason, to be declining; or their estates, which they apprehend to be wasting away, and abject poverty and beggary stare them in the face. Not unfrequently this disease alienates the mind entirely from religion, and the unhappy victim of it refuses to attend upon any religious duties, or to be present where they are performed. Frequently it assumes the form of *monomania,* or a fixed misapprehension in regard to some one thing. The celebrated and excellent William Cowper laboured, for years, under one of the most absurd hallucinations, respecting a single point; and in that point, his belief—though invincible—was repugnant to the whole of his religious creed. He imagined, that he had received from the Almighty a command, at a certain time, when in a fit of insanity, to kill himself; and as a punishment for disobedience, he had forfeited a seat in paradise. And so deep was this impression, that he would attend on no religious worship, public or private; and yet at this very time took a lively interest in the advancement of Christ's kingdom; and his judgment was so sound on other matters, that such men, as John Newton and Thomas Scott, were in the habit of consulting with him on all difficult points. The case of this man of piety and genius, was used by the enemies of religion, and particularly by the enemies of Calvin ism, as an argument against the creed which he had embraced; whereas his disease was at the worst, before he had experienced any thing of religion, or had embraced the tenets of Calvin. And, let it be remembered, that it was by turning his attention to the consolations of religion, that his excellent physician was successful in restoring his mind to tranquillity and comfort; and the world will one day learn, that of all the remedies for this malady, the pure doctrines of grace are the most effectual to resuscitate the melancholy mind. This is, in fact, a bodily disease, by which the mind is influenced and darkened. Thus it was received by the ancient Greeks; for the term is compounded of two Greek words which signify *black bile.* How near they were to the truth, in assigning the physical cause which produces the disease, I leave to others to determine. Casuists have often erred egregiously, by referring all such cases to mental or moral causes. It is probable, even when the disease is brought on by strong impressions on the mind, that, by these, physical derangement occurs. To reason with a man against the views which arise from melancholy, is commonly as inefficacious, as reasoning against bodily pain! I have long made this a criterion, to ascertain whether the dejection experienced was owing to a physical cause; for, in that case, argument though demonstrative, has no effect. Still such persons should be affectionately conversed with; and their peculiar opinions and views should rarely be contradicted. Cases often occur, in which there is a mixture of moral and physical causes; and these should be treated in reference to both sources of their affliction. Melancholy is sometimes hereditary, and often constitutional. When such persons are relieved for a while, they are apt to relapse into the same state, as did William Cowper. The late excellent and venerable James Hall, D. D. of North Carolina, was of a melancholy temperament; and, after finishing his education at Princeton, he fell into a gloomy dejection, which interrupted his studies and labours for more than a year. After his restoration, he laboured successfully and comfortably in the ministry for many years, even to old age; but at last was overtaken again, and entirely overwhelmed by this terrible malady. Of all men, that I ever saw, he had the tenderest sympathy with persons labouring under religious despondency. When on a journey, I have known him to travel miles out of his way to converse with a sufferer of this kind; and his manner was most tender and affectionate in speaking to such.

I have remarked, that persons who gave no symptoms of this disease until the decline of life, have then fallen under its power; owing to some change in the constitution at that period, or some change in their active pursuits. I recollect two cases of overwhelming melancholy in persons, who appeared in their former life, as remote from it as any that I ever knew. The first was a man of extraordinary talents, and eloquence; bold and decisive in his temper, and fond of company and good cheer. When about fifty-five or six years of age, without any external cause to produce the effect, his spirits began to sink, and feelings of melancholy to seize upon him. He avoided company; but I had frequent occasion to see him, and sometimes he could be engaged in conversation, when he would speak as judiciously as before; but he soon reverted to his dark melancholy mood. On one occasion he mentioned his case to me, and observed with emphasis, that he had no power whatever to resist the disease, and, said he, with despair in his countenance, "I shall soon be utterly overwhelmed." And so it turned out, for the disease advanced until it ended in the worst form of *mania*, and soon terminated his life. The other was the case of a gentleman who had held office in the American army, in the revolutionary war. About the same age, or a little later, he lost his cheerfulness, which had never been interrupted before, and by degrees, sunk into a most deplorable state of melancholy, which as in the former case, soon ended in death. In this case, the first thing which I noticed, was, a morbid sensibility of the moral sense, which filled him with remorse, for acts, which had little or no moral turpitude attached to them.

I would state then, as the result of all my observation, that religion, in its regular and rational exercise, has no tendency to melancholy or insanity, but the contrary; and that, religion is the most effectual remedy for this disease, whatever be its cause. But melancholy persons are very apt to seize on the dark side of religion, as affording food for the morbid state of their minds. True Christians, as being subject to like diseases with others, may become melancholy; but not in consequence of their piety: but in this melancholy condition, they are in a more comfortable, as well as in a safer state, than others. They may relinquish all their hopes; but they cannot divest themselves of their pious feelings.

I have said nothing respecting the supposed tendency of strong religious feelings to produce insanity, for what has been said respecting melancholy is equally applicable to this subject. Indeed, I am of opinion, that melancholy is a species of insanity; and in its worst form, the most appalling species; for, in most cases, insane persons seem to have many enjoyments, arising out of their strange misconceptions, but the victim of melancholy is miserable; he is often suffering under the most horrible of all calamities, black despair. When a child, I used to tremble when I read Bunyan's account, in his Pilgrim, of the man shut up in the iron cage. And in the year 1791, when I first visited the Pennsylvania Hospital, I saw a man there who had arrived a few days before, said to be in a religious melancholy, and to be in despair. He had made frequent attempts on his own life, and all instruments, by which he might accomplish that direful purpose, were carefully removed. Having never been accustomed to see insane persons, the spectacle of so many, deprived of reason, made an awful impression on my mind; but although some were raving and blaspheming, in their cells, and others confined in strait-jackets, the sight of no one so affected me, as that of this man in despair. Although near half a century has elapsed since I beheld his sorrowful countenance, there is still a vivid picture of it in my imagination. We spoke to him, but he re turned no answer; except that he once raised his despairing eyes; but immediately cast them down again. Whether this man had been the subject of any religious impressions, I did not learn. But this one thing, I must testify, that I never knew the most pungent convictions of sin to terminate in insanity; and as to the affections of love to God, and the lively hope of everlasting life producing insanity, it is too absurd for any one to believe it. I do not dispute, however, that enthusiasm may have a tendency to insanity; and some people are so ignorant of the nature of true religion as to confound it with enthusiasm. I will go further and declare, that, after much thought on the subject of enthusiasm, I am unable to account for the effects produced by it, in any other way, than by supposing that it is a case of real insanity. Diseases of this class are the more dangerous, because they are manifestly contagious. The very looks and tones of an enthusiast are felt to be powerful by every one; and when the nervous system of any one is in a state easily susceptible of emotions from such a cause, the dominion of reason is overthrown, and wild imagination and irregular emotion govern the infatuated person, who readily embraces all the extravagant opinions, and receives all the disturbing impressions which belong to the party infected. Without a supposition such as the foregoing, how can you account for the fact, that an educated man and popular preacher, and a wife, intelligent and judicious above most, having a family of beloved children, should separate from each other; relinquish all the comforts of domestic life, and a pleasant and promising congregation, to connect themselves with a people who are the extreme of all enthusiasts—the Shakers? But such facts have been witnessed in our own times, and in no small numbers. In a town in New Hampshire, the writer, when in the neighbourhood, was told of the case of a young preacher, who visited the Shaker settlement, out of curiosity, to see them dance, in which exercise their principal worship consists: but, while he stood and looked on, he was seized with the same spirit, and began to shake and dance too; and never returned, but remained in the society. But, there being no demand for his learning or preaching talents, whatever they might be—and he being an able bodied man, they employed him in building stone fences. This species of infatuation, which is called enthusiasm, is apt to degenerate into bitterness and malignity of spirit, towards all who do not embrace it, and then it is termed fanaticism. This species of insanity, as I must be permitted to call it, differs from other kinds in that it is social, or affects large numbers in the same way, and binds them together by the link of close fraternity. It agrees with other kinds of monomania, in that the aberration of mind relates to one subject, while the judgment may be sound in other matters. No people know how to manage their agricultural, horticultural, and mechanical business more skilfully and successfully, than the Shakers. And the newer sect of Mormons, would soon settle down to peaceable industry, if the people would let them alone. This country promises to be the theatre of all conceivable forms of enthusiasm and fanaticism; and as long as these misguided people pursue their own course, without disturbing other people, they should be left to their own delusions, as it relates to the civil power; but if any of them should be impelled by their fanatical spirit, to disturb the peace, they should be treated like other maniacs.

The causes of melancholy and insanity, whether physical or moral, cannot easily be explored. The physician will speak confidently about a lesion of the brain, but when insane persons have been subjected to a post-mortem examination, the brain very seldom exhibits any appearance of derangement. The casuist, on the other hand, thinks only of moral causes, and attributes the disease to such of this class as are known to have existed, or flees to hypothesis, which will account for every thing. There is a remarkable coincidence, however, which has fallen under my observation, between those who assign a moral and those who assign a physical cause for melancholy and madness, in regard to one point. Some forty or fifty years ago, the writer, about the same time, read Shepard's "Sincere Convert," and Robe on "Religious Melancholy," and he noticed, that they both ascribe the deep and fixed depression of spirits, frequently met with, to a secret, criminal indulgence. Well, in the statistics of several insane asylums and penitentiaries which have been published recently, the most of the cases of insanity are confidently ascribed to the same thing, as its physical cause. This increasing evil is of such a nature that we cannot be more explicit. Those who ought to know the facts, will understand the reference. It must, after all, be admitted that the claims of intemperance in the use of intoxicating drinks, to a deleterious influence on the reason, stand in the foremost rank; but the madness produced by this cause is commonly of short duration. I do not speak of that loss of reason which is the immediate effect of alcohol on the brain; but of that most tremendous form of madness called *delirium tremens*. I have said that it was short, because it is commonly the last struggle of the human constitution, under the influence of a dreadful poison, which has now consummated its work—and death soon steps in and puts an end to the conflict.

After spending so much time in speaking of melancholy as a disease, I anticipate the thoughts of some good people, who will be ready to say, What, is there no such thing as spiritual desertion—times of darkness and temptation, which are independent of the bodily temperament? To which I answer, that I fully believe there are many such cases; but they deserve a separate consideration, and do not fall within the compass of my present design. The causes, symptoms, and cure of such spiritual maladies are faithfully delineated by many practical writers; and although these cases are entirely distinct from melancholy, they assume, in many respects, similar symptoms, and, by the unskilful casuist, are confounded with it. These two causes, as I have before intimated may often operate together, and produce a mixed and very perplexed case, both for the bodily and spiritual physician.

After all that has been said, the fact, with which we commenced, is that religious exercises are very much modified by the temperament, and in some cases, by the idiosyncrasy of the individual. The liquor put into an old cask, commonly receives a strong tincture from the vessel. Old habits, although a new governing principle is introduced into the system, do not yield at once; and propensities, apparently extinguished, are apt to revive, and give unexpected trouble. It is a comfortable thought, that those bodies cannot go with the saints to heaven, until they are completely purified. What proportion of our present feelings will be dropped with the body, we cannot tell. How a disembodied spirit will perceive, feel, and act, we shall soon know by consciousness; but, if ever so many of the departed should return and attempt to communicate to us their present mode of existence, it would be all in vain; the things, which relate to such a state, are inconceivable, and unspeakable. What Paul saw in the third heaven he dare not, or he could not communicate; but he did not know whether he saw these wonderful things in the body or out of the body. This was a thing known, as he intimates, only to God.

CHAPTER V.

Effect of sympathy illustrated.—Cautions in relation to this subject.—A singular case in illustration.

THE causes, already considered, which modify religious experience, relate to Christians as individuals but man is constitutionally a social being; and religion is a social thing; so that we cannot have a complete view of this subject, without considering them as they stand connected with others; and, especially, as they are influenced by one another. There is a mysterious bond, called *sympathy*, by which not only human beings, but some species of animals are connected. It is much easier, on this subject, to state facts than to account for them. A man cannot go into any company without being sensible of some change in his feelings. Whatever passion agitates those around him, he involuntarily participates in the emotion; and the mere external expression of any feeling, often produces the same expression in himself, whether it be yawning, smiling, crying, or coughing, and this must be effected by an assimilation of the mind of the beholder, to the state of mind which produced the external act. The wilder and stronger the passions which agitate others, the more are we affected by them. This operation of mutual sympathetic excitement, when many persons are brought together under some agitating influence, produces a stream of emotion which cannot easily be resisted; and far above what any one of the crowd would have felt, if the same cause had operated on him alone. Hence the ungovernable fury of mobs, carrying desolation, and often murder in their train; and yet the ringleaders, had they been alone, would have experienced no such violence of passion; and hence the danger, in large cities, of permitting multitudes of undisciplined people to assemble promiscuously. A mob is an artificial body, pervaded by one spirit; by the power of sympathy; for which the French have an appropriate phrase, *esprit du corps.* If there be any thing in animal magnetism, which has of late made so much noise, beside sheer imposture, it must be grafted on this principle; for the extent to which human beings may influence each other, by contact or proximity, in certain excitable states of the nervous system, has never been accurately ascertained. In those remarkable bodily affections, called the *jerks,* which appeared in religious meetings some years ago, the nervous irregularity was commonly produced by the sight of other persons thus affected; and if, in some instances, without the sight, yet by having the imagination strongly impressed by hearing of such things. It is a fact, as undoubted as it is remarkable, that, as this bodily affection assumed a great variety of appearances, in different places, nothing was more common, than for a new species of the *exercise,* as it was called, to be imported from another part of the country, by one or a few individuals. This contagion of nervous excitement is not unparalleled; for whole schools of young ladies have been seized with spasmodic or epileptic fits, in consequence of a single scholar being taken with the disease. There are many authentic facts ascertained in relation to this matter, which I hope some person will collect and give to the public, through the press. It will not be thought strange then, that sympathy should have a powerful influence in increasing and modifying the feelings which are experienced in religious meetings; nor is it desirable that it should be otherwise. This principle, no doubt, is liable to abuse, and when unduly excited, may be attended with disagreeable and injurious effects, but without it, how dull and uninteresting would social worship be. When a whole assembly, in listening to the same evangelical discourse, or praising God in the same divine song, or sitting together around the same sacramental table, are deeply affected, they form, as it were, one body, and the whole mass is melted down and amalgamated into one grand emotion. They seem to have but one heart and one soul; and as harmoniously as their voices mingle in the sacred song of praise to the Redeemer, do their feelings amalgamate in one ascending volume, towards heaven. The preacher, who is privileged to address such an assembly, seems to have before him one great body, having many eyes, but one soul. Hence we see the reason, why a company thinly scattered over a large house, always appears cold and uncomfortable; while the same persons brought near together, in a small house, have an entirely different appearance; and also we see why social meetings in private houses, are felt by sincere Christians to be more profitable, often, than the more solemn assemblies of the church. And, upon the same principle, all worshippers feel more animated when surrounded by a multitude. But, it is in times of revival, or general awakening, that the power of this principle manifests itself most evidently and it is no evidence of a spurious work, that the sympathies of the people are much awakened, or that many are led to seriousness by seeing others affected. God often blesses this instinctive feeling in this very way. But, is it not to be expected that, at such a time, many will be affected by mere sympathy? And will not such as are thus affected, be in great danger of being deceived, by taking these tender emotions of sympathy to be the exercises of true repentance, especially, as they fall in with those convictions of conscience, which all who hear the gospel experience? Is it then judicious, by impassioned discourses, addressed to the sympathies of our nature, to raise this class of feelings to a flame? or to devise *measures*, by which the passions of the young and ignorant may be excited to excess? That measures may be put into operation, which have a mighty influence on a whole assembly, is readily admitted; but are excitements thus produced really useful? They may bring young people, who are diffident, to a decision, and as it were, constrain them to range themselves on the Lord's side, but the question which sticks with me, is, does this really benefit the persons? In my judgment, not at all, but the contrary. If they have the seed of grace, though it may come forth slowly, yet this principle will find its way to the light and air, and the very slowness of its coming forward, may give it opportunity to strike its roots deep in the earth. If I were to place myself on what is called an *anxious seat*, or should kneel down before a whole congregation to be prayed for, I know that I should be strangely agitated, but I do not believe that it would be of any permanent utility. But if it *should* produce some good effect, am I at liberty to resort to any thing in the worship of God which I think will be useful? If such things are lawful and useful, why not add other circumstances to increase the effect? Why not require the penitent to appear in a white sheet, or to be clothed in sackcloth, with ashes on his head? and these, re member, are Scriptural signs of humiliation. And on these principles, who can reasonably object to holy water, to incense, and the use of pictures or images in the worship of God? All these things come into the church upon this same principle, of devising *new measures* to do good; and if the *anxious seat* is so powerful a means of grace, it may soon come to be reckoned among the sacraments of the church. The language of experience is, that it is unsafe and unwise to bring persons, who are under religious impressions, too much into public view. The seed of the word, like the natural seed, does not vegetate well in the sun. Be not too impatient to force into maturity the plant of grace. Water it, cultivate it, but handle it not with a rough hand. The opinion entertained by some good people, that all religion obtained in a revival is suspicious, has no just foundation. At such times, when the Spirit of God is really poured out, the views and exercises of converts are commonly more clear and satisfactory, than at other times, and the process of conversion more speedy. But doubtless, there may be expected a considerable crop of spurious conversions, and these may make the greatest show; for the seed on the stony ground, seems to have vegetated the quickest of any. And this is the reason that, after all revivals, there is a sad declension in the favourable appearances; because that which has no root must soon wither. In looking back, after a revival season, I have thought, how would matters have been if none had come forward, but such as persevere and bring forth fruit? Perhaps things would have gone on so quietly, that the good work would not have been called a *revival*. But ministers cannot prevent the impressions which arise merely from sympathy—neither should they attempt it; but, when they are about to gather the wheat into the garner, they should faithfully winnow the heap; not that they can discern the spirits of men, but the word of God is a discerner of the thoughts and intents of the heart. The church is no place of safety for the unconverted. Hundreds and thousands are shielded from salutary convictions, by their profession and situation in the church. Let ministers be "wise as serpents," as well as "harmless as doves." "Be not many masters, (διδασκαλοι) knowing that ye shall receive the greater condemnation." "They watch for souls as they that must give account,"—AWFUL ACCOUNT!

From what has been said about the power of sympathy, some may be ready to conclude that all experimental religion, and all revivals may be accounted for, on this principle, without the necessity of supposing any supernatural agency to exist; and if no effects were produced but those excitements which often mingle with religious exercises, this would be no irrational conclusion. But under the preaching of the gospel we find a permanent change of moral character taking place: so great a change, that, even in the view of the world who observe it, the subject appears to be "a new man." An entire revolution has taken place in his principles of action as well as in his sentiments respecting divine things. Now those who would ascribe all experimental religion to mere natural feelings, artificially excited, must believe that there are no such transformations of character as have been mentioned; and that all who profess such a change are false pretenders. But this ground is manifestly untenable; for no facts are more certain than such reformations; and if there be men of truth and sincerity in the world, they are to be found among those who have undergone this moral transformation. Surely there are no phenomena now taking place in our world half so important and worthy of consideration, as the repentance of an habitual sinner; so that he utterly forsakes his wicked courses, and takes delight in the worship of God and obedience to his will. Let it be remembered, that these are effects observed only where the gospel is preached, and in some instances, numerous examples of such conversions from sin to holiness occur about the same time, and in the same place No series of miracles could give stronger evidence of the divine origin and power of the gospel, than the actual and permanent reformation of wicked men; and the skeptic may be challenged to account for such effects on any natural principles. But it may still be asked how the person who is the subject of these new views and exercises, can know that they are the effects of a supernatural agency? It is readily admitted that we cannot be conscious of the agency of another spirit on ours, because our consciousness extends only to our own thoughts, and often when new feelings arise in our minds we are unable to trace them to their proper cause. In this case, if we had no revelation from God, we might not be able with certainty to account for such effects; but in the word of God we are distinctly and repeatedly informed, that God by his Spirit will continue to operate on the minds of men, to turn them from iniquity, and to cause them to engage with delight in his service; and when we find these very effects taking place, in connexion with the means appointed to produce them, we can have no doubt about their divine origin; and our faith is confirmed in this doctrine of divine agency by observing the wonderful change produced by the preaching of the gospel upon the most depraved and degraded of the heathen. The transformation of character, in thousands of instances now existing, is enough to produce conviction in any mind, not rendered obdurate by the prejudices of infidelity. It may be objected, that, in many instances, the change professed is not permanent, but temporary, and they who appear saints to-day, may be found wallowing in the mire of iniquity, to-morrow. These are facts which we cannot gainsay; but we do deny that they go to invalidate the argument from the examples of a permanent and thorough change which do really take place. If there were only one real, sound conversion, and reformation, in a hundred of those who may be religiously impressed, still, the conclusion in favour of a divine influence, would be valid. In the spring we behold the trees clothed and adorned with millions of blossoms, which never produce mature fruit; but when in autumn, we find here and there, apples, large, sweet, and mellow, do we hesitate to believe that this is a good tree which produces good fruit? For reasons already given, it ought not to be expected that all serious impressions should eventuate in a sound conversion. External appearances may be the same to our view, where the causes are entirely diverse. This is especially to be expected when a great many are affected at once, and meet in the same assembly. And if these transient appearances did not take place under the preaching of the gospel, our Saviour's doctrine of the various effects of the word would not be verified. Ministers of the gospel cannot be blamed for these temporary impressions; unless they use unauthorized means to work upon the sympathies of their hearers. That, through ignorance, vanity and enthusiastic ardour, many preachers in our day, have attempted to produce such excitements, cannot be denied, and by the true friends of vital piety, is greatly lamented. Perhaps nothing has so much prejudiced the minds of sensible men against experimental religion, as the extravagance and violence of those factitious excitements which have been promoted, in various places, by measures artfully contrived to work upon the passions and imagination of weak and ignorant people. And as the preacher must have his reward of glory for his efforts, all this must be so brought out, that their number may be counted and published to the world. Alas! alas! poor human nature! I believe that all respectable denominations, among us, are becoming more and more sensible, that something more is requisite in the ministry than fiery zeal. Some who, within our remembrance, disparaged a learned ministry, are now using noble exertions to erect seminaries, and encourage their young preachers to seek to be learned. This is a matter of rejoicing, and augurs well for the American Church hereafter. I should be unwilling to bring before the public all the scenes that I have witnessed under the name of religious worship. But as the subject of sympathy is still under consideration, I will relieve the reader by a short narrative. Being in a part of the country where I was known, by face, to scarcely any one, and hearing that there was *a great meeting* in the neighbourhood, and a *good work* in progress, I determined to attend. The sermon had commenced before I arrived, and the house was so crowded that I could not approach near to the pulpit, but sat down in a kind of shed connected with the main building where I could see and hear the preacher. His sermon was really striking and impressive, and in language and method, far above the common run of extempore discourses. The people were generally attentive, and, so far as I could observe, many were tenderly affected, except that in the extreme part of the house, where I sat, some old tobacco-planters kept up a continual conversation in a low tone, about tobacco-plants, seasons, &c. When the preacher came to the application of his discourse he became exceedingly vehement and boisterous, and I could hear some sounds in the centre of the house which indicated strong emotion. At length, a female voice was heard, in a piercing cry, which thrilled through me and affected the whole audience. It was succeeded by a low murmuring sound from the middle of the house; but, in a few seconds, one and another arose in different parts of the house, under extreme and visible agitation. Casting off bonnets and caps, and raising their folded hands, they shouted to the utmost extent of their voice; and in a few seconds more, the whole audience was agitated, as a forest when shaken by a mighty wind. The sympathetic wave, commencing in the centre, extended to the extremities; and at length it reached our corner, and I felt the conscious effort of resistance as necessary as if I had been exposed to the violence of a storm. I saw few persons through the whole house who escaped the prevailing influence; even careless boys seemed to be arrested and to join in the general outcry. But what astonished me most of all was, that the old tobacco-planters, whom I have mentioned, and who, I am persuaded, had not heard one word of the sermon, were violently agitated. Every muscle of their brawny faces appeared to be in tremulous motion, and the big tears chased one another down their wrinkled cheeks. Here I saw the power of sympathy. The feeling was real, and propagated from person to person by the mere sounds which were uttered; for many of the audience had not paid any attention to what was said; but nearly all partook of the agitation. The feelings expressed were different, as when the foundation of the second temple was laid; for while some uttered the cry of poignant anguish, others shouted in the accents of joy and triumph. The speaker's voice was soon silenced, and he sat down and gazed on the scene with a complacent smile. When this tumult had lasted a few minutes, another preacher, as I suppose he was, who sat on the pulpit steps, with his handkerchief spread over his head, began to sing a soothing and yet lively tune, and was quickly joined by some strong female voices near him; and in less than two minutes the storm was hushed, and there was a great calm. It was like pouring oil on the troubled waters. I experienced the most sensible relief to my own feelings from the appropriate music; for I could not hear the words sung. But I could not have supposed that any thing could so quickly allay such a storm; and all seemed to enjoy the tranquillity which succeeded. The dishevelled hair was put in order, and the bonnets, &c. gathered up, and the irregularities of the dress adjusted, and no one seemed conscious of any impropriety. Indeed, there is a peculiar luxury in such excitements, especially when tears are shed copiously, which was the case here. But I attended another meeting in another place where there had been a remarkable excitement, but the tide was far on the ebb; and although we had vociferation and outcrying of a stunning kind, I did not hear one sound indicative of real feeling, and I do not think that one tear was shed during the meeting.

CHAPTER VI.

Erroneous views of regeneration.—The correct view.—The operation of faith.—Exercises of mind, as illustrated in President Edwards's narrative.—The operations of faith still further explained.

It is proper now to inquire, what are the precise effects of regeneration, or the exercises of a newly converted soul? As the restoration of depraved man to the image of God, lost by the fall, is the grand object aimed at in the whole economy of salvation, it can easily be said, in the general, that by this change a principle of holiness is implanted, spiritual life is communicated, the mind is enlightened, the will renewed, and the affections purified and elevated to heavenly objects. Such general descriptions do not afford full satisfaction to the inquiring mind; and as we have taken into view many of those circumstances which diversify the exercises of grace, in different subjects, let us now endeavour to ascertain, with as much precision as we can, what are those things which are essential to the genuineness of this work, and which, therefore, will be found in every sincere Christian. But in this attempt, great difficulty must be met in conveying our ideas with precision. Even those terms which are most used in the Holy Scriptures, to designate the essential exercises of piety are differently understood, and when used, convey different ideas to different persons. I will endeavour, however, to avoid this difficulty, as much as possible, by defining the terms which I employ. I have all along admitted, that the mode of the Spirit's operation, in regeneration, is altogether inscrutable: and an attempt to explain it, is worse than folly. We may, however, without intruding into things unseen, or attempting to dive into the unsearchable nature of the divine operations, say, that God operates on the human mind, in a way perfectly consistent with its nature, as a spirit, and a creature of understanding and will. On this principle some suppose, that there can be no other method of influencing a rational mind but by the exhibition of truth, or the presentment of motives: any physical operation, they allege, would be unsuitable. Their theory of regeneration, therefore, is, that it is produced by the moral operation of the truth, contemplated by the understanding, and influencing the affections and the will, according to the known principles of our rational nature. But respecting what is necessary to bring the truth fairly before the mind, the abettors of this theory divide into several parts. The Pelagian, believing human nature to be uncontaminated, and needing nothing but a correct knowledge of the truth, rejects all supernatural aid, and maintains, that every man has full ability to perform all good actions, and to reform what is amiss, by simply attending to the instructions of the word, and exercising his own free will, by which he is able to choose and pursue what course he pleases. The semi-Pelagian agrees with the views given, except in one particular. He believes that the truth, if seriously contemplated, will produce the effects stated, but that mankind are so immersed in the world of sensible objects, and so occupied and filled with earthly thoughts and cares, that no man will, or ever does contemplate the truth so impartially and steadily, as to produce a change in his affections and purposes, until he is influenced by the Holy Spirit; and, according to him, the only need of divine agency, in regeneration, is to direct and fix the attention on divine things. This being done, the truth, as contained in the divine word, and as apprehended by the natural understanding, is adequate to produce all the desired effects on the active principles of our nature. There is still a third party, who attribute regeneration to the simple operation of the truth on the mind, whose views are neither Pelagian nor semi-Pelagian. They hold, that the natural man cannot discern the things of the Spirit of God, and that if a man should ever so long contemplate the truth with such views as natural reason takes of it, it would never transform him into the divine likeness; but that, by the illumination of the Holy Spirit, the sinner must obtain new, spiritual views of divine things, by which he is renovated or regenerated: yet, these deny that any operation on the mind itself is necessary, as they allege that these spiritual views of truth will certainly draw after them the exercise of those affections, in which holiness essentially consists. Now, in my judgment, this theory is defective, only in one point, and that is, it supposes the mind, which is already in possession of doctrinal knowledge of the truth, to have this same truth presented to it in an entirely new light, without any operation on the soul itself. Just as if a man was blind, but standing in the clear shining of the sun's rays. These he feels, and can talk philosophically about the sensation of light and colours; while he has not in his mind the first simple perception of any object of sight. Could this man be made to perceive the visible objects around him, without an operation on the eyes to remove the obstruction, or to rectify the organ? The case of the soul is entirely analogous. Here is light enough; the truth is viewed by the intellect of unregenerate man, but has no transforming efficacy. The fault is not in the truth, which is perfect, but the blindness is in the mind, which can only be removed by an influence on the soul itself; that is, by the power of God creating "a new heart," to use the language of Scripture. The apostle Paul was sent to the Gentiles "to open their eyes, and to turn them from darkness to light." Two things are always necessary to distinct vision, the medium of light, and a sound organ; either of these without the other, would be useless; but combined, the beauties of nature, and the glory of God in the visible world, are seen with delight. It is so in the spiritual world. The truth is necessary; but until the mind is brought into a state in which it can perceive it in its beauty and glory, it is heard, and read, and contemplated, without any transforming effect—without drawing the affections to God, or subduing the power of selfish and sensual desires. The fault existing in the percipient being, there must be such an exertion of divine power as will remove it, and this is regeneration. Then, all the effects of the truth will take place, as according to the former theory. But I seem to hear the common objection, that if the soul be the subject of any operation, this must be *physical*, and what is this but to make man a mere machine, or to deal with him as if he were a block? I believe that a more ambiguous, unhappy word could not be used than *physical;* the best way to get clear of the mists which surround it, is to drop its use altogether in this connexion. Indeed, it is a term which properly belongs to another science—to natural philosophy. If the operation must have a name, let it receive it from the nature of the effect produced; this being spiritual, let it be called a *spiritual* operation; or, as the effect produced, is confessedly above the powers of unassisted nature, let us call it *supernatural*, which is the precise technical term, used by the most accurate theologians. Can the Almighty, who made the soul, operate upon it in no other way than by a mechanical force? Cannot he restore its lost power of spiritual perception and susceptibility of holy feeling, without doing any violence to its free and spiritual nature? But I shall be told, that there neither is, nor can be, any moral or spiritual nature, or disposition prior to volition, in the mind—for morality consists, essentially, in choice; and to suppose morality to have any other existence, than in the transient act, is an absurdity. If this be sound moral philosophy, then my theory must fall. This is a question not requiring or admitting of much reasoning. It is a subject for the intuitive judgment of the moral faculty. If there are minds so constituted, that they cannot conceive of permanent, latent dispositions in the soul, both good and evil, I can do no more than express my strong dissent from their opinion, and appeal to the common sense of mankind.

Some of my most serious readers, I know, will object to my theory of the mind's operations, in one important particular. They are so far from thinking that any illumination of the mind will produce holy affections, that it is a radical principle in their philosophy of religion, that light always increases or stirs up the enmity of an unregenerate heart; that the more unholy beings know of God, the more they will hate him, as is supposed to be proved by the experience of thousands under conviction of sin; and by the case of the devils who believe and tremble, but never love. The difference between me and these persons is not so great as at first view it seems. Their error consists, if I am right, in making too wide a severance between the understanding and the will; between the intellect and the affections. I am ready to admit that all the knowledge which you can communicate to a man remaining unregenerate, may have the tendency of increasing or stirring up his enmity to God and his law; but, observe, that I make illumination the first effect of regeneration. And I hold that no unregenerate man is, while in that state, any more capable of spiritual perception than a blind man is of a perception of colours. The blind man, however, has his own ideas about colours, and may understand their various relations to each other, and all the laws which regulate the reflection and refraction of light as well as those who see. This was remarkably exemplified in the case of Dr. Sanderson, who, though blind from his early infancy, delivered an accurate course of lectures, on light and colours, in the University of Oxford. Just so, an unregenerate man may be able to deliver able lectures on all the points in theology, and yet not have one glimpse of the beauty and glory of the truth, with which he is conversant. The sacred Scriptures represent all unconverted men, as destitute of the true knowledge of God. If there be a clear truth in the laws of mental operation, it is, that the affections are in exact accordance with the views of the understanding. If men are unaffected with the truth known, it must be because they do not know it aright: neither can they perceive it in its true nature until they are regenerated. Did any man ever see an object to be lovely and not feel an emotion corresponding with that quality? And what unconverted man ever beheld in Christ, as represented in Scripture, the beauty and glory of God? Hence that doctrine is not true, which confines depravity or holiness to the will; and which considers the understanding as a natural and the will as a moral faculty. The soul is not depraved or holy by departments; the disease affects it, as a soul; and of course all faculties employed in moral exercises, must partake of their moral qualities. There is, however, no propriety in calling either of them a *moral* faculty; for although both understanding and will are concerned in every moral act, yet not one hundredth part of the acts of either partakes of a moral nature. The will is just as much a natural faculty as the understanding; and the understanding is as much a moral faculty as the will. But in strict propriety of speech, the only faculty which deserves to be called a moral faculty is conscience; because, by it only are we capable of moral perceptions or feelings.

I am afraid that I have gone too far into abstruse distinctions, for most of my readers; but there are thousands of plain, private Christians, in our country, who not only can enter into such disquisitions, but will relish them.

I come now to what I intended when I began this subject, to describe as exactly as I can, what are the exercises of the new heart, or the regenerate man. And here my appeal is to no theories, but to experience, combined with the word of God. Every man, on whom this divine operation has passed, experiences *new views of divine truth.* The soul sees, in these things, *that* which it never saw before. It discerns, in the truth of God, a beauty and excellence, of which it had no conception until now. Whatever may be the diversity in the clearness of the views of different persons, or in the particular truths brought before the mind, they all agree in this, that there is a new perception of truth; whether you ascribe it to the head or the heart, I care not. It is a blessed reality, and there are many witnesses of sound mind, and unquestionable veracity, who are ready to attest it as a verity, known in their own delightful experience. But, as the field of truth is very wide, and divine things may be perceived under innumerable aspects and relations, and as there is no uniformity in the particular objects which may first occupy the attention of the enlightened mind, it is impossible to lay down any particular order of exercises which take place. The case may be illustrated by supposing a great multitude of blind persons restored to sight by an act of divine power. Some of them would be so situated, that the first object seen would be the glorious luminary of day; another might receive the gift of sight in the night, and the moon and stars would absorb his wondering attention; a third might direct his opened eyes to a beautiful landscape; and a fourth might have but a ray of light shining into a dark dungeon without his knowing whence it came. Of necessity, there must be the same endless variety in the particular views of new converts; but still they all partake of new views of divine truth; and the same truths will generally be contemplated, sooner or later; but not in the same order, nor exhibited to all with the same degree of clearness. Now, according to the views which I entertain, this spiritual knowledge granted to the regenerated soul is nothing else but saving faith; for knowledge and belief involve each other. To know a thing and not believe it is a contradiction; and to believe a thing and not know it is impossible. Faith is simply *a belief of the truth*, when viewed as distinct, and discriminated from all other mental acts. Some will be startled at this nakedness of faith; and many will be ready to object, that it is to make faith to be no more than a bare assent of the understanding to the truth: well, if it be uniformly accompanied by all holy affections and emotions what is the difference? But I deny that as described, it is a naked assent of the understanding, as those words are commonly understood. The wide distinction between the understanding and will, which has very much confounded our mental philosophy, has come down to us from the schoolmen. But in making the distinction, they made simple verity, the object of the understanding. And that is what we commonly mean by bare assent; it relates to the simple truth; but the will, has respect, they said, to *good*—every species of good. Now the faith of which I have spoken, at the same time contemplates the truth, and the beauty, excellency, and goodness of the object, and also its adaptedness to our necessities: all these things are comprehended in the views which the Holy Spirit gives to the mind. Therefore, though faith be a simple uncompounded act, a firm belief, or persuasion, it comprehends the objects ascribed both to the understanding and the will. Here I shall be met by a definition of faith, which makes the act simple also, but considers that act to be *trust* or *confidence*. This the reader will remember is Dr. Dwight's definition of Faith. And the only objection to it, is, that it is too narrow to comprehend all that belongs to the subject. Trust is nothing else than the firm belief or persuasion of the truth of a promise. When we say that we trust, or have confidence in a person, it relates to some promise. This definition comprehends all acts of faith, which have a promise of God for their object, and these are certainly the most important acts, and accompanied with the most sensible emotions. But all divine truth is not in the form of a promise. The whole word of God is the proper object of a true faith; and a large part of divine revelation is taken up with histories, prophecies, doctrines, and precepts. The Christian believes all these, as well as the promises!

Here faith is the first act of the regenerated soul; and the most important act, for it draws all holy affections and emotions in its train. But though it sweetly mingles with every other grace, it is distinct from them all. All its diversified acts arise from the nature of the truths believed, and men may enumerate and name as many of these acts as they please; still the nature of faith remains simple. It is a firm persuasion or belief of the truth, apprehended under the illumination of the Holy Spirit. It necessarily works by love and purifies the heart, for divine things thus discerned, cannot but excite the affections to holy objects, by which sinful desires and appetites will be subdued; and when we are persuaded of the truth of God's gracious promises, there will always be a sweet repose of soul, because the promises contain the very blessings which we need; and to be assured that there are such blessings for all who will receive them, and especially if the soul is conscious that it is exercising faith, will produce sweet consolation—There is "joy and peace in believing."

According to the view of faith now given, there is nothing mysterious about it. To believe in divine truth is an act of the mind, precisely the same as to believe in other truth; and the difference between a saving faith and a historical or merely speculative faith, consists not in the truths believed, for in both they are the same; nor in the degree of assent given to the proposition, but in the evidence on which they are respectively founded. A saving faith is produced by the manifestation of the truth, in its true nature to the mind, which now apprehends it, according to the degree of faith, in its spiritual qualities, its beauty, and glory, and sweetness; whereas a historical or speculative faith may rest on the prejudices of education, or the deductions of reason; but in its exercise, there is no conception of the true qualities of divine things. The humblest, weakest believer possesses a knowledge of God, hidden from the wisest of enlightened men; according to that saying of Christ, "I thank thee, O Father, Lord of heaven and earth, that thou hast hid these things from the wise and prudent, and hast revealed them to babes."

On the subject of experimental religion our dependence must not be on the theories of men, but on the unerring word of God, and on the facts which have been observed in the experience of true Christians. In the exercises of new converts there is, in some respects, a remarkable similarity, and in others a remarkable variety. All are convinced of sin, not only of life but of heart. All are brought to acknowledge the justice of God, in their condemnation, and to feel that they might be left to perish, without any derogation from the perfections of God; and that they have no ability to bring God under any obligations to save them, by their prayers, tears, or other religious duties. All true Christians, moreover, love the truth which has been revealed to their minds, and are led to trust in Christ alone for salvation; and they all hunger and thirst after righteousness, and resolve to devote themselves to the service of God, and prefer his glory above their chief joy. But, besides those varieties already described, as arising from several causes, there is often much difference in their exercises, arising from the particular truths which they are led to contemplate when their eyes are first opened. I do not mean to go over the ground which we have already passed, otherwise than by a statement of facts from authentic sources, which may serve to corroborate and illustrate the statements already given. Perhaps no man, who has lived in modern times, has had a better opportunity to form an accurate judgment of facts of this kind, than President Edwards; and few men, who ever lived, were better qualified to discriminate between true and false religion. It is a thing much to be prized, that this great and good man has left a record of that most remarkable revival which took place in Northampton, New England, in the year 1734 and onwards. This narrative was written soon afterwards, and was communicated to Dr Watts and Dr. Guyse, who united in a preface which accompanied the narrative, when published in London. In this account, carefully drawn up, we have a satisfactory account of the exercises of the subjects of the work, with the varieties which were observed in the experience of different persons. The leading facts have here been selected from the narrative, so as to occupy the least possible room. To any, who take an interest in this subject, these facts cannot but be gratifying; and however the narrative may have been perused by some, yet it will not be disagreeable to them to have some of the prominent traits of the religious exercises, at that time, presented to them in a condensed form. Mr. Edwards informs us, "that there was scarcely a single person in the town, old or young, left unconcerned about the great things of the eternal world;" and although he does not pretend to know the precise number of converts, he is of opinion that it could not be less, in the judgment of charity, than three hundred. Our object is not to abridge the narrative, but merely to select the account of the variety of exercises experienced, as there given. "There is a great variety," says he, "as to the degree of trouble and fear, that persons are exercised with, before they attain any comfortable evidence of pardon and acceptance with God. Some are from the beginning carried on with abundantly more hope and encouragement than others. Some have had ten times less trouble than others, in whom the work yet appears the same in the issue..... The awful apprehensions persons have had of their misery have, for the most part, been increasing, the nearer they have approached to deliverance. Sometimes they think themselves wholly senseless, and fear that the Spirit of God has left them, and that they are given up to judicial hardness, yet they appear very deeply exercised with that fear, and in great earnestness to obtain conviction again. Many times, persons under great awakenings were concerned because they thought they were not awakened, but miserably hard-hearted, senseless, sottish creatures still, and sleeping on the brink of hell....... Persons are sometimes brought to the borders of despair, and it looks as black as midnight to them, a little before the day dawns on their souls. The depravity of the heart has discovered itself in various exercises, in the time of legal convictions. Sometimes it appears as in a great struggle, like something roused by an enemy. Many, in such circumstances, have felt a great spirit of envy towards the godly; especially towards those thought to have been recently converted. As they are gradually more and more convinced of the corruption and wickedness of their hearts, they seem to themselves to grow worse and worse, harder and blinder, more desperately wicked instead of growing better..........When awakenings first begin, their consciences are commonly more exercised about their outward vicious courses, but afterwards are much more burdened with a sense of heart sins, the dreadful corruption of their nature, their enmity against God, the pride of their hearts, their unbelief, their rejection of Christ, the stubbornness of their will, and the like.........Very often, under first awakenings, they set themselves to walk more strictly, confess their sins, and perform many religious duties, with a secret hope of appeasing God's anger. And sometimes, at first setting out, their affections are so moved, that they are full of tears, in their confessions and prayers, which they are ready to make much of, as if they were some atonement, and conceive that they grow better apace, and shall soon be converted; but their affections and hopes are short-lived, for they quickly find that they fail, and then they think themselves to be grown worse again. When they reflect on the wicked working of their hearts against God, they have more distressing apprehensions of his anger, and have great fears that God will never show mercy to them; or perhaps, that they have committed the unpardonable sin, and are often tempted to leave off in despair.........When they begin to seek salvation, they are commonly profoundly ignorant of themselves. They are not sensible how blind they are, and how little they can do, to bring themselves to see spiritual things aright, and towards putting forth gracious exercises in their own souls. When they see unexpected pollution in themselves, they go about to wash their own defilements and make themselves clean; and they weary themselves in vain, till God shows them that it is in vain; and that their help is not where they have sought it. But some persons continue to wander in such a labyrinth ten times as long as others, before their own experience will convince them of their own insufficiency—so that it is not their own experience at last, that convinces them, but the Spirit of God. There have been some who have not had great terrors, but yet have had a very quick work. Some, who have not had very deep convictions *before* their conversion, have much more of it *afterwards*. God has appeared far from limiting himself to any certain method, in his proceedings with sinners, under legal convictions. There is in nothing a greater difference in different persons, than with respect to the *time* of their being under trouble: some but a few days, and others for months and years. As to those in whom legal convictions seem to have a saving issue, the first thing that appears after their trouble, is a conviction of the justice of God in their condemnation, from a sense of their exceeding sinfulness. Commonly, their minds, immediately before the discovery of God's justice, are exceedingly restless—in a kind of struggle or tumult; and sometimes in mere anguish; but commonly, as soon as they have this conviction, it immediately brings their minds to a calm and unexpected quietness and composure; and most frequently, then, though not always, the pressing weight upon their spirits is taken off; or a general hope arises, that some time God will be gracious, even before any distinct, particular discoveries of mercy. Commonly, they come to a conclusion, that they will lie at God's feet and *wait his time*......... That calm of spirit which succeeds legal conviction, in some instances, continues some time before any special and delightful manifestation is made to the soul, of the grace of God, as revealed in the gospel. But, very often some comfortable and sweet views of a merciful God, of a sufficient Redeemer, or of some great and joyful things of the gospel, immediately follow, or in a very little time. And in some, the first sight of their desert of hell, of God's sovereignty in regard to their salvation, and a discovery of all-sufficient grace, are so near, that they seem to go together. The gracious discoveries, whence the first special comforts are derived, are, in many respects, very various. More frequently, Christ is distinctly made the object of the mind, in his all-sufficiency and willingness to save sinners; but some have their thoughts more especially fixed on God, in some of his sweet and glorious attributes, manifested in the Gospel and shining forth of Jesus Christ. Some view the all-sufficiency of the grace of God—some chiefly, the infinite power of God and his ability to save them, and to do all things for them—and some look most to the truth and faithfulness of God. In some, the truth and certainty of the Gospel, in general, is the first joyful discovery they have: in others, the certain proof of some particular promise. In some, the grace and sincerity of God, in his invitations, very commonly, in some particular invitation, is before the mind. Some are struck with the glory and wonderfulness of the dying love of Christ; and others with the sufficiency of his blood, as offered to make an atonement for sin; and others again, with the value and glory of his obedience and righteousness. In many, the excellency and loveliness of Christ chiefly engage their thoughts, while in some, his divinity; being filled with the idea, that He is indeed the Son of the living God; and in others, the excellency of the way of salvation by Christ, and the suitableness of it to their necessities........There is often in the mind, some particular text of Scripture, holding forth some particular ground of consolation; at other times, a multitude of texts, gracious invitations, and promises, flowing in one after another, filling the soul more and more with comfort and satisfaction. Comfort is first given to some while reading some portion of Scripture; but in others, it is attended with no particular Scripture at all. In some instances, many divine things seem to be discovered to the soul at once; while others have their minds fixed on some one thing; and afterwards a sense of others is given; in some, with a slower, in others, a swifter succession.

"It must be confessed, that Christ is not always distinctly and explicitly thought of in the first sensible act of grace—though most commonly he is—but sometimes he is the object of the mind only implicitly. Thus when persons have evidently appeared stripped of their own righteousness, and have stood condemned, as guilty of death, they have been comforted with a joyful and satisfactory evidence, that the mercy and grace of God is sufficient for them—that their sins, though never so great, shall be no hindrance to their being accepted—that there is mercy enough in God for the whole world, &c.—while they give no account of any particular or distinct thought of Christ; but yet it appears, that the revelation of mercy, in the gospel, is the ground of their encouragement and hope; yet such persons afterwards obtain distinct and clear discoveries of Christ, accompanied with lively and special actings of faith and love towards him. Frequently, when persons have had the gospel ground of relief opened to them, and have been entertaining their minds with the sweet prospect, they have thought nothing at that time of their being converted. The view is joyful to them as it is in its own nature glorious; gives them quite new and delightful ideas of God and Christ, and greatly encourages them to seek conversion, and begets in them a strong resolution to devote themselves to God and his Son. There is wrought in them a holy repose of soul in God through Christ, with a secret disposition to fear and love him, and to hope for blessings from him in this way, yet they have no conception that they are now converted; it does not so much as come into their minds. They know not that the sweet complacence they feel in the mercy and complete salvation of God, as it includes pardon and sanctification, and is held forth to them through Christ, is a true receiving of this mercy, or a plain evidence of their receiving it. Many continue a long time in a course of gracious exercises and experiences, and do not think themselves to be converted, but conclude otherwise; and none knows how long they would continue so, were they not helped by particular instructions. There are undoubted instances of some who lived in this way for many years together. Those who, while under legal convictions, have had the greatest terrors, have not always obtained the greatest light and comfort; nor has the light always been most speedily communicated; but yet I think the *time* of conversion has been most sensible in such persons. Converting influences commonly bring an extraordinary conviction of the certainty and reality of the great things of religion; though in some, this is much greater, sometime after conversion, than at first."

The religious exercises, contained in the preceding statement, will not be new to those who have been at all conversant with revivals. Such will recognize, in the account, what they have observed, and will be gratified to find the same facts which they have observed, recorded and published by such a master in Israel. Almost the only remark which I feel disposed to make, is, that it is too commonly supposed that the time of receiving comfort, is always the time of regeneration; whereas, this might rather be termed the time of conversion; for then the exercises of the renewed soul came to a crisis, and faith, which was before weak and obscure, shines forth with vigour. Perhaps it is the prevalent opinion among orthodox writers, that the first views of the renovated soul are views of Christ; and when mere legal convictions are immediately followed by such views and their attendant consolations, this opinion may be correct; but in many cases, it is reasonable to believe, that the convictions experienced are those of the true penitent. And as, in almost all cases here recorded and observed by others, there is a distinct view and approbation of God's justice in the condemnation of the sinner, I cannot but think, agreeably to what was stated in a former chapter, that the soul has passed from death unto life, before these feelings are experienced; and that may help to account for the remarkable *calm* which now succeeds the dark and stormy night. This revelation of Jesus Christ in the believer, may be compared to the birth of a child into the light of this world; but its conception was long before. And so this interesting point in experience is the *new birth*, but the principle of spiritual life commonly exists before. Besides, comfort is no sure evidence of a genuine birth; some who become strong men in the Lord are born in sorrow. They weep before they are able to smile; but, in the spiritual birth, joy and sorrow often sweetly mingle their streams.

There are two reasons why faith, though one of the simplest exercises of the mind, is represented as having so many different acts; the one is, the great variety in the truths believed; and the other, that, commonly, various exercises are included in the account of faith, which do always accompany or follow a true faith, but do not appertain to its essence. As faith has all revealed truth for its object, the feelings produced in the mind correspond with the particular nature of the truth which is, at any time, in the contemplation of the mind. If, by the soul under the illumination of the Holy Spirit, the law is viewed in its spirituality and moral excellence, while there will be experienced an approbation of the will of God thus expressed, yet a lively sense of the sinfulness of our hearts and lives, must be the predominant feeling. This discovery of the purity of the law, and this deep feeling of the evil of sin, commonly precede any clear view of Christ, and the plan of salvation; and this has given rise to the prevalent opinion, that repentance goes before faith in the natural order of pious exercises. But, according to our idea of faith, as given above, it must necessarily precede and be the cause of every other gracious exercise. Commonly, indeed, when we speak of faith, we describe its maturity; but there are often many obscure but real acts of faith, before the soul apprehends the fulness, and excellency, and suitableness of Christ. And in many cases, when some view of the plan of salvation is obtained, the single truth believed is, the ability of Christ to save; and even the full persuasion of this gives rise to joy, when the soul has been long cast down with gloomy forebodings of everlasting misery, and with the apprehension that, for such a sinner, there was no salvation. As faith does no more than bring the truth before the mind in its true nature, every act of faith must, of course, be characterized by the qualities of the truth thus presented, and by its adaptation to the circumstances and convictions of the sinner. All those acts of faith which bring the extent and spirituality of the law of God fully into view must be accompanied with painful emotions, on account of the deep conviction of disconformity to that perfect rule, which cannot but be experienced, when that object is before the mind. But all those invitations, promises, and declarations which exhibit a Saviour, and the method of recovery, when truly believed, under a just apprehension of their nature, must be accompanied, not only with love, but joy, and hope, and a free consent to be saved in God's appointed way; and when the previous distress and discouragement have been great, and the views of gospel truth clear, the joy is overflowing, and as long as these views are unclouded, peace flows like a river. But even in the discoveries which faith makes of Christ, there is a great variety in the extent and combination of divine truth which comes before the mind at any one time. Probably no two persons, in believing, have precisely the same truths in all their relations, presented to them; and not only so, but it is hardly credible, that the same believer, in his various contemplations of divine truth, takes in exactly the same field of view at different times. Hence it appears, that the whole power of faith is derived from the importance, excellence, amiableness, and suitableness of the truths believed. And when faith is " imputed for righteousness," it is not the simple act of faith which forms a righteousness. If any exercise of the renewed mind could constitute a righteousness, it would be love—which according to its strength, is " the fulfilling of the law ;" but when the soul by faith is fully persuaded that Christ is the end of the law for righteousness, this righteousness of the Surety, when received by faith, is imputed; and by this alone, which is perfect, can God be just in justifying the ungodly. " Faith thus receiving and resting on Christ and his righteousness, is the alone instrument of justification; yet is not alone in the person justified, but is ever accompanied with all other saving graces, and is no dead faith: but worketh by love." "By this faith, a Christian believeth to be true, whatsoever is revealed in the word, for the authority of God himself speaking therein; and acteth differently, upon that which each particular passage thereof containeth; yielding obedience to the commands, trembling at the threatenings, and embracing the promises of God for this life, and that which is to come. But the principal acts of faith are, accepting and resting upon Christ alone for justification, sanctification, and eternal life, by virtue of the covenant of grace." This quotation, taken from a formulary, known to many of my readers, contains as just and comprehensive a view of the nature of saving faith as could be given in words.

But another reason why so many divine acts are attributed to faith is, because other exercises are included in the description of faith, which though they always accompany it, ought not to be confounded with it. It was, two hundred years ago, a question much agitated among the divines of Holland, whether *love* or charity entered into the essence of faith? And in our own country, faith and love have not been kept distinct. A very prevalent system of theology makes the essence of faith to be *love*. Much evil arises from confounding what are so clearly distinguished in the word of God. If faith and love were identical, how could it be said that "faith works by love?" The apostle Paul speaks of faith, hope, and charity, or *love*, as so distinct, that, although they are all necessary, they may be compared, as to excellency—" The greatest of these is charity." The celebrated Witsius, in his " Economy of the Covenants," in describing faith, among the various acts which he attributes to this divine principle, reckons "love of the truth," and " hungering and thirsting after Christ." Now, it is an abuse of language to say that faith *loves* or *desires;* faith works by love, and excites hungering and thirsting desires after Christ. But, it may be asked, if these graces are inseparably connected, why be so solicitous to distinguish them? First, because in so doing, we follow the sacred writers; secondly, because it has a bad effect to use a Scriptural word to express what it was never designed to express; and, thirdly, because of the special office of faith in a sinner's justification; in which neither love, nor any other grace has any part, although they are the effects of faith. When love is confounded with a justifying faith, it is very easy to slide into the opinion that as love is the substance of evangelical obedience, when we are said to be justified by faith, the meaning is, that we are justified by our own obedience. And accordingly, in a certain system of divinity, valued by many, in this country, the matter is thus stated: faith is considered a comprehensive term for all evangelical obedience. The next step is—and it has already been taken by some—that our obedience is meritorious, and when its defects are purged by atoning blood, it is sufficient to procure for us a title to eternal life. Thus have some, boasting of the name of Protestants, worked around, until they have fallen upon one of the most offensive tenets of Popery. But, it would be difficult to bring a true penitent to entertain the opinion, that his own works were meritorious, or could, in the least, recommend him to God. The whole of God's dealings with the souls of his own people, effectually dispel from their minds every feeling of this kind. The very idea of claiming merit is most abhorrent to their feelings.

But while it is of importance to distinguish faith from every other grace, yet it is necessary to insist on the fact, that that faith, which does not produce love and other holy affections, is not a genuine faith. In the apostles' days, a set of libertines arose, who boasted of their faith, but they performed no good works to evince the truth of their faith. Against such the apostle James writes, and proves that such a faith was no better than that of devils, and would justify no man; that the faith of Abraham and other believers, which did justify, was not a dead faith, but living; not a barren faith, but productive of good works, and proved itself to be genuine by the acts of duty which it induced the believer to perform.

While then faith stands foremost in the order of gracious exercises, because it is necessary to the existence of every other, love may be said to be the centre, around which all the virtues of the Christian revolve, and from which they derive their nature. Love, of some kind, is familiar to the experience of all persons; and all love is attended with some pleasure in its exercise; but it varies on account of the difference of the objects of affection. Divine love is itself a delightful and soul-satisfying exercise. The soul which has tasted the goodness of God, is convinced, that nothing more is necessary to complete felicity, than the perfection of love. This supposes, however, that our love to God is ever accompanied with some sense of his love to us. Love, unless reciprocated, would not fill up the cup of human happiness. But to love, and be beloved, this is heaven. And "we love Him because he first loved us." In the first exercises of a renewed mind, love to God and love to man are both brought into action; but often the prospect of deliverance from eternal misery which threatened, may absorb the attention. It is indeed a marvellous deliverance, to be snatched from the verge of hell, and assured of everlasting life; what a tumult of feeling must it create? But notwithstanding this, it frequently happens, that in the first discoveries of the plan of salvation, the soul loses sight of its own interest, and is completely occupied in contemplating and admiring the wisdom, love, and justice of God, as exhibited in the cross of the Lord Jesus Christ. Indeed, the believer, when these spiritual discoveries are afforded, thinks nothing of the nature of those acts which he is exercising; and it may not be till long afterwards, that he recognizes these outgoings of soul to be true love to the Saviour.

There are two affections, distinct from each other in their objects, which are included under the term *love*, the one terminates on the goodness or moral excellence of its object, and varies according to the particular view, at any time enjoyed, of the divine attributes. This comprehends all pious affections and emotions arising from the contemplation of the perfections of God; and some of them, such as reverence and humility, would not fall under the name of love, when taken in a strict sense; but when used as a general term for our whole obedience, it must comprehend them all. This may, for convenience, be called the love of *complacency*, in which the rational soul delights in the character of God as revealed in his word. The other affection, called love, has not the character of the person beloved for its object, but his happiness. It may be intensely exercised towards those in whose moral qualities there can be no complacency, and is called the love of benevolence. God's love to sinners is of this kind; and this is the kind of love which Christians are bound to exercise to all men in the world, even to those that hate and persecute them. Though the love of benevolence may exist without the love of complacency, yet the converse cannot be asserted. No one ever felt love to the character of another without desiring his happiness. Before conversion, the soul is sordidly selfish, but no sooner does this change take place, than the heart begins to be enlarged with an expansive benevolence. The whole world is embraced in its charity. "Good will to man" is a remarkable characteristic of the "new creature;" and this intense desire for the salvation of our fellow men, and ardent wish that they may all become interested in that Saviour, whom we have ound to be so precious, is the true source of the missionary spirit, and is the foundation, often, of laborious and long continued exertions to prepare for the holy ministry; and prompts and inclines delicate females to consent to leave all the endearments of home, for arduous labour in a foreign, and sometimes a savage land.

But, however lively the affection of love in the exercises of the real Christian, he never can lose sight of his own unworthiness. Indeed, the brighter his discoveries of the divine glory, and the stronger his love, the deeper are his views of the turpitude of sin. The more he is elevated in affection and assured hope, the deeper is he depressed in humility and self-abasement. His penitential feelings, from the nature of the case, keep pace with his love and joy; and when his tears flow in copious showers, he would be at a loss to tell, whether he was weeping for joy or for sorrow. He might say, for both; for in these pious exercises, these opposite emotions sweetly mingle their streams; and so delightful is this mingling of affections naturally opposite, that the person could hardly be persuaded, that the sweet would be as agreeable without, as with, the bitter. One hour spent under the cross, while the soul is thus elevated, thus abased—thus joyful, and thus sorrowful—is better than a thousand of earthly delights. Observe, Bunyan does not make the burden of Christian fall off instantly on his entering in at the strait gate; but when, as he travelled, he came in sight of the cross. Then, in a moment, those cords which had bound it to his back, and which none could loose, were burst asunder, and his burden fell off, and never was fastened on him again; although he lay so long in the prison of Giant Despair. The feelings of a renewed heart, are never afterwards the same as under legal conviction. There are scenes, in the experience of the lively Christian, of which the wise men of the world never dream; and which, if they were told of them, they would not believe; and these things, while they are hidden from the wise and prudent, are revealed unto babes. The secret of the Lord is with them that fear him. The soul, which has thus returned from its wanderings to the Bishop and Shepherd, feels under the strongest obligations to live for God—to deny itself—to forsake the world— to do any thing—be any thing—or suffer any thing, which may be for the honour of its divine Master. Hence a new life commences—a new spirit is manifested—and the *new man*, maugre all his remaining ignorance and imperfection, gives lucid evidence to all who carefully observe him, that he has been with Jesus, and has been baptized with the Holy Ghost; and, the more frequently these views and exercises are reiterated, the more spiritual and heavenly is his conversation. This is a light which cannot be hid and which ought to shine more and more unto the perfect day. Hear then the exhortation of the apostle Jude, "But ye, beloved, building up yourselves on your most holy faith, praying in the Holy Ghost, keep yourselves in the love of God, looking for the mercy of our Lord Jesus Christ unto eternal life."

CHAPTER VII.

Considerations on dreams, visions, &c.—Remarkable conversion of a blind infidel from hearing the Bible read.

THERE are many professors of religion in our country, who, if they should peruse this work would imagine a great defect in the account given of a sinner's conversion, because nothing has been said about dreams and visions, or voices and lights, of a supernatural kind. During the various religious excitements which extended over the Southern States, under the preaching of different denominations, there was mingled with the good influence by which sinners were converted and reformed, no small degree of enthusiasm, which led the people to seek and expect extraordinary revelations, which were supposed to be granted in dreams or visions. Indeed, at one time, the leaders in a very general excitement, which occurred in Virginia, about the commencement of the Revolutionary war, were impressed with the idea, that they possessed precisely the same gifts and powers which had been bestowed upon the apostles; and this enthusiastic idea would have spread widely, if they had not failed, in some private attempts, to work miracles. But the opinion, that certain persons had an extraordinary call from God to preach, and that they needed neither learning nor study, to enable them to preach the gospel, continued to prevail for a long time; and this species of enthusiasm is not entirely passed away even to this day. Such preachers were much in the habit of declaiming in every sermon, against letter-learned and college-bred ministers, and they seldom failed to inform their hearers, that they had selected the subject of discourse, after entering the pulpit; and some of them even gloried that they had never learned to read, as they believed, that all learning interfered with the inspiration of the Spirit, which they were confident that they possessed. While this notion of an extraordinary call and immediate inspiration was common, it is not surprising that the people should have entertained wild opinions respecting the nature of conversion. As it was customary to give the narratives of religious experience in public, not only in the presence of the church, but of a promiscuous assembly, there was a strong temptation to tell an extraordinary story; and the more miraculous it was, the higher evidence it was supposed to afford of being the work of God; concerning the genuineness of which the subject never expressed a doubt. Seldom was a narrative of experience heard, which did not contain something supernatural; such as a remarkable prophetic dream; an open vision; a sudden and brilliant light shining around, as in the case of Paul; or an audible voice, calling them by name, or uttering some text of Scripture, or some other encouraging words. Sometimes, however, the cause of experimental religion was sadly dishonoured by the ludicrous stories of poor ignorant people—especially the unlettered slaves; for this religious concern seized upon them with mighty force, and many of them, I doubt not, were savingly converted.

The philosophy of dreams is very little understood: and it is not our purpose to entertain or perplex the reader with any theories on the subject. Dreams have by some been divided into natural, divine, and diabolical. The wise man says, "A dream cometh through the multitude of business." Most dreams are undoubtedly the effect of the previous state of the mind, and of the peculiar circumstances and state of the body, at the time. Most persons find their thoughts, in sleep, occupied with those things which gave them concern when awake; and every cause which disorders the stomach or nerves, gives a character to our dreams. Most persons have experienced the distress of feverish dreams. But there are sometimes remarkable dreams, which leave on the mind the strong impression that they have a meaning, and portend coming events. And that there have been dreams of this description, we learn from the authority of the Bible; and these prophetic dreams were not confined to the servants of God, as we learn from the instances of the butler and baker, in the prison of Pharaoh, and from the remarkable dream of Pharaoh himself. All these must have proceeded from some supernatural influence, as, when interpreted by Joseph, they clearly predicted future events, of which the persons dreaming had not the least knowledge. So, Nebuchadnezzar's dream contained a symbolical representation of future events of great importance, which, however, neither he nor his wise men understood, but which was interpreted by Daniel, by divine inspiration. Why God so frequently made his communications to his servants by dreams, is not easily explained. Perhaps, the mind is better prepared for such revelations, when external objects are entirely excluded; or, it might have been to obviate that terror and perturbation to which all men were subject, when an angel or spirit appeared to them. Whether God ever now communicates any thing by dreams is much disputed. Many, no doubt, deceive themselves, by fancying that their dreams are supernatural; and some have been sadly deluded by trusting to dreams; and certainly people ought not to be encouraged to look for revelations in dreams. But there is nothing inconsistent with reason or Scripture, in supposing, that, on some occasions, certain communications, intended for the warning or safety of the individual himself, or of others, may be made in dreams. To doubt of this, is to run counter to a vast body of testimony in every age. And if ideas, received in dreams, produce a salutary effect, in rendering the careless serious, or the sorrowful comfortable, in the view of divine truth, very well; such dreams may be considered *providential*, if not divine But if any are led by dreams, to pursue a course repugnant to the dictates of common sense or the precepts of Scripture, such dreams may rightly be considered diabolical. Some persons have supposed that they experienced a change of mind while asleep. They have gone to rest with a heart unsubdued and unconverted, and their first waking thoughts have been of faith and love. Some have sunk to sleep, worn down with distress, and in their sleep have received comfort, as they supposed, from a believing view of Christ. Such changes are suspicious; but if they are proved to be genuine by the future life of the person, we should admit the possibility of God's giving a new heart, just as he does to the infant. Or, truth may be as distinctly impressed on persons' minds in sleep, as when they are awake. Some persons appear to have their faculties in more vigorous exercise, in some kinds of sleep, than when their senses are all exercised. The Rev. John Fletcher, vicar of Madely, relates that he had a dream of the judgment day, the effect of which was a deep and abiding impression of eternal things on his mind. As the scene was vividly painted on his imagination, and the representation of truth was as distinct and coherent as if he had been awake, it may be gratifying to the reader to have the account of it, set before him. He had been variously exercised about religion before this. "I was," says he, "in this situation, when a dream, in which I am obliged to acknowledge the hand of God, roused me from my security. On a sudden, the heavens were darkened, and clouds rolled along in terrific majesty, and a thundering voice like a trumpet, which penetrated to the bowels of the earth, exclaimed, 'arise ye dead and come out of your graves.' Instantly the earth and the sea gave up the dead which they contained, and the universe was crowded with living people who appeared to come out of their graves by millions But what a difference among them! Some, convulsed with despair, endeavoured in vain to hide themselves in their tombs, and cried to the hills to fall on them, and the mountains to cover them from the face of the holy Judge; while others rose with seraphic wings above the earth which had been the theatre of their conflicts and their victory. Serenity was painted on their countenances, joy sparkled in their eyes, and dignity was impressed on every feature. My astonishment and terror were redoubled when I perceived myself raised up with this innumerable multitude into the vast regions of the air, from whence my affrighted eyes beheld this globe consumed by the flames, the heavens on fire, and the dissolving elements ready to pass away. But what did I feel, when I beheld the Son of man coming in the clouds of heaven, in all the splendour of his glory, crowned with the charms of his mercy, and surrounded with the terrors of his justice; ten thousand thousands went before him, and millions pressed upon his footsteps. All nature was silent. The wicked were condemned, and the sentence was pronounced—the air gave way under the feet of those who surrounded me, a yawning gulf received them and closed upon them. At the same time He that sat upon the throne exclaimed, 'Come, ye blessed of my Father, inherit the kingdom prepared for you from the foundation of the world. Happy children of God! I cried, You are exalted in triumph with your Redeemer, and my dazzled eyes will soon lose sight of you, in the blaze of light which surrounds you. Wretch that I am, what words can express the horrors of my situation! A fixed and severe look from the Judge, as he departed, pierced me to the heart, and my anguish and confusion were extreme, when a brilliant personage despatched from the celestial host, thus addressed me, 'Slothful servant, what dost thou here? Dost thou presume to follow the Son of God, whom thou hast served merely with thy lips, while thy real love to God, and a living faith in his Son? Ask thy conscience what were the motives of thy pretended good works? Dost thou not see that pride and self-love were the source of them? Dost thou not see that the fear of hell rather than the fear of offending God, restrained thee from sin?' After these words he paused; and regarding me with a compassionate air, seemed to await my reply. But conviction and terror closed my mouth, and he thus resumed his discourse, 'Withhold no longer from God the glory which is due him. Turn to him with all thy heart, and become a new creature. Watch and pray, was the command of the Son of God; but instead of having done this by working out thy salvation with fear and trembling, thou hast slept the sleep of security. At this very moment dost thou not sleep in that state of lethargy and spiritual death, from which the word of God, the exhortations of his servants, and the strivings of his grace have not been sufficient to deliver thee? Time is swallowed up in eternity. There is no more place for repentance. Thou hast obstinately refused to glorify God's mercy in Christ Jesus—go then, slothful servant and glorify his justice.' Having uttered these words he disappeared, and, at the same time, the air gave way under my feet—the abyss began to open—dreadful wailings assailed my ears, and a whirlwind of smoke surrounded me. The agitation of my mind and body awoke me; the horror of which nothing can equal, and the mere recollection of which still makes me tremble. O how happy I felt on awaking to find that I was still in the land of mercy, and the day of salvation! O my God, I cried, grant that this dream may continually influence my sentiments and my conduct! May it prove a powerful stimulus to excite me to prepare continually for the coming of my great Master!"

By this dream Mr. Fletcher was convinced that he had been indulging vain hopes, and that his mind was still unrenewed. His conviction of this truth, however, did not rest entirely, nor chiefly on what had been told him in his dream, but he now set to work in sober earnest to examine his religious principles and motives, by the Scriptures; and the more he examined the more fully was he convinced that he was yet in an unconverted state. From this time he began with all earnestness to seek for justification through the blood of Christ; and never rested until he found peace with God by a living faith in the truth and promises of God.

The dream of John Newton, which he had long before his conversion, when in the harbour of Venice, is probably known to most of our readers.—" I thought," says he, " that it was night, and my watch upon the deck—a person came to me and brought me a ring, with an express charge to keep it carefully; assuring me that while I preserved that ring, I should be happy and successful; but if I lost or parted with it, I must expect nothing but trouble and misery. I accepted the present and the terms willingly, not in the least doubting my own care to preserve it, and highly gratified to have my happiness in my own keeping. I was engaged in these thoughts, when a second person came to me and observing the ring on my finger, he took occasion to ask me some questions concerning it. I readily told him its virtues, and his answer expressed a surprise at my weakness, in expecting such effects from a ring. I think he reasoned with me some time on the impossibility of the thing; and at length urged me in direct terms to throw it away. At first, I was shocked at the proposal; but his insinuations prevailed. I began to reason and doubt, and at last plucked it off my finger, and dropped it over the ship's side into the water, which it had no sooner touched, than I saw, at the same instant, a terrible fire burst out from a range of mountains (the Alps) which appeared at some distance behind the city of Venice. I saw the hills as distinct as if awake, and that they were all in flames. I perceived too late my folly; and my tempter, with an air of insult, informed me that all the mercy God had in reserve for me was comprised in the ring which I had wilfully thrown away. I trembled and was in great agony, and stood self-condemned, when a third person, or the same who gave me the ring, came to me and demanded the cause of my grief. He blamed my rashness, and asked me if I thought I should be wiser, if I had my ring again. I could hardly answer, but thought it gone beyond control. He went down under the water, and soon returned, bringing the ring with him. The moment he came on board, the flames were extinguished. I approached to receive the ring, but he refused to restore it, saying 'If you should receive this ring again, you would soon bring yourself into the same distress. You are not able to keep it; but I will preserve it for you, and whenever it is needful will produce it in your behalf.' Upon this I awoke in a state of mind not to be described. I could hardly eat or sleep or transact necessary business for two or three days, but the impression soon wore off, and in a little time I totally forgot it, and I think it hardly occurred to my mind till several years afterwards."

I will conclude this *unsubstantial* discussion by citing the words of that remarkable young sage of remote antiquity, Elihu, the reprover of both Job and his friend, and the sublime defender of God and his dispensations. "For God speaketh once, yea twice, yet man perceiveth it not. In a *dream*, in a vision of the night, when deep sleep falleth upon men, in slumberings upon the bed. Then he openeth the ears of men and sealeth their instruction."

Sometime in the year 1811, as well as he remembers, the substance of the following narrative was put into the hands of the writer, by the Rev. Dr. William M. Tennent, of Abington, Pennsylvania, when this excellent man was on his death-bed, and near his end. It will be seen that it was drawn up with a view to publication as soon as the subject of the memoir, who was then alive in Dr. Tennent's congregation, should be called home to his rest. That event occurred sometime since; and in communicating this memoir to the public, the writer considers himself as fulfilling an implied promise, when he accepted the manuscript.

Having, however, ascertained that Mrs. Ann Snowden, of Philadelphia, was the lady at whose house this gentleman resided, and that she was the person by whom the Scriptures were read; and knowing, also, that she was both pious and intelligent, the writer requested her to put down on paper an exact account of this pleasing and remarkable event; which she did with the utmost readiness. From these authentic sources, the following narrative is derived; and will be given with very slight verbal alterations, in the very words of the respected persons named.

Dr. Tennent's memoir is prefaced by the following words:

"Unfinished memoir of Mr. George Inglis, who has been a member of the Presbyterian church in Abington from 1790 till the present time, 1810. It is expected, that some fit person into whose hand these sketches of his character may fall, will, after his decease, prepare them for the press; as it is hoped the Church of Christ may derive some advantage from them."

The narrative then proceeds as follows: "Mr. George Inglis was born in the city of Philadelphia, of honourable parentage, and received a liberal education in the university of that city, which was completed between his 16th and 17th year. Having served a regular apprenticeship to a merchant, he entered into the mercantile business, and settled in the island of Jamaica, where he continued about eleven years. Very early in life he began to drink in iniquity like water, discovered strong prejudices against serious persons and serious things; associated with the gay, libertine, and dissipated; never read the Scriptures except so much of them as enabled him to construe his Greek lessons, whilst in college. His propensities to sinful indulgences increased with his years, and in the island where he resided, temptations being increased, and the means of restraint from vicious courses diminished, he became more and more confirmed in the habits of sin, until at length he was given up to almost every species of iniquity. Amidst his open and avowed enmity to God and religion, at the close of the afore mentioned period, an awful tornado fell upon that part of the island where he resided, by which he lost the greater part of his property, and was compelled to return to the continent. This happened during the revolutionary war. All this made no alteration in his morals for the better; but the more he was corrected, the more hardened he grew; casting off the fear of God, and putting to defiance the scourges of Jehovah. Thus he continued, till some years afterwards, being in the town of Manchester, Virginia, without any natural (known) cause, to produce the effect, he was smitten by the immediate hand of God, whilst in the possession of good health, with the total loss of sight within a few days. In this situation his mind was all distraction. His cry was to man only for help; but to God his Maker, who giveth songs in the night to the afflicted and oppressed, he had not learned to cry. This lesson, however, he was taught not long afterwards."

Thus far the narrative has been given in the words of Dr. Tennent; it will now be proper to hear Mrs. Snowden's account of the conversion of this man, as she was the only human instrument made use of in bringing him to the knowledge of the truth It is in the form of a letter addressed to the writer.

"Rev. and Dear Sir—I will now endeavour to fulfil the promise made to you some time ago, by giving such information as is within my recollection, respecting the case of Mr. George Inglis. That gentleman, a native of Philadelphia, had received a classical education, and with it every indulgence which a father's partiality could bestow. Brought up in the gay world, it is to be feared there was but little attention paid to his immortal interests. After spending the time necessary to acquire the knowledge of mercantile affairs, he left the city for the West Indies, where he was, for a while, successful in business, and found himself in circumstances to visit England; and, while in London, throwing aside every restraint, he indulged himself in all the amusements and levities of that gay metropolis. Returning to America, he engaged in business in the state of Virginia. After residing some time there, it pleased the Lord to deprive him of his sight; an affliction at that time looked upon by him as insupportable, for he saw not the hand from whence it came; but after he was made sensible that he was a brand snatched from the burning, often have I heard him bless the chastisement as that of a tender Father.

"Mr. Inglis had weak eyes from an early age, but his blindness came on him suddenly. Finding no relief from the physicians where he resided, he left Virginia for Philadelphia; and upon the application of his friends, was received, with his servant, into my house, as a boarder. I found him a man of strong passions, impatient under sufferings, and not willing to submit to restraints of any kind. When the physicians of the city were consulted, they gave his friends no hope of the recovery of his eyesight: him they soothed with the promise of a further consideration of his case. A few weeks after he came to my house, a gentleman, very much celebrated as an oculist, came to the city. Mr. Inglis applied to him for advice. He did not tell him that his was an incurable case, but said that he would see him again. He bore this very impatiently, observing to me that life was now becoming an intolerable burden; but that he had this consolation, that he had it in his power at any time to lay it down. It was but to increase the quantity of opium (he was in the habit of taking opium) and all his sufferings would be at an end; and that, after another visit from the doctor, if he found there was no hope of his recovering his sight, he would certainly take that method of putting an end to his existence. I remonstrated with him on the impropriety of his behaviour; alleging, that he had no more right to take away his own life, than he had to take away the life of his neighbour; asking him if he had considered the consequences of rushing uncalled into the presence of his Maker. His answer was, that he had considered it well; and he advocated his opinion on this principle, that he was by a merciful Creator placed on this earth to enjoy the good things of this life as far as it was in his power honestly to obtain them—that the duties required of him were, to be as useful to his friends in particular, and society at large, as his circumstances would admit of—that having lost his sight, he should no longer enjoy any happiness here, would become a burden to his friends, and could be of no use in the world. He alleged, that the purposes for which life was given to him were now defeated; of course there would be no impropriety in laying it down. I made some remarks on what he had advanced as his sentiments, and to strengthen what I said, quoted some passages of Scripture. These he treated in a very light manner—spoke of the Bible as the work of men, contrived to keep the vulgar in awe—with many other observations too common with men of deistical principles. I then inquired if he had ever read the Bible; he frankly acknowledged that he had not since he left school. Upon asking him if he had not read the works of those that were opposed to the Scriptures, he admitted that he had. If so, I observed, he must have formed his opinions from the avowed enemies of that sacred book. Was this a fair method of proceeding? Was it just? That I thought he would not act thus, on any other occasion. This book you acknowledge you have not read since you were a boy. All that you know about it, you have from the enemies of the Christian religion. Taking these things into consideration, I hope you will no more speak against the Bible, as it is a book that you have never read since you were capable of forming a judgment of its contents. He apologized for what he had said, in a handsome manner, acknowledged that he was wrong in speaking as he had done, and expressed a wish to have it read to him. This I declined, and gave my reasons for so doing, which were, that a man so prejudiced, as he appeared to be was not likely to profit by the reading of the Bible that he would most probably cavil at, and perhaps ridicule it; in so doing, he would wound my feelings without benefitting himself; for I considered it as the word of God, and my hopes of eternal salvation rested on the truths contained in it. He then assured me on the word of a gentleman, that if I would read to him, whatever his opinions might be, he would carefully avoid saying any thing that might have a tendency to wound my feelings, or give offence, in the smallest degree. There was an earnestness in his manner of addressing me which satisfied my mind, that he was sincerely desirous to have the Scriptures read to him; and the next day was fixed upon for that purpose. It appeared to me that he waited impatiently for the arrival of the appointed hour, for, no sooner did the time come, than he sent for me. Before we began, I observed to him, that as in the New Testament he would find the fulfilment of the promises of the Saviour, I would point out those promises as they should occur in reading the Old Testament; which it would be necessary for him to take notice of as we proceeded. Beginning then with the first chapter of Genesis, before we had gone through the chapter, he stopped me to express his admiration of the language. 'It was sublime beyond any thing he had ever read.' While I was reading, he was all attention; and when the time arrived when I was under the necessity of leaving off, it was with regret that he observed that I had finished; putting me in mind, at the same time, of my promise to attend to him, on the next day. I think it was on the second day of my reading to him, that he cried out, 'What a wretch am I to have spoken against such a book! a book that I knew nothing of, having never given it an attentive perusal.' I went on for a few days, reading to him according to the plan laid down, which was one hour every day; when the distress of his mind greatly increased. There was now no more said about a second visit to the doctor—no complaints—no murmurings, on account of the loss of sight. He now saw the hand of

God in the dispensation of his providence, and would acknowledge that it was less, far less, than he deserved. My family duties preventing me from being with him as much as I wished, I now called in the aid of some of my religious friends, among whom was Mr. Joseph Eastburn, to converse with him and to assist in reading to him. Several religious books were now occasionally read to him, among which were Boston's Fourfold State, Newton's Works, Hervey's Dialogues, &c. The descriptive parts of the last mentioned author, were at his request passed over, except where it more fully served to explain the doctrines of free grace—a subject to him of the deepest interest. Though totally deprived of sight, and unaccustomed to go out, he now neglected no opportunity of hearing the word of God; attending sermons on Sabbaths, and weekly societies as often as was in his power. As might be expected, his natural disposition, sometimes getting the better of the good resolutions he had formed, would betray him into a fretfulness that was troublesome to his friends, and occasioned much uneasiness to himself. On such occasions I have heard him lament deeply over his sinful nature, accusing himself of ingratitude to that God who had mercifully stopped him in his career of vice, by depriving him of the light of day, and enlightening his darkened mind, and had enabled him to understand the truths contained in his blessed word. I do not recollect how long he staid with me, but it was something less than a year, when his friends thought it would be best to remove him to the country; and boarding was obtained for him in the neighbourhood of the Rev. Dr. Tennent, of Abington."

Dr. Tennent, in the memoir already quoted, after mentioning some circumstances which have been given in detail in a former page, goes on to say, "It pleased God, by these means to bring him to very serious and deep impressions of his moral character, and to constrain him, after some time, to attempt to pray. This [change] was effected in the gentleness, kindness, and tenderness of infinite mercy, and with out those horrors which often precede the conversion of high-handed and daring sinners. In his case, all was mercy, without extraordinary terror. He was embraced in the arms of redeeming love, and delivered from the fiery pit without beholding its awful flames. In his first attempt to supplicate the Deity, he was principally affected with a sense of the baseness of his conduct, and vile ingratitude for the mercies bestowed, and this exercise was accompanied with an involuntary flow of tears, and a desire to call God his Father, and afterwards to mention the blessed name of Jesus, the Saviour. Probably, this was the beginning of his new birth, and the hour of his conversion; which was not long afterwards confirmed by a remarkable vision of two books, with a glorious light shining in the midst of them, as he was lying in his bed; which he apprehended to be the Old and New Testaments of the living God, presenting to, and impressing on his mind this sacred declaration, but without a voice, " This is the way," and filling his soul at the same time, with inexpressible joy."

What is here related, is no doubt strictly true, but there is no propriety in calling it "a vision," since it can easily be accounted for by a vivid impression on the imagination. A vision is something supernatural seen with the bodily eyes; but this man was totally blind; the objects so clearly discerned must then have been from impressions on the imagination. But in saying this, it is not intended to deny that the cause was the Spirit of God. This divine Agent can, and does produce vivid impressions on the imagination, which have so much the appearance of external realities, that many are persuaded that they do see and hear what takes place only in their own minds.

"In the year 1790, Mr. Inglis was removed to Abington, and became a boarder in the house of the Rev. William M. Tennent, and soon afterwards was admitted to the communion of the church, in that place, with which he hath walked steadfastly in the faith ever since; exemplifying in a striking and high degree the power of God's grace in the 'new creation.'

From the beginning of his *turn* to God, there was abundant proof that 'old things had passed away, and that all things had become new.' Before, a blasphemer, but now a worshipper of the true God. Before, a drunkard, and a Sabbath-breaker, unclean, a ridiculer of holy things, and indulging habitually in all ungodliness and wickedness—led captive by the prince of the power of the air, who ruleth in the children of disobedience, but now, freed from his bonds and made by sovereign grace to rejoice in the liberty of the gospel. Before, a hater of good men and good things, but now a lover of both. He was made to hunger and thirst after righteousness—after the bread of life—after the knowledge of His will; and seemed only to be happy when he had a glimpse of his glory. For more than a year after his conversion, he could not bear to hear any other book read to him than the Holy Scriptures; and the most practical authors on religion. He shunned all political conversation, the reading of newspapers, and whatever might divert his thoughts from holy meditations and a further knowledge of his Redeemer.

"Whilst residing in his first permanent lodgings in the country, it may not be improper to mention a second remarkable vision which he had. Walking in the garden one day, as he usually did for sacred meditation, he was suddenly arrested and overcome with a most affecting view of his Saviour, as suspended on the cross, and bearing his very sins. In this vision of redeeming love he was so lost that he knew not where he was—overwhelmed with unutterable joy, and the most affecting gratitude for the discharge of the immense debt which he owed to the justice of a holy God. The impressions then made are still kept in strong remembrance. How long he was in this state he knew not, but was finally conducted to the house, after having called for a guide—full of joy and gladness: a second remarkable proof of his interest in gospel redemption."

We will simply repeat our objection to the use of the word "vision" to represent what was nothing more than a strong, believing view of the scene of the crucifixion, accompanied, no doubt, with a vivid imagination of the bleeding, dying Saviour, suffering for his sins.

"The writer will only add, that he has frequently, within the term of twenty years, heard Mr. Inglis say, he would not, if it had been within the power of a wish, have had his natural sight restored, having found his eyes such an avenue to sin. His whole conduct since his conversion has corresponded with his profession as a Christian disciple. He has, in the view of his brethren where he resides, made a visible growth in grace, even in the knowledge of our Lord and Saviour Jesus Christ. He has, with others travelling to the same blessed country, been on the mount and in the valley—an humble, meek, patient, self-denying Christian, rejoicing in the hopes of a better country—weeping on account of his own unfruitfulness—looking for strength to vanquish his enemies, and hoping for victory by the merits of the great Redeemer. Hitherto steadfast, may he hold fast unto the end! and may many such be added unto the Lord! Blessed be God for the gift of his Son, for the revelation of his incomprehensible love and grace, and for the crown of glory which is laid up for all who are looking and longing for his second appearance!"

The foregoing account was written about thirty years ago, and Mr. Inglis, who was then in years, did not depart this life until two or three years since. As the Rev. Robert Steel succeeded Dr. Tennent, as pastor of the Presbyterian church at Abington, I requested him to give me notice of the old gentleman's death, with an account of his state of mind in his latter days. This he did, and I regret that I have mislaid his letter, so that I cannot at present put my hands on it. But I confess that I was much disappointed in not finding something more memorable in the closing scene of one who had been so manifestly snatched "as a brand from the burning." As well as I recolect, Mr. Steel represents that the spirituality and ardour of Mr. Inglis's religion considerably declined in his later years; that he became somewhat worldly minded, and appeared to be too much concerned about his little property; and that he had nothing remarkable in the exercises of his mind, while on his death-bed: but no one, I believe, ever doubted the reality of the change which he had experienced; neither was he ever left to do any thing to bring discredit on the profession which he had made. [See p. 12.]

One reflection which occurred to me on reading Mr. Steel's letter was, that it is not desirable for a Christian to live to be very old; especially when all active service in the cause of Christ is precluded. Old age is a peculiarly unfavourable season for growth in grace. Many of the natural auxiliaries to piety are then removed; and at the same time, many infirmities cluster around us; so that a declension in religion is not uncommon in the protracted years of the aged.

Another solemn reflection was, that a man is never too old nor too decrepit to be covetous. Covetousness is peculiarly the vice of the aged, and when indulged, strikes its roots deeper, the older we grow. What Christ says to all, may with emphasis be addressed to the aged, "Take heed, and beware of covetousness." The writer remembers to have seen and conversed with the old gentleman in the church at Abington, soon after Dr. Tennent's death. At that time he was always in his place in the house of God, and attracted attention by his venerable and solemn appearance. It was agreed that his taste and judgment in regard to preaching were uncommonly sound and good; but nothing would pass with him in which Christ was not made conspicuous. Purely evangelical preaching was that in which he delighted; and at that period, his conversation was in a strain of warm and pious feeling.

My closing remark is, that we should despair of the conversion of no one; and we should use all our efforts to prevail on skeptical men to read the Bible. The Bible has converted more infidels than all the books of "evidences" which exist.

CHAPTER VIII.

Religious Conversation.—Stress laid by some on the knowledge of the time and place of Conversion.—Religious experience of Halyburton.

It is often a question among serious people, whether every person, who is a real Christian, knows not only that he is such, but the time and place of his conversion. This subject has already been partially discussed in these essays, but demands a more particular and extended consideration.

It is well known to all, that the Christian denominations, which exist in this country, differ from one another in their views of various doctrines and rites of religion; but the fact is not so well known, that the religious experience of the individuals of the several denominations is as various as their doctrines and external forms of worship. To those who view these things at a distance, and superficially, all religious people appear alike; and many, when they hear of a number converted, take it for granted that they have all passed through the same train of exercises, to whatever sect they belong. There are some serious people, well indoctrinated in the Scriptures, who, while they hold a sound theory respecting the nature of regeneration, never speak of their own religious exercises; believing that such exposures are not for edification, as they tend to foster spiritual pride and vain glory, and afford a temptation to hypocrisy, which is commonly too strong for the deceitful heart. Among such professors, you hear nothing of conviction and conversion; and when any of this class fall into a distressing case of conscience which urges them to seek spiritual counsel, they always propose the case in the third person. They will talk to you by the hour and the day, about the doctrines of religion, and show that they are more conversant with their Bibles, than many who talk much of their religious feelings. There are two objections to this practice. The first is, that it has the effect of keeping out of view the necessity of a change of heart. The second is, that it is a neglect of one effectual means of grace. Religious conversation, in which Christians freely tell of the dealings of God with their own souls, has been often a powerful means of quickening the sluggish soul, and communicating comfort. It is in many cases, a great consolation to the desponding believer, to know that his case is not entirely singular; and if a traveller can meet with one who has been over the difficult parts of the road before him, he may surely derive from his experience some salutary counsel and warning. The Scriptures are favourable to such communications. "Come and hear," says David, "all ye that fear God, and I will declare what he hath done for my soul." "Then they that feared the Lord spake often one to another, and the Lord hearkened and heard it, and a book of remembrance was written before him for them that feared the Lord, and that thought upon his name." Paul seldom makes a speech or writes a letter, in which he does not freely speak of his own religious joys and sorrows, hopes and fears. There is, no doubt, an abuse of this means of grace, as of others; but this is no argument against its legitimate use, but only teaches that prudence should govern such religious intercourse. The opposite extreme is not uncommon in some denominations; as where professors are publicly called upon, and that periodically, for their experience; or where, when professors are met, it is agreed that every one, in turn, shall give a narrative of his or her experience, in religion. Such practices are not for edification. There are, however, cases in which it may be expedient—it may be delightful—for a few select friends to enter into a full detail of the dealings of God with their souls, respectively. The writer, in another place, published an account of such a conference in Holland, which he received from the late Rev. Dr

Livingston, of New Brunswick. A company of pious friends having met for religious conversation, the subject which came up was the striking similarity of the experience of God's people in all ages, and in all countries; when some one observed, that there were present, four persons from the four quarters of the world, respectively, and who had embraced religion in their native country. One was from the Dutch settlements in the East Indies, a second from the Cape of Good Hope, the third a young nobleman of Holland, and the fourth Dr Livingston himself, from the United States of America. It was then proposed as an illustration of the subject of conversation, that each should give a narrative of his Christian experience. The company in attendance expressed the highest gratification, and were no doubt greatly edified. It is much to be lamented, that many persons who are fond of religious conversation, deal so much in cant phrases, and assume an air so affected and sanctimonious. This is the thing which disgusts grave and intelligent Christians; and often occasions the wicked to ridicule or blaspheme. "Let not your good be evil spoken of." Be not public nor indiscriminate in your communications of this kind. "Take heed that you cast not your pearls before swine, lest they trample them under their feet, and then turn again and rend you."

It is a fact, that what passes for conversion in one sect, will be condemned as altogether insufficient in another. A few years since there was, what was called a great revival, in a Presbyterian congregation, in New Jersey. The Presiding Elder of the Methodist Society, for that district, having classes of his church mingled with the people of that congregation, so that he had the opportunity of conversing with a number of the subjects of this work, gave it as his opinion, to a person who communicated the fact to me, that none with whom he spoke, were converted, for he did not meet with one who would say, that he *knew* his sins were pardoned. On the other hand, many of the conversions which take place at camp meetings, and other meetings, where there is much excitement, though the subjects do profess to know that their sins are pardoned, are not believed to be cases of sound conversion by Presbyterians; and they are confirmed in this opinion, often, by the transitory nature of the reformation produced. We have known instances of persons professing conversion at a camp-meeting, and filling the camp with their rejoicing, who relapsed into their old habits of sin, before reaching their own dwellings. In these strong excitements of the animal sensibilities, there is great danger of deception. When feelings of distress are wound up to a very high pitch, there often occurs a natural re-action in the nervous system, by which the bodily sensations are suddenly changed, and this, attended with some text of Scripture impressed on the mind, leads the person to believe, that he was in that moment converted, when in reality no permanent change has been effected. It is one thing to be persuaded of the truth of the gospel, and quite another to be certain that I have believed, and that my sins are pardoned. Mr Wesley was for several years in the ministry, and a missionary to America before he had this joyful sense of the forgiveness of sins, and he seems to intimate, that until this time he was an unconverted man; and most of his followers make this joyful sense of pardoned sin, the principal evidence of conversion, and one which all must experience. Most serious, intelligent readers, however, will be of opinion, that Mr. Wesley was as humble and sincere a penitent, before this joyful experience, as afterwards; and that it is a dangerous principle to make a man's opinion of his own state, the criterion by which to judge of its safety. Certainly, we should greatly prefer to stand in the place of some broken-hearted, contrite ones, who can scarcely be induced to entertain a hope respecting their acceptance, to that of many who boast that they never feel a doubt of their own safety. Men will not be judged in the last day by the opinion which they had of themselves. For this confidence, it would seem, never forsakes some to the last, who nevertheless will be cast into outer darkness. "Not every one that saith unto me Lord, Lord, shall enter into the kingdom of heaven, but he that doeth the will of my Father which is in heaven. Many will say unto me in that day, Lord, Lord, have we not prophesied in thy name, and in thy name have cast out devils, and in thy name done many wonderful works? And then will I profess unto them, I never knew you, depart from me ye workers of iniquity." In early life, the writer knew some high professors of his own denomination, who could tell the day and hour when God had mercy on them. One of these, a fair spoken, plausible man, who had spent the former part of his life in pleasure and dissipation, gave such an account of his conversion as was adapted to produce envy and discouragement in professors who had been less favoured; and not only could designate the month and day of the month, but the hour of the day, when he obtained reconciliation with God. No one doubted of his piety—but mark the event. This high professor, a few years afterwards, was excommunicated from the church, for manifest perjury! Another, whose experience was remarkable and his conversion sudden, became a preacher, then a fanatic—and finally an infidel. This man told me, that though often in great spiritual distress, he never doubted of the goodness of his state. They who believe that a man may be a saint to-day and a devil to-morrow, not in appearance only, but in reality, easily account for these apostasies, but we are inclined to hold fast by what the beloved disciple says about such, in his time. "They went out from us, but they were not of us, for if they had been of us they would no doubt have continued with us; but they went out, that they might be made manifest that they were not all of us."

Few men in later times appear to have arisen to greater eminence in piety than Henry Martyn, the missionary. The strength of the principle of holiness, in his case, was manifested in his habitual spirituality of mind, and constant exercise of self-de nial; yet, as far as is related, his incipient exercises of religion were by no means strongly marked, but seem to have been rather obscure and feeble. The same is the fact respecting those two distinguished men of God, Philip and Matthew Henry, the father and the son. The early exercises of these men were not in any respect remarkable. Indeed, they both became pious when very young; and we rarely get a very distinct and accurate account of the commencement of piety in early life. But no one, who is acquainted with the lives of these eminent ministers, will deny that they grew up to an uncommon degree of piety, which in the experience of both, though characterized by genuine humility, was free from any mixture of gloom or austerity. True religion can rarely be found exhibiting so cheerful a mien and so amiable an aspect, and yet, with these men every thing became a part of their religion; to this one object their whole lives were devoted. I have derived much satisfaction, and I hope, profit, from the account which Halyburton gives of his religious experience; especially, because the account was given when the writer was advanced in years, and when his judgment was fully matured. Many youthful narratives of pious exercises are very fervent, but they are frothy, and marked with that kind of ignorance and self-confidence which arise from inexperience. Halyburton is an example of a person brought up under religious discipline and instruction, and under constant restraint, whose convictions of sin were nevertheless exceedingly pungent and awful. His conversion too was sudden, and his first exercises of faith clear and strong. "I cannot," says he, "be very positive about the day or the hour of this deliverance; nor can I satisfy many other questions about the way and manner of it. As to these things I may say with the blind man, 'One thing I know, that whereas I was blind, now I see.' It was towards the close of January, or the beginning of February, 1698, that this seasonable relief came; and, so far as I can remember, I was at secret prayer, in very great extremity, not far from despair, when the Lord seasonably

11*

stepped in and gave this merciful turn to affairs When I said there was none to save, then 'his arm brought salvation.' God, who commanded the light to shine out of darkness, 'shined into my mind,' to give the light of the knowledge of the glory of God in the face of Jesus Christ. That which afforded me relief was a discovery of the Lord, as manifested in his word. He said to me, 'thou hast destroyed thyself, but in me is thy help.' He let me see that there are forgivenesses with him, that with him is mercy and plenteous redemption. He made all his goodness pass before me, and proclaimed his name. 'The Lord, the Lord God, merciful and gracious, long-suffering, and abundant in goodness and truth, keeping mercy for thousands, forgiving iniquity and transgression and sin;' who will be gracious to whom he will be gracious, and will show mercy to whom he will show mercy. This was a strange sight to one who before looked on God as a 'consuming fire' which I could not see and live. He brought me from Sinai and its thunderings, to Mount Zion, and to the Mediator of the new covenant, and to the blood of sprinkling that cleanseth from all sin, and speaketh better things than the blood of Abel. He revealed Christ in his glory. I now with wonder beheld his glory, the glory as of the only begotten of the Father, full of grace and truth. And I was made, by this sight, to say, 'Thou art fairer than the sons of men.'...... And I was hereby further satisfied, that not only was there forgiveness of sins and justification by free grace, through the redemption that is in Christ Jesus, whom God hath set forth to be a propitiation through faith in his blood, to declare his righteousness for the remission of sins that are past, through the forbearance of God—but I saw moreover, with wonder and delight, how God by this means might be just even in justifying the ungodly, who believe in Jesus. How was I ravished with delight when made to see that the God in whom a little before I thought there was no help for me, or any sinner in my case—if indeed there were any such—notwithstanding his spotless purity, his deep hatred of sin, his inflexible justice and righteousness, and his unimpeachable faithfulness pledged in the threatenings of the law, might not only pardon, but without prejudice to his justice or his other attributes, might be just even in justifying the ungodly...... And the Lord further opened the gospel-call to me, and let me see that even to me, was 'the word of this salvation sent. All this was offered unto me, and I was invited to come and freely take of the waters of life, and to come in my distress unto the blessed rest....... He, to my great satisfaction, gave me a pleasing discovery of his design in the whole, that it was, 'that no flesh might glory in his sight,' but that he who glories, should glory only in the Lord; and that he might manifest the riches of his grace, and be exalted in showing mercy, and that we in the end might be saved. The Lord revealed to my soul the full and suitable provision, made in this way against the power of sin—that as there is righteousness in him, so there is strength, even 'everlasting strength' in the Lord Jehovah, to secure us against all enemies...... When this strange discovery was made of a relief, wherein full provisions were made for all the concerns of God's glory, and my salvation in subordination thereto, my soul was, by a sweet and glorious power, carried out to rest in it, as worthy of God, and every way suitable and satisfying in my case. 'They that know thy name will put their trust in thee.' All these discoveries were conveyed to me by the Scriptures only. It was not indeed by one particular promise or testimony of Scripture, but by the concurring light of a great many, seasonably set home, and most plainly expressing the truths above mentioned. The promises and truths of the Bible, in great abundance and variety, were brought to remembrance, and the wonders contained in them, were set before my eyes in the light of the word. 'He sent his word and healed me.'...... But it was not the Bible alone that conveyed the discovery; for most of these passages whereby I was relieved, I had formerly in my distress, read and thought upon, without finding any relief in them. But now the Lord shined into my mind by them. Formerly, I was acquainted only with the letter, which profits not, but now the Lord's words were spirit and life, and in his light I saw light. God opened my eyes to see wonders out of his law. There was light in his words; a burning light by them shone into my mind, not merely some doctrinal knowledge, but 'the light of the knowledge of the glory of God in the face of Jesus Christ.' The light, that I now had, shone from heaven; it was not a spark kindled by my own endeavours, but it shone suddenly about me; it came by the word of God, a heavenly means. It opened heaven and discovered heavenly things, even the glory of God; and it led me up as it were to heaven. Its whole tendency was heavenward. It was a true light, giving manifestations of God, even the one true God, and the one Mediator between God and man; and giving a true view of my state with respect to God...... It was a pleasant and a sweet light: it had a heavenly satisfaction in God attending it. It led to a pleasure in the fountain whence it came. It was a distinct and clear light, not only representing spiritual things, but manifesting them in their glory. It put all things in their proper place, in due subordination to God, and gave distinct views of their genuine tendency. It was a satisfying light. The soul rested in the discoveries that it made and was satisfied; it could not doubt of what it saw, and that things were as they were represented. It was a quickening, refreshing and healing light; when 'the Sun of Righteousness' arose, there was 'healing under his wings.' It was a great light: it made discoveries which were easily distinguished from any former discoveries it had ever made. And it was a powerful light; it dissipated that thick darkness which had overspread my mind, and made all those frightful temptations, which had formerly disturbed me, fly before it. It was composing: not like a sudden flash of lightning, which fills the soul with fear and amazement, but it composed and quieted my soul and put all my faculties, as it were, in their due posture, and gave me the exercise of them. It destroyed not, but improved my former knowledge. But, as the true idea of light is not conveyed by the ear; so no words can convey the idea of light to the blind And he who has eyes, will need no words to describe it. It is like the new name that none knows, save he that has it.

"The first discernible effect of this light was, an approbation of God's way of saving sinners by Jesus Christ, to the glory of his grace. And this I take to be the true Scriptural notion of justifying faith; for it not only answers the Scripture descriptions of it, by receiving, coming, looking, trusting, believing, &c., but it really gives God that glory which he designed by all this contrivance—the glory of his wisdom, grace, mercy, and truth. Now this discovery of the Lord's name brought me to trust in him, and glory only in the Lord. I found my soul fully satisfied in these discoveries, as pointing out a way of relief, altogether and in all respects suitable to the need of a poor, guilty, self-condemned, self-destroyed sinner, driven from all other reliefs. In this I rested, as in a way of full peace, comfort, security, and satisfaction, as providing abundantly for all those ends I desired to have secured. And this approbation was not merely for a time; but ever after in all temptations it discovered itself, by keeping in me a fixed assent and adherence of mind to this truth, and full persuasion of it, that God hath granted unto us eternal life, and this life is in his Son.

"The next remarkable effect of this discovery was, that it set me right as to my chief end, and made me look to the glory of God, for which formerly I had no real concern. Now mine eye was made, in some measure, single in eyeing the Lord's honour. It manifested itself in frequent desires, that the Lord might be honoured and glorified, in my life, or by my death. It kept my soul fixed in the persuasion that it was every way meet that I should take shame and confusion to myself as what only belonged to me; and that the glory of my salvation was only and entirely the Lord's due.

"A third discernible effect was, that I was led to look upon his yoke to be easy and his burden light; and to count that his commandments were not grievous, but 'right concerning all things.'—This was very contrary to my former temper. I now came to a fixed persuasion that the law was not only just, such as I could make no reasonable exception against, but holy, and such as became God; and good, such as was every way suited to my true interest and peace, and advantage—which I could never think before. The duties to which my heart was most averse had now become agreeable and refreshing.

"A fourth remarkable effect of this discovery was, the exercise of evangelical repentance, which was very different, in many respects, from that sorrow with which I was before acquainted. It differed in its rise. Sorrow before flowed from the discovery of sin as it brings on wrath; now it flowed from a sense of sin as containing wretched unkindness to ONE, who was himself astonishingly kind to an unworthy wretch. I looked on him whom I had pierced, and did mourn. Sorrow formerly wrought death, alienated my heart from God, and thus dispirited me for duty, and made me fear hurt from him; but this sorrow filled my heart with kindness to God and to his ways, sweetened my soul, and endeared God to it. It flowed from a sense of his favour to an unworthy wretch that deserved none, and was thus a godly sorrow leading to kindness to God, and a drawing near him, but with much humble sense of my own unworthiness, like the returning prodigal. The more God manifested of his kindness, the more still did this feeling increase: when he was pacified, then was I ashamed and confounded. The sorrow I had before I looked on as a burden: it was nothing but selfish concern for my own safety, and a fear of the righteous resentment of God. But this sorrow was sweet and pleasant, as being the exercise of filial gratitude; and I took pleasure in the surprising manifestations of God's favour to one so unworthy, and in acknowledging my own unworthiness. This sorrow was a spring of activity, and I was glad to be employed in the meanes' errand that might give opportunity to evidence how deeply I was grieved for my former disobedience. It resulted in a return to the way of life, and to such a course, as upon a review, I did not repent of, but delighted in, and in which I desired continually to advance. It wrought carefulness to avoid sin, anxiety to please God, indignation against sin, fear of offending God again, vehement desire of having sin removed, the Lord glorified, and obedience promoted.

"A fifth discernible effect was, an humble, but sweet and comfortable hope, and persuasion of my own salvation, answerable to the clearness of the discovery. When the Lord gave me this view of the way of salvation, he satisfied me, that it was a way full of peace and security, the only way which I might safely venture. Hereby I was freed from the disquieting fear that the ground of my trust would fail. I was satisfied I could not fail, otherwise than by missing the way. While I held fast and reposed with satisfaction on what I was convinced was safe, I could not but be quiet and composed about the result. This shows how nearly allied faith and assurance are, though they are not the same, no wonder the one should be taken for the other. This discovery, manifested that salvation was in the way of self-denial, and trust in the Lord alone; for nothing so soon marred this hope, as the least appearance of self, and stirring of pride. Whenever the glory of the Lord appeared and he spake peace, I was filled with shame, and the deeper this humiliation was, the more the humble confidence of my safety increased.

"A sixth discernible difference was, with respect to the ordinances of the Lord's appointment. I was drawn to follow them as the Lord's institutions, and his appointed means of our obtaining discoveries of his beauty. I desired 'to behold the beauty of the Lord, and to inquire in his temple.' I was brought to exercise more liveliness when the Lord discovered himself; 'my soul then followed hard after him.' When the Lord enlarged me and caused me to approach to him and see his glory, he still humbled me, discovered self, and put me in opposition to it. I was now acquainted, in some measure, with that boldness and freedom of access, with humble confidence, to God as on a throne of grace, manifesting himself in Christ. In a word, I was in some measure, sensible of the Lord's hiding or manifesting himself, according as I performed my duty, and of the necessity of the exercise of grace, particularly faith, in all approaches to God."

Although in the preceding authentic narrative of religious experience, we have entered more into detail than usual, yet we are persuaded, that the serious reader will not think the account too long or too particular. I have not met with any account of Christian experience which is so full and satisfactory as this; and when it is known to have been written by a man of sound understanding, and most exemplary piety, at a late period of life, when his judgment was matured by much experience, it cannot but furnish a decisive proof of the reality of experimental religion, which cannot be gainsaid. In these exercises there is not a tincture of enthusiasm. Indeed, holy affections thus produced by the contemplation of truth are the very opposite of enthusiasm; which always substitutes human fancies or impulses for the truths of God, which it uniformly undervalues. In this case, we see also, how high the exercises of Scriptural piety may rise, without degenerating into any extravagance. Many Christians seem not to know or believe that such spiritual discoveries of the beauty of holiness and the glory of the Lord, are now attainable: but still there are some, and often those of the humbler class of society, who are privileged with these spiritual discoveries, and prize them above all price. The language of such is, "One day in thy courts is better than a thousand. I would rather be a doorkeeper in the house of God, than dwell in the tents of sin." "Return unto thy rest, O my soul, for the Lord hath dealt bountifully with thee." It is delightful to trace the effects of God's truth in producing every holy affection, when it is discerned by the light of the Holy Spirit. Faith is almost identified with this view; love flows out sweetly and spontaneously; evangelical repentance is enkindled; the soul is clothed with humility; zeal for God's glory is predominant; his ordinances are sought with desire, and found to be channels which freely communicate with the rich fountain of grace beneath the throne of God. So far are right views of free grace from leading those who entertain them to indulge in indolence, or be careless about holy living, that they impart the only true cause of activity and diligence in the work of the Lord. In the foregoing account, the reader may learn the nature of true religion more clearly than from many sermons and long treatises; but the humble, doubting Christian must not make the measure of grace which this favoured saint enjoyed, the standard by which to judge of the reality of his own religious experience. The same light may shine with vastly different degrees of clearness, from the meridian blaze down to the faint crepuscular dawn, but the rays come from the same source; and that which is now but just discernible in the midst of shades of departing night, will go on to increase, until it shines more and more to the perfect day. Let not the extraordinary clearness and distinctness discourage those who are sincerely desirous to see " the beauty of the Lord," but let them rather take fresh courage in a pursuit, which from this example, they find may be crowned with glorious success. " They that wait upon the Lord shall renew their strength; they shall mount up with wings as eagles, they shall run and not be weary, and they shall walk and not faint."

CHAPTER IX.

Christian experience of R —— C ——. Narrative of Sir Richard Hill's experience.

THE following extracts, from a narrative of the Christian experience of R—— C——, will serve to illustrate some points which have heretofore been treated; particularly the gradual manner in which some persons are brought to the knowledge of the truth; and the extreme difficulty of ascertaining, in many cases, where common grace ends and special grace commences.

"I grew up," says the narrator, "to manhood with very little thought of religion, and without experiencing any serious impressions, except the alarm occasionally produced by the death of a companion, or relative. Whilst I habitually cherished a great dislike to strict religion, which frowned upon a life of pleasure and amusement, I entertained a strong prejudice in favour of Christianity in general, and that particular denomination to which my parents and ancestors belonged. I call this a prejudice, for I knew nothing of the evidences of the truth of Christianity, and had only a very vague and confused notion of what the Scriptures contained; except that, when a child, I had read, frequently, many portions of the historical parts of the Bible. In this state of mind, I was exposed to the common objections of infidels; which arose from reading history, and finding that all nations had their respective religions, in which they believed as firmly as we did in ours; and the thought occurred, often, 'Why may they not be in the right, and we in the wrong?' But, about this time, infidelity began to prevail, and its abettors to be bold in declaring their opinions. My mind was so completely unfurnished with arguments in favour of Christianity, that the only thing on which I could fix was, that it had come down from my ancestors, and the people with whom I was conversant, generally believed in it. But this was far from satisfying my mind. I began to feel uneasy for fear that we were all wrong in our belief; but the thought was never pleasing to my mind. As to books of evidences, I knew nothing about them, and cannot remember that I had ever heard of such works. And I was so situated that I had no one to whom I could apply for instruction. The only person with whom I had any communication, on literary subjects, was a gentleman, who though he said nothing to me on the subject, was deeply imbued with skeptical opinions. Being separated from the companions of my youth, and placed in a secluded situation, where, except on particular occasions, I saw little company, and where there were few opportunities of hearing instructive preaching, I was cast upon my own thoughts, and my reflections were often not very pleasing. One day—it was the Lord's day—as I was looking over some books, which I had in a trunk, my eye caught the words, 'Internal Evidences of the Christian Religion.' I had often seen the same book, and never so much as thought what the subject of it was; but in my present perplexity, I seized it with avidity, and began to read. The work was the celebrated treatise of Soame Jenyns, Esq. I never removed from where I was sitting until I had finished it, and as I proceeded, the light of evidence poured in upon my mind with such power of demonstration, that at the conclusion, I had the idea of the room being full of resplendent light. I enjoyed a pleasure which none can appreciate but those who have been led to the contemplation of the truth, in like perplexing circumstances. Not only were all my doubts removed, but I wanted no more evidence. My conviction of the truth of Christianity was complete. I believe it could not have been increased.

"But still I knew scarcely any thing of the method of salvation, revealed in the gospel. I entertained the common legal notions of thousands of ignorant people, 'that at a convenient time I would become good,' never doubting, for a moment, of my ability to do all that was requisite. The only thing which gave me uneasiness was, the fear of a sudden death, which would not afford me the opportunity of repenting and making my peace with God. But the hope prevailed, that I should die a lingering death, and be in my senses, and then I would do all that was requisite to prepare me for heaven; while at the same time, I had no definite idea, what that preparation was. During this period, I was exposed to few temptations; but still some sins had dominion over me. One day a child brought to me a small book and said that Mrs. T. requested that I would read it, and return it soon, as it was borrowed. The title was, 'Jenks on Submission to the Righteousness of God.' I read the book through at a single sitting, and again a new light sprung up in my mind. The author, in the introduction, gives an account of his ignorance of the true method of a sinner's justification, until he had been for years a preacher. He was a minister of the Church of England. I now found that I likewise had been all my life ignorant of the way of salvation; for I entertained the same legal and unscriptural notions which he proves to be utterly erroneous. Although these new views seem to have been merely intellectual, yet they afforded me a great satisfaction. I had now a distinct knowledge of the gospel method of justification, which I ever afterwards retained. Another copy of this book I have never seen.

"The preaching, to which I had access, was mostly of a wild, fanatical kind, and the way in which I heard the *new birth* described, tended to prejudice me against the doctrine of regeneration. I had never before heard any thing about this change, and yet I was sure that I knew some very good and religious people. I began to be troubled to know, whether sober, intelligent Christians believed in this doctrine. It also became a subject of discussion in the little circle with which I was conversant; and I found that one person in the company professed to have experienced this change; another was convinced of its reality, but professed to be merely an inquirer; a third was of opinion, that it related to the conversion of Jews and infidels, and that there was no other regeneration, except in baptism; and the fourth was the skeptical gentleman, already mentioned, who was incredulous about the whole matter. In these conversations, I, being young and ignorant, took no part, but I listened to them with intense interest. I had recourse to such books as I had access to, but could find nothing that was satisfactory; for my range of religious books was very narrow, and few of these of an evangelical cast. The person of my acquaintance, who professed conversion, one day gave me a narrative of the various steps and changes experienced in this transition from darkness to light. As I entertained a favourable opinion of the veracity and sincerity of the individual, I began to think there might be something in it. Although I had experienced no remarkable change thus far, I knew that the subject of religion had become one of much more frequent thought, and excited much more interest in my mind than formerly. One evidence of this was, that I commenced secret prayer, a duty utterly neglected until this time, except when some one of the family was dangerously sick. I had selected a retired spot, surrounded by a thick growth of trees and bushes, on the margin of a brook. Here I made a kind of arbour, over a little plat of green grass, and in the summer evenings I would resort to this sequestered spot. It was on the afternoon of a Sunday, I was reading a sermon on the long-suffering and patience of God, in waiting with delaying sinners; and so many things applied so exactly to my own case, that I became so much affected with a sense of the divine goodness and forbearance, in sparing me, and waiting so long with me, while I was living in neglect of him, that I felt impelled to go out and weep. I was reading the sermon aloud to the family, by request. I laid down the book abruptly, and hastened to my retirement, where I poured out a flood of tears, in prayer. And, suddenly, I was overwhelmed with a flood of joy. It was exstatic beyond any thing which

I had ever conceived; for though I thought religion a necessary thing, I never had an idea that there was any positive pleasure in its exercises. Whence this joy originated, I knew not. The only thing which had been on my mind was, the goodness and patience of God, and my own ingratitude. Neither can I now say how long it continued; but the impression left was, that I was in the favour of God, and should certainly be happy for ever. When the tumult of feeling had subsided, I began to think that this was conversion—this was the great change, of which I had recently heard so much. It occurred to me, when walking home, that if this was indeed the change called *the new birth*, it would be evinced by my forsaking all my sins. This suggestion appeared right, and I determined to make this the test of its reality. All the evening, my mind was in a delightful calm; but the next day my feelings had returned into their old channel. I was grieved at this, and resorted to the same place where I had experienced such a delightful frame, in hopes, that by some kind of association, the same scene would be renewed; but though *there* was the place and all the objects of yesterday, the soul-ravishing vision was not there; and after a feeble attempt at prayer, and lingering for some time, I returned without meeting any thing which I sought and desired. It was not long before I was subjected to the test which I had fixed; a temptation to a besetting sin was presented, and I had no strength to resist but was instantly overcome. This failure gave me inexpressible pain, on reflection. I did not know how dear were my cherished hopes until they were wrested from me. I never felt a keener regret at any loss which I ever experienced.

"Although I was constrained to admit, that I was not a regenerated person, I was sensible of a considerable change in my views and feelings on the subject of religion. I had no longer any doubt of the necessity of regeneration, and entertained some consistent notions of what its effects must be. I had, as before stated, acquired evangelical views of the way in which a sinner must be justified; and entertained different feelings from what I had formerly towards religious people. Formerly they were objects of dread and aversion, now I felt a sincere regard, and high respect for the same characters; and was pleased, when I heard of any of my friends becoming religious, or more serious than before. I had now an opportunity of hearing an able minister preach an evangelical sermon on the text, 'For our righteousnesses are as filthy rags,' &c., and I cannot tell the gratification I experienced, in hearing the doctrine of justification, which I had fully embraced, preached distinctly and luminously from the pulpit: but when I looked around on the audience, I had the impression, that they were all, or nearly all, ignorant of what he was saying, and were still trusting to their own works. It gave me pleasure, also, now, to converse on the doctrines of religion; and I felt a real abhorrence of vicious courses. This was my state of mind when Providence cast my lot where a powerful revival had been in progress for some time. I had witnessed something of this kind in a wild, fanatical sect, where bodily agitations were common and violent; but this was a different scene. The principal conductor and preacher was a man of learning and eloquence; and his views of experimental religion, as I think, most correct and scriptural. If he erred, it was on the safe side, in believing in the thorough conversion of but a small number of those who appeared impressed. In entering into this scene, I experienced various new, and conflicting feelings. The young converts spoke freely, in my presence, of their conviction and conversion; but often with a degree of levity, which surprised me. In their conversations I could take no part, and although my general purpose was to consider myself an unawakened, unconverted sinner, yet when I heard the marks of true religion laid down, and especially by the distinguished preacher, before mentioned, I could not prevent the thought arising continually, 'If this is religion, then you have experienced it.' This seemed to me to be the suggestion of a false hope, by the enemy, to prevent my falling under conviction. Still the idea was continually presented to my mind, and with the appearance of truth. I took occasion to state the matter to the clergyman above alluded to, as soon as I could gain access to him; for I was diffident and timid, and had never opened my case to any one, freely. I told him all my former exercises, and stated distinctly, that they had not been sufficient to break the habit of sinning, to which I was addicted. As soon as I mentioned this part, he said, in a peremptory tone, 'then surely your exercises were not of the nature of true religion; and you must seek a better hope or you will never be admitted into heaven.' This decisive answer drove away, from that moment, every idea of my being in a state of grace; and I felt relieved from what I had myself considered a temptation, to entertain a false hope. Now I began to seek *conviction*, as a necessary preliminary to conversion; and hoped that every sermon which I heard, would be the means of striking terror into my soul. I read the most awakening discourses, went to hear the most arousing preachers; endeavoured to work on my own mind by imagining the awful realities of the judgment, and the torments of the damned. I strove to draw the covering from the pit, that I might behold the lake of fire, and hear the wailings of the damned. But the more I sought these awful feelings of conviction, the further they seemed to fly from me. My heart seemed to grow harder every day. I was sensible of nothing but insensibility. I became discouraged; and the more, because I was obliged to remove from the scene of the revival, to a place where there was no concern about religion, in the people generally; and where, I expected the preaching to be cold and lifeless I spent a day before my departure, in secret, and in solemn reflection on my deplorable and hopeless case. I ran over all the kind dispensations of God's providence towards me, and reflected on the many precious means of grace, which I had recently enjoyed, without effect. The conclusion which seemed now to be forced on my mind was, that God had given me up to a hard heart, and that I never should be so happy as to obtain religion. This conclusion had, to my mind, all the force of a certainty; and I began to think about the justice of God in my condemnation: and no truth ever appeared with more lucid evidence to my mind. I fully justified God in sending me to hell. I saw that it was not only right, but I did not see how a just God could do otherwise. And *I seemed to acquiesce in it, as a righteous and necessary thing.* At this moment, my mind became more calm than it had been for a long time. All striving and effort on my part ceased, and being in the woods, I recollected that it was time for me to return to the house, where I expected to meet some friends. Here I found a minister waiting for me, whom I had seen but never spoken to. He took me aside, and began to represent the many privileges which I had enjoyed, and expressed a hope that I had received some good impressions. I told him that it was true, that I had been highly favoured; but that I had now come to a fixed conclusion that I should certainly be for ever lost; for under all these means, I had not received the slightest conviction, without which my conversion was impossible. He replied, by saying, 'that no certain degree of conviction was necessary—that the only use of conviction was, to make us feel our need of Christ as a Saviour; and appealed to me, whether I did not feel, that I stood in need of a Saviour.' He then went on to say, 'Christ is an advocate at the right hand of God, and stands ready to receive any case which is committed to his hands, and however desperate your case may now appear to be, only commit it to him and He will bring you off safely, 'for He is able to save to the uttermost all that come unto God by Him.' Here, a new view broke in on my mind. I saw that Christ was able to save *even me*, and I felt willing to give my cause into his hands. This discovery of the bare possibility of salvation, was one of the greatest deliverances I ever experienced. I was affected exceedingly with the view, which I had of this truth, so as to be unable to speak. Hope now sprung up in my desolate soul—not that I was pardoned or accepted. Such a thought did not occur—but that it was yet possible, that I might be, hereafter, and I was resolved never to give over seeking, until I obtained the blessing. All that evening I was sweetly composed, and precious promises and declarations of the word of God came dropping successively into my mind, as if they had been whispered to me. I never could have believed, unless I had experienced it, that the mere possibility of salvation would produce such comfort.

" About this time, next morning, probably—when I retired to the woods—where my secret devotions were usually performed, I experienced such a melting of heart from a sense of God's goodness to me, as I never felt before or since. It seemed as if my eyes—so hard to weep commonly—were now a fountain of tears. The very earth was watered with their abundance. Indeed, my heart itself seemed to be dissolved, just as a piece of ice is dissolved by the heat of the sun. Of the particular exercises of this melting season, my memory does not retain a distinct recollection.

" For some months I attended to religious duties, with various fluctuations of feeling. Sometimes I entertained a pleasing hope that I was indeed a Christian—a renewed person; but, at other times, I was not only distressed with doubts, but came to the conclusion, that I was still in my sins. The only thing which I deem it important to mention during this period, was, a deeper discovery of the wickedness of my own heart. This conviction of deep-rooted, inherent depravity, distressed me much; but I obtained considerable relief from reading Owen on 'Indwelling Sin.' This book exhibited the state of my heart much better than I could have done myself. Still, however, I was much dissatisfied with myself, because after so long a time, I had made so little progress. On one occasion, at the close of the exercises of the Sabbath, I was so deeply sensible that my soul was still in imminent danger of perdition, that I solemnly resolved to begin a new and more vigorous course of engagedness to secure my salvation. I had spent much time in reading accounts of Christian experience, and those which lay down the marks and evidences of true religion, such as 'Owen on Spiritual Mindedness,' 'Edwards on the Affections,' 'Guthrie's Trial of a Saving Interest in Christ,' 'Newton's Letters,' 'Pike and Hayward's Cases of Conscience,' &c. I also conversed much with old and experienced Christians, as well as with those of my own age. - But all these having, as it then seemed to me, very little facilitated my progress, and the evils of my heart seeming rather to increase, I hastily resolved to lay aside all books, except the Bible, and to devote my whole time to prayer and reading, until I experienced a favourable change. In pursuance of this purpose, I withdrew into a deeply retired spot, where I knew I should be free from all intrusion from mortals, and began my course of exertion with fasting and strong resolution never to relinquish my efforts, until I found relief. For five or six hours I was engaged alternately in reading the Scriptures and attempting to pray; but the longer I continued these exercises, the harder did my heart become, and the more wretched my feelings, until at length I was exhausted and discouraged, and began to despair of help, and was about returning from my chosen retirement, in gloomy despondence, when it occurred to me with peculiar force, that if I found I could do nothing to help myself, yet I might call upon God for mercy. Accordingly, I fell down before him, and said little more than is contained in the publican's prayer, 'God be merciful to me a sinner;' but this I uttered with a deep and feeling conviction of my utter helplessness. The words were scarcely out of my mouth, when God was pleased to give me such a manifestation of his love in the plan of redemption through Christ, as filled me with wonder, love, and joy. Christ did indeed appear to me as altogether lovely, and I was enabled to view Him as *my* Saviour, and to see that his sufferings were endured for *me*. At no time before had I the full assurance of being in the favour of God; but now every doubt of this was dissipated. I could say, for the first time with unwavering confidence, 'My beloved is mine, and I am his.' And this assurance of God's favour arose not from any suggestion or impulse directly made to my mind, but from the clear view, that Christ, as a Saviour, was freely offered, and from a conscious assurance, that I did truly accept the offer. I now opened my Bible and began to read at the 18th chapter of John and onward. Every word and sentiment appeared glorious. I seemed to be reading a book which was perfectly new, and, truly, the sacred pages seemed to be illuminated with celestial light. And I rejoiced to think that the Sacred Scriptures would always be read in the same manner. How little did I know of the spiritual warfare! After my feelings had a little subsided, but while the glorious truths of the Gospel were still in full view, I made a formal and solemn dedication of myself to God, the Father, Son, and Holy Spirit; and having writing materials with me, I wrote down the substance of this covenant, and subscribed it with my hand.

"I now believed, assuredly, that I was reconciled to God through Jesus Christ; but being naturally inclined to be suspicious of myself, I resolved to make the Holy Scriptures the test of the genuineness of my exercises, and to leave the final determination to the fruits produced, as our Lord says, 'By their fruits ye shall know them.' I remembered that it was written, that faith works by love and purifies the heart. I hoped, therefore, that I should now be delivered from those evils of the heart with which I had been lately so much affected. But, alas! in a few days I found that the 'old man' was not dead, but had power to struggle in a fearful manner. I must acknowledge, therefore, that, after a few weeks, I was much in the same spiritual condition in which I was before this remarkable manifestation."

* * * * *

Here the narration breaks off abruptly. It will not escape the notice of the attentive reader, that in this account all circumstances are avoided which could lead to the discovery of the writer. The true reason of this, I have reason to believe is, that the writer is still alive, and has no desire to be made conspicuous. It would be attended with no advantage to explain by what means this imperfect narrative came into my possession. The use which I make of it is not contrary to the wishes of the writer, while the injunction is peremptory, that no hint shall be given to the public, by which it may be conjectured who it is.

It may be remarked, in the first place, on this narrative, that sometimes persons are brought along very gradually in their acquisition of the knowledge of the truth. One discovery is made at one time, and another truth is revealed at another time; and between these steps there may be a long interval. It may again be remarked, that commonly before a person comes to the knowledge of a truth, the need of information is sensibly felt; and the appropriate means of communicating it are provided. A book, a sermon, a casual conversation, may be intimately connected with our salvation. Those, who commence a religious life, though they may appear sincere, should always be urged to go forward; there is much before them which they have not yet experienced. If they are not yet in the right way they may arrive at it. In looking over the various exercises here detailed, I am utterly at a loss to say when the work of grace commenced. Perhaps, scarcely any two persons, taken at random, would agree in this point; for, while some would scarcely admit, that there was any exercising of saving faith until the last manifestation here described, others would be for carrying it back to the very beginning of the exercised soul's serious attention to religion. However this matter may be decided, one thing, I think, is evident, that it is a great practical error to suppose, that nothing, connected essentially with the sinner's conversion, is experienced or done, until the moment of his conversion. He may have to unlearn many erroneous opinions, taken up through prejudice or inclination. He must learn the truth of the Christian religion, if unhappily he has adopted skeptical notions. He must learn to know what the Bible teaches, as to man's duty, and the true method of salvation. God's methods of bringing his chosen into the paths of truth and holiness are often wonderful. They are, at every step, led in a way which they knew not. How remarkably true is this, as it relates to conviction of sin! When the sinner is most convinced, he thinks he has no conviction at all. And in regard to conversion, what a different thing does it turn out to be in experience, from what it was conceived to be beforehand! Whilst the anxious soul was expecting something miraculous, or entirely out of the way, he experiences a new train of thought, new and pleasing views of truth, with corresponding emotions, by which the mind is so occupied, that it has no time nor inclination to scrutinize the nature or cause of these pleasing exercises. He believes and hopes without asking himself the question, are these the views and feelings of a renewed soul? Afterwards, he can look back and see that faith was exercised in these very acts, and that the peace which he then enjoyed was the peace of reconciliation through our Lord Jesus Christ. But when the love of God is shed abroad in the heart by the Holy Ghost, as described in the last part of this narrative, the distressed soul is made sensible at once of its happy state, and is made to rejoice in the smiles of the divine favour. Then he can no more doubt that God is reconciled and has lifted upon him the light of his countenance, than that the sun is shining at mid-day. All Christians, however, are not favoured with these bright discoveries, but always walk in a degree of darkness, or at best in a mere crepuscular light; yet they fear the Lord and obey the voice of his servants. I have known instances of some persons changing their opinion of the time of their own conversion, several times, and fixing it at different periods of their experience, as their sentiments became more correct and mature; and those converts who shine forth more brightly at first, are not always they who appear best after the lapse of years.

The following narrative of the experience of Sir Richard Hill, written by himself, is found in his life, by the Rev. Edwin Sidney, and has been inserted in the Christian Observer of London, for September, 1839. We make no apology for its length, as we are confident that all who have a taste for this kind of reading, will be gratified to have the whole of this interesting account, without curtailment.

"It would not be an easy matter for me to ascertain the time, when the first dawnings of divine light began to break in upon my soul; but I remember particularly that, when I was about eight or nine years of age, being then at a neighbouring school, and repeating the catechism one Sunday evening with some other boys, to the master, I found my heart sweetly drawn up to heavenly objects, and had such a taste of the love of God, as made every thing else appear insipid and contemptible. This was but a transitory glimpse of the heavenly gift; and I was no sooner withdrawn with the rest of my school-fellows, than my religious impressions vanished, and I returned to folly with the same eagerness as before. But God did not leave me to myself; I had frequent checks of conscience, and the thoughts of death sometimes came forcibly into my mind. I remained about two years at the school before mentioned, after which I was removed to Westminster, where my convictions still pursued me, and forced me to several superficial repentances and resolutions; but these, being all made in my own strength, soon came to nothing.

"When I had been about four or five years at Westminster, I was to be confirmed with several more of my school-fellows. I looked upon this as going into a new state, and therefore made the most solemn resolutions of becoming a new creature. But, alas! my happiness and conversion were far from beginning here, as I had fondly imagined. The adversary, now finding that he was not likely to make me continue any longer in a state of practical wickedness by his former stratagems, began to attack me on another side, viz. by suggesting horrible doubts concerning the very fundamentals of all religion—as the being of a God—the immortality of the soul, and the divine origin of the Scriptures. I endeavoured to reason myself into the belief of these truths, but all in vain. However, I thought I might easily get some book that should convince me of their certainty. Accordingly, I borrowed Dr. Beveridge's Private Thoughts, of a clergyman's widow, with whom I boarded, she having first read to me a few pages in that excellent work. It was, to the best of my remembrance, whilst she was reading, that such glorious instantaneous light and comfort were diffused over my soul, as no tongue can express; the love of God was shed abroad in my heart, and I rejoiced with joy unspeakable and full of glory. However, these comforts, I think, did not last above half an hour at most, but went off by degrees, when the same doubts succeeded; upon which I again had recourse to Bishop Beveridge's Thoughts, or to conversation on the subject of religion; and for several times as I did this, I experienced the same manifestations of divine love, which were sometimes of longer, sometimes of shorter duration.

"At length I began to be tired of this state of uncertainty, especially as the comforts I had before felt began to be few and faint. Add to this the bad example of my school-fellows, and the despair I began to be in of obtaining satisfaction of the truth of what is called natural as well as revealed religion, contributed not a little to make me lay aside my inquiries, and to fall into many sins that youth and strong passions prompted me to; and this I did with the more eagerness, as I was desirous of laying hold of every opportunity of turning my thoughts from within myself.

"I believe I might now be about eighteen years of age, when, having gone through the school at Westminster, I was entered at Magdalen College, Oxford, where I continued between four and five years. After which I went abroad for about two years more, returning to England in 1757, being then about the age of twenty-three or twenty-four. During my residence at Oxford and in foreign parts, notwithstanding all the wretched pains I took to lull conscience asleep, still my convictions pursued me; yea, the more I endeavoured to put from me the thoughts of my soul by drinking deeper draughts of iniquity, the more strongly did the insulted Spirit plead with me, and often in the very act of sin, would so embitter my carnal gratifications, and strike me with such deep remorse, that, oh! horrid to think! I have even been ready to murmur, because God would not let me alone, nor suffer me to sin with the same relentless satisfaction which I observed in my companions.

"But He that hath loved me with an everlasting love, had all this while thoughts of mercy towards me, and would not take his loving kindness utterly away from me. He therefore waited that he might be gracious unto me, and followed me with such loud and constant convictions as often brought me upon my knees, and sometimes forced me to break off my sins for a month, or a quarter of a year together; for, though I still remained full of doubts as to the truth of religion, yet I thought that, if there was a God and a future state, and if Jesus Christ was indeed the true Messiah and the author of eternal salvation to those who obey him, I could by no means be saved in the state I was in; and that, being uncertain whether these things were so or not, it was the highest infatuation to leave the eternal happiness or misery of my soul at a peradventure, especially as I could be no loser by admitting the truths of religion, and living under their influence; whereas, were I to continue in sin under the supposition of their being false, I might find myself fatally mistaken, when it would be too late to recant or retrieve my error. But, notwithstanding I came to this conclusion, and plainly saw its reasonableness, yet were my religious fits of no long continuance, but every temptation that offered itself hurried me impetuously away, and I became seventimes more the child of hell than before.

Nevertheless, every new fall increased my anguish of spirit, and set me upon praying and resolving; insomuch, that I frequently bound myself under the most solemn imprecations.

"But alas! alas! I was, all this while, as ignorant of my own weakness, as of Him on whom my strength was laid; and therefore no wonder all my attempts to make myself holy, were attended with no better success than if I had tried to wash the Ethiopian white, and answered no other end than to distress my soul a thousand times more than if I had never made such solemn vows; for, all this while, I had no other notion of religion than that it consisted in something which I was to do in order to make God amends for my past sins, and to please him for the time to come; in consideration of which I should escape hell and be entitled to everlasting life.

"In this manner I went on vowing and breaking my vows, sinning, and repenting, till my most merciful God and Saviour, seeing that all his gracious calls would not overrule the horrible perverseness of my will, instead of giving me up, as in just judgment he might have done, or pronouncing against me that dreadful sentence, 'Cut it down, why cumbereth it the ground?' —I say, instead of this, he began to deal with me after a far more violent method than he had hitherto done, filling my soul with the most unimaginable terrors, insomuch that I roared for the very disquietness of my heart. The arrows of the Almighty stuck fast in me, the poison whereof drank up my spirits, and the pains of hell gat hold upon me.

"From this time, which was about October, 1757, I may say that sin received its mortal blow. (I mean its reigning power, for God knows the body of sin yet is far from being done away,) and I set myself to work with all the earnestness of a poor perishing mariner, who is every moment in expectation of shipwreck. I fasted, prayed, and meditated; I read the Scriptures, communicated, and gave much alms. But these things could bring no peace to my soul; on the contrary, I now saw, what I never had seen be fore, that all my works were mixed with sin and imperfection. Besides this, Satan furiously assaulted me with suggestions that I had committed the unpardonable sin against the Holy Ghost, and had let my day of grace slip; that therefore my prayers were cast out by God, and were an abomination to him, and that it was too late to think of mercy, when it was the time of judgment.

"It is beyond the power of conception, much more of expression, to form an idea of the dreadful agonies my poor soul was now in. What to do, or to whom to have recourse, I knew not; for, alas, I had no acquaintance with any body who seemed to have the least experience in such cases. However, those about me showed the greatest concern for my situation, and offered their remedies for my relief, such as company, physic, exercise, &c., which, in order to oblige them, I complied with; but my disorder not being bodily, but spiritual, was not to be removed by these carnal quackeries, as they were soon convinced.

"I recollected, however, that once, if not oftener, the Rev. Mr. Fletcher, then tutor to two neighbouring young gentlemen, but since vicar of Madely, in this county, had, in my hearing, been spoken of in a very disrespectful manner, for things which seemed to me to savour of a truly Christian spirit. I therefore determined to make my case known to him, and accordingly wrote him a letter, without mentioning my name, giving him some account of my situation, and begging him for God's sake, if he had a word of comfort to offer to my poor, distressed, despairing soul, to meet me that very night at an Inn in Salop, in which place I then was. Though Mr. Fletcher had four or five miles to walk, yet he came punctually to the appointment, and spoke to me in a very comfortable manner, giving me to understand that he had very different thoughts of my state from what I had myself. After our discourse, before he withdrew, he went to prayer with me; and among other petitions that he put up in my behalf, he prayed that I might not trust in my own righteousness, which was an expression, that, though I did not ask him its import, I knew not well what to make of.

"After my conversation with Mr. Fletcher, I was rather easier, but this decrease of my terrors was but for a few days' duration; for, though I allowed that the promises and comforts he would have me apply to myself belonged to the generality of sinners, yet I thought they were not intended for me, who had been so dreadful a backslider, and who, by letting my day of grace slip, had sinned beyond the reach of mercy. Besides I concluded that they could be made effectual to none but such as had faith to apply them; whereas I had no faith, consequently they could avail me nothing. I therefore wrote again to Mr. F., telling him, as nearly as I can remember, that however others might take comfort from the Scripture promises, I feared none of them belonged to me, who had crucified the Son of God afresh, and sinned wilfully after having received the knowledge of the truth. I told him also, that I found my heart to be exceeding hard and wicked; and that, as all my duties proceeded from a slavish dread of punishment, and not from the principles of faith and love, and were withal so very defective, I thought it was impossible God should ever accept them. In answer to this, the kind and sympathizing Mr. F. immediately wrote me a sweet and comfortable letter, telling me that the perusal of the account I had given him had caused him to shed tears of joy to see what great things the Lord had done for my soul, in convincing me experimentally of the insufficiency of all my own doings to justify me before God, and of the necessity of a saving faith in the blood of Jesus. He also sent me 'The Life and Death of Mr. Halyburton, Professor of Divinity in the University of St. Andrews,' which book I read with the greatest eagerness, as the account Mr. H. therein gives of himself, seemed in a very particular manner to tally with my own experience. I therefore thought that what had been, might be; that the same God who had showed himself so powerfully, on the behalf of Mr. H., and delivered him out of all his troubles, was able to do the same for me.

"You will wonder how I could hold out under all these pressures, the half of which, I might say, has not been told; and indeed it was impossible I could have held out, had it not been that, at those very times when I thought all was over with me, there would, now and then, dart in upon me some comfortable glimmering of hope, which kept me utterly from fainting.

"In this situation I continued from September 1757, to January 1758, when the Vinerian Professor of Oxford being to read a course of lectures upon the Common Law, I resolved to set out for that place, not through any desire I had to attend the lectures, for I had no heart for any such thing, but because I knew I should have chambers to myself in college, and thereby have an opportunity of being much alone, and of giving way to those thoughts, with which my heart was big, as also of seeking the Lord with greater diligence, if peradventure I might find him. Accordingly, when I arrived at the University, though to save appearances, I dragged my body to several of the lectures, yet my poor heavy-laden soul engrossed all my attention; and so sharp was the spiritual anguish I laboured under, that I scarcely saw a beggar in the streets, but I envied his happiness, and would most gladly have changed situations with him, had it been in my power. O, thought I, these happy souls have yet an offer of mercy, and a door of hope open to them, but it is not so with me; I have rejected God so long, that now God has rejected me as he did Saul; my day of grace is past, irrecoverably past, and I have forever shut myself out of all the promises.

"All this while, one thing that greatly astonished me was, to see the world about me so careless and unconcerned, especially many that were twice my age amongst the Doctors of Divinity, and fellows of the college. Surely, thought I, these people must be infatuated indeed, thus to mind earthly things and to follow the lusts of the flesh, when an eternity of happiness or misery is before them, when they know not how short a time they have to live, and their everlasting state depends on the present moment.

"It was now the season of Lent, the first or second Sunday in which, the sacrament of the Lord's Supper is always administered in Magdalen College Chapel. I therefore besought the Lord with strong cryings, that he would vouchsafe me some token for good, some sense of his love towards me, and willingness to be reconciled to me, that I might wait upon him at his table without distraction, and partake of those blessings which that ordinance is instituted to convey to the souls of true believers.

"And O, for ever and for ever blessed be his holy name, he did not reject the prayer of the poor destitute; he heard me what time the storm fell upon me, and, I make no doubt, had heard, and, in his purpose at least, answered me, from the first day he inclined my heart to understand, and to seek after him. But he knew better than I did myself, when it was meet to speak peace to my soul, and therefore waited that he might be gracious unto me; first in order to convince me the more deeply of the exceeding sinfulness of sin, and the desert thereof; secondly, to show me more experimentally my own weakness and the insufficiency of any righteousness of my own to recommend me to his favour; thirdly, to make me prize more highly, and hunger and thirst more earnestly, for Jesus Christ, and the salvation that is in him. These ends being in some measure answered, on Saturday, February 18th, to the best of my remembrance, the night before the sacrament, it pleased the Lord, after having given me, for a few days before, some taste of his love, first to bring me into a composed frame of spirit, and then to convey such a thorough sense of his pardoning grace and mercy to my poor soul, that I, who was just before trembling upon the brink of despair, did now rejoice with joy unspeakable and full of glory! The love of God was shed abroad in my heart through the Holy Ghost that was given unto me, even that perfect love which casteth out fear; and the Spirit itself bore witness with my spirit that I was a child of God.

"For some time after these sensible manifestations of God's love were withdrawn, my mind was composed and my hope lively; but I had still, at seasons, secret misgivings and many doubts as to the reality of my conversion, which put me seriously to examine my state, whether the Scripture marks of a work of grace were really to be found in me or not; and in these examinations I had great help from those excellent books, Guthrie's Trial of a Saving Interest in Christ, and Palmer's Gospel New Creature. Add to this, that being now in London, I had there the opportunity of hearing that faithful minister of Christ, the Rev. Mr. Romaine, whose discourses were so exactly descriptive of, and adapted to, my own experience, that they afforded me a good confirmation that I was indeed passed from death unto life, and from the power of Satan unto God.

"During my stay in London, it pleased God to make me acquainted with many of his people, to whom my heart was immediately knit with the closest affection; yea, so great was my love to all those, in whom I discerned the Divine image of the Lord Jesus, that the yearnings of Joseph's heart towards his brethren will but very faintly express it. Be they who or what they would, high or low, rich or poor, ignorant or learned, it mattered not; if I had reason to believe they were born of God and made partakers of a divine nature; they were equally dear to me; my heart was open to receive them without reserve, and I enjoyed the sweetest fellowship and communion with them, whilst all other company was insipid and irksome.

"For about two years after this, I was, in a good measure, relieved from those piercing terrors and that deep distress with which I was before overwhelmed. This, you will say, was living upon frames and experiences, more than upon the exceeding great and precious promises made to returning sinners in Christ

Jesus. It is true it was so, and of this God soon convinced me; for I now began to doubt whether these great comforts I had set so high a value upon, might not be all delusion, or proceed from the workings of my own spirit; and if so, my case was just as bad as ever. My day of grace might still be past, and nothing yet remain for me but 'a fearful looking for of judgment and fiery indignation.'

"This was in April, 1759, soon after my return from London into Shropshire, where I had not been long before I wrote to Mr. Fletcher, giving him an account of my state. After this it pleased the Lord to remove my burthen, and to exchange these sharp terrors of the spirit of bondage, for the sweet reviving comforts of the spirit of adoption, showing me the rich treasures of Gospel promises, and that they, and not my own frames, were to be the ground of my hope and my stay in every time of need. Since this time, I may say with Bishop Cowper, that my soul has never experienced the like extremity of terror; and though I have had many ups and downs, many grievous temptations and sharp conflicts, much aridity of soul, deadness, and strong corruptions to fight against, yet have I always found the Lord to be a very present help in trouble; his grace has been sufficient for me in every hour of need, and I doubt not but all his dealings with me, however thwarting to my own ideas of what was fit and meet for me, have some way or other been subservient to my spiritual interest, since his most sure promise is that all things work together for good, to them that love God and are the called according to his purpose."

CHAPTER X.

Imperfect sanctification.—The spiritual warfare.

It may be difficult to account for the fact, that when the power of God was as sufficient to make the sinner perfect, in the new creation, as to implant a principle of spiritual life, he should have left the work imperfect; and that this imperfection, according to our views of Scripture, and of the fact as made known by experience, should continue through the whole period of human life, to whatever extent it may be protracted. Some, indeed, seem to suppose, that the remainders of sin in believers are seated in the body, and therefore as long as this sinful body continues, this inbred corruption will manifest itself, more or less. This opinion seems to have been imbibed, at a very early period of the history of the church, and was probably derived from the Platonic philosophy, which considers matter to be the origin of evil. From this view of the seat of indwelling sin, men, in all ages, who entertained it, have been led to lay great stress on fasting and other bodily austerities, by which the body was enfeebled and emaciated. But, the principle assumed being false, all that is built upon it must be false likewise. The body, though infected with the pollution of sin, through its connexion with the soul, is not, and cannot be the source of iniquity. Mere matter, however curiously organized and animated, is, apart from the soul, no moral agent, and therefore not susceptible of moral qualities. Sin must have its origin and seat in the free rational soul; and the appetites and passions, which have their seat in the body, partake of the nature of sin, by their excess and irregularity, and by their cravings, often influence the will to choose that which is not good, or is not the best. Still, however, the body is a great clog to the soul, and the appetites and passions, which are seated in the body, being very urgent in their cravings for gratification, greatly disturb the exercises of piety, and sometimes prevail against the higher principles which by grace have been implanted. As the body is also subject to various diseases, these, on account of the close connexion between the soul and body, mightily affect the mind, and often create a great hinderance to devotion, and the exercises of piety.

Where two opposite principles exist in the same

soul, there must be a perpetual conflict between them, until "the weaker dies." But as the "old man," though crucified, never becomes extinct in this life, this warfare between the flesh and the spirit never ceases until death. As these opposite moral principles operate through the same natural faculties and affections, it is a matter of course, that as the one gains strength, the other must be proportionably weakened; and experience teaches that the most effectual way to subdue the power of sin, is, to cherish and exercise the principle of holiness. But, if the love of God grows cold, or declines in vigour, then the motions of sin become more lively, and the stirring of inbred corruption is sensibly experienced. Just then, in the same proportion, will the principle of evil be diminished, as the principle of grace is strengthened. Every victory, over any particular lust, weakens its power; and by a steady growth in grace, such advantage is obtained over inbred sin, that the advanced Christian maintains the mastery over it, and is not subject to those violent struggles which were undergone when this warfare commenced. Young Christians, however, are often greatly deceived by the appearance of the death of sin, when it only sleeps, or deceitfully hides itself, waiting for a more favourable opportunity to exert itself anew. When such an one experiences, in some favoured moment, the love of God shed abroad in his heart, sin appears to be dead, and those lusts which warred against the soul, to be extinguished; but when these lively feelings have passed away, and carnal objects begin again to entice, the latent principle of iniquity shows itself; and often that Christian who had fondly hoped that the enemy was slain and the victory won, and in consequence, ceased to watch and pray, is suddenly assailed and overcome by the deceitfulness of sin. Christians are more injured in this warfare, by the insidious and secret influence of their enemies lulling them into the sleep of carnal security, than by all their open and violent assaults. No duty is more necessary, in maintaining this conflict, than watchfulness. Unceasing vigilance is indispensable. "Watch and pray that ye enter not into temptation,"—"and what I say unto you, I say unto all, Watch." Lawful pursuits are more frequently a snare than those which are manifestly sinful. It is a duty "to provide things honest in the sight of all men," but while this object is industriously pursued, the love of the world gradually gains ground. The possession of wealth is viewed as important. Eternal things are out of view, or viewed as at a great distance, and the impression from them is faint. Worldly entanglements and embarrassments are experienced; the spiritual life is weakened. A sickly state commences, and a sad declension ensues. Alas! for the Christian now. Where is the burning zeal with which he commenced his course? Where now are the comforts of religion, with which he was so entirely satisfied, that the world was viewed as an empty bauble? Where now is his spirit of prayer, which made this duty his delight? Where his love of the Bible, which drew him aside often from worldly business to peruse its sacred instructions? O! what a change! Reader, it is, perhaps, thy own case. "Thou art the man" who hast thus fallen, and left thy first love. "Repent, therefore, and do the first works," lest some heavy judgment fall upon thee. God holds a rod for his own children, and when the warnings and exhortations of the word, and the secret whispers of the Spirit are neglected, some painful providence is sent—some calamity, which has so much natural connexion with the sin, as to indicate that it is intended as a chastisement for it. These strokes are often very cutting and severe, but they must be so to render them effectual. "No chastening for the present, seemeth to be joyous, but grievous, nevertheless, afterward it yieldeth the peaceable fruit of righteousness unto them which are exercised thereby." Our heavenly Father afflicteth not willingly, but "for our profit, that we might be partakers of his holiness." The followers of Dr. Hawker, in England, who are ultra Calvinists, entertain the opinion, that "the law in our members" is not, in the least, affected or weakened, by our regeneration or sanctification, but that through life, it remains the very same, no how weakened in its strength, by any progress in the divine life which the Christian may make. But this is contrary to the word of God, which speaks of "dying daily unto sin"—of "mortifying the deeds of the body" —"crucifying the flesh," &c. The same opinion, or one near akin to it, was held by Mr. William Walker, of Dublin, which he brings to view in his able "address to the Wesleyan Methodists." His opinion, however, I think, was, that there is no such thing as a progressive work of sanctification which word properly means a *consecration* to God.

In a former chapter, I mentioned the different views of different denominations of Christians respecting the nature of the soul's exercises in conversion, but this difference is far more considerable as it relates to the spiritual conflict and sanctification. It is far from the wish of the writer to give offence to any body of Christians, much less to provoke controversy. This is no proper field for controversy. In the midst of this militant state, there ought to be one peaceful ground, where all true followers of Jesus might sit down together and compare their experiences of the loving kindness and faithful dealings of their Lord and Master. But surely it ought not to be offensive to any body of Christians simply to state what their views are in regard to experimental religion, and how far they agree or differ from those of other Christians. If there be mistakes, or erroneous views, on any side, they should be considered and corrected. And the writer of these essays will be thankful to any one who will kindly point out any mistakes in regard to matters of fact into which he may happen to fall. There has long been a difference of opinion respecting the true interpretation of the seventh chapter of the epistle to the Romans, in regard to Paul's description of the spiritual conflict, whether he describes the exercises of a convinced sinner, whom he personates; or whether he does not express honestly the feelings of his own heart, and describe the painful conflict between the powers of sin and holiness which was going on in his own bosom. The latter, undoubtedly, is the obvious meaning, for the apostle speaks in the first person, and gives no notice of introducing a person of another character; and some of the expressions here employed, are as strongly descriptive of a regenerate heart as any in the Bible. Who, but a regenerate man, can say, "I delight in the law of God after the inward man!" And the closing words show clearly enough, that the apostle was detailing the exercises of his own soul; for he gives thanks to God for giving him the victory, in this severe conflict, but still intimates that the two irreconcilable principles continued, according to their respective natures, to operate within him. "I thank God, through Jesus Christ our Lord. So then, with the mind, I MYSELF serve the law of God, but with the flesh, the law of sin." Arminius began his career of departure from the commonly received opinions of the reformed churches, by writing a book in exposition of the vii. of the Romans; and it is a remarkable coincidence that Faustus Socinus, in Poland, was engaged at the same time in writing a book on the same subject, and to support the same views. This subject is excellently treated in one of President Dickinson's Letters; and more largely by "Frazer on Sanctification." The same subject is also treated accurately and judiciously by Dr. Hodge, in his commentary on the Epistle to the Romans. It is understood that the followers of Mr. John Wesley, hold, in conformity with his recorded opinion, that SANCTIFICATION is not a gradual and progressive work, which remains imperfect in the best, in this life, but that, like regeneration, it is instantaneous, and that the result is a complete deliverance from indwelling sin; so that from that moment they are perfectly holy, and sin no more—unless they fall from this high state of grace—in thought, word, or deed. Here then there can be no similarity between the religious experience of an Arminian, who has attained sanctification, and a Calvinist, who is seeking to grow in grace and in the knowledge of our Lord Jesus Christ. The one is conscious of no sin,

14*

inward or outward, of nature or of act, and must have perpetual joy—a heaven on earth; while the other is groaning under a deep sense of inherent depravity, which works powerfully against his will, and continually interrupts and retards his progress. His frequent language is "O wretched man that I am, who shall deliver me from the body of this death!" Here, indeed, we have a wide difference in the religious experience of professing Christians; and it must be acknowledged, that if the experience of the Arminian is in accordance with the word of God, he has greatly the advantage over the contrite, broken hearted penitent, whose complaints are so great that they often cause him to wet his couch with tears. How to reconcile these widely different views of our condition as sanctified sinners, I know not. There must be a grand mistake somewhere; and I sincerely pray to God, that if my views on this subject are erroneous, they may be corrected!

The Christian is a soldier, and must expect to encounter enemies, and to engage in many a severe conflict. The young convert may well be likened to a raw recruit just enlisted. He feels joyous and strong, full of hope and full of courage. When the veteran Christian warns him of coming dangers and formidable enemies, and endeavours to impress on his mind a sense of his weakness and helplessness without divine aid, he does not understand what he says. He apprehends no dangers or enemies which he is not ready to face, and is ready to think that the aged disciples, with whom he converses, have been deficient in courage and skill, or have met with obstacles which are now removed out of the way. He views the contests, of which they speak, as the young soldier does the field of battle at a distance, while he is enjoying his bounty-money, and marches about with a conscious exultation, on account of his military *insignia*, and animated with martial music. The young Christian is commonly treated by his Lord with peculiar tenderness. He is like the babe, dandled on the knee, and exposed to no hardships. His frames are lively, and often joyous, and he lives too much upon them. His love to the Saviour and to the saints is fresh and fervent, and his religious zeal, though not well regulated by knowledge, is ardent. He often puts older disciples to the blush by the warmth of his affections, and his alacrity in the service of his Redeemer; and it is well, if he does not sometimes indulge a censorious spirit, in judging those who have been long exercised in the spiritual life. This is indeed the season of his "first love" which began to flow in the day of his espousals; and though occasionally dark clouds intercept his views, these are soon forgotten, when the clear sunshine breaks forth to cheer him on his way. During this period he delights in social exercises, especially in communion with those of his own age; and in prayer, and in praise, and spiritual conversation, his heart is lifted up to heaven, and he longs for the time, when he may join the songs of the upper temple. But ere long the scene changes. Gradually the glow of fervent affections subsides. Worldly pursuits, even the most lawful and necessary, steal away the heart; and various perplexing entanglements beset the inexperienced traveller. He begins to see that there were many things faulty in his early course. He blames his own weakness or enthusiasm; and, in avoiding one extreme he easily falls into the opposite, to which human nature has a strong bias. He enters into more intercourse with the world, and, of course, imbibes insensibly some portion of its spirit. This has a deadening effect on his religious feelings; and his devotions are less fervent and less punctual; and far more interrupted with vain, wandering thoughts, than before; and he is apt to fall into a hasty or formal attendance on the daily duties of the closet; and a little matter will sometimes lead him to neglect these precious seasons of grace. A strange forgetfulness of the presence of God, and of his accountableness for every thought, word, and action, seizes upon him. Close self-examination becomes painful, and when attempted, is unsuccessful. New evils begin to appear springing up in the heart. The imagination, before he is aware, is filled with sensual imagery, which afford ing carnal pleasure, the train of his thoughts is with difficulty changed. A want of prompt resolution is often the occasion of much guilt, and much unhappiness. Pride is sure to lift its head when God is out of view; and it is wonderful how this and kindred evils will get possession and grow, so as to be visible to others, while the person himself is not aware of the disease. Anger, impatience, fretfulness, envy, undue indulgence of the appetites, love of riches, fondness for dress and show, the love of ease, aversion to spiritual duties, with numerous similar and nameless evils are now bred in the heart, and come forth to annoy and retard the Christian in his course. His pride makes him unwilling to open his ear to friendly and fraternal reproof; such words fall heavily on him, and wound his morbid sensibility, so that a conflict takes place between a sense of duty and unmortified pride. He inwardly feels that the rebuke of a brother is just, and should be improved to the amendment of the evil pointed out; but pride cannot brook the thought of being exposed and humbled; and he tries to find something in the manner or circumstances which can be censured; or suspicion will ascribe it to a bad motive. If in this spiritual conflict, pride should gain the victory, alas! how much sin follows in its train;—resentment towards a kind brother, hypocrisy in concealing the real dictates of conscience, and approbation of the inner man; and a neglect of all efforts at improvement. The person thus circumstanced, is instinctively led to endeavour to persuade himself that he has done right. Still, however, the language of his better part is that of self-condemnation. But he hushes it up, and assumes an air of innocence and boldness, and thus the Spirit is grieved. Who can describe the train of evils which ensue, on one defeat of this kind? The mind becomes dark and desolate; communion with God is interrupted, and a course of backsliding commences, which sometimes goes on for years, and then the wanderer is not arrested and brought back without severe chastisement. In such cases the judgments of God against his own straying children are fearful; and if any experience them not, who have thus declined, it is because they are not children; "for what son is he whom the father chasteneth not?"

Worldly prosperity has ever been found an unfavourable soil for the growth of piety. It blinds the mind to spiritual and eternal things, dries up the spirit of prayer, fosters pride and ambition, furnishes the appropriate food to covetousness, and leads to a sinful conformity to the spirit, maxims, and fashions of the world. Some few have been enabled to pass this ordeal, without serious injury; and have come forth like the three children from Nebuchadnezzar's furnace, without the smell of fire on their garments; but this could not have been unless the Son of Man had been with them. Such persons use all their health, influence, and wealth in promoting the kingdom of Christ; but generally, God in mercy, refuses to give worldly prosperity to his children. He "hath chosen the poor of this world, rich in faith;" that is, he hath commonly chosen poverty as the safest condition for his children. His are "an afflicted and poor people, and they shall trust in the name of the Lord." But the poor have their conflicts and temptations, as well as the rich. They are continually tempted to discontent, to envy at the prosperity of the rich, and sometimes to use unlawful means to satisfy their craving wants. On account of the dangers of both these conditions, Agur prayed, "Give me neither poverty nor riches; feed me with food convenient for me; lest I be full and deny thee, and say, who is the Lord; or lest I be poor and steal, and take the name of my God in vain." But in whatever state Providence has placed us, we should therewith be content. Certainly when Christians make haste to be rich, they are not governed by the wisdom which cometh from above. No wonder that they pierce themselves through with many sorrows, and are often in danger of eternal perdition. If we sought wealth from no other motive but to use it for God's glory, it would do us no harm; for this principle would regulate the pursuit; so that it would not be detrimental to the kingdom of God within us.

The enemies of the Christian have been commonly divided into three classes, the world, the flesh, and the devil; but though these may be conceived of, and spoken of separately, they resist the Christian soldier by their combined powers. The devil is the agent, the world furnishes the bait or the object of temptation, and the flesh, or our own corrupt nature, is the subject on which the temptation operates. Sometimes, indeed, Satan injects his fiery darts, enkindled in hell, to frighten the timid soul, and drive it to despair; but in this he often overshoots his mark, and drives the poor trembling soul nearer to his Captain, whose broad shield affords ample protection. And we are not to suppose that we are not often led astray by the enticements of sin within us, without the aid of Satan; but we need not be afraid of charging too much evil upon this arch adversary. He is ever on the alert, and is exceedingly cautious in his approaches. Long experience has doubtless greatly increased his power and subtlety, unless he should be more restrained than formerly. Some people make a mock of Satan's temptations, as though they were the dreams of superstitious souls. Not so Paul, and Peter, and John—not so Luther, and Calvin, and Zuingle. Not so any who understand the nature of the spiritual warfare. It is to the great injury of many professors, that they are not constantly on the watch against the wiles of the devil. If you wish to know where he will be likely to meet you, I would say, in your closet, in the church, on your bed, and in your daily intercourse with men. A single thought which suddenly starts up in your mind, will show that the enemy is near, and is suggesting such thoughts, as without his agency never can be accounted for. "Watch, therefore," "resist the devil, and he will flee from you."

CHAPTER XI.

Narrative of G—— A—— S——, an Episcopal Clergyman.—Narrative of a young Officer in the Army.

THE following is the religious experience of G—— A—— S——, an Episcopal Clergyman in H——, which he recently communicated to the author of these essays, to be used as he might think proper.

" I entered the military academy at West Point, in the summer of 1825; the second year of the present Bishop McIlvaine's residence there as chaplain. I sat under his preaching 'as with the Spirit of God,' with eyes that did not see, and ears that did not hear. The chaplain departed, the curse was still upon my soul. Finally, I became much involved in the spirit of infidelity, together with several others. One evening, in particular, I trembled at the thoughts of our conversation: in the darkness of our minds, we had denied all. A few days afterwards, one of my companions, noted for his brightness of intellect, called at my room, and said, I have been reading Alexander's ' Evidences of the Christian Religion,' and it has almost persuaded me to be a Christian. I well remember with what great delight I received the communication, resolving to get the book, and 'see if those things were so;' not however, with any view or desire of becoming a Christian at PRESENT. In due time, the book was procured, I retired to my room, my heart as hard as the mill-stone, the heavens over my head as brass, and the earth beneath my feet as iron. I opened to the introduction, the most blind of unbelievers; all around me was perfect clouds and darkness. I began to read, I had proceeded half way through the introduction, *and was suddenly impressed that the religion of Christ was of God.* I did not doubt its truth more than I did my life: yet I was entirely without argument. At that time I could have given no reason, yet I did not doubt. I felt *a perfect belief* that an Omnipotent Spirit did it.

Before, I hardly believed there was a God: now I felt it as by a two-edged sword. It was a most awfully sublime moment; yet I had *not the least fear*. *I did not even think of sin.* The next impression was that I was undergoing a conversion. This, I *would not then:* the thought was very pleasant, that now I knew Christ died for the world; and that at some future time, I would go further in his love. I was happy, sublime; no terror; a thought did not enter my mind of the consequence of delay. To avoid the progress of conversion, I threw down the book perfectly satisfied, for I had attained to one of the most splendid pieces of consciousness imaginable; a sight beyond the veil, within eternity, worth thousands of worlds to me. I turned to think of something else. And oh! the horrors of hell, how they came flooding in upon my soul. I felt that an Omnipotent hand was guiding them there. Commensurate with my agony, was my awful sense of sinfulness; a conviction of sin, righteousness, and judgment to come, rose before my eyes in immense reality. I felt no anguish, no fear, no sin, *until I resolved not to attend to these things at present*. My anguish of soul became insupportable, it thickened and darkened, I could not endure it longer. And *with the sole view* of escaping my present misery, I resolved to yield to the will of that Mighty Being who was rending my soul. I instantly caught up the book, and offered a prayer for mercy. The intensity of my anguish began immediately to subside. The wrath of God seemed to mitigate, in a few moments, I settled down into a state of deep and solemn conviction of sin; a state more tolerable than the former; but still one of gloom so thick that it could be felt. A mountain weight pressed upon my soul; how to remove it I knew not, for the spirit still held me bound. I did not know but this was to continue through life. I endeavoured to lose my feelings, and feel at ease, but I could not. I knew nothing of the way of salvation; I had no spiritual guide; but in order to keep my present sorrow as light as possible, I continued to read and pray for mercy. Thus I continued in the wilderness for about a week: when, sitting by my fireside, dwelling upon my despair, a sudden light came down from heaven; I saw the open gate—' the *way*, the *truth*, and the *life*'—a new song was put into my mouth, and I rejoiced with joy unspeakable, and full of glory! Unspeakable gratitude be to the Father, Son, and Holy Ghost, for ever and ever. I have thought that two particulars in the above are worthy of notice. 1st. The motives that actuated me. 2d. That being perfectly ignorant of the way of salvation, the Spirit was a perfect teacher."

There are several things very remarkable in the preceding narrative. The delight at finding an infidel companion convinced, or almost convinced of his error; the desire to see the book which had produced this effect; the sudden persuasion of the truth of the Christian religion, by a sudden impression on the mind; the elevated happiness experienced on account of having discovered the truth; the determination still not to become a Christian at present; the horror and anguish consequent on this resolution; the relief obtained by resuming attention to religion; and finally, the discovery of the way of salvation through Christ, when the moment before, no idea was entertained of such a way, are all remarkable circumstances; and to some, may seem to savour of enthusiasm. But we cannot prescribe limits to the Holy Spirit, in his ways of leading benighted souls into the path of life. Still, it may be asked, how could there be a rational conviction of the truth of Christianity, when the individual knew no reasons or arguments in favour of it? To which it may be answered, that Christianity has a light of its own, independent of all external evidences; and if the Spirit of God cause one ray of this divine light to irradiate the mind, the truth becomes manifest. This person was on the borders of atheism. By an awful impression on his mind, God caused him to feel and know that He existed, and held him in his hand; and at the same time, let a ray of light from Divine Revelation into his mind. Suppose a number of human beings to be educated in a dark cavern, where they never saw the light of heaven; but being visited by one and another who testified to them the existence of the celestial luminaries, the candid among them, upon weighing the evidence, would acknowledge the existence of such bodies; although, of necessity, their conceptions of these objects would be very inadequate. But some, depending on their own reason, might reject the testimony as a mere fabrication, since what was related was totally contrary to all their own experience. Suppose then that the guardian of these subterranean inhabitants, should take one of these skeptics to a point where a single ray of light from the sun should be let in upon his eyes, how wonderful the sensation, how sublime the emotion, how strong now the persuasion of the existence of such a bright luminary! The doubts of such an one, however deep and inveterate, would be dissipated in a moment; not by argument: where we possess intuition, argument is superfluous. So, in the case before us, one ray of divine light produced instantaneously the undoubted persuasion of the divine existence, and that the Christian religion was from God. The next ray of light opened to the astonished view of the man, the awful sinfulness of his character, and discovered to him that he was in the hands of an angry God, from whose terrors he could not escape; and the third cast a clear light on the way of salvation, filling the soul with joy unspeakable. The only thing which seems contrary to our common theory is, that the person supposed that he was taught the method of salvation by the Spirit, without any aid from the external teaching of the word. Now, this is very possible; but it would be of the nature of *inspiration* and not mere *illumination*. I am, therefore, of opinion, that there was within the knowledge of the individual so much acquaintance with Christ and his mediatorial work, that, agreeably to his usual method, the Spirit took of the things of Christ, and showed it unto him. And **although** *now*, when inspiration has ceased, the Spirit makes no new revelations to men; yet he often brings to their remembrance truths once known, but which may have been long forgotten; according to John xiv. 26: see also xvi. 8—14. One single evangelical text may be made the object of saving faith.

It is exceedingly gratifying to be made acquainted with such cases. It shows that the Holy Spirit, who operates where and when he will, is often at work on the minds of those whom we would least suspect to be thus visited. Here a thoughtless cadet at our Military Academy, falls into infidelity, yea, atheism; is surrounded by companions in the same state of mind. Providence throws a book of "Evidences" in his way; and, while he reads, a new light darts into his mind; not from the book, but from the Father of lights, and this infidel young man becomes a preacher of that very gospel, which he aimed to destroy. Laus Deo. To God be all the glory!

The writer of the following narrative, is a young officer of high promise, belonging to the American army. It is a pleasing thing to find that men, who, by their profession, are commonly far removed from the usual means of grace, are not beyond the reach of the divine mercy. It is much to be desired that both our army and navy should be supplied with a competent number of pious and exemplary chaplains; but this want seems to be very little felt, and therefore is very imperfectly provided for. When men of either of these professions embrace religion, they are commonly remarkable for the eminence of their piety. The fact is, that they are exposed to so much ridicule and opposition, that unless their religious impressions were strong, and their resolutions firmly fixed, they would not be able to stand up against the opposing current.

This narrative will at least encourage the hearts of pious parents, who have sons in exposed situations, not to despair of their conversion, but to be incessant in their prayers, that God would graciously follow them with the strivings of his Holy Spirit, and in due season bring them to the foot of the cross. And may it not be a good opportunity to remind all praying persons, that in the variety of their intercessions, the young men in our army and navy should not be forgotten? As long as such institutions are needed, they who are set for the defence of our country, by sea and land, should not be forgotten in the prayers of Christians and of the Church.

"I entered the Military Academy in 1828. As was customary with my parents, I was furnished with a Bible, with the injunction to read it often, and make it the rule of my life. Like most other youths, however, I kept it in my trunk; and I blush while I say it, I do not believe that during the whole time I was there, four years, I took it out to read more than six times; and then, probably, I had a desire to, if I did not actually, conceal the act from my room-mates around me. How strange the aversion to that good Book, and yet how general this antipathy in the thoughtless around us! I must confess, however, that though my aversion to it was strong, I had a firm belief in its truth, and though in such a body of young men, I could not, but now and then, hear an effort on the part of one or another around me, to convince himself of its untruth, yet, I must say, that I never could get rid of the fear of God in my heart, or of the firm conviction of the truth of His word. Still, however, I graduated an impenitent sinner; and being let loose from scholastic restraint, and left to my own guidance, like most other youths under the same circumstances, I followed the ways of pleasure and worldly gratification.

"After graduating, in 1832, I went home. But, alas, how changed! My father and brother had both gone during my absence, to that bourne from which no traveller returns. Their spirits had fled—it is hoped to heaven. I did not see them in their dying hours; but their spirits, though gone, still spake. I was told of the anxiety they both expressed, just before death, on my account; and in particular the reply of my father, to the question asked him, if he had any word to send to me: 'No, only to read my letters,' was his reply. Yes, father, I have read those letters, and long shall they be treasured up in recollection of thy solicitude. But I must continue my narrative. Though the scenes at home, this visit, were impressive, yet they did not result in producing within me the conviction that I was a sinner. I left my home again as impenitent as I had come. This time my sister furnished me with a Bible, with the prayer written in it, that I 'would make it the rule of my conduct and the guide of my life.' As before, I stowed it away in my trunk; thence scarcely, if ever at all, to come out. Probably for years together, I did not so much as look into it, and during all this time, except when at home, I was as much a stranger to the church, as I was to the Bible. Indeed, what is more shameful, in 1836, I, in some unaccountable way lost my Bible; so that, from that time till the latter part of the year 1838, or during an interval of two years, I was entirely without one: and during all this time, besides having no Bible, (I did not dream of buying one,) I was so situated, at least for much the greater portion of the time, that I could not have access to any church. I was serving with the army, against the Indians at the South, and every one knows how ill calculated an active life in the field is to produce serious impressions. Still, I may say, during all this time I had the fear of God before my eyes; though not to the extent as to cause me to love and serve Him, or to cut off any of my darling pleasures. And yet how good the Lord was! Though I went on sinning, day after day, and was often thrown into discussion with infidels around me, who strove their utmost to argue or laugh me out of what they would call my early prejudices, and though I indulged in reading infidel productions, Tom Paine's work among the number, yet still *His* Spirit would strive with me, and would not give me entirely over to my own devices.

"I returned North in the fall of 1838, and again saw my widowed mother; her who had nurtured me with a Christian's care, and who had early instilled into me those religious principles and feelings, which, by the grace of God, had never been entirely lost to me, and

15*

to which under the same spiritual influence, I must attribute my having been kept from utterly falling away I saw her again, exhibiting as before, the chastening influences of the religion she professed. The same calm and resigned countenance; the same sweet smile of welcome, still showed the powerful influence of the Holy Spirit upon her heart. I thought I could see the workings of her feelings in my behalf; and I could not but imagine that in every look she gave me, she offered up a prayer on my account.

"I left her for a station North. I may say I went away this time with better feelings than I ever did before. I had had, by this time, some experience of the world, and had already thought of the nothingness of its pleasures; and, besides, the calm, peaceful, and happy deportment of my mother, made me anxious to become a partaker also of religion I went away with the firm determination of at least looking more into the Bible, and of thus taking the first step towards making myself better. Another sister, this time, on my leaving her, presented me with a Testament. This, when I got to my station, I read, or attempted to read, every evening. I tasked myself to one chapter. But a late return from a party, or ball, would cause me to defer it till the morning; and then if the breakfast bell should arouse me from my slumbers, I would neglect it till the evening. And so, between the parties and balls, and indolence in the morning, my reading of the Testament was very irregular. But still, I had a great respect for religion, and admired the truths of the gospel. I would always uphold good principles of conduct in those around me, and would as often reprobate those that were bad. But all my ideas of virtue were founded on a wrong basis. I believed that it was in the power of every individual, of himself, to do good and eschew evil. And, therefore, when I did see good principles in those around me, my admiration was upon the individual himself and not upon the Holy Spirit which restrained him; and when I saw wickedness in those around me, my condemnation, (and my self-righteousness could not make it too strong,) was upon the individual and not upon the sin which impelled him.

"But still, though I strongly criticised the conduct of others, upholding the good and denouncing the bad; yet I felt that I was not a Christian, in the Bible sense of the term. I knew this from my utter inability to pray. On retiring, I had often attempted to realize the overshadowing presence of a God above me; but all was hard, dark, and impenetrable. I could not realize the existence of an all merciful Saviour. During all this time, I regularly attended divine service, at least once a day, every Sunday. I was delighted to either hear or read a good sermon. But I heard, or read it, more with the feelings of a critic than of an humble follower of the lowly Jesus, desiring the sincere milk of the word. And so, whenever the preacher expatiated upon the beauties of virtue, though I received pleasure from his discourse, yet I had none of the consciousness that virtue was to be followed because God had commanded it; but because it seemed to be a necessary element in society; and, perhaps, because its votary reciprocally recommended himself to society, by its pursuit. I recollect, in particular, that Dr. Chalmers's sermons afforded me great satisfaction. But the beautiful imagery in them, as well as his elegant diction, probably pleased me quite as much as the truths he inculcated.

"Things went on in this way, for nearly a year, when at the close of this time, I began to feel myself strongly tempted by the evil one, though, at the time, I did not attribute it to this unseen spirit. Probably, it is better to say, (to use the language I would have then used,) I was uneasy, discontented, looked at things awry, extracted more of the bitter than the sweet from the things and circumstances around me; or, in other words, was extremely miserable. I could experience no joy from the things of earth, and of the joys of heaven, I knew nothing.

"But thanks to a good and righteous God, *he* was pleased to let me into this state, to show me that al. my hopes of happiness from earthly things were vain.

I was in the act of throwing myself on the settee, when I carelessly took up the Bible, which happened to be lying near me. The first chapter I opened at, was the 1st Epistle general of Peter, chapter 1st. But how shall I describe my feelings, the moment I cast my eyes upon its pages! My heart was melted into deep contrition. I felt the love of God shed abroad in my whole being. I was convinced that I had the Holy Spirit at work within me. I was affected to tears at his goodness. *I wept like a child.* I felt that I had been a sinner. My ingratitude came like a flood upon me. I was overcome with gratitude for *his* mercy. It completely possessed my whole being. I rejoiced in the thought, that though I had been a wanderer from *him*, yet *he* was a good and kind Saviour, and was ready to forgive me all the injuries I had done *him*. I could indeed say, with deep conviction, as I read the passage which presented itself to me: 'Blessed be the God and Father of our Lord Jesus Christ, which, according to his abundant mercy, hath begotten us again unto a lively hope, by the resurrection of Jesus Christ, from the dead.' Indeed, this whole chapter seemed to be perfectly adapted to my state. I recollect, in particular, the eighth verse was singularly pleasing to me. 'Whom having not seen, ye love; in whom though now ye see him not, yet believing, ye rejoice with joy unspeakable, and full of glory.'

"Another remarkable circumstance connected with this display of divine goodness, was, the wonderful acuteness of intellect I felt myself to have, in reading the word of God. And not only could I perceive things in the gospel that I never saw before, but I felt my whole character changed. I felt not only a strong love to God, but to every body around me. I could have wept upon the bosom of my bitterest enemy. Oh! the joys of that moment! But, alas! how vain and impotent are the attempts of man, unless the Holy Spirit of God remains with him. I recollect very well, that I thought I would go and see the minister, and tell him what had passed. But not acting up to the suggestion immediately, I neglected it, and soon again, sad to say, I had relapsed into my former forgetfulness of the Lord. The fear of the ridicule of the world had been too strong for my faith, and I felt, too, that I could not yet give up the world, and declare myself on the Lord's side. But still *he* would not let me go. He would not give me up. I was removed shortly afterwards to another station, and here I can see the all gracious design of Providence in this change. I was by this means thrown into the society of several pious officers. One in particular, whom I valued very highly, and who, the very evening he conversed with me upon the goodness of God, in twice leading him back from signal relapses into sin, was seized with the fever, that in five days carried him to his grave, was in particular of great service to me, under the divine blessing, in confirming me in my resolves to renounce the world, and cleave unto the Lord; and so indeed were all the others. Suffice it to say, that not many months after I came among them, I openly proclaimed myself on the Lord's side, and sealed the covenant by partaking of the emblems of *his* body and blood. And it is an additional source of happiness for me to state, that it was not long after, that the partner of my bosom also renounced the world, and joined me in the race set before us in the gospel.

"The foregoing narrative, I have thought would be of some interest to you. But if it serve no other purpose than to show you how good the Lord has been to me, it will answer its end."

CHAPTER XII.

The spiritual conflict. — Satan's Temptations. — Evil thoughts. — A case in illustration.

WE have spoken of the Christian's enemies, in the general, it is now intended to enter into a more partic ular view of the conflict which is experienced by the pilgrim to Zion. Swarms of vain thoughts may be reckoned among the first and most constant enemies of the servant of God. The mind of man is like a fountain which is continually sending forth streams. There is not a moment of our waking time when the rational soul is entirely quiescent. How it may be in our sleeping hours, this is not the place to inquire—as we are not in that state engaged in this warfare. Perhaps, this is saying too much. I believe that sin may be committed in sleep; for there is often a deliberate choice of evil, after a struggle between a sense of duty and an inclination to sin. And often the same vain and impure thoughts, which were too much indulged in waking hours, infest us when asleep, and may find much readier entertainment than when we have all our senses about us. It is difficult indeed, to say when moral agency is suspended, so as to render the person inculpable for his volitions; and many know that they consent to temptations in sleep, when they abhor the evil as soon as they are awake. And, in other cases, inclination is indulged, where there is not the least sense of the moral turpitude of the act. But, in other cases, persons in sleep consent to sin with a clear apprehension of the evil of the thing to which they consent. Here, there must be some guilt; for, if there was not an evil nature, prone to iniquity, such volitions would not take place. Two things are in our power, and these we should do: first, to avoid evil thoughts and such pampering of the body as has a tendency to pollute our dreams; and, secondly, to pray to God to preserve us from evil thoughts, even in sleep. Particularly, we should pray to be delivered from the influence of Satan during our sleeping hours. Mr. Andrew Baxter, in his work on the Soul, is of opinion that dreams can in no way be accounted for, but by the agency of other spirits acting on ours. While I do not adopt this theory of dreaming, I am inclined to believe, that, some how or other, both good and evil spirits have access to our minds in sleep. They actually seem to hold conversation with us, and suggest things of which we had never thought before. To return from this digression—it may be safely asserted that no human mind, in this world, is free from the incursion of vain thoughts. The proportion of such thoughts depends on the circumstances of the individual, and the degree of spirituality and self-government to which he has attained. The question very naturally arises here, Is the mere occurrence of vain or wicked thoughts sinful? This is a nice question in casuistry, and should not be answered inconsiderately. It is said in Scripture, "the thought of foolishness is sin;" but by thought, in this place, we should probably understand "intention." The wise man would teach that sin may be committed in the mind without any external act; a doctrine abundantly taught in other parts of Holy Writ. Or, we may understand it to mean that, when thoughts of evil are entertained and cherished in the mind, there is sin. But as our thoughts are often entirely involuntary, arising from we know not what causes, it cannot be that every conception of a thing wrong is itself sinful. If I conceive of another person stealing, or murdering, or committing adultery, if my mind abhors the deed, the mind is not thereby polluted. Thoughts may not in themselves be sinful, and yet they may become so, if they fill and occupy the mind to the exclusion of better thoughts. Ideas of present scenes and passing transactions, are not, in themselves, sinful, because necessary, and often required by the duties which we have to perform; but if the current of these thoughts is so continuous that they leave no room for spiritual meditations, they become sinful by their excess. Again, as every Christian has set times for prayer and other devotional exercises; if the mind, on such occasions, wanders off from the contemplation of those objects, which should occupy it, such forgetfulness of God's presence, and vain wandering of the thoughts, are evidently sinful. And here is an arena on which many a severe conflict has been undergone, and where, alas! many overthrows have been experienced by the sincere worshipper of God. How our perfectionists dispose of this matter, and what their professed experience is, I know not. I suppose, however, that they are, at best, no more exempt from wandering thoughts than other Christians; and if so, they must practise a double hypocrisy, first, in persuading themselves that there is no sin in all this; and, secondly, in denying, or concealing from others, their real experience on this subject. But is it not true, that from the very laws of association of ideas, there will often be an involuntary wandering of the thoughts? This is admitted; and it is conceded, also, that it may be impossible, in all cases, to determine with precision which of our straying thoughts contracts guilt, and how much blame attaches to us, when our thoughts suddenly start aside from the mark like a deceitful bow. There are, however, some plain principles which sound casuistry can establish. If, when the thoughts thus start aside, they are not immediately recalled, then there is sin; for the mind has this power over its thoughts, and, when it is not exercised, it argues negligence, or something worse. Again, if this deviation of our thoughts would have been prevented by a solemn sense of the divine presence and omniscience, then it is sinful; for such impressions should accompany us to the throne of grace. And, finally, if the true reason of these erratic trains of thought, at such seasons, is owing to a secret aversion to spiritual things, and a preference, at the moment, to some carnal or selfish indulgence—then, indeed, there is not only sin, but sin of enormous guilt. It is the direct acting of enmity against God. There are many, it is to be feared, who take little or no account of their thoughts; and who, if they run through the external round of duties, feel satisfied. Multitudes are willing to be religious and even punctilious in duty, if no demand is made upon them for fixedness of attention, and fervency and elevation of affection. The carnal mind hates nothing so much as a spiritual approach to God, and the remainders of this enmity, in the pious, are the very "law in their members, which wars against the law of the mind." This is the very core of their inbred sin, from which all evil thoughts proceed, on account of which they need to be humbled in the dust, every day that they live. There is much reason to fear, however, that many who appear to be serious Christians, are not at all in the habit of watching their thoughts, and ascertaining the evil that is in them. I knew a person, nearly half a century ago, who, being greatly troubled with wandering thoughts in times of devotion, was solicitous to know whether any other person was troubled in the same way, and to the same degree, with such swarms of vain thoughts. He carefully wrote down what he experienced in this way, and then took it to two serious professors, of whose piety he had a good opinion, and, without intimating that it was his own experience, inquired whether they were acquainted with any thing like this. They both acknowledged that they were often interrupted with wandering thoughts in prayer; but, in the degree described in the paper, they were not, and could not believe that any real Christian was. There may be, and no doubt is, a constitutional difference among men in regard to this matter. In some minds the links of association are so strong, that, when a particular idea is suggested, the whole train must come along, and thus the object previously before the mind is lost sight of, and will not be recovered without a resolute effort.

An old writer says, "what busy flies were to the sacrifices on the altar, such are vain thoughts to our *holy services;* their continued buzzing disturbs the mind and distracts its devotion." St. Bernard complained much of these crowds of vain thoughts. He said—" Introëunt et exeunt," they pass and repass, come in and go out, and will not be controlled. "Amovere volo, nec valeo," I would fain remove them, but cannot. This is in perfect accordance with Paul's experience, "when I would do good, evil is present with me." And Chrysostom says, "that nothing is more dreadful to the godly than sin. *This is death—this is hell.*" Therefore, though nothing amiss be discerned by man, yet is he afflicted, deeply afflicted on account of his rebellious thoughts, which being in the secret closet of the heart, can only appear unto God.

The old writer, before mentioned, introduces a struggling soul, mourning on this account. "O the perplexing trouble of my distracting thoughts! How do they continually disturb the quiet of my mind, and make my holy duties become a weariness of my soul! They cool the heart, they damp the vigour, they deaden the comfort of my devotions. Even when I pray God to forgive my sins, I then sin whilst I am praying for forgiveness; yea, whether it be in the church, or in the closet, so frequently and so violently do these thoughts withdraw my heart from God's service, that I cannot have confidence he hears my suit, because I know by experience, I do not hear myself; surely therefore God must need be far off from my prayer, whilst my heart is so far out of his presence, hurried away with a crowd of vain imaginations." To whom he applies the following consolations: "1. These vain thoughts, being thy burden, shall not be thy ruin; and though they do take from the sweetness, they shall not take from the sincerity of thy devotions. 2. It is no little glory which we give to God in the acknowledgment of his omnipresence and omniscience, that we acknowledge Him to be privy to the first risings of our most inward thoughts. 3. It is much the experience of God's children, even the devoutest saints, that their thoughts of God and of Christ, of heaven and holiness, are very unsteady and fleeting. Like the sight of a star through an optic glass, held by a palsied hand, such is our view of divine objects. 4. Know thou hast the gracious mediation of an all-sufficient Saviour to supply thy defects, and procure an acceptance of thy sincere though imperfect devotions. 5. As thou hast the gracious mediation of an all-sufficient Saviour to supply thy defects, so hast thou the strengthening power of his Holy Spirit to help thy infirmities; which strength is made perfect in weakness.—When thou art emptied it shall fill thee; when thou art stum bled, it shall raise thee. The experience of God's saints will tell thee, that they have long languished under this cross of *vain thoughts:* yet, after long conflict, have obtained a joyful conquest, and from mourning doves have become mounting eagles."

The conflict with vain and wandering thoughts is common to all Christians, and is the subject of their frequent and deep lamentations: but there are other conflicts, which seem to be peculiar to some of God's children, or are experienced in a much greater degree by some than others. These arise from horribly wicked thoughts, blasphemous, atheistical, or abominably impure, which are injected with a power which the soul cannot resist, and sometimes continue to rise in such thick succession, that the mind can scarcely be said to be ever entirely free from them. I have known persons of consistent piety and sound intellect, who have been infested with the continual incursion of such thoughts, for weeks and months together: so that they had no rest during their waking hours; and even their sleep was disturbed with frightful dreams; and whilst thus harassed, they had no composure to attend on religious duties; but when they attempted to pray, Satan was present with his terrific suggestions; and when they presented themselves with God's people, in his house, they found no comfort there; for the thought was continually introduced into their minds, that there was no truth in the Bible, or any of its doctrines. And it is wonderful what new and unthought of forms of blasphemy and infidelity do, in such cases, arise; so that the ideas which occupy their minds are often inexpressible, and indeed not fit to be expressed, in words. These may emphatically be called "the fiery darts of the wicked one." They may be compared to balls or brands of fire cast into a house full of combustibles. The object of the enemy, by such assaults, is, to perplex and harass the child of God, and to drive him to despair; and as many, who are thus tempted, are ignorant of Satan's devices, and of the "depths" of his subtlety, and charge upon themselves the fault of all these wicked thoughts, the effect aimed at does actually take place. The tempted, harassed soul is not only distressed above measure, but, for a season, is actually cast down to the borders of despair. We know of no affliction, in this life, which is more intolerable than such a state of temptation, when continued long. It, no doubt, is true, that there are certain states of the physical system which favour the effect of these temptations; but this does not prove that these thoughts do not proceed from Satan. This arch-fiend is deeply versed in the physiology of human nature; and wherever he discovers a weak point, there he makes his assault. The melancholic, and persons wasted and weakened with excessive grief, are peculiarly susceptible of injury from such temptations; as is that class of doubting, mourning Christians, who are for ever disposed to look on the dark side of the picture; and who are wont "to write bitter things against themselves." On uninstructed minds, the effect often is to induce the belief that they have sinned the sin unto death, by blaspheming the Holy Ghost; or, that they have sinned beyond the reach of mercy, and that God has abandoned them to be a prey to sin and Satan. But it is not upon ignorant, weak, and diseased persons only that these furious assaults are made; such a man as Luther, was in frequent conflicts of this kind; and he was so persuaded that these were the temptations of the devil, that he speaks of his presence with as much confidence as if he had seen him by his side.

A friend of the writer, who is yet alive, was for months so harassed by these fiery darts of the wicked one, that I never saw any human being in a more pitiable condition of extreme suffering; and although there was no intermission, during his waking hours, there were seasons when these blasphemous suggestions were injected with peculiar and terrifying violence. Knowing this person to be discreet, as well as pious, I requested, by letter, some account of this dreadful state of mind, if there was a freedom to make the communication. In answer, I received recently, a letter, from which the following is an extract: "I feel a singular reluctance to speak of my religious experience. I have felt that my case was a very remarkable one. I have thought, at times, that *no one* could recount a similar experience. It has appeared to me so uncommon, that I have refrained from disclosing the peculiar exercises of my mind to the most intimate friend. I know not that I ever opened to you my case, with the exception of that distressing point to which you refer, and even then I think I was not very particular. That was a season far more distressing than any I ever experienced—

I well remember mine afflictions and my misery; the wormwood and the gall.' My deliverance from it was an unspeakable mercy. I have no doubt that the state of my health had some connexion with the mental sufferings I then endured. My constitution, which had always been feeble, had given to my disposition a proneness to melancholy; and in my bereaved and desolate state I was peculiarly susceptible of gloomy impressions. My nervous system was deeply affected. Sleep at one time forsook my pillow for successive nights. It was under these circumstances that I sunk into the darkness and distress which you witnessed. In all this there was nothing very remarkable. I think very many can record a similar experience. It was not the fact that in a feeble state of health I was dark and comfortless in spirit, that has so much tried me, but the peculiarity of my case seemed to consist in the *nature* of my spiritual conflicts. You may, perhaps, recollect that I stated to you that my chief distress arose from *blasphemous suggestions*—*unnatural*, *monstrous*, and *horrid*, which seemed to fill my mind, and hurry away my thoughts, with a force as irresistible as a whirlwind. I strove against them—I prayed against them; but it was all in vain. The more I strove, the more they prevailed. The very effort to banish them appeared to detain them. My soul all this while was wrapped in midnight darkness, and tossed like the ocean in a storm. It seemed to me as if I was delivered over to the powers of darkness, and that to aggravate my wretchedness, some strange and awfully impious association would be suggested by almost every object that met my eye. You ask me to describe my deliverance. It was gradual. A return of domestic comforts, a restoration of health, and an OCCUPATION OF THE MIND WITH DUTY, were the means which God was pleased to bless to the removal of this distressing experience. For twelve or thirteen years I have had no return of this state of mind, except to a partial extent; yet I have, at times, been greatly harassed with these fiery darts of the wicked one, which I can truly say, are my sorest affliction. I have always remarked, that these painful exercises of mind have attended seasons of special examination and prayer. When I have thought most of my obligation to God, and endeavoured to meditate most on divine things, then it has been, that my mind has suffered most from the intrusion of thoughts, at which my soul is filled with anguish, and from which I desire deliverance more than from death. This fact is mysterious to me. I cannot but think I love God. I am sure I do desire an entire consecration to Christ. It is my daily prayer to attain holiness. I esteem the way of salvation glorious; and justification through the alone righteousness of Christ is a precious doctrine. But did ever any Christian experience such trials, is a question which I am ready often to ask. I know of no uninspired writer that has come nearer a description of what I have experienced than John Bunyan and John Newton. The hymn of the latter, commencing with 'I asked the Lord that I might grow,' &c., contains many thoughts remarkably accordant with my experience.

"You see, I have nothing to relate, that is instructive or cheering—and yet I sometimes feel thankful for the terrible conflicts which I endure, for there is nothing which so constantly drives me to a throne of grace — nothing that strips me so entirely of self-dependence, and creates within me such longing after holiness. I am much inclined to think that Satan is far less dangerous when he comes as 'a roaring 'ion,' and frightens the soul with his horrid blasphemies, than when 'he transforms himself into an angel of light,' and seduces our affections gradually and secretly away from God, and attaches them sinfully to the world.

"P. S.—The most discouraging fact in all my experience has been, what I have already alluded to—the rushing in of a tide of unutterably impious thoughts or imaginations, at a time when I have sought the most elevated and glorious views of God, breaking up my peace and comfort, when I have tried to fix my mind most intently on spiritual objects. Is the onset of the enemy to drive one from a close communion with God? or is it to be traced to a law of association recalling past experiences?

"If I had more confidence in my religious experience I think I could suggest many thoughts that might be useful to Christians under temptation; and especially, when suffering under certain physical disorders. One thing, I am free to say, USEFUL OCCUPATION is essential to the restoration and peace of some minds."

Many other eminent servants of God have experienced, in various forms, the same conflicts with the great adversary: and when we describe these temptations as not unfrequent in the experience of the children of God, we do not speak without authority. Paul says, "For we wrestle not against flesh and blood, but against principalities, against powers, against the rulers of the darkness of this world, against spiritual wickedness in high places." From this passage, it is evident, that our spiritual foes are numerous, and powerful, and that the believer's conflict with them is violent: it is a "wrestling," or a contention which requires them to put forth all their strength, and to exercise all their skill. Therefore, it was, that the apostle, who was himself engaged in this conflict, urges it upon Christians to put on the panoply of God. Against such enemies, armour, offensive and defensive, is requisite. And blessed be God, there is a magazine, from which such armour may be drawn. Hear Paul's enumeration of the several parts of this panoply: "The girdle of truth, the breast-plate of righteousness,—sandals of gospel peace,—the shield of faith." This he places highest, as being an indispensable defence against "the fiery darts of the wicked"—"the helmet of salvation," "the sword of the Spirit, which is the word of God." To all which must be added prayer and watchfulness. As one of God's methods of comforting and strengthening his mourning children is by good books, I will embrace this opportunity of recommending to those engaged in the spiritual warfare, "Gurnall's Christian Armour." In such cases, there is almost a necessity of referring to old authors; for, some how or other, our modern sermons and tracts touch but seldom on these things, which filled so many of the pages of our fathers.

The soul struggling with the intrusion of wicked thoughts may be supposed to express its feelings in language like the following: "O my wretchedly wicked heart, which is the fountain from which proceed such streams of abominable thoughts! Sure if I had ever been washed in the fountain of Christ's blood, or at all purified by his Spirit, so foul a corruption could never cleave unto my soul. Wo is me! for so far am I from being a holy temple of the Lord, that my heart rather seems to be the cage of every unclean bird, and even a den of devils. The flames of hell seem to flash in my face, and the amazing terrors of cursed blasphemies torture my soul and wound my conscience even unto death. I would rather choose to die ten thousand deaths than undergo the fears, and frights, and bitter pangs of my amazing thoughts and dreadful imaginations. In every place in every action—in the church and in the closet—in my meditations and in my prayers, these abominable and tormenting thoughts follow and harass me; so that I loathe myself and am a burden to myself. 'O wretched man, that I am, who shall deliver me from the body of this death!' Alas! I perish! whilst ashamed to speak what I abhor to think, I must needs despair of a cure, not knowing how to lay open my sore."

To a complaint of this kind, the pious Robert Mossom, addresses the following grounds of consolation:

1. "The horrid blasphemies which affright thy soul, though they are thy thoughts, yet are they Satan's suggestions; and not having the consent of thy will, they bring no guilt upon thy conscience. It is agreeable to the truth of God's word, and the judgment of all divines, ancient and modern, that where the will yields no consent, there the soul may suffer temptation, but act no sin. Again, 'The importunity and frequency of these suggestions which weary the soul, resisting, shall bring a greater crown of glory in its overcoming.' True it is, that, 'he that is born of God, keepeth himself, and that wicked one toucheth him not.' But how toucheth him not? Is it meant of wicked temptations? No, sure, but of wilful transgressions. He toucheth him not so as to leave the impress of sin and guilt upon the soul. It is no sin to be tempted; for Christ our Lord and Saviour, was tempted, 'but without sin. To admit the temptation with allowance or delight, that is sin.

2. "That these foul and frightful suggestions have not the consent of thy will appears by this, that thou hast a loathing and abhorring of them; which speaks the greatest aversion, and so is far from a consenting of the will. What is forcibly cast into the mind cannot be said to be received with our consent. It is out of our power to prevent Satan from suggesting evil thoughts. These arise not from thy own corrupt nature: they are *brats* laid at thy door, not thine own lawful children. These are the *buffetings* of Satan. Paul had 'a messenger of Satan to buffet him,' which was as a 'thorn in his flesh,' constantly pricking and keeping him uneasy, and tempting him to impatience; and he prayed earnestly and repeatedly to be delivered from this cross, but his request was not granted; yet he received an answer more gracious and beneficial than the removal of the thorn would have been;

for God said unto him, 'My grace is sufficient for thee.'"

The heart assailed by Satan, is like a city besieged, within which there lie concealed many traitors, who, as far as they dare, will give encouragement and aid to the enemy without. And this creates the chief difficulty in the case of many temptations; for although there is not a full consent, or a prevailing willingness, yet there is something which too much concurs with the temptation; except in shocking blasphemies, which fill the soul with terror. The soul afflicted with these temptations is apt to think its case singular. It is ready to exclaim, "Never were any of God's children in this condition. It must be some strange corruption which induces the enemy thus to assault me, and some awful displeasure of God towards me, which makes him permit such a temptation." To which it may be replied, "Afflictions, of this kind, are no new thing; and that with the real children of God. Such cases are not uncommon, in every age, and occur in the pastoral experience of every faithful minister. Some persons have, for years, been so afflicted with these temptations, that they have pined away and have been brought near the gates of death; and these, too, persons of no ordinary piety. Take then the following directions: 1. Learn to discriminate between the temptations and the sin of temptation. 2. Examine with care, what transgressions may have occasioned this sore affliction. 3. Humble yourself before God with fasting and prayer, and supplicate the throne of grace to obtain the mercy of God through the merits of thy Saviour, for the full and free pardon of whatever sin has occasioned these temptations; beseeching God to rebuke Satan; and then make an unreserved resignation of thyself into the hands of Jesus, the Great Shepherd of the flock, that he may keep thee as a tender lamb, from the paw and teeth of the roaring lion. 4. If still these thoughts intrude, turn thy mind quickly away from them; they are most effectually subdued by neglect. 5. "O thou afflicted, tossed with tempests and not comforted," do as children with their parents when they see any thing frightful: they *cling closer and hold faster.* So do thou with thy God and Saviour. Satan's aim is to drive thee from God into some desperate conclusions, or into some ruinous act; but thou mayest disappoint this subtle adversary, by running to Christ as thy refuge, and cleaving to him with humble, believing confidence; and when Satan sees this, he will soon cease from the violence of his temptations. And when the devil hath left thee, angels will come and minister unto thee; especially the ANGEL OF THE COVENANT, CHRIST JESUS. He shall rejoice thy soul with the quickening graces and cheering comforts of his Spirit.

CHAPTER XIII.

Growth in grace.—Signs of it.—Practical directions how to grow in grace.—Hinderances to it.

WHEN there is no growth, there is no life. We have taken it for granted, that among the regenerate, at the moment of their conversion, there is a difference in the vigour of the principle of spiritual life, analogous to what we observe in the natural world; and no doubt the analogy holds, as it relates to growth. As some children, who were weak and sickly in the first days of their existence, become healthy and strong, and greatly outgrow others who commenced life with far greater advantages; so it is with the "new man;" some who enter on the spiritual life with a weak and wavering faith, by the blessing of God on a diligent use of means, far outstrip others who, in the beginning, were greatly before them.

It is often observed, that there are professors who never appear to grow, but rather decline perpetually, until they become, in spirit and conduct, entirely conformed to the world, from whence they professed to come out. The result, in regard to them, is one of two things; they either retain their standing in the Church, and become dead formalists, "having a name to live while they are dead;" "a form of godliness, while they deny the power thereof;" or they renounce their profession and abandon their connexion with the Church, and openly take their stand with the enemies of Christ, and not unfrequently go beyond them all in daring impiety. Of all such we may confidently say, "they were not of us, or undoubtedly they would have continued with us." But of such I mean not now to speak further, as the case of backsliders will be considered hereafter.

That growth in grace is gradual and progressive is very evident from Scripture; as in all those passages where believers are exhorted to mortify sin and crucify the flesh, and to increase and abound in all the exercises of piety and good works. One text on this subject will be sufficient: "Grow in grace and in the knowledge of our Lord and Saviour Jesus Christ." And this passage furnishes us with information of the origin and nature of this growth. It is *knowledge;* even the knowlege of our Lord and Saviour Jesus Christ. Just so far as any soul increases in spiritual knowledge, in the same degree it grows in grace. Persons may advance rapidly in other kinds of knowledge, and yet make no advances in piety; but the contrary. They may even have their minds filled with correct theoretical knowledge of divine truth; and yet its effect may not be to humble, but to "puff up." Many an accurate and profound theologian has lived and died without a ray of saving light. The natural man, however gifted with talent, or enriched with speculative knowledge, has no spiritual discernment. After all his acquisitions, he is destitute of the knowledge of Jesus Christ. But it should not be forgotten, that divine illumination is not independent of the word, but accompanies it. Those Christians, therefore, who are most diligent in attending upon the word in public and private, will be most likely to make progress in piety. Young converts are prone to depend too much on joyful frames, and love high excitement in their devotional exercises; but their heavenly Father cures them of this folly, by leaving them for a season to walk in darkness, and struggle with their own corruptions. When most sorely pressed and discouraged, however, he strengthens them with might in the inner man. He enables them to stand firmly against temptation; or, if they slide, he quickly restores them, and by such exercises they become much more sensible of their entire dependence, than they were at first. They learn to be in the fear of the Lord all the day long, and to distrust entirely their own wisdom and strength, and to rely for all needed aid on the grace of Christ Jesus. Such a soul will not readily believe that it is growing in grace; but to be emptied of self-dependence, and to know that we need aid for every duty, and even for every good thought, is an important step in our progress in piety. The flowers may have disappeared from the plant of grace, and even the leaves may have fallen off, and wintry blasts may have shaken it, but it now is striking its roots deeper, and becoming every day stronger, to endure the rugged storm. One circumstance attends the growth of a real Christian, in grace, which renders it exceedingly difficult for him to know the fact, upon a superficial view of his case, and that is, the clearer and deeper insight which he obtains into the evils of his own heart. Now this is one of the best evidences of growth; but the first conclusion is apt to be, "I am growing worse every day"—"I see innumerable evils springing up within me which I never saw before." This person may be compared to one shut up in a dark room, where he is surrounded by many loathsome objects. If a single ray of light be let into the room, he sees the more prominent objects; but if the light gradually increase, he sees more and more of the filth by which he has been surrounded. It was there before, but he perceived it not. His increased knowledge of the fact is a sure evidence of increasing light. Hypocrites often learn to talk by rote of the wickedness of their hearts;

but go to them and seriously accuse them of indulging secret pride, or envy, or covetousness, or any other heart sins, and they will be offended. Their confessions of sin are only intended to raise them in the opinion of others, as truly humble persons; and not that any should believe that corruption abounds within them. Growth in grace is evinced by a more habitual vigilance against besetting sins and temptations, and by greater self-denial, in regard to personal indulgence. A growing conscientiousness in regard to what may be called minor duties, is also a good sign. The counterfeit of this is, a scrupulous conscience, which sometimes haggles at the most innocent gratifications, and has led some to hesitate about taking their daily food. Increasing spiritual mindedness is a sure evidence of progress in piety; and this will always be accompanied by deadness to the world. Continued aspirations to God, in the house and by the way, in lying down and rising up, in company and in solitude, indicate the indwelling of the Holy Spirit, by whose agency all progress in sanctification is made. A victory over besetting sins by which the person was frequently led away, shows an increased vigour in the renewed principle. Increasing solicitude for the salvation of men, and sorrow on account of their sinful and miserable condition, and a disposition tenderly to warn sinners of their danger, evince a growing state of piety. It is also a strong evidence of growth in grace, when you can bear injuries and provocations with meekness, and when you can from the heart desire the temporal and eternal welfare of your bitterest enemies. An entire and confident reliance on the promises and providence of God, however dark may be your horizon, or however many difficulties environ you, is a sign that you have learned to live by faith: and humble contentment with your condition, though it be one of poverty and obscurity, shows that you have profited by sitting at the feet of Jesus. Diligence in the duties of our calling, with a view to the glory of God, is not an evidence to be despised. Indeed, there is no surer standard of spiritual growth, than a habit of aiming at the glory of God in every thing. That mind which is steady to the main end, gives as good evidence of being touched by divine grace, as the tendency of the needle to the pole proves that it has been touched by the magnet. Increasing love to the brethren is a sure sign of growth; for as brotherly love is a proof of the existence of grace, so exercising brotherly love is, of vigour in the divine life. This love, when pure, is not confined within those limits which party spirit circumscribes, but overleaping all the barriers of sects and denominations, it embraces the disciples of Christ. wherever it finds them. A healthy state of piety is always a growing state; that child which grows not at all must be sickly. If we would enjoy spiritual comfort, we must be in a thriving condition. None enjoy the pleasures of bodily health, but they who are in health. If we would be useful to the Church and the world we must be growing Christians. If we would live in daily preparation for our change, we must endeavour to grow in grace daily. The aged saint, laden with the fruits of righteousness, is like a shock of corn fully ripe, which is ready for the garner; or like a mature fruit, which gradually loosens its hold of the tree, until at last it gently falls off. Thus the aged, mature Christian, departs in peace. As growth in grace is gradual, and the progress from day to day imperceptible, we should aim to do something in this work every day. We should "die daily unto sin and live unto righteousness." Sometimes the children of God grow faster when in the fiery furnace than elsewhere. As metals are purified by being cast into the fire, so saints have their dross consumed and their evidences brightened, by being cast into the furnace of affliction. "Beloved, think it not strange concerning the fiery trial which shall try you, as though some strange thing happened unto you," but rejoice, because " the trial of your faith, being much more precious than of gold that perisheth, though it be tried with fire shall be found unto praise, and honour, and glory."

We shall here present some practical directions how to grow in grace, or make progress in piety.

1. Set it down as a certainty that this object will never be attained without vigorous, continued effort; and it must not only be desired and sought, but must be considered more important than all other pursuits, and be pursued in preference to every thing which claims your attention.

2. While you determine to be assiduous in the use of the appointed means of sanctification, you must have it deeply fixed in your mind, that nothing can be effected in this work without the aid of the Divine Spirit. "Paul may plant and Apollos water, but it is God that giveth the increase." The direction of the old divines is good; 'use the means as vigorously as if you were to be saved by your own efforts, and yet trust as entirely to the grace of God, as if you made use of no means whatever.'

3. Be much in the perusal of the Holy Scriptures, and strive to obtain clear and consistent views of the plan of redemption. Learn to contemplate the truth in its true nature, simply, devoutly, and long at a time, that you may receive on your soul the impression which it is calculated to make. Avoid curious and abstruse speculations respecting things unrevealed; and do not indulge a spirit of controversy. Many lose the benefit of the good impression which the truth is calculated to make, because they do not view it simply in its own nature, but as related to some dispute, or as bearing on some other point. As when a man would receive the genuine impression which a beautiful landscape is adapted to make, he must not be turned aside by minute inquiries respecting the botanical character of the plants, the value of the timber, or the fertility of the soil; but he must place his mind in the attitude of receiving the impression which the combined view of the objects before him, will naturally produce on the taste. In such cases the effect is not produced by any exertion of the intellect; all such active striving is unfavourable, except in bringing the mind to its proper state When the impression is most perfect,

we feel as if we were mere passive recipients of the effect. To this there is a striking analogy in the way in which the mind is impressed with divine truth. It is not the critic, the speculative or polemic theologian, who is most likely to receive the right impression, but the humble, simple-hearted, contemplative Christian. It is necessary to study the Scriptures critically, and to defend the truth against opposers; but the most learned critic and the most profound theologian must learn to sit at the feet of Jesus in the spirit of a child, or they are not likely to be edified by their studies.

4. Pray constantly and fervently for the influences of the Holy Spirit. No blessing is so particularly and emphatically promised in answer to prayer as this; and if you would receive this divine gift, to be in you as a well of water springing up to everlasting life, you must not only pray, but you must watch against every thing in your heart or life which has a tendency to grieve the Spirit of God. Of what account is it to pray, if you indulge evil thoughts and imaginations almost without control; or if you give way to the evil passions of anger, envy, pride and avarice, or bridle not your tongue from evil speaking? Learn to be conscientious; that is, obey the dictates of your conscience uniformly. Many are conscientious in some things, and not in others; they listen to the monitor within, when he directs to important duties; but in smaller matters, they often disregard the voice of conscience, and follow present inclination. Such cannot grow in grace.

5. Take more time for the duties of the closet, and for looking into the state of your soul. Redeem an hour daily from sleep, if you cannot obtain it otherwise; and as the soul's concerns are apt to get out of order, and more time is needed for thorough self examination, than an hour a day, set apart, not periodically, but as your necessities require, days of fasting and humiliation before God. On these occasions, deal faithfully with yourself. Be in earnest to search out all your secret sins, and to repent of them. Re

new your covenant with God, and form holy resolutions of amendment in the strength of divine grace and if you find upon examination, that you have been living in any sinful indulgence, probe the festering wound to the core, and confess your fault before God, and do not rest until you have had an application of the blood of sprinkling. You need not ask why you do not grow, while there is such an ulcer within you. Here, it is to be feared, is the root of the evil. Sins indulged are not thoroughly repented of and forsaken; or the conscience has not been purged effectually, and the wound still festers. "Come to the fountain opened for the washing away of sin and uncleanness." Bring your case to the great Physician.

6. Cultivate and exercise brotherly love more than you have been accustomed to do. Christ is displeased with many of his professed followers, because they are so cold and indifferent to his members on earth; and because they do so little to comfort and encourage them; and with some, because they are a stumbling block to the weak of the flock; their conversation and conduct not being edifying, but the contrary. Perhaps these disciples are poor, and in the lower walks of life, and therefore you overlook them, as beneath you. And thus would you have treated Christ himself, had you lived in his time; for he took his station among the poor and afflicted; and he will resent a neglect of his poor saints with more displeasure than he would of the rich. Perhaps they do not belong to your party or sect, and you are only concerned to build up your own denomination. Remember how Christ condescended to treat the sinful woman of Samaria, and the poor woman of Canaan, and remember what account he has given of the last judgment, when he will assume to himself all that has been done, or neglected to be done, to his humble followers. There should be more Christian conversation and friendly intercourse between the followers of Christ. In former days, "They that feared the Lord spake often one unto another, and the Lord hearkened

and heard it, and a book of remembrance was written for them that feared the Lord and thought upon his name."

7. If you are in good earnest to make greater progress in piety, you must do more than you have done for the promotion of God's glory and of Christ's kingdom on earth. You must enter with livelier, deeper feeling, into all the plans which the Church has adopted to advance these objects. You must give more than you have done. It is a shame to think how small a portion of their gains some professors devote to the Lord. Instead of being a tithe, it is hardly equal to the single sheaf of first fruits. If you have nothing to give, labour to get something. Sit up at night and try to make something, for Christ hath need of it. Sell a corner of your land and throw the money into the treasury of the Lord. In primitive times many sold houses and lands, and laid the whole at the Apostles' feet. Do not be afraid of making yourselves poor by giving to the Lord, or to his poor. His word is better than any bond, and he says, "I will repay it." Cast your bread on the waters, and after many days you will find it again. Send the Bible—send missionaries—send tracts to the perishing heathen.

8. Practise self-denial every day. Lay a wholesome restraint upon your appetites. Be not conformed to this world. Let your dress, your house, your furniture, be plain and simple, as becometh a Christian. Avoid vain parade and show in every thing. Govern your family with discretion. Forgive and pray for your enemies. Have little to do with party politics. Carry on your business on sober, judicious principles. Keep clear of speculation and suretiships. Live peaceably with all men as much as in you lies. Be much in ejaculatory prayer. Keep your heart with all diligence. Try to turn to spiritual profit every event which occurs; and be fervently thankful for all mercies.

9. For your more rapid growth in grace, some of you will be cast into the furnace of affliction. Sick

ness, bereavement, bad conduct of children and relatives, loss of property, or of reputation, may come upon you unexpectedly, and press heavily on you. In these trying circumstances, exercise patience and fortitude. Be more solicitous to have the affliction sanctified, than removed. Glorify God while in the fire of adversity. That faith which is most tried, is commonly most pure and precious. Learn from Christ how you ought to suffer. Let perfect submission to the will of God be aimed at. Never indulge a murmuring or discontented spirit. Repose with confidence on the promises. Commit all your cares to God. Make known your requests to him by prayer and supplication. Let go your too eager grasp of the world. Become familiar with death and the grave. Wait patiently until your change cometh; but desire not to live a day longer than may be for the glory of God.

If we are on the watch we often may find good things when they were least expected. It is seldom that I consult an almanac for any purpose, but wishing, the other day, to see when the moon would change, I opened the calendar at the current month, and the first thing which struck my eye was the heading of a paragraph in the very words which I had selected as the subject of this essay—" Hinderances to Growth in Grace." Of course I perused the short paragraph, and I was so well pleased with what I read, that I resolved to take it for my text—and here it is, word for word:

" The influence of worldly relatives and companions—embarking too deeply in business—approximations to fraud for the sake of gain—devoting too much time to amusements—immoderate attachment to a worldly object—attendance on an unbelieving or unfaithful ministry—languid and formal observance of religious duties—shunning the society and religious converse of Christian friends—relapse into known sin—oversight and of course non-improvement of graces already attained."

Now, all this is very good and very true; the only

objection is, that several of the particulars mentioned should rather be considered as the effects of a real declension in religion than the mere hinderances to growth; although it is true, that nothing so effectually hinders our progress as an actual state of backsliding. It seems desirable to ascertain, as precisely as we can, the reasons why Christians commonly are of so diminutive a stature and of such feeble strength in their religion. When persons are truly converted they always are sincerely desirous to make rapid progress in piety; and there are not wanting exceeding great and gracious promises of aid to encourage them to go forward with alacrity. Why then is so little advancement made? Are there not some practical mistakes very commonly entertained, which are the cause of this slowness of growth? I think there are, and will endeavour to specify some of them. And first, there is a defect in our belief of the freeness of divine grace. To exercise unshaken confidence in the doctrine of gratuitous pardon is one of the most difficult things in the world; and to preach this doctrine fully without verging towards antinomianism is no easy task, and is therefore seldom done. But Christians cannot but be lean and feeble when deprived of the proper nutriment. It is by faith, that the spiritual life is made to grow; and the doctrine of free grace, without any mixture of human merit, is the only true object of faith. Christians are too much inclined to depend on themselves, and not to derive their life entirely from Christ. There is a spurious legal religion, which may flourish without the practical belief in the absolute freeness of divine grace, but it possesses none of the characteristics of the Christian's life. It is found to exist in the rankest growth, in systems of religion which are utterly false. But ven when the true doctrine is acknowledged, in theory, often it is not practically felt and acted on. The new convert lives upon his frames, rather than on Christ; and the older Christian still is found struggling in his own strength; and failing in his expectations of success, he becomes discouraged first.

and then he sinks into a gloomy despondency, or becomes, in a measure, careless; and then the spirit of the world comes in with resistless force. Here, I am persuaded, is the root of the evil; and, until religious teachers inculcate clearly, fully, and practically, the grace of God as manifested in the gospel, we shall have no vigorous growth of piety among professing Christians. We must be, as it were, identified with Christ—crucified with him, and living by him, and in him by faith, or rather have Christ living in us. The covenant of grace must be more clearly and repeatedly expounded in all its rich plenitude of mercy, and in all its absolute freeness.

Another thing which prevents growth in grace, is, that Christians do not make their obedience to Christ comprehend every other object of pursuit. Their religion is too much a separate thing, and they pursue their worldly business in another spirit. They try to unite the service of God and Mammon. Their minds are divided, and often distracted with earthly cares and desires, which interfere with the service of God; whereas they should have but one object of pursuit, and all that they do and seek, should be in subordination to this. Every thing should be done for God and to God; whether they eat or drink, they should do all to his glory. As the ploughing and sowing of the wicked is sin, because done without regard to God and his glory; so the secular employments and pursuits of the pious should all be consecrated, and become a part of their religion. Thus they would serve God in the field and in the shop, in buying and selling, and getting gain—all would be for God. Thus their earthly labours would prove no hinderance to their progress in piety; and possessing an undivided mind, having a single object of pursuit, they could not but grow in grace, daily. He whose eye is single shall have his whole body full of light.

Again, another powerful cause of hinderance in the growth of the life of God in the soul, is, that we make general resolutions of improvement, but neglect to extend our efforts to particulars; and we promise ourselves that in the indefinite future, we will do much in the way of reformation, but are found doing nothing each day in cultivating piety. We begin and end our days without aiming or expecting to make any particular advance on that day. Thus our best resolutions evaporate without effect. We merely run the round of prescribed duty, satisfied if we do nothing amiss, and neglect no external service which we feel to be obligatory. We resemble the man who purposes to go to a certain place, and often resolves with earnestness that he will some day perform the journey, but never takes a step towards the place. Is it at all strange that that person who on no day makes it his distinct object to advance in the divine life, at the end of months and years is found stationary? The natural body will grow without our thinking about it, even when we are asleep, but not the life of piety, which only increases by, and through the exercises of the mind, aiming at higher measures of grace. And, as every day we should do something in this good work, so we should direct our attention to the growth of particular graces; especially of those in which we know ourselves to be defective. Are we weak in faith? let us give attention to the proper means of strengthening our faith; and, above all, apply to the Lord to increase our faith. Is our love to God cold and hardly perceptible, and greatly interrupted by long intervals in which God and Christ are not in all our thoughts? let us have this for a daily lamentation at the throne of grace—let us resolve to meditate more on the excellency of the divine attributes, and especially on the love of God to us—let us be much in reading the account of Christ's sufferings and death, and be importunate in prayer, until we receive more copious effusions of the Holy Spirit; for the fruit of the Spirit is love, and the love of God is shed abroad in our hearts by the Holy Ghost which is given unto us. And so we should directly aim at cultivating and increasing every grace; for the divine life, or "new man," consists of these graces, and the whole cannot be in health and vigour, while the constituent parts are feeble and in a state of decay. The same remarks are applicable to the mortification of sin; we are prone to view our depravity too much in the general, and under this view to repent of it, and humble ourselves on account of it; whereas, in order to make any considerable progress in this part of sanctification, we must deal with our sins in detail. We must have it as a special object, to eradicate pride and vain glory, covetousness, indolence, envy, discontent, anger, &c. There should be appropriate means used, suited to the extirpation of each particular vice of the mind. It is true, indeed, that if we water the root we may expect the branches to flourish; if we invigorate the principle of piety, the several Christian virtues will flourish; but a skilful gardener will pay due attention both to the root and the branches; and, in fact, these graces of the heart are parts of the root, and it is by strengthening these, that we do invigorate the root. The same is true, as it relates to the remaining principle of sin; we must strike our blows chiefly at the root of the evil tree; but those inherent vices which were mentioned, and others, should be considered as belonging to the root, and when we aim at their destruction particularly, and in detail, our strokes will be most effectual.

I shall mention, at present, but one other cause of the slow growth of believers in piety, and that is the neglect of improving in the knowledge of divine things. As spiritual knowledge is the foundation of all genuine exercises of religion, so growth in religion is intimately connected with divine knowledge. Men may possess unsanctified knowledge and be nothing the better for it; but they cannot grow in grace without increasing in the knowledge of our Lord Jesus Christ. "Being," says Paul, "fruitful in every good work, and increasing in the knowledge of God." "Grow in grace," says Peter, "and in the knowledge of our Lord Jesus Christ." Mr. Edwards remarks, that the more faithful he was in studying the Bible, the more he prospered in spiritual things. The reason is plain, and other Christians will find the same to be true.

CHAPTER XIV.

Backsliding.—The Backslider restored

THERE is a perpetual, and there is a temporary backsliding. The first is the case of those who, being partially awakened and enlightened by the word accompanied by the common operations of the Spirit, make a profession of religion, and, for a while, seem to run well, and to outstrip the humble believer in zeal and activity; but having no root in themselves, in the time of temptation, fall totally away, and not only relinquish their profession, but frequently renounce Christianity itself, and become the bitterest enemies of religion. Or, seduced by the pride of their own hearts, they forsake the true doctrines of the gospel, and fall in love with some flattering, flesh-pleasing form of heresy; and spend their time in zealous efforts to overthrow that very truth, which they once professed to prize. Or, thirdly, they are overcome by some insidious lust or passion, and fall into the habitual practice of some sin, which at first they secretly indulge, but after a while cast off all disguise, and show to all that they are enslaved by some hurtful and hateful iniquity. Persons who thus apostatize from the profession and belief of Christianity, or who fall into a habitual course of sinning, are commonly in the most hopeless condition of all who live in the midst of the means of grace. When they openly reject Christianity, their infidelity is commonly accompanied by contempt and a malign temper, which often prompts them to blasphemy; and they are, according to our apprehension, in great danger of committing the unpardonable sin; and some who in these circumstances are actuated by inveterate hatred to the truth, and who make use of their tongues to express the feelings of enmity which rankle in them, do often fall into this unpardonable sin. The case of such seems to be described by Paul, in the sixth chapter of his Epistle to the Hebrews. "For it is impossible for those who were once enlightened, and have tasted of the heavenly gift, and were made partakers of the Holy Ghost, and have tasted the good word of God and the powers of the world to come, if they shall fall away, to renew them again to repentance, seeing they crucify to themselves the Son of God afresh and put him to an open shame." Some suppose that the Apostle here describes the character of the true Christian, and that he merely supposes the case, if such should fall away, what would be the fearful consequence; but this seems to us a forced construction. It seems more reasonable to believe that he is describing a case which may, and often does occur, and that the description applies to such professors as had received the miraculous endowments of the Holy Spirit, and yet apostatized: and by crucifying the Son of God afresh he probably alludes to the manner in which those who went back to the Jews, were required to execrate the name of Christ in the Synagogues, and to profess that he deserved to be crucified as he had been, and thus put him to an open shame. But whether such apostates do actually commit the unpardonable sin or not, seems in most cases to be of little consequence, for they commonly die in their sins, and all sin unrepented of is unpardonable. In some cases, however, apostates stop short of infidelity and blasphemy, and while they stand aloof from religion, content themselves with decency, and do not treat religion with disrespect; yet it will be found on examination, that the hearts of such are extremely callous, and their consciences are seared as with a hot iron. The Spirit of God, evidently has left them, and strives no more with them; and they often die as they have lived, fearfully insensible, having "no bands in their death." But sometimes conscience is let loose upon them in their last hours, and they are left to die in the horrors of despair. In the days of the apostles, they seem to have had some way of knowing when a man had committed "the sin unto death," and for such, Christians were not to pray, as their destiny was irretrievably fixed; but such knowledge cannot be possessed now, and we may therefore pray for all, as long as they are in the place of repentance.

But when we speak of backsliding, we commonly mean those sad departures of real Christians from God, which are so common, and often so injurious to the cause of religion. These cases are so common, that some have thought that all Christians have their seasons of backsliding; when they left their first love, and lost the sweet relish of divine things, and were excluded from intimate communion with God. But, however common backsliding may have been among Christians, there is no foundation for the opinion, that it is common to all; we find no such declension in the experience of Paul or John; and in the biographies of some modern saints we find no such sad declension. We could refer to many recorded accounts of personal experience, but it will be sufficient to mention Mr. Baxter, Col. Gardiner, G. Whitfield, and Mr. Brainerd. No doubt all experience short seasons of comparative coldness and insensibility, and they who live near to God have not always equal light, and life, and comfort, in the divine life. Those fluctuations of feeling, which are so common, are not included in the idea of a state of backsliding. This occurs when the Christian is gradually led off from close walking with God, loses the lively sense of divine things, becomes too much attached to the world and too much occupied with secular concerns; until at length the keeping of the heart is neglected, closet duties are omitted or slightly performed, zeal for the advancement of religion is quenched, and many things once rejected by a sensitive conscience, are now indulged and defended.

All this may take place, and continue long before

the person is aware of his danger, or acknowledges
that there has been any serious departure from God.
The forms of religion may be still kept up, and open
sin avoided. But more commonly backsliders fall
into some evil habits; they are evidently too much
conformed to the world, and often go too far in par-
ticipating in the pleasures and amusements of the
world; and too often there is an indulgence in known
sin, into which they are gradually led, and on account
of which they experience frequent compunction, and
make solemn resolutions to avoid it in future; but
when the hour of temptation comes, they are overcome again and again, and thus they live a miserable
life, enslaved by some sin, over which, though they
sometimes struggle hard, they cannot get the victory.
There is in nature no more inconsistent thing than a
backsliding Christian. Looking at one side of his
character, he seems to have sincere, penitential feelings, and his heart to be right in its purposes and
aims; but look at the other side, and he seems to be
"carnal, sold under sin." O wretched man! how he
writhes often in anguish, and groans for deliverance,
but he is like Sampson shorn of his locks, his strength
is departed, and he is not able to rise and go forth, at
liberty, as in former times. All backsliders are not
alike. Some are asleep; but the one now described is
in a state of almost perpetual conflict, which keeps
him wide awake. Sometimes when his pious feelings
are lively, he cannot but hope that he loves God and
hates sin, and is encouraged; but oh, when sin pre-
vails against him, and he is led away captive, he cannot think that he is a true Christian. Is it possible
that one who is thus overcome, can have in him any
principle of piety? Sometimes he gives up all hope,
and concludes, that he was deceived in ever thinking
himself converted; but then again, when he feels a
broken and contrite heart, and an ardent breathing
and groaning after deliverance, he cannot but conclude, that there is some principle above mere nature,
operating with him.

The sleeping backslider is one who, by being sur

rounded with earthly comforts, and engaged in secular pursuits, and mingling much with the decent and respectable people of the world, by degrees, loses the deep impression of divine and eternal things; his spiritual senses become obtuse, and he has no longer the views and feelings of one awake to the reality of spiritual things. His case nearly resembles that of a man gradually sinking into sleep. Still he sees dimly, and hears indistinctly, but he is fast losing the impression of the objects of the spiritual world, and sinking under the impression of the things of time and sense. There may be no remarkable change in the external conduct of such a person; except that he has no longer any relish for religious conversation, and rather is disposed to waive it. And the difference between such an one, and the rest of the world, becomes less and less distinguishable. From any thing you see or hear, you would not suspect him to be a professor of religion, until you see him taking his seat at the Lord's table. Such backsliders are commonly awakened by some severe judgments; the earthly objects on which they had too much fixed their affections are snatched away; and they are made bitterly to feel that it is an evil thing to forget and depart from the living God.

There is still another species of backsliding, where by a sudden temptation, one who appeared to stand firm, is cast down. Such was the fall of Peter, and many others have given full evidence that a man's standing is not in himself; for frequently men are overcome in those very things in which they were least afraid, and had most confidence in their own strength. These cases are usually more disgraceful than other instances of backsliding, but they are less dangerous; for, commonly, where there is grace they produce such an overwhelming conviction of sin, and shame for having acted so unworthily, that repentance soon follows the lapse, and the person, when restored, 's more watchful than ever against all kinds of sin, and more distrustful of himself. Such falls may be compared to a sudden accident by which a bone is broken, or put out of joint, they are very painful, and cause the person to go limping all the remainder of his life, but do not so much affect the vitals, as more secret and insidious diseases, which prey inwardly without being perceived.

There are many persons, who never made a public profession of religion, who for a while, are the subjects of serious impressions, whose consciences are much awake, and whose feelings are tender. They seem to love to hear the truth, and in a considerable degree fall under its influence, so as to be almost persuaded to be Christians; and for a season give to the pious, lively hopes of their speedy conversion. They are such as the person to whom Christ said, "thou art not far from the kingdom of God." But through the blinding influence of avarice or ambition, or some other carnal motive, they are led away and lose all their serious thoughts and good resolutions. Such persons usually lose their day of grace. I have seen an amiable young man, weeping under the faithful preaching of the gospel, and my hopes were sanguine, that I should soon see him at the table of the Lord; but alas! I believe that, on that very day, he quenched the Spirit, and has been going further and further from the Lord ever since!

The backsliding believer can only be distinguished from the final apostate by the fact of his recovery; at least, when Christians have slidden far back, no satisfactory evidence of the genuineness of their piety can be exhibited; nor can they have any which ought to satisfy their own minds. In the course of pastoral visitation I once called upon a habitual drunkard who had been a flaming professor. I asked him what he thought of his former exercises of religion. He said, that he was confident that they were genuine; and expressed a strong confidence that the Lord would recover him from his backsliding state. Now here was the very spirit of Antinomianism. Whether he was ever recovered from his besetting sin, I cannot tell; but I rather think that he continued his intemperate habits to the very last. I have often remarked how tenaciously the most profane and obstinate sinners will cleave to the hope of having been once converted, if they have ever been the subjects of religious impressions. One of the profanest men I ever heard speak, and one of the most outrageous drunkards, when asked on his death-bed, to which he was brought by intemperance, respecting his prospects beyond the grave, said, that when a very young man, he had been among the Methodists, and thought that he was converted; and though he had lived in the most open and daring wickedness for more than twenty years since that time, yet he seemed to depend on those early exercises. Miserable delusion! But a drowning man will catch at a straw. An old sea-captain, whom I visited on his death-bed, seemed to be trusting to a similar delusion. He related to me certain religious exercises which he had when he first went to sea, but of which he had no return ever since, though half a century had elapsed. I have met with few persons who had neglected to cherish and improve early impressions, who were ever afterwards hopefully converted. They are generally given up to blindness of mind and hardness of heart. But some of these are sometimes brought in, in times of revival; or, at a late period, driven to the gospel refuge, by severe affliction. The conviction of a Christian backslider is often more severe and overwhelming than when first awakened. When his eyes are opened to see the ingratitude and wicked rebellion of his conduct, he is ready to despair, and to give up all hopes of being pardoned. He sinks into deep waters where the billows of divine displeasure roll over him; or he is like a prisoner, in a horrible pit, and in the miry clay. All around him is dark and desolate, and he feels himself to be in a deplorably helpless condition. His own strivings seem to sink him deeper in the mire; but, as his last and only resource, he cries, out of the *depths*, unto God. As his case is urgent he cries with unceasing importunity, and the Lord hears the voice of his supplications, and brings him up out of the horrible pit, and places his feet upon a rock, and establishes his goings, and puts a new song into his mouth, even of praise to the Redeemer. The freeness of pardon to the returning backslider is a thing which is hard to be believed, until it is experienced. No sooner is the proud heart humbled, and the hard heart broken into contrition, than Jehovah is near with his healing balm. To heal the broken in heart, and to revive the spirit of the contrite ones, is the delight of Immanuel. And he receives the returning penitent without reproaches. He pardons him freely, and sheds abroad his love in his heart, and fills him with the joy of the Holy Ghost. It is, in fact, a new conversion; though there is but one regeneration. We never hear of a sinner being born a *third time*—but we remember that Christ said unto Peter, " when thou art converted, strengthen thy brethren." Indeed, the exercises of the soul on these occasions may be so much more clear and comfortable than on its first conversion, that the person is disposed to think that this is the real commencement of spiritual life, and to set down all his former experience as spurious; or, at least, essentially defective. Christians, when recovered from backsliding, are commonly more watchful, and walk more circumspectly than they ever did before. They cannot but be more humble. The remembrance of their base departure from God fills them with self-loathing. Whenever spiritual pride would lift up its head, one thought of a disgraceful fall will often lay the soul in the dust. And whether the backslider's sins have been open or secret, the recollection of his traitorous behaviour fills him with shame and self-abhorrence. When such persons have so conducted themselves as to bring upon them the censures of the church, so as to be separated from the communion of his people, at first, it is probable, resentment will be felt towards the officers of the church who perform this painful duty; but after reflection, these resentments are turned against themselves, and they pass much heavier censures on themselves than the church ever did. Judicious, seasonable discipline is a powerful means of grace, and often would be the effectual means of recovering the backslider, if exercised as it should be. Indeed, this may be said to be one main design of its appointment. If whenever there is an appearance of declension in a church member, the pastor, or some other officer of the church, would go to the person, and, in the spirit, and by the authority of Christ, would address a serious admonition to him, and then a second, and a third, and if these were unheeded, then to bring him before the church, backsliding, in most cases, would be arrested before it proceeded far. But every member of the church has a duty to perform towards erring brethren. When they see them going astray, they should not act towards them as if they hated them, but should in any wise rebuke them. Christian reproof from one Christian to another seems to be almost banished from our churches. There is a quick eye to discern a brother's faults, and a ready tongue to speak of them to others; but where do we now find the faithful reprover of sin, who goes to the man himself, without saying a word to any one, and between themselves, faithfully warns, exhorts, and entreats a straying brother to return. The serious discipline of formal accusations, and witnesses, &c., by such a course would be, in a great measure, rendered unnecessary; but the practice is, to let the evil grow until it has become inveterate, and breaks out into overt acts, and then there is a necessity to pay attention to the matter, and to put in force the discipline of the church. But even this often proves salutary, and is a powerful means of reclaiming the offender; or, if he persists in his evil courses, it serves to separate an unworthy member from the communion of saints. But when church officers and private Christians utterly fail in their duty towards backsliding brethren, God himself often makes use of means of his own, which do not require the intervention of men. He smites the offender with his rod, and causes him to smart in some tender part. He sends such afflictions as bring his sins forcibly before his conscience. He deprives him of the objects for the sake of which he forsook the Lord.—It may be the wife of his youth, or a beloved child, on which his affections were too fondly fixed, so as to become idolatrous. Or, if it was the love of the world which was the seductive cause of his backsliding, riches are caused to "make to themselves wings and flee away like the eagle to heaven." Or, was the love of ease and indulgence of the sensual appetites the cause of his delinquency, the stroke falls on his own body. He is brought low by sickness, and is tried upon his bed with excruciating pains, until he cries out in his distress, and humbly confesses his sins. Or, if he was carried away by an undue love of the honour that cometh from men, it is not unlikely that his reputation, which he cherished with a fondness which caused him to neglect the honour of his God, will be permitted to be tarnished by the tongue of slander, and things may be so situated, that although innocent, he may not have it in his power to make the truth appear. Children, too much indulged, become, by their misconduct, fruitful causes of affliction to parents; and thus they are made to suffer in the very point where they had sinned. Look at the case of Eli and of David. All afflictions, however, are not for chastisement, but sometimes for trial; and those whom God loves best are most afflicted in this world. They are kept in the furnace, and that heated seven times, until their dross is consumed, and their piety shines forth as pure gold, which has been tried in the fire. But we are now concerned only with those afflictions which are most effective to bring back the backslider; the virtue of which the Psalmist acknowledges when he says, "It is good for me to be afflicted, for before I was afflicted I went astray." It may be truly said, that many who had backslidden, never would have returned had it not been for the rod; other means seemed to have lost their power, but this comes home to the feelings of every one. Whether a believer is ever permitted to go out of the world in a backslidden state, is a question of no practical importance; but it seems probable that Christians die in all conditions in which any of this character are ever found. No one has any right to presume, that if he backslides, death may not overtake him in that unprepared condition. Backsliding then is a fearful evil; may we all be enabled to avoid it; or if fallen into it, to be recovered speedily from so dangerous a state!

CHAPTER XV.

The rich man and the poor.—The various trials of believers.

THEY are not the happy whom the blinded world think to be such. The man of successful enterprise, and increasing wealth had some enjoyment while busily occupied in making a fortune; but now when he has arrived at a higher pitch of wealth than his most sanguine hopes had anticipated, he is far from being happy, or even contented. The desire of acquisition has grown into an inveterate habit, and he cannot stop in his career; he must find out some new enterprise; he must engage in some new speculation; and before all is over, it is well if he loses not all he had gained; and being accustomed to live high, he is unprepared to meet poverty; and to preserve his family from such a mortifying change of circumstances, he contrives ways and means to defraud his creditors. This man is not happy in his prosperity, and under a reverse of fortune, he is truly miserable. He has put away a good conscience, which is the most essential ingredient in that peace which Christ gives to his disciples. His reputation too, if not tarnished, remains under a dark cloud of suspicion, which never can be removed. Abroad, he meets with neglect and sometimes contempt, from those on whom he once looked down; at home he has before him the sad spectacle of a family degraded from their former rank, and under all the feelings of mortified pride, struggling to conceal their poverty from the gaze and contempt of an unpitying world. But ever. if no reverse is experienced, and the man continues to be successful in all his enterprises; and if at the close of his career, he can calculate millions, in the bank, or in real estate; his only remaining difficulty is, how to dispose of such a mass of wealth. He has a son, it is true, but he is a base profligate, and in a single year, would, by reckless speculation, or at the gaming table, dissipate the whole which has been so carefully hoarded up And yet this man could scarcely be induced to give a dollar to any benevolent object, lest he should lessen the amount which he was by every means raking together, for this unworthy son. He has daughters, too, whose husbands in selecting them had more respect to their fortunes, than to any personal qualifications, and these are impatient, that the old man should live so long, and hold the purse-strings with so close a grip. Though they will go through all the *ceremonial* of deep grief, and mourn as decently, and as long as fashion requires; yet no event is heard with more heart-felt pleasure, than that their aged relative is at last obliged to give up all his possessions.

Are the rich happy? not such as have been described. But there are a favoured few who seem to have learned the secret of using wealth so as to do much good, and to derive from it much enjoyment. They are desirous of making increase too, but it is all for the Lord; not to be hoarded, until they are obliged to leave it, and then to be distributed among benevolent societies. No; they are continually contriving methods of making it produce good, *now.* They are parsimonious to themselves, that they may be liberal to the poor; and may be able to enrich the treasury of the Lord. Such men are blessed, in their deed; and though unostentatious in their charities, their light cannot be hid. A few rich men of this description have lived in England, and even our new country records with gratitude, the names of a few benefactors of the public; and we trust in God that the number will be multiplied. Reader, go and do likewise.

But, more commonly, the elect of God are not called to glorify him in this way. Wealth is a dangerous talent, and is very apt so to block up the way to heaven, that they who do press in, have, as it were, to squeeze through a gate as difficult of entrance as the eye of a needle to a camel: and alas! many professors who bid fair for heaven, when in moderate circumstances, after becoming rich, are found "drowned in perdition"—"pierced through with many sorrows." Poverty and suffering are by infinite wisdom judged best for the traveller to Zion. Let the Lord's people be contented with their condition, and thankful that they are preserved from snares and temptations, which they would have found it difficult to withstand. God will not suffer them to be tempted above what they are able to bear, but with the temptation provides a way for their escape. The rich are exposed to suffering as well as the poor; though their sufferings may be of a different kind. The poor man may be forced by necessity to live on coarse bread; the rich man also, while tantalized with the daily sight of the finest of the wheat, is obliged for the sake of his health, to live upon bran. The poor man lies on a hard bed, because he can afford to get no better; the rich man lies as hard to preserve himself from aches and pains, which are the natural fruit of luxury. The poor man has little of the honours of the world, but then he is envied by none, and passes along in obscurity, without being set up as a mark to be shot at, by envy and malignity, which is often the lot of the rich. When sickness comes, the rich man has some advantages, but when oppressed with painful sickness, neither a bed of down, nor rich hangings and carpets, contribute any thing to his relief; and in such a time of distress, the privations of the poor, though the imagination readily magnifies them, add not much to the pain produced by disease. But we have dwelt too long on this comparison between the real sufferings of the rich and the poor. More after all depends upon the submission and patient temper of the mind, than upon external circumstances; and, indeed, so short is the time of man's continuance upon earth, and so infinite the joys or miseries of the future world, that to make much of these little differences would be like estimating the weight of a feather when engaged in weighing mountains. Who thinks it a matter of any concern, whether the circumstances of persons who lived a thousand years ago were affluent or destitute, except, so far as these external enjoyments and privations contributed to their moral improvement, or the contrary? If we could be duly impressed with the truths which respect our eternal condition, we should consider our afflictions here as scarcely worthy of being named. Thus the apostle Paul seemed to view his own sufferings, and those of his fellow Christians, when he said, "For I reckon that the sufferings of this present time, are not worthy to be compared with the glory which shall be revealed in us." Compared with the sufferings of others, those of the apostle were neither few nor small; but in the view of eternity by faith, he calls them "these light afflictions which are but for a moment;" and he had learned the happy art, not only of being contented, in whatever state he was, but of rejoicing in all his tribulations; not that tribulation, considered in itself, could be a matter of rejoicing, for who ever found pain and reproach to be pleasant? But he rejoiced in these things on account of their salutary effects, "for," says he, "tribulation worketh patience, and patience experience, and experience hope, and hope maketh not ashamed, because the love of God is shed abroad in our hearts by the Holy Ghost." The primitive Christians were encouraged to bear patiently and joyfully, their present sufferings, on account of the rich and gracious reward which awaited them in the world to come. Upon the mere principle of contrast, our earthly sorrows will render our heavenly joys the sweeter. But this is not all:—hear the words of Jesus himself, "Blessed are they who are persecuted for righteousness' sake, for theirs is the kingdom of heaven. Blessed are ye when men shall revile you, and persecute you, and say all manner of evil against you falsely, for my sake: rejoice and be exceeding glad, for great is your reward in heaven." Peter also testifies, " and if ye suffer for righteousness' sake, happy are ye,"—"for it is better, if the will of God be so, that ye suffer for well doing than for evil doing. For Christ once suffered, the just for the unjust." He was also of the same opinion with his brother Paul, that Christians ought to rejoice in all their sufferings for righteousness' sake. " Beloved," says he, " think it not strange concerning the fiery trial which is to try you, as though some strange thing happened unto you : but rejoice, inasmuch as ye are partakers of Christ's sufferings, that when his glory shall be revealed, ye may be glad also with exceeding joy. If ye be reproached for the name of Christ, happy are ye, for the Spirit of God resteth on you." " If any man suffer as a Christian, let him not be ashamed, but let him glorify God on this behalf." Let Zion's mourners lift up their heads and rejoice, for though weeping may endure for a night, joy cometh in the morning! Let all Christians manifest to others the sweetness and excellency of religion, by rejoicing continually in the Lord. The perennial sources of their spiritual joy can never fail—for while God lives and reigns, they ought to rejoice. Since Christ has died, and ever lives to make intercession for them, they have ground of unceasing joy. While the throne of grace is accessible, let the saints rejoice; let them rejoice in all the promises of God, which are exceeding great and precious, and are all yea and amen in Christ Jesus to the glory of God.

In one sense, all our sufferings are the fruits of sin, for if we had never sinned, we should never have suffered : but, in another sense, the sufferings of believers are produced by love : " whom the Father loveth, he chasteneth and scourgeth every son whom he receiveth." As in the economy of salvation, God leaves his chosen people to struggle with the remain ders of sin in their own hearts; so he has ordained, that their pilgrimage to the heavenly Canaan, shall be through much tribulation. From the beginning the saints have generally been a poor and afflicted people, often oppressed and persecuted; and when exempt from sufferings from the hands of men, they are often visited with sickness, or have their hearts sorely lacerated by the bereavement of dear friends, are punished with poverty, or loaded with obloquy and reproach. There seems to be an incongruity in believers enjoying ease and prosperity, in this world, when their Lord was "a man of sorrows and acquainted with grief." It seems, indeed, to be a condition of our reigning with Him, that we should suffer with Him. When James and John, under the influence of ambition, asked for the highest places in his kingdom, he said to them, "Can ye drink of the cup which I drink of, and be baptized with the baptism that I am baptized with?" They seem not to have understood his meaning, for, with self-confidence, they answered, "We are able." He replied, "Ye shall, indeed, drink of the cup that I drink of, and be baptized with the baptism that I am baptized with." For the Christian to seek great things for himself here, does not become the character of a disciple of the meek and lowly Jesus. The early Christians were called to endure much persecution, but they did not count their lives dear unto them. When the apostles, after our Lord's ascension, were publicly beaten for preaching that the Saviour was risen, they rejoiced together that they were counted worthy to suffer such things for his name's sake. It is a striking peculiarity in the religion of Christ, that, in the conditions of discipleship, "taking up the cross" is the first thing. He never tempted any to follow him with the promise of earthly prosperity, or exemption from suffering. On the contrary, he assures them that in the world they shall have tribulation. He does, indeed, promise to those who forsake father and mother, wife and children, brothers and sisters, houses and lands, a compensation of a hundred fold more than they had left; but he permits them not to fall into the delusion that this hundred fold was to consist in earthly good things, for he immediately adds, "*with persecution.*" Whosoever will not take Christ with his cross, shall never sit with him on his throne. "*No cross, no crown,*" holds out an important truth in few words. Christ, in his intercessory prayer, does request, for his disciples, that they may be kept from the evil, which is in the world, but he means from the "evil one,"—from the evil of sin, and from temptations above their strength to endure.

The reasons why Christ has chosen that his people should be afflicted, and often sorely persecuted, are not difficult to be ascertained. In the former essay, it was shown that the rod is one of God's means for recovering backsliders from their wanderings; but afflictions are also employed to prevent Christians from backsliding. In prosperity, pride is apt to rise and swell; carnal security blinds their eyes; the love of riches increases; spiritual affections are feeble; and eternal things are viewed as far off, and concealed by a thick mist. These circumstances are, indeed, the common precursors of backsliding; but to prevent this evil, and to stir up the benumbed feelings of piety, the believer is put into the furnace. At first, he finds it hard to submit, and is like a wild bull in a net. His pride and his love of carnal ease resist the hand that smites him; but severe pain awakes him from his sleep, and he finds himself in the hands of his heavenly Father, and sees that nothing can be gained by murmuring or rebelling. His sins rise up to view, and he is convinced of the justice of the divine dispensations. His hard heart begins to yield, and he is stirred up to cry mightily to God for helping grace. Although he wishes and prays for deliverance from the pressure of affliction; yet he is more solicitous that it should be rendered effectual to subdue his pride, wean him from the love of the world, and give perfect exercise to patience and resignation, than that it should be removed. He knows that the furnace is the place for purification. He hopes and prays that his dross may be consumed; and that he may come forth as gold which has passed seven times through the refiner's fire.

Paul attributes a powerful efficacy to afflictions; so as to place them among the most efficacious means of grace. "For," says he, "our light affliction which is but for a moment, worketh out for us a far more exceeding and eternal weight of glory." "Furthermore, we have had fathers of our flesh, which corrected us, and we gave them reverence; shall we not much rather be in subjection to the Father of spirits and live? For they, verily, for a few days, corrected us after their own pleasure, but He for our profit, that we might be partakers of his holiness. Now, no chastening for the present seemeth to be joyous but grievous; nevertheless, afterward it yieldeth the peaceable fruit of righteousness unto them who are exercised thereby." When faith is in very lively exercise, believers can rejoice even in tribulation. Not that they cease to feel the pain of the rod —for then it would cease to be an affliction—but while they experience the smart, they are convinced that it is operating as a salutary though bitter medicine; and they rejoice in the prospect, or feeling of returning health. But, again, God pours not the rich consolations of his grace into a heart that is not broken. "He sendeth the rich empty away." "The whole need not a physician;" but when by affliction he has broken the hard heart, and emptied it of self-confidence, he delights to pour in the joy of the Holy Ghost. Therefore, it often occurs, that the believer's most joyful seasons are his suffering seasons. He has, it is true, more pungent pain, than when in prosperity and ease, but he has also richer, deeper draughts of consolation. Though sorrow and joy are opposite, there is a mysterious connexion between them. Sorrow, as it were, softens and prepares the heart for the reception of the joy of the Lord. As the dispensations of God towards his children, are exceedingly diverse, in different ages, so his dealings with individual believers, who live at the same time, are very different. Why it is so we cannot tell; but we are sure, that he has wise reasons for all that he does. In some cases, pious persons appear to pass through life with scarcely a touch from his rod; while others, who to us do not appear to need more chastisement than those, are held the greater part of their life under the heavy pressure of affliction, with scarcely any intermission. Here is a Christian man who has nearly reached the usual termination of human life, and has hardly known what external affliction is, in his own experience. Prosperity has attended him through his whole course. But there is a desolate widow who has been bereaved of her husband and children, and has neither brother nor sister, nephew nor niece, and for eight years has been confined to her bed, by wasting and painful disease, and has no hope of relief on this side of the grave. Such a disparity is striking; but we see only the outside of things. There are sore afflictions of the mind, while the body is in health. That man may have had severer chastisement than this afflicted, desolate widow. I have heard an aged Christian declare, that though he had experienced much sickness, lost many dear friends, and met with many sore disappointments in life, his sufferings on these accounts were not to be compared with the internal anguish which he often endured, and of which no creature had the least conception. This shows that we are not competent to form an accurate judgment of the sufferings of different persons. Besides, when affliction has been long continued, we become, in a measure, accustomed to it, and, as it were, hardened against it; but when we judge of such cases, we transfer our own acute feelings to the condition, which are no correct standard of the sufferings, of the patient, under a lingering disease. The widow, to whom I referred, was not a fictitious, but a real person. I once visited her, and conversed with her, and found her serene and happy; desiring nothing but a speedy departure, that she might be absent from the body, and present with the Lord; but she was not impatient; she was willing to remain and suffer just as long as God pleased. Her heart was truly subdued to the obedience of Christ. There was only one earthly object for which she seemed to feel solicitude, and that was the little forsaken, and almost desolate church of which she was a member. For a series of years, disaster after disaster had fallen upon this little flock. Their house of worship had been accidentally burnt, they had been so long without a pastor, that they dwindled down to a few disheartened and scattered members, and only one aged elder remained. Seldom was there an occasional sermon in the place, as they had no convenient house of meeting on the Sabbath. Now, although this poor widow could not have attended, if there had been preaching every Lord's day, yet that little church lay as a burden on her mind; and I heard a minister who knew the circumstances say, that as once a poor wise man saved a city, so this poor, pious widow, by her prayers, saved a church from extinction. For before her death, a neat, new church was erected, and a pastor settled, and a number of souls hopefully converted, and gathered into the church. I was once on a visit to a friend, who requested me to accompany her to see a sick woman, supposed to be near her end. The house was not a cabin, but a mere wreck of a once comfortable dwelling. Every appearance of comfort was absent. The partitions appeared to have been taken down, and the whole house was turned into one large room. There was no glass in the windows—but that mattered not, it was summer. Upon entering this desolate place, I saw the sick woman lying on a miserable bed, unable to raise her head from the pillow, and attended only by an aged mother above eighty years of age, and a little daughter about seven or eight. Here, indeed, seemed to be the very picture of wretchedness; and I was told that her brutal husband generally came home drunk, and never gave her a kind or soothing word.—Hear the conclusion—I verily thought before I left the house, that this was the happiest woman

I ever saw. Her devout and tender eye was sweetly fixed on heaven. Her countenance was serene, and illumined with a heavenly smile.

CHAPTER XVI.

Death-bed of the Believer.

WE have arrived now, at a very solemn part of our subject. The writer feels that it is so to himself, as he knows that he must soon be called to travel the road which leads to the narrow house, appointed for all living. If after having gone through this scene, he were permitted to return, and finish these papers on Religious Experience, by narrating what the soul suffers in passing the gate of death; and more especially, what are its views and feelings, the moment after death, he would be able to give information which at present no mortal can communicate. The thought has often occurred, when thinking on this subject, that the surprise of such a transition as that from time to eternity, from the state of imprisonment in this clay tenement, to an unknown state of existence, would be overwhelming even to the pious. But these are short-sighted reflections. We under take to judge of eternal things, by rules only suited to our present state of being, and our present feel ings. That the scene will be new and sublime, beyond all conception, cannot be doubted; but what our susceptibilities and feelings will be, when separated from the body, we cannot tell. Is it not possible, that our entrance on the unseen world, may be preceded by a course of gradual preparation for the wonderful objects which it contains, analogous to our progress through infancy in the present world? That knowledge of future things will be acquired gradually, and not instantaneously, we are led to believe from the constitution of the human mind, and from all the analogies of nature. The soul may therefore have to go to school again, to learn the first elements of celestial knowledge; and who will be the instructers, or how long this training may continue, it would be vain to conjecture. Whether in this gradual progress in the knowledge of heavenly things, our reminiscence of the transactions in which we were engaged upon earth, will be from the first vivid and perfect, or whether these things will at first be buried in a sort of oblivion, and be brought up to view gradually and successively, who can tell us? But I must withdraw my imagination from a subject, to which her powers are entirely inadequate. Though I have been fond of those writings of Dick, Taylor, and Watts, which give free scope to reasonings from analogy, in regard to the future condition of the believer, yet I am persuaded, that they add nothing to our real knowledge. Their lucubrations resemble the vain efforts of a man born blind to describe to his fellow sufferers, the brilliance of the stars, the splendours of the sun, or the milder beauties of a lovely landscape. While he seems to himself to approach nearest to the object, he in fact is most remote from any just conceptions of it. This brings to recollection, what has often appeared highly probable, in regard to the developement of our mental powers; that as in infancy some of our most important faculties, as for example, reason, conscience, and taste, are entirely dormant, and gradually and slowly make their appearance afterwards; so, probably, this whole life is a state of infancy in relation to that which is to come, and there may exist *now*, in these incomprehensible souls of ours, germs of faculties never in the least developed in this world, but which will spring into activity as soon as the soul feels the penetrating beams of celestial light; and which will be brought to maturity just at the time when they are needed. The capacity of the beatific vision may now be possessed by the soul, deeply enveloped in that darkness which conceals the internal powers of the mind even from itself, except so far as they are manifested by their actual exercise. How shallow then, is all our mental philosophy, by which we attempt to explore the depths of the human mind! But are these conjectural speculations for edification? Do they bring us any nearer to God, and to our beloved Redeemer? I cannot say, that they do. At the best, they are no more than an innocent amusement; and in indulging them, we are in great danger of becoming presumptuous, and even foolish, by supposing that we possess knowledge, when in fact our brightest light is but darkness. Vain man would be wise. Let us then cease from man—let us cease from our own unsubstantial dreams, and lay fast hold of the sure word of prophecy as of a light shining in a dark place. "To the law and to the testimony; if they speak not according to these, there is no light in them," or as some render the passage, "light shall never rise to them." One simple declaration of the word of God is worth more to a soul descending into the valley and shadow of death, than all the ingenious and vivid imaginings of the brightest human minds.

Considering the absolute and undoubted certainty of our departure out of life, it seems passing strange that we should be so unconcerned. If even one of a million escaped death, this might afford some shadow of a reason for our carelessness; but we know that "it is appointed unto men once to die." In this warfare there is no discharge, and yet most men live as if they were immortal. I remember the foolish thought which entered my childish mind, when my mother informed me that we all must die. I entertained the hope that before my time came, some great change would take place, I knew not how, by which I should escape this dreaded event. I have nothing to do with the death of the wicked at present. The dying experience of the believer is our proper subject, and we read that one object of Christ's coming into the world was "to deliver such as were all their life time in bondage through fear of death." Death, in itself considered, is a most formidable evil, and can be desirable to none. The fear of death is not altogether the consequence of sin; the thing is abhorrent to the constitution of man. Death was held up in terror to our first parents when innocent, to prevent their transgression, and having entered the world by their sin in whom we all sinned, this event has been, ever since, a terror to mortals—"THE KING OF TERRORS." Man instinctively cleaves to life; so does every sentient being. There are only two things which can possibly have the effect of reconciling any man to death. The first is, the hope of escaping from misery which is felt to be intolerable: the other an assurance of a better, that is a heavenly country. The captain of our salvation conquered death, and him that had the power of death, that is the Devil, by dying himself. By this means, he plucked from this monster his deadly sting, by satisfying the demands of God's holy law. "For the sting of death is sin, and the strength of sin is the law." All those, therefore, who are united to Christ, meet death as a conquered and disarmed enemy. Against them he is powerless. Still, however, he wears a threatening aspect, and although he cannot kill, he can frown and threaten, and this often frightens the timid sheep. They often do not know that they are delivered from his tyranny, and that now he can do nothing but falsely accuse, and roar like a hungry lion disappointed of his prey. There are still some who all their lifetime are subject to bondage "through fear of death." Their confidence is shaken by so many distressing doubts, that though sincerely engaged in the service of God, they can never think of death without sensible dread; and often they are afraid, that when the last conflict shall come, they will be so overwhelmed with terror and despair, that they shall prove a dishonour to their Christian profession. I recollect a sickly, but pious lady, who with a profusion of tears, expressed her anxiety and fear in the view of her approaching end; and there seemed to be ground for her foreboding apprehensions, because, from the beginning of her profession, she had enjoyed no comfortable assurance, but was of the number of those who, though they "fear God, and obey the voice of his servant, yet walk in darkness and have no light" of comfort. But mark the goodness of God, and the fidelity of the Great Shepherd. Some months afterwards I saw this lady on her death-bed, and was astonished to find that Christ had delivered her entirely from her bondage. She was now near to her end and knew it, but she shed no tears now but those of joy and gratitude. All her darkness and sorrow were gone, and her heart glowed with love to the Redeemer, and all her anxiety now was to depart and be with Jesus. There was, as it were, a beaming of heaven in her countenance. I had before tried to comfort her, but now I sat down by her bedside to listen to the gracious words which proceeded from her mouth, and could not but send up the fervent aspiration, "O let me die the death of the righteous, and let my last end be like hers." Then I knew that there was one who had conquered death, and him who has the power of death; for Satan, to the last moment, was not permitted to molest her.

No arguments have ever so powerfully operated on my mind, to convice me of the reality and power of experimental religion, as witnessing the last exercises of some of God's children. Some of these scenes, though long past, have left an indelible impression on my memory; and I hope a salutary impression on my heart.

Another lady, and a near relative of the former, I had often observed passing along her way, humble, gentle, silent, evidently not seeking to be conspicuous, but rather to remain unnoticed and unknown. She had a few chosen female friends, with whom she freely communicated, for her heart was affectionate, and her disposition sociable—to these she poured out her inmost soul, and received from them a similar return. She was crushed under a habitual feeling of domestic affliction; but not of that kind which freely utters its complaints, and engages the sympathy of many; but her sorrows were such as her delicacy of feeling did not permit her even to allude to; the conduct of an imprudent father, weighed heavily on her spirits; but towards him—and her mother being dead, she kept his house—she was assiduously respectful; and while he made himself the laughing stock of his acquaintances, she endeavoured to make his home comfortable. But often, I thought, that her lively sensibility to the ridicule and reproaches which fell upon him, would be an injury to her delicate constitution; and the more so, because this was a subject on which she would not converse, even with the intimate, confidential friends, before mentioned. It was evident, that her health was slowly giving way, and that the disease which carries off nearly one half of the adults in this land, was secretly consuming her vitals. But she never complained, and seemed rather to become more cheerful, as her eye became more brilliant and her cheeks more pallid. She was for a long time after this, seen occupying her humble retired place in the house of God, and still went her accustomed rounds among her poor and sick neighbours, while doing every thing to render home comfortable to her restless, unhappy parent. At length, however, her strength failed, and she was obliged to confine herself to the house, and before long to her bed. Being informed of this, as being her pastor, I visited her. Hitherto her extreme modesty and retired habits had prevented me from having much personal acquaintance with this excellent woman. I was accompanied to the house by one of her intimate friends, who still lives, and if she should see this paper will readily recognize the portrait of her beloved friend. The house was a cottage, and all its furniture of home manufacture; but upon the whole there was impressed a neatness and order, which indicated a superior taste in her who had long had the sole management. I did not know but that from her habitual reserve and silence, she would be embarrassed in her feelings, and reserved in her communications; but I was happily disappointed. She received me with an affectionate smile, and a cordial shake of the hand, and said that she was pleased that I had thought it worth my while to come and see a poor dying woman. Not many minutes were spent in compliments, or general remarks; she entered freely and most intelligently, into a narrative of her religious exercises, which had commenced at an early period of her life, but expatiated in the sweetest manner, on the divine excellencies of the Saviour; not as one who was speaking what she had learned from others, or from the mere exertion of her own intellect; but as one who felt in the heart every word which she uttered. There was a gentleness, a suavity, and a meek humility expressed in every tone of her voice, and the same depicted on every lineament of her countenance. Though, when in health, she was never reckoned beautiful, yet there was now in her countenance, animated with hope and love, and religious joy, or rather peace, a beauty of countenance which I never saw equalled. It was what may without impropriety be called *spiritual beauty.* I found what I had not known before, that her mind had been highly cultivated by reading. and this was manifest in the propriety, and indeed I may say, elegance of her language. Not that she aimed at saying fine things. Such an idea never entered her humble mind; but possessing, naturally, a good understanding, which she had carefully improved by reading, especially the best religious authors, and being now animated with a flow of pious affection, which seemed never to ebb; all these things gave her language a fluency, a glow, and a vividness, which was truly remarkable. I have often regretted that I had not put down, at the time, her most striking expressions, but the mere words could convey no more than the shadow of such a scene. It has often been remarked, that the speeches of great orators, when written and read, have scarcely a resemblance to the same speeches, delivered with all the pathos, the grace, and the varied intonations and gestures of the orator. The same may more truly be said of the sayings of the lying Christian; we may catch the very words, but the spirit, the sacred and solemn tones, free from all affectation, the heavenly serenity of countenance, and the nameless methods of manifesting the pious affections of the heart, never can be preserved, nor distinctly conveyed, by words, to others. The mind of this young lady possessed a uniform serenity, undisturbed with fears, doubts, or cares. Every thing seemed right to her submissive temper. It was enough, that her heavenly Father appointed it to be so. For many weeks she lay in this state of perfect tranquillity, as it were in the suburbs of heaven; and I believe no one ever heard a complaint from her lips. Even that grief which had preyed on her health, when able to go about, had now ceased to cause her pain. Hers was, in my apprehension, the nearest approximation to complete happiness which I ever saw upon earth; yet there was no violence of feeling, no agitation, no rapture. It was that kind of happiness which from its gentleness and calmness, is capable of continuance. As it was her request that I should visit her often, I did so as frequently as the distance of my residence, and other avocations would permit; not, as I often said, with any expectation of communicating any good to her, but of receiving spiritual benefit from her heavenly conversation. O! how often did I wish that the boldest infidels—and they were rampant at that time—could have been introduced into the chamber of this dying saint. I often, especially after witnessing this scene, endeavoured to describe to such as attended preaching, the power of religion to sustain the soul in the last earthly conflict; but they were incredulous as to the facts, or ascribed them to some strange enthusiasm which buoyed up the soul in a preternatural manner. But here there was no enthusiasm—nothing approaching to what may be called a heated imagination. All was sober—all was serene—all was gentle—all was rational; and, although five and forty years have passed since this scene was witnessed, the impression on my mind, is distinct and vivid. The indescribable countenance, calm but animated, pale with disease, but lighted up with an unearthly smile; the sweet and affectionate tones of voice—the patient, submissive, cheerful, grateful temper, are all remembered with a vividness and permanence with which I remember nothing of recent occurrence. When I think of such scenes, I have often thought and said, "if this be delusion, then let my soul for ever remain under such delusion."

If the foregoing was a sample of the death-bed exercises of all Christians, then would I say, that his last days are his best days, and the day of death happier than the day of birth. This, however, is far from being a true view of the general fact. It is a select case—one of a thousand—upon the whole, the happiest death I ever witnessed. I have, indeed, seen dying persons agitated with a kind of delirious rapture; in which the imagination has been so excited, that the person looked and spoke, as if the objects of another world were actually present to the view. In such case, the nervous system loses its tone, and when the general feelings are pious, and the thoughts directed heavenward, the whole system is thrilled with an indescribable emotion. And we have a number of recorded death-scenes, which partake of this character; and are greatly admired and extolled by the injudicious and fanatical. Scenes of this kind are frequently the effect of disease, and sometimes of medicine operating on the idiosyncrasy of particular persons. Such persons may be pious, but the extraordinary exhilaration and exstasy, of which they are the subjects, ought not to be ascribed to supernatural influence, but to physical causes. Between such experiences, and the case described above, there is no more resemblance, than between a blazing meteor, which soon burns itself out, and the steady, genial beams of the vernal sun. I once witnessed an extraordinary scene of this kind in a skeptic, who neglected religion, and scoffed at its professors, till very near the close of life; and then seemed to be agitated and exhilarated with religious ideas and feelings, leading him to profess his faith in Christ, and to rejoice, and exult in the assurance of salvation, and all this without any previous conviction of sin, and unmingled at the time with deep penitential

20*

feelings. Well, why might it not have been an instance of sovereign grace, like that of the thief on the cross? It is *possible*. As in life, that piety which is founded on knowledge, and in which the faculties of the mind continue to be well balanced, and the judgment sound, is by far the least suspicious; so those death-bed exercises, which are of a similar character, are much to be preferred to those which are flighty, and in which reason seems to regulate the helm no longer; but an excited, and irregular imagination assumes the government of the man. According to this rule, some glowing narratives of death-scenes will be set aside, as, if not spurious, yet not deserving to be admired and celebrated as they often are.

CHAPTER XVII.

Death bed Exercises of Andrew Rivet.

I PROPOSE now to give a summary view of the recorded experiences of several eminent persons on their death-bed; and as comparisons among the living are odious, so also among the dead I will endeavour to act the part of an impartial and faithful narrator, but having given my analysis I will leave my readers to judge respecting the genuineness of the devotion of the persons whose exercises shall be introduced. Our accounts of the death-scenes of the apostles are too brief to enable us to say much about them; but judging from their epistles, we may conclude, that they met death, not only with firmness, but with joy. Not one of them ever expresses the least fear of death; but on the contrary, Paul speaks with exultation of the prospect before him; for he exclaims, " I am now ready to be offered up and the time of my departure is at hand. I have fought a good fight, I have finished my course, I have kept the faith;

henceforth there is laid up for me a crown of righteousness, which God, the righteous Judge, will give me at that day, and not to me only but to all who love his appearing." And Peter who knew that he was to go out of the world by a violent death as Christ had showed him; yet seems to be no how troubled about it, but when old, speaks of it with the utmost composure. "Yea, I think it meet," says he, "as long as I am in this tabernacle, to stir you up by putting you in remembrance; knowing that shortly I must put off this my tabernacle, even as our Lord Jesus Christ hath showed me." No doubt, John, the beloved disciple, sweetly fell asleep, with "love" upon his lips and in his heart. His whole soul seems to have been dissolved into love, and to such a man death could have no terrors. His brother James, who was slain by the sword of Herod, is the only one of the apostles of whose death we have an account in the sacred word; except the awful account of the suicide of the traitor. Of the circumstances of the death of James, who seems to have been one of the most distinguished, and who always, when a selection was made to witness any particular scene, was one of them; the historian, with characteristic brevity, says, " Now about that time, Herod the king, stretched forth his hands to vex certain of the church. AND HE KILLED JAMES, THE BROTHER OF JOHN, WITH THE SWORD." From this we may learn, that in order to go safely to heaven, it is not necessary, that we should have a laudatory obituary on earth. I have often been shocked with the thought, that while a man's eulogy is pronounced upon earth, the poor soul may be writhing and blaspheming in the torments of hell! Among the primitive members of the Church, Stephen was the first martyr, and his death was—I will not say heroic—for heroes know nothing of Christ or heaven—but I will say it was CHRISTIAN; which is a much better style of dying, than any of the heathen heroes or heroines knew any thing about. He was well prepared, for he had just before been favoured with a direct view into heaven, and saw

Christ on the right hand of God. No wounds on the body would be felt by one absorbed in such a heavenly vision. O how little can they harm us, who can do no more than kill the body! They rushed upon the man and hurried him to the place of execution, and stoned him, "calling on [God,] and saying, Lord Jesus, receive my spirit. And he kneeled down and cried with a loud voice, Lord, lay not this sin to their charge. And when he had said this, he fell asleep." There was nothing wanting here to render this a glorious death. And as he is called the protomartyr, so his death was a prototype of the deaths of succeeding martyrs. The accounts given of the joys and triumphs of some of them, approximate to miracle; but we know not how insensible to bodily pain, the soul may be rendered, which is overflowing with the love of Christ. This is the true secret of their ambition to be crucified or burnt, or cast to the wild beasts. But as these martyrs seem to have been another race of men from us, and lived in times very different from ours, let us come down and contemplate the dying Christian in circumstances similar to our own; and see what grace can do, in these latter days. And I propose to select the experiences of men of different countries. The accounts which I shall bring forward are not new: to some of my readers they may all be familiar; but as the men were eminent in the church, and distinguished for talents, their biographies being commonly known, will answer the end in view, better than the death-bed exercises of unknown persons, of whose lives we could have no satisfactory information.

The first person of whose dying exercises I propose to give a condensed narrative is ANDREW RIVET, a Frenchman by birth and education, but who spent the greater part of his life in Holland; where, at Leyden, he was professor of theology. The learned need not be informed, that in that age when theology was more thoroughly studied, than in any other since the apostles' days, Andrew Rivet had no superior, whether you contemplate him as an exegetical or polemical theologian. His acquaintance with the Christian fathers was most exact and extensive; and he knew how to estimate their labours, and what deference was due to their authority, of which he gave full evidence, in the work entitled CRITICI SACRI, which is now the best guide on this subject, which the young theologian can follow. Rivet's theology was as sound as it was extensive. His great learning did not turn his head or lead him into heresy; but it will be seen by the following narrative abridged from Middleton, how little value he set on all his learning, compared with the teaching of the divine Spirit.

Having preached a sermon on Christmas day, he was, immediately afterwards, taken ill, with a constipation of the bowels. Of a beloved niece, who attended on him, he asked what she thought of his disease, which he thought would prove mortal. She answered, that she was of the same opinion, but that he had nothing to fear, having been long prepared to follow God, when he should call—and that his life had already been long, and nothing remained to be desired, but that it should be crowned with a happy and glorious end! "Thou speakest right," said he, "and I pray thee always address thyself to me with like speeches, and while my sickness continues, depart not from me, day nor night. Promise me now that thou wilt keep a cheerful countenance, and that thou wilt speak nothing to me, but what may administer joy and support to me. Although I fear not death, yet I fear the trial of those pains which I have always had a very sharp feeling of." Then, suddenly turning his speech unto God, he said, "Great God, thou art my Father, thou hast given me both life and a new life; thou hast taught me from my youth, and I have declared thy wonderful works; forsake me not now in my old age. Hitherto, through thy peculiar favour, thou hast preserved me sound in my body and my faculties, and the functions of my mind have not been impaired, so that a little before I was oppressed by this disease, I found myself as apt and ready for the exercise of my vocation, as in my flour ishing youth. O Lord God! if it be thy will that I should longer attend upon thy service, thou canst assuage my disease in one moment; but if thou hast decreed otherwise, *thy will be done.* This one thing I beg with most inward affections, that thou wilt make me conformable to thy good will—let not thy good Spirit depart from me, that in this conflict thy strength may make me a conqueror; accomplish this, O Lord, for thine own sake, and since thou hast employed me in thy work, grant that I may die an honourable death, and such as may be an example unto others: that I may stand fast in that sound doctrine which I have taught, and may make a good confession thereof before witnesses—that thereby thy church may be both instructed and edified. Let me apply to myself by a lively faith, all the promises of the gospel, and let them put forth their efficacy in me, unto my joy and eternal consolation, that nothing in the world, neither affliction nor distress, may separate me from thee, or cause me to doubt of thy love and favour. Thou knowest my weakness and infirmities: permit not the grievousness of my pain to cast me into impatience or murmuring. Either make my pains tolerable, or furnish me with fortitude and constancy sufficient to bear them: that I may not offend with my tongue, keep thou the door of my lips!" The pains of his disease were very great, but he continued to call upon God for help and for support. His expressions of his own sinfulness and weakness were of the most abasing kind. Confessing himself to be a miserable sinner, and casting away all confidence in any good thing which he had done in his life, he accused his own defects, and ascribed unto God all the good which he had ever done, often repeating such expressions as these: " It is God that hath wrought the work for me; shall I allege or plead my own righteousness before Him? Far be that from me. If I should justify myself, my own mouth would condemn me. I will rather open my sin before Him in a most humble confession of it, and pray that He will increase in me the grace of true repentance; yea, let Him wear out this body with sorrow, it matters not, so He give to me a broken and a contrite spirit, which is a sacrifice acceptable unto himself. As for my part, I do most willingly offer up myself. Accept, O Lord, this imperfect sacrifice, and supply the defects thereof by the perfect righteousness of that great High Priest, who, through the eternal Spirit, offered himself unto God without spot. Let me be accepted as a living sacrifice, holy, and well pleasing unto God, which is our reasonable service. Crucify, O Lord, this old man, that the body of sin may be utterly destroyed, and that I may rise to newness of life. *The wages of sin is death, but the gift of God is eternal life, through Jesus Christ, our Lord."* He repeated the word GIFT, and added, " it is mere grace, not of works, but of him that calleth." *" Who shall lay any thing to the charge of God's elect? It is God that justifieth. Who is he that condemneth? It is Christ that died; yea, rather, that is risen again, who is even at the right hand of God, who also maketh intercession for us."*

After a short sleep, he proceeded, in the following strain: " I am God's, and He will save me. He hath honoured me with a holy calling, and hath not suffered his gift to be altogether useless in me, as to the edification of his church. As to myself, I can most truly affirm, that I have not served Him for filthy lucre, but with a sincere heart; and that I myself was first persuaded of the truth of the gospel, before I preached it to others. I tasted the good word of God, which, by its power, pierceth to the dividing asunder of soul and spirit, and is a discerner of the thoughts and intents of the heart. Thou hast known my heart, O eternal God! Thou knowest that I am not ashamed of the gospel of Christ, but have esteemed it my only honour to serve thee; and that I have delighted myself in the pleasure of obeying thy will. Such was thy goodness to me. I truly and humbly acknowledge that whatsoever good thing was in me, flowed from thy grace; but my defects ought to be ascribed to my inbred corruption. Alas! I acknowledge this with humble and serious repentance. How often have I sinned in so holy a charge, not only by omitting many things which I ought to have done, but also by doing many things amiss. Long since had I been cast off, were it not that I had to do with so good a Lord, who hath borne with me, and hath been so gracious to me, as not to exact a severe account of my words and works. Alas! O Lord my God! enter not into judgment with thy servant; for in thy sight shall no man living be justified. Let me be found, not having my own righteousness, but the righteousness of thy Son; for the sake of whom I beg thy favour. Pardon, O my God! pardon the iniquity of thy servant, who is devoted to thy fear. I refuse not thy discipline—I know it is necessary. Only this I earnestly beg, that it may turn to my salvation. 'Chasten me, O Lord, but in measure, lest thou bring me to nothing.' Let not my trial exceed my strength, lest I sin through impatience, and become a scandal to those I should edify." He uttered many similar expressions, for which we have not room.

To Renessius, a doctor of divinity, who came to see him, he said, "I pray you testify unto all men, that I die in the faith and the doctrine which I have always delivered, both in preaching and writing; and if in some things I have erred, I pray God, that He will make perfect all my imperfections."

He received the visits of all who expressed a desire to see him, and would have none hindered from coming to him. "Let all that will," said he, "have access to visit me. I ought to give an example of dying to other men." And to those who stood around his bed, he said, "Come, see a man, who is an example of the great mercy of God. What shall I render unto him? All his benefits overwhelm me. He hath so disposed my life, that in my whole course, I have had a healthy body. He hath heaped upon me both temporal and spiritual blessings; and now, before I am rendered feeble or morose, through old age, he comes unto me and prevents me. He has both called me, and made me willing to follow at his call. And now, when the end of my life is within my view, he still affords me the perfect use of reason, that I may praise my God in the land of the living, and instruct my neighbours by my example. Pray for me, my friends, that this grace may be continued unto me, until I draw my last breath; that He will strengthen my faith, confirm my patience, and raise my hope. He hath already captivated all my affections to his will. I have cast the care of me, of mine, of life, and all my affairs, upon him. Let him do with my body as it pleaseth him, so it may but be well with my soul. * * * And now there is nothing I am concerned about, neither is my life dear unto me, so that I may finish my course with joy, and fulfil the ministry which I have received of the Lord; which is best done at the last."

He would not permit any clergyman who came to see him, to go away without praying with him. It grieved him much that his wife, who was of feeble health, should be subjected to so much fatigue and watchfulness in attending on him. But as she was unwilling to leave him, he said, "Since thou wilt have it so, tarry; it is a pleasure to me to see thee. The Lord strengthen thee!" Friday night was spent in grievous pains, and in most ardent prayers for the church of God, for the princes, who were defenders of it, for the people that lived under their jurisdiction, and for the pastors, to whom the care of souls was committed. He seemed to be greatly interested in behalf of the United Provinces of Holland. "O God," said he, "withdraw not thy protection from these Provinces; neither remove thy candlestick away. Let not thine anger burn against them, because of that impiety and profaneness which hath made too great a progress. Rather bow their hearts unto repentance, and convert them, that thy judgments may be prevented. Let them coalesce in one body; especially let them be joined unto thee, without whom all union is but conspiracy. Preside in their Assembly; and bend their hearts, so that all their decrees may lean to the good of the Commonwealth, and especially of the church," &c.

His sufferings were exceedingly great, but he bore them with wonderful patience, and whenever there was the least interval of ease, he was engaged in prayer or exhortation. On the last day of December, which closed the current year, Mr. Rivet, after having endured indescribable agonies from the disease, and from the remedies made use of, offered up the following fervent prayer for the church:—" O Lord, it is thy possession, which thou hast purchased with thy own blood. Forsake not thy own work—let a holy jealousy be kindled in thee. Lift up on high the arms of thy power, and bring down the audacious ones, which tyrannize over thy flock. Rebuke thou the negligent that heal her wounds slightly. Reduce in the right way those that wander, and strengthen those ready to fall through division. Gather both the one and the other to thyself, into one body, building them up upon the foundations of the apostles and prophets, Jesus Christ himself being the chief corner stone, in whom all the building fitly framed together, groweth into a holy temple in the Lord." And then making a little pause, he said, " I have been one of those builders; I have brought what I received from the Lord that I might put to my helping hand, with others, towards the building of the temple; and I myself shall be a living stone in the house."

On the first day of the year 1651, and the Lord's day, upon opening his eyes, he said, " O Lord, thou hast granted me to see the beginning of the year. Thou hast measured out my time until the middle of this age." Having sent to the Hague for his son, he inquired respecting the weather, and being informed that the cold was sharp and severe, he prayed thus, " O my God, bring my son unto me, that I may see him, embrace him, and bless him, before I die." Then turning to his wife, he said, " dost thou think that this earnest desire to see my son proceeds from mere natural affection? Nothing less. Truly I love no man any more according to the flesh. I earnestly desire his eternal salvation, and I hope to have such discourses with him, which may increase his zeal in adorning his spiritual vocation." (His son was a minister.) "I have yet spirit and utterance sufficient for this work. Let none be hindered from coming to me. It is usual for a man in my station, by admonishing others, publicly to make profession of his own faith. Not for the sake of a little vain-glory, O Lord, thou knowest; for it little concerns me to be approved unto men, provided I may approve myself unto God. But I desire the salvation of many, and to give testimony to the truth of those things which I have publicly taught."

Some officers of the garrison having come to see him, two or three of whom were from France, he addressed them in the following manner, "I rejoice that I have an opportunity to make a confession of my faith before you that are my countrymen; and I pray you to keep it in memory, and give testimony of it, where it shall be necessary. You see before you, a man, weak indeed, but without guile, who solemnly protesteth, that he hath never published in his writings, nor taught with his lips, any thing that did not agree with the sense of his heart, and the doctrine which hath been delivered to us by the prophets and apostles, which is the same with that laid down in the Confession of Faith of our churches, in which I have lived, and in which I purpose to die. The Lord God Almighty confirm you in that faith, so that nothing may move you from it. 'For what will it profit a man if he gain the whole world and lose his own soul?' Seek ye first the kingdom of God, and the righteousness thereof, and then all other things shall be added unto you. Learn to number your days, and get a wise heart. Look upon me, and let me be as an example unto you. It is but eight days since I preached to you of man's frailty, being myself in health and lively at that time, and now you see the truth of what I said, in myself." And then taking leave of them he said, "The Lord deliver you from the allurements of the world, and give you an increase of his fear and of all spiritual gifts."

When his visiters were all gone, and his own family stood around his bed, he said to his niece, "My daughter, do not depart from me, but persist with me in the duty of prayer. Do not fear to rehearse all those words to me, which God shall suggest unto thy heart or mouth. This sweet and pleasing communication shall help to pass over the night with the more ease. And God will be with us and assist our good intentions. He will help our weaknesses and afford us matter of supplications, and thanksgivings. Such discourses are pleasing unto him. He attends unto them that fear him, when they talk together of those things that belong to the salvation of their souls." And then, as one in a rapture, he exclaimed, " My God, thou hast drawn me and I was drawn. Thou hast known me from my mother's womb with a merciful and efficacious knowledge. Thou hast called me by name. Thou hast bored mine ears, and I was attentive. I have declared thy message in the congregation, and thy word was sweeter than honey in my mouth. Who am I, O God, but dust and ashes, an earthen and a frail vessel, into which, notwithstanding, thou hast been pleased to pour a holy liquor, and seed of immortality. Thou livest, and thou makest me to live. I shall not die, but live for ever, with that 'life which is hid with Christ in God.' Blessed and holy is he who hath a part in the first resurrection: over him the second death shall have no power. 'Behold I am dead, and also raised from the dead. I live, but not in myself, but in the life of the Son of God, who loved me, and gave himself for me.' Thou hast chosen me before thou gavest me a being. And it pleased thee that I should be born of believing parents, and especially of a mother eminent in holiness, who dedicated me to thy service from my tender years. With what care and affection did she implant the seeds of piety in me. And the Almighty God, who worketh in all, gave his blessing to this diligent nurture, and heard her ardent prayers; and my ministry hath been accepted of him. I am thy servant, O my God, thou hast taught me from my youth; and I have taught thy wonderful works, and thy grace unto this day; for thy gifts have not been without fruit in me. Thou usest weak instruments for the accomplishing of thy work. Thou hast pardoned, thou hast helped me, thou hast accepted the truth and sincerity of my heart. And now, O my God, seeing it is evident that thou wilt have me retire from this valley of miseries, do not thou forsake me in this last and important act. If it be thy will, that I die, that also is my will. I am ready—my heart is prepared. I give thee my heart, for that is it which thou requirest. Let this gift be approved by thee. Receive this gift which is thy own, from him to whom thou hast given all things—who gives himself to thee. O Lord, I give thee thanks; thou instructest me, thou enlightenest me, thou talkest with my soul, O Lord. Thou embracest me in the arms of thy mercy. Grant also that I may embrace thee, by a lively faith, and that I may apply unto myself the promises of the gospel, which I have proposed unto others. Let them be effectual in me, that by them I may be supported against all pains, yea, death itself."

Mr. Rivet had a brother in the ministry nearly as eminent as himself, whom he loved with a very sincere and tender affection. The niece who now attended on him, was the daughter of this brother, and that he might know the gracious dealings of God towards him in his sickness, he requested his niece to write down whatever he might say, from time to time, and communicate it to her father. "Not," says he, "that I would procure praise to myself, but I would have it known to all, that the religion which I have professed and taught in the name of God, is the true religion, and that alone which leads men unto salvation; and, particularly, I would have my brother informed of that inestimable grace which I have received of God, that he may be abundantly comforted and strengthened in his expectation of a better life, which I already enjoy. O! with how great love have I loved and esteemed him! Yea, I have loved the gifts of God in him, and shall love them to the last. I pray God, who is the giver of every good gift, that he will strengthen and make perfect his own work in him. O Lord God, I pray not only for my brother, but for all those in France to whom thou hast committed the conduct and rule of the churches. Bless their persons, sanctify their gifts, grant that they may return to the simplicity which is in Christ, and that they detract not from the glory of God, to ascribe unto man what belongs to his salvation." He now broke out in an extraordinary transport, "O great and immense mercy! who can but be rapt into admiration? He gives both being and well-being,—he bestows his gifts, he supporteth, he pardoneth, he worketh in us both to will and to do, according to his good pleasure, and when himself hath given and wrought all this, yet he gives to us an eternal reward." But not satisfied with sending messages to his brother, on the second day of January he requested to be raised up and placed in a chair, that he might write to him; and, accordingly, he penned, with his own hand, a farewell letter, full of solemnity and tenderness. He wrote also to his nephew,—after which exertion he found himself much exhausted. But the only thing which gave him any uneasiness of mind, was, lest he should be disappointed in seeing his son. But his comforts were not uninterrupted. After his regular physicians had given him up, some persons who had known relief, in such cases, from a particular remedy, urged that it should be tried. He submitted, but while the experiment put him to great pain, it produced no change for the better; and when it was over, his mind appeared to be perturbed and uncomfortable. "Alas!" said he, "He is departed from me, that made glad my heart. I have grieved that Holy Spirit, the comforter, who had filled my soul with peace and joy. I have been so wretched and unhappy as to give ear to those who spoke to me of my returning to the world. I have been tickled with the desire of living, and how could such a thing be, after the fruits of the heavenly Canaan had been tasted?" Here he appeared much distressed, and casting his arms about the neck of his beloved niece, exclaimed, "my dear niece, help me, continue to discourse of good things to me.—Call upon the Comforter to return and renew that excellent work which he had begun in me. O, return! return! confirm me with thy strength before I go hence and be seen no more." He remained in this state of distress for a short time—when he was reminded of the precious promises of God; but being exhausted, he fell into a swoon. When he opened his eyes, he said to his wife, who was by him, " my dearest yoke-fellow, we have lived together in peace for thirty years, and I thank thee for thy help, which hath been a great comfort unto me, for I did cast all domestic cares on thee; continue, I beseech thee, to love my children with that pious affection which thou hast hitherto," (the children were by a former wife.) Then turning to his son, who had arrived that morning, he said, "and thou my son, love and honour this dearest companion of my life, the partner of all my joys and my sorrows, who hath done the duty of a mother towards thee.—This I desire of thee, and this I command thee, as thou expectest a blessing from God upon what I have gotten for my labour,—divide it between you, without quarrelling or contention, according to what is just and right." Then taking hold of both their hands and joining them together, he said, " promise that you will maintain a holy and mutual friendship with each other,"—to which they gave their assent. Then turning to his wife, he said, "the Lord bless thee, my dear love, and strengthen thee. He is a husband to the widow, and a father of the fatherless."

And to his son, " The Almighty Father bless thee, my son, guide thee in all thy ways, enrich thee with all Christian virtues, and plentifully make thee to abound in all spiritual and temporal blessings! Regard not the world, nor its deceitful hopes, for the world passeth away, and the lusts thereof. Place all thy felicity in the blessing of God. Be strong in faith, and prepared unto every good work. Let the peace of God dwell in thee, and make thee peaceable and kind." And to his niece, he said, "Farewell, my dear niece, we have a kindred in the heavens, which shall endure for ever."

After many other discourses, similar to those recorded, he again collected his family and blessed them, and desired all to retire and leave him alone. His niece, who scarcely ever went out of his sight, asked if he wished her to withdraw also. He said, "Do not go from me, but be thou a witness of my last hours." After he had exhausted himself with conversation with his son, Mr. Hulsius, and others, he was asked how he did. He said, "Very well—I feel no pain—I am filled with the grace of God—I am not sensible of cold or heat—I fear, no more, the inconveniences of temporal life—the Spirit of God strengthens me, and affords me abundant consolations. I have no doubt of my salvation. He hath set me on high. He hath hid me in his hiding place. He hath fenced me round about, and hath perfected whatsoever concerns me. I am like a vessel filled with pure water which no agitation troubles. It is God that justifieth me, who shall condemn? It is Christ that died, yea rather is risen again." * * * "O my God, I thank thee that thou hast given me the spirit of humility, sincerity and truth. I have not been as a tinkling cymbal. O Lord, thou knowest the secrets of my soul, and my inmost thoughts. Thou hast taught me in the school of true doctrine, and I have above all sought the glory of thy name. O Lord, I wait for the moment which thou hast determined. I believe, I persevere, I am not troubled. The Spirit of God witnesseth with my spirit that I am a child of God."

Though every day was expected to be his last, yet the strength of his constitution enabled him to hold out until Saturday, January 7, 1651. To the last, he continued to spend his whole time, when awake, in prayer, and in such discourses as we have recorded. On Thursday morning, when he saw the light of day, he said, "It is day-light. I shall shortly no more know the difference between day and night. I am come to the eve of that great and eternal day, and am going to that place, where the sun shall no more give light. God will be an everlasting light unto me; and already, O Lord, thou sendest the rays of that light into my soul, and openest my eyes that I may perceive them. O how powerfully dost thou work in me! While this old man decays, thou puttest on me the new man, which is renewed in knowledge after the image of him that created it. Deliver me from this prison, that I may celebrate thy name; yet neither do I so contemn this body, as not to think of its restoration; for I know the dead shall live, yea, my dead body. It is sown in corruption, it shall be raised in incorruption; it is sown a vile body, but it will rise a glorious body; it is sown in weakness, but it shall be raised again in power. In a word, it shall be conformed to the glorious body of our Lord Jesus Christ, who is become the first fruits of them that sleep. I shall see him in my flesh —mine own eyes shall see him—I shall behold his face in righteousness, and shall be satisfied with his likeness when I awake." The whole of this day was spent in such like discourses. Among other things, he said, "The sense of divine favour increaseth in me every moment. My pains are tolerable, and my joys inestimable. I am no more vexed with earthly cares. I remember when any new book came out, how earnestly I have longed after it—but now all that is but dust. Thou art my all, O Lord, my good is to approach unto thee. O, what a library have I in God, in whom are all the treasures of wisdom and knowledge! Thou art the teacher of spirits—I have learned more divinity in these ten days that thou hast come to visit me, than I did in fifty years before." The last words he attempted to utter, were those of Paul, "I have fought a good fight," &c. and when others assisted him to finish them, he said, AMEN.

CHAPTER XVIII.

Death-bed exercises and speeches of the Rev. Thomas Halyburton

HAVING in a former chapter given an account of Halyburton's conversion, written by himself, in mature age, it will be gratifying to the pious reader to learn how he ended his course; and how his religion sustained him in the last trying conflict. And here, as in the case of Rivet, much opportunity was given to this holy man to leave behind him an ample testimony of the preciousness of the Lord Jesus Christ, and of the power of divine grace to support and comfort the true believer, even in the pangs of dissolution. When first seized with mortal sickness, he experienced, for a while, a terrible conflict, in which he was afraid that his faith would fail; but his God was merciful and faithful to his promises, and came to his relief. To one who came to see him, he said, "I have a great conflict, and my faith is like to fail. O that I may be kept now in this last trial, that is ensuing, from being an offence to God and his people." When some of his brethren came to see him, he said, "I am but young, and have but little experience, but this death-bed now makes me old, and therefore I use the freedom to exhort you to faithfulness in the Lord's work. You will never repent this. He is a good Master, I have always found him so. If I had a thousand lives, I would think them all too little to employ in his service." But for several days he was under a cloud, and his spiritual joys had deserted him; and when a friend came in, he said, "O what a terrible conflict I had yesterday; but now I can say, 'I have fought the good fight, I have kept the faith.' Now he has filled my mouth with a new song. 'Jehovah Jireh, in the mount of the Lord.' Praise, praise is comely for the upright. Shortly I shall get a different view of God from what I have ever had, and shall be more qualified to praise him than ever. O! the thoughts of an incarnate God are sweet and ravishing. And how do I wonder at myself that I do not love him more. O that I could honour him! What a wonder that I enjoy so much composure under all my bodily trouble, and in view of approaching death. O what a mercy, that I have the use of my reason till I have declared his goodness unto me." To his wife he said, " He came to me in the third watch of the night, walking upon the waters, and he said unto me, 'I am Alpha and Omega, the beginning and the end. I was dead and am alive, and live for ever more, and have the keys of hell and death.' 'He stilleth the tempest, and O there is a sweet calm in my soul.'" To one who requested him to be careful of his health, he replied, " I'll strive to last as long as I can, and I'll get my rest ere it be long. I have no more to do with time, but carefully to measure it out for the glory of God." Then he said, "I shall see my Redeemer stand on the earth at the last day; but I hope to see him before that, the Lamb in the midst of the throne. O it will be a beautiful company, 'The spirits of just men made perfect, and Jesus the Mediator of the New Covenant. O for grace, grace, to be patient to the end.'" When one said, "Keep the light of the window from him," he said, " Truly light is sweet, and a pleasant thing it is to behold the sun—the Sun of Righteousness. O glorious light, when the Lamb is the light of the temple. We cannot have a conception of it now, eye hath not seen, nor ear heard," &c. Seeing his youngest child, he caused them to bring her to him, and said, " Mary, my dear, the Lord bless you. The God of your father and of my father bless you.—The God that fed me all my life, the Angel that redeemed me from all evil, bless you and the rest, and be your portion. That is a goodly heritage, better than if I had crowns and sceptres to leave you. My child, I received you from him, and I give you to him again." To his wife he said, " Encourage yourself in the Lord He will keep you, even though you come into enemies' hands, surely he will cause the enemy to treat you well." He then declared his willingness to part with his dearest relatives, and said, "For this is the practical part of religion; to make use of it when we come to the strait. This is a lesson of practical divinity." When the physician came in, he addressed him in the following solemn and pungent language; " Doctor, as to this piece of work, you are nearly at an end with it. I wish you to lay it to heart; death will come to your door also. And it is a business of great moment to die like a Christian; and it is a rare thing. Christ himself has told us that there are few that shall be saved even among them who are outwardly called. I wish the Lord himself may show you kindness. The greatest kindness I am now capable of showing you is, to recommend serious religion to you. There is a reality in religion, doctor, but this is an age that hath lost the sense of it. 'He has not said to the house of Jacob, seek ye my face in vain.' Atheists will one day see whether it be so or not. I bless God that I was educated by godly parents in the principles of the Church of Scotland. I bless him that when I came to riper years, I did, on mature deliberation, make these principles my choice. I bless the Lord, I have been helped ever since to adhere to them, without wavering. I bless him that I have seen, that holiness yields peace and comfort in prosperity and adversity. What should I seek more, or desire more to give me evidence of the reality of religion? Therefore I am not ashamed of the gospel of Christ; for it is the power of God unto salvation to every one that believeth. I am so far from altering my thoughts of religion by reason of the present contempt thrown on it, and opposition made to it, that these things endear it the more to me." After much more of the same kind, he said, "Well, doctor, the Lord be with you, and persuade you to be in earnest. I return you thanks for your attention." After a pause, he proceeded; "Every one that is in Christ Jesus must be a new creature: he must have union with Christ and a new nature. That is the ground work of religion. The Christian religion is little understood by the most of us. O! the gospel of Christ, how purely was it preached in this place, when I was at the University; though I found not the sweetness of it, at that time, as I have found it since. It has fallen on me like showers on the mown grass. Verily there is a reality in religion. Few have lively impressions of it. Now get acquaintance with God. The little acquaintance I have had with God these two days, has more than ten thousand times repaid the pains I have in all my life taken about religion. It is a good thing to have God to go to, when we are turning our face to the wall. 'He is known for a refuge in the palaces of Zion, a very present help in trouble.' O! there is a strange hardness in the heart of man."

To his children, he said, "My children, I have nothing to say to you, but that ye be seekers of God. Fulfil my joy. Alas! that I was so long in beginning to seek God! and yet I was touched with convictions that God was seeking me, before I arrived at the years of some of you." To his eldest daughter he said, "Margaret, you seem sometimes to have convictions; beware of them—they are the most dangerous things you ever meddled with: for although you may seek not God, every one of them is God's messenger; and if you despise God's messenger, he will be avenged on you. My dear, seek the Lord, and be your mother's comfort."

He requested that the 138th of Mr. Rutherford's letters should be read to him, and then said, "This is a book I would recommend to you all; there is more practical religion in that letter, than in some large volumes."

When the three ministers of the place came to see him, he addressed them with great fidelity and affection: —"Dear brethren, it is not from any confidence in myself, but out of a sincere love to you, and from what I myself have experienced, that for your encouragement I presume to say, when the Lord helped me to diligence in studying and meditating, I found him then remarkably shining upon me, and testifying his approbation of a sincere mind. There is nothing to be had with a slack hand." And to one of them who had recently entered the ministry, " Your entry into the ministry, is likely to fall on an evil day; but there is one thing for your encouragement: you have a call. The times will make hard work for you in this place; but that which makes your work the harder is, that the people are hardened under a long course of pure gospel ordinances. However, be faithful, and God will strengthen his own work. I will not say that you will get things brought to the state you would desire; but I'll tell you I have one thought, and I'll abide by it, if ministers will ply their work, though they cannot bring sinners to the Lord, they may make their consciences, that a prophet has been among them, speak for the Lord, whether they will or not."

"Now, brethren, give diligence, hold fast what ye have. I must say a word unto my brethren, it is on my heart. I am young, but I am near the end of my life, and that makes me old. It becomes me to take advice from you, however, I only wish to exhort you to diligence in the common salvation.—I repent I did no more, but I have peace in reflecting that what I did, I did sincerely. He accepts of the mite. It was the delight of my heart to preach the gospel, and it made me sometimes neglect a frail body. I ever thought if I could contribute to the saving of a soul, it would be to me a star, a crown—a glorious crown. I know this was the thing that I aimed at—I desired to decrease, that the bridegroom might increase; and to be nothing, that He might be all, and I rejoice in his exaltation." To two ministers who came from the country, he said, " Brethren, we have need to take care, with the great apostle, lest when we have preached Christ to others, we ourselves should be castaways. We have need to fear, lest it be so. Happy is the man that feareth always. Be diligent in preaching the gospel—let it be your care not only to be diligent in composing sermons, but, above all, to scan your own hearts, to enable you to dive into consciences, to awaken hypocrites, and to separate the precious from the vile—and to do it with such accuracy as not to make sad the hearts of those whom God would have made glad. The great point in religion, and in the management of your ministry, is, that you may obtain the testimony of the great Shepherd, when he shall appear. As to the work of the ministry, it was my delight and my deliberate choice : and were my days lengthened out much more, and the times as troublesome as they are likely to be, I would rather be a contemned minister of God, than the greatest prince on earth. I preached the gospel of Christ with pleasure, and loved it, for my own soul's salvation was upon it; and since I lay down, I have not changed my thoughts about it. I commend it to you all to double your diligence. There may be hard conflicts; you have a prospect of difficulties between you and the grave. We all appear good when untried, but we have need to have on the whole armour of God, to watch and be sober."

To his successor in the parish which he had served before he came to the University, he said, "I have this to say, as to my congregation, that people were my choice. With much peace and pleasure I preached as I could, though not as I should, the gospel of Jesus Christ. Though, in all things, I own myself to have sinned exceedingly before the Lord, yet I have the consolation that I anxiously aimed at leading them to the Lord Jesus, and another foundation can no man lay. I hope you will build on that same foundation, for, as you will in that way save your own soul, so it is the way to save them that hear you. From experience I can say, that the pursuing this sincerely, is the way of salvation. Signify to them, that if it please the Lord to take me away, I die, rejoicing in the faith, and in the profession of what I preached to them, under a low state of body; and, that without this I could have no comfort. I would have my people understand, that the gospel which I recommended to them, if not received, will be a wit ness against them." His successor remarked, "I am persuaded you have seals to your ministry in that parish." He answered, "we are like our Master, set for the fall and rising again of many, though we can do no more; if we are faithful, they shall know that a prophet has been among them."

Mr. Halyburton conversed much with his friends, and most of his discourses have been preserved, but we have only room for a small part of what he uttered on his death-bed. A specimen, however, will serve to show the spirit of the man, and the state of his mind, as well as the whole. There are still some of his dying speeches so excellent, that I cannot think that their insertion will appear tedious to the pious reader. But besides his discourses with his friends and visiters, he drew up a paper in the form of a last will or testimony, in which he gives at large, his views of doctrine and worship. The whole of this paper is highly worthy of attention, but we can only insert the following extract:

"Every thing in God's way and in his word is glorious, honourable, and like himself. He needs none of our testimonies; but it is the least that we can do to signify our wishes to have his praises celebrated. And I, being so many ways obliged, take this solemn occasion to acknowledge, before I leave the world, these, among my other innumerable obligations; and I desire to bequeath this as my last, best legacy, to my family, even my serious and solemn advice, that they should make choice of God for their God. He has been my father's God: the God both of my wife's predecessors and mine; and he has been, we hope, our God; and I recommend him to my children, for their God; solemnly charging them, even all of them, as they will be answerable on the great day, to make it their first care, to seek after peace with God, and reconciliation through Christ crucified; and being reconciled, to make it their constant care to please him in all things. I beseech them with all the bowels of a father, as they love their souls, that they sit not down short of a saving acquaintance with him; that they wait diligently upon the means of grace, and attend the worship of God in all duties, especially secret and family duties, and that they carefully attend public ordinances. Beware of contenting yourselves with the mere form of these duties, but cry to the Lord for communion with Him in them; and for the outpouring of the Spirit, whereby ye may be enabled to worship God who is a Spirit, in spirit. It is my charge to you, and that in which I am more concerned than in any thing relating to you, that you follow him fully, without turning to the right hand, or to the left. In this way I dare promise you blessedness. If you follow this way, I do bless you all, and pray that He who blesses and they are blessed, may bless you all. I have, often as I could, devoted all of you to God; and there is nothing I have so much at heart, as that ye may indeed be the Lord's. And if ye turn aside from this way, I would have this be a standing witness against you, in the day of the Lord. O! that God himself by his grace, may, in a day of his power, determine your tender hearts to seek him early; for then will He be a good portion unto you."

When some people came in to see him, he said, "For these fourteen or fifteen years, I have been studying the promises; but I have seen more of the book of God this night, than in all that time. O the wisdom that is laid up in the book of God! I know, a great deal that comes from a dying man will go for canting and raving, but I bless God, that he has preserved to me the little judgment that I had, and I have been enabled, with composure, to reflect on his dealing with me. I am sober and composed, if I ever was so. And whether men will hear or forbear, this is my testimony. The operations of the Spirit of God, are ridiculed in this day; but if we take away the operations and influences of the Spirit of God, in religion, I know not what is left. He promised the Spirit to lead us into all truth. O! that this generation would awake to seek after the quickening influences of the Spirit. O! for a day of the down-

22 *

pouring of the Spirit from on high, in a work of conversion!—For such a day as that, when the Spirit of God effectually reached our fathers, and brought forth great men, and caused others to be conquered by them! 'The residue of the Spirit is with him.' "

The state of the church was much on his mind, and he was greatly concerned for Scotland, lest a dry, formal, and merely rational religion should prevail; of which he saw some symptoms. He expressed also strong apprehensions that the judgments of God were about to be inflicted on his country. The welfare of his pupils also engaged much of his attention. He often expressed a desire to have them around him, that he might give them one practical lecture from his death-bed. But as this could not be done, it being vacation, he dictated a letter to the students of theology, in which he gives them solemn and useful advice. He recommended to them the perusal of the writings of the great Dr. Owen; but immediately added, "But the word of God, in dependence on the Spirit of God, must be your study and meditation, day and night. Words cannot express what I have found of God, since I came to this bed of languishing. I am bold to recommend to you this work, as the most noble, honourable, and advantageous you can be employed in. And I am this day sure, from experience, that it is better to serve the Lord in the gospel of his Son, than to serve the greatest princes on earth, in the highest station. If God help you in this service, the reward is too great to be expressed. My thoughts, my words are swallowed up, and my affection toward you is such, that my body would quite sink to speak what is in my heart, of love to you, and desire to have you acquainted with my dearest Lord, to whom I was always deeply obliged, but am now so much indebted that I fear to mention how good he has been to my soul. O! choose him—cleave to him—serve him—study to know him more and more—live in communion with him. Never rest until you reach eternal communion with him. I have desired my brother-in-law to sign this in my name. I wish nothing more than that when you have done much service to the church here, I may have the happiness of hearing you approved by the Great Shepherd."

As his disease was a pulmonary consumption, he lasted long, and retained the uninterrupted exercise of his reason, and after the first severe conflict, of which mention was made, he enjoyed peace and joy without intermission, and manifested in various ways, and particularly by his heavenly discourse, the power of divine grace, and the eminence of that faith in Christ, by which he was so remarkably supported to the end. He lost no opportunity of seeking to benefit all who approached him, and often addressed himself to his wife and children individually, in the most tender and earnest manner. And as many ministers came to see him, he exercised great fidelity in his solemn exhortations to them, to be diligent and faithful in the work of the Lord. At length the powers of nature were exhausted, and for some days he was in a dying state. Among his last words were, "Free grace, free grace—not unto me." And when his speech had utterly failed, when one said, "I hope you are encouraging yourself in the Lord," he lifted up his hands and clapped them.

CHAPTER XIX.

Dying Experience of Mr. John Janeway, the Rev. Edward Payson, and Rev. Samuel Finley, D. D.

Mr. JANEWAY was a young man who had just entered the holy ministry, when he was called away, and exchanged earth for heaven. He was never permitted to preach more than two sermons, before his lungs were so affected, that he was obliged to cease from his earthly labours. During his last days, he was absorbed in the contemplation of Christ and heaven. His meditations, his discourses, his whole deportment, made it evident, that he was ripening for glory. His faith had grown up to a full assurance, and he often feasted on the rich provisions of God's house, and enjoyed many foretastes of future blessedness. The Lord often called him up to the mount and let him see his glory. In the midst of earthly comforts, he longed for death, and his thoughts of the day of judgment were refreshing to him. He would say, " What if the day of judgment were come, even this hour? I would be glad with all my heart. I should behold such lightnings, and hear such thunderings as Israel did at the mount, and I am persuaded, my heart would leap for joy. The meditation of that day, hath even ravished my soul; and the thoughts of its certainty and nearness, are more refreshing to my soul, than all earthly comforts. Surely nothing can more revive my spirit, than to behold the blessed Jesus, who is the life and joy of my soul." When he began to sink rapidly under his complaint, his soul was so devoutly occupied in the contemplation of Christ and heaven, that he almost forgot his pains and sickness. His faith, his love, and his joy, exceedingly abounded. He would frequently exclaim, "O! that I could let you know what I feel! O! that I could show you what I now see! O! that I could express the thousandth part of that sweetness which I now find in Christ! You would then all think it worth while to make religion your chief business. O! my dear friends, you little think what Christ is worth upon a death-bed. I would not now for a world, nay, for a million of worlds, be without Christ and pardon. I would not for a world live any longer, and the very thought of a possibility of recovery, makes me tremble. I do tell you, that I so long to be with Christ, that I could be content to be cut in pieces, and put to the most exquisite tortures, so I might die and be with Christ. O! how sweet Jesus is. 'Come, Lord Jesus, come quickly.' Death do thy worst. Death has lost its terrors. Through grace, I can say, death is nothing to me. I can as easily die as shut my eyes. I long to die—I long to be with Christ." He charged his friends most earnestly, not to pray for his life. "O! the glory, the unspeakable glory which I behold—my heart is full—my heart is full. Christ smiles, and I am constrained to smile. Can you find it in your hearts to stop me, now I am going to the complete and eternal enjoyment of Christ? Would you keep me from my crown? The arms of my blessed Saviour are open to receive me. The angels stand ready to carry my soul into his bosom. O! did you see but what I see, you would cry out with me, 'Dear Lord, how long.' 'Come, Lord Jesus, come quickly.' 'O! why are thy chariot wheels so long in coming?'" A minister having spoken to him of the joys of heaven, he said, " Sir, I feel something of it. My heart is as full as it can hold in this lower state. I can hold no more. O! that I could but let you know what I feel. Who am I, Lord, who am I, that thou shouldst be mindful of me? Why me, Lord, why me? and pass by thousands to look on such a wretch as I? O! what shall I say unto thee, thou Preserver of men? O! blessed, and for ever blessed, be free grace. Why is it, Lord, that thou shouldest manifest thyself unto me and not to others? 'Even so, Father, because it seemed good in thy sight.' Thou wilt have mercy, because thou wilt have mercy. And if thou wilt look on such a worm, who can hinder? Who would not love thee, O blessed Father? O! how sweet and gracious hast thou been to me! O! that He should have me in his thoughts before the foundation of the world."

On one occasion, after his brother had been praying with him, his joys became unutterable; he broke out in such exclamations as these, "O! He is come—He is come—how sweet, how glorious, is the blessed Jesus! He is altogether lovely. How shall I speak the thousandth part of his praise? O! for words to set forth a little part of his excellency! Come look on a dying man and wonder. Was there ever greater kindness? Were there ever more sensible manifestations of grace? O! why me, Lord, why me? Surely this is akin to heaven, and if I were never to enjoy more than this, it is more than a sufficient recompense for all that men and devils could inflict. If this be dying, it is sweet. The bed is soft. Christ's arms, and smiles, and love, surely would turn hell into heaven. O! that you did but see and feel what I do. Behold a dying man, more cheerful than you ever saw a man in health, in the midst of his sweetest worldly enjoyments. O! sirs, worldly pleasures are poor, pitiful, sorry things, when compared with this glory in my soul." He often exhorted those around him to assist him in his praises. "O!" said he, "help me to praise God. Henceforth, through eternity, I have nothing else to do but to love and praise the Lord. I cannot tell what to pray for, which is not already given me. I want only one thing, and that is, a speedy lift to heaven. I expect no more here. I desire no more—I can bear no more. O! praise, praise, praise that boundless love which hath wonderfully looked upon my soul, and hath done more for me, than for thousands of his children. Bless the Lord, O my soul, and all that is within me bless his holy name. O my friends, help me, help me, to admire and praise Him who hath done such astonishing wonders for my soul. He hath pardoned all my sins and filled me with his goodness. He hath given me grace and glory, and no good thing hath He withheld from me. All ye mighty angels, help me to praise God. Let every thing that hath being help me to praise Him. Praise is my work now, and will be my work for ever. Hallelujah, Hallelujah, Hallelujah!"

A few hours before his death he had his mother and brothers and sisters called around his bed, when in a most solemn and affecting manner, he addressed himself in turn to each, and took leave of them. To his mother he offered his thanks for her tender love, and expressed his desire that she might see Christ formed in the hearts of all her children, and meet them all with joy at the day of judgment. Then he took his brothers and sisters in order, and offered an appropriate petition for each. He then said. "O!

that none of us may be found among the unconverted in the day of judgment! O! that we may all appear with our honoured father and dear mother, before Christ with joy. O! that we may live to God here, and live with God hereafter. And now, my dear mother, brothers, and sisters, farewell!" His last words were, "Thy work is done—I have fought a good fight," &c. " Come, Lord Jesus, come quickly." After which he immediately expired.

No man, in our country, has left behind him a higher character for eminent piety, than the Rev. Edward Payson. His views and exercises, when near death, will answer well to be placed by the side of those of Mr. John Janeway.

When this faithful pastor found that his end was approaching, he felt a strong desire to address some advice to his flock. He therefore had it announced from the pulpit, that he would be pleased to see as many of them as could make it convenient to come to his house, and appointed them a time. To them, when assembled, he spake nearly as follows: " It has often been remarked that people who have gone to the other world, cannot come back to tell us what they have seen; but I am so near the eternal world, that I can see almost as clearly, as if I were there; and I see enough to satisfy myself, at least, of the truth of the doctrines which I have preached. I do not know that I should feel at all surer had I been there. It is always interesting to see others in a situation in which we know we must shortly be placed ourselves; and we all know that we must die. And to see a poor creature, when, after an alternation of hopes and fears, he finds that his disease is mortal, and death comes to tear him away from every thing he loves, and crowds him to the very verge of the precipice of destruction, and then thrusts him down headlong;—there he is cast into an unknown world; no friend, no Saviour to receive him:—O! how different is this, from the state of a man who is prepared to die! He is not obliged to be crowded along, but the other world comes like a great magnet to draw him away from this; and he knows that he is going to enjoy—and not only knows but begins to taste it—perfect happiness, for ever, for ever, and ever. And now God is in this room. I see Him! and O! how unspeakably lovely and glorious does he appear! worthy of ten thousand hearts, if we had so many. He is here, and hears me pleading with the creatures that he has made, whom he preserves and loads with blessings, to love him. And how terrible does it appear to me to sin against this God—to set up our wills in opposition to his. It makes my blood run cold to think how miserable I should now be without religion. To lie here and see myself tottering on the verge of destruction,—O! I should be distracted. And when I see my fellow creatures in this situation, I am in an agony for them, that they may escape the danger before it be too late. Suppose we should hear the sound of some one pleading earnestly with another, and we should inquire, What is that man pleading for so earnestly? O! he is only pleading with a fellow creature, to love his God, his Saviour, his Preserver, his Benefactor. He is only pleading with him, not to throw away his immortal soul; not to pull down everlasting wretchedness on his own head. He is only persuading him to avoid eternal misery and accept eternal happiness. 'Is it possible,' we should exclaim, 'that any persuasion can be necessary for this?' And yet it is necessary. O! my friends! do, *do* love this glorious Being. Do seek for the salvation of your immortal souls. Hear the voice of your dying minister, while he entreats you to care for your souls."

On another occasion, he said, "I find satisfaction in looking at nothing that I have done. I have not fought, but Christ has fought for me. I have not run, but Christ has carried me. I have not worked, but Christ has wrought in me. Christ has done all." The perfections of God were to him a well-spring of joy, and the promises were breasts of consolation, whence his soul drew aliment and comfort. "O!" exclaimed he, "the loving kindness of God. His oving kindness! This afternoon, while I was meditating, the Lord seemed to pass by and proclaim himself, 'THE LORD GOD, MERCIFUL AND GRACIOUS.' 'O how gracious!' Try to conceive of that—'his *loving kindness*,' as if it were not enough to say *kindness*, but *loving kindness!* What must be the loving kindness of the Lord who is himself infinite in love? It seemed, as if Christ had said to me, ' You have often wandered, and been impatient of the way, by which I have led you; but what do you think of it now?' And I was cut to the heart, when I looked back and saw the goodness by which I had been guided, that I could ever for a moment distrust his love."

To a minister who called upon him, he said, "That the point in which he believed ministers failed most, and in which he had certainly failed most, was in doing duty professionally, and not from the heart." He said also, " I have never valued as I ought, the doctrines which I have preached. The system is great and glorious, and is worthy of our utmost efforts to promote it. The interests depending will justify us in our strongest measures. In every respect we may embark our all upon it; it will sustain us."—" I was never fit to say a word to a sinner, except when I had a broken heart myself; when I was subdued and melted into penitence, and felt just as if I had received pardon to my own soul; and when my heart was full of tenderness and pity." He seemed to be greatly affected with a view of the grace of God, in saving lost men; and especially, that it should be bestowed on one so ill-deserving as himself. " O how sovereign! O how sovereign! Grace is the only thing that can make us like God. I might be dragged through heaven, earth, and hell, and I should still be the same sinful, polluted wretch, unless God himself should renew and cleanse me."

In conversation with his eldest daughter, being asked whether self-examination was not a very difficult duty for young Christians, " Yes," he replied, " and for old ones, too; because it is displeasing to the pride of the heart, because wandering thoughts are then most apt to intrude, and because of the deceitfulness of the heart. When a Christian first looks into his heart, he sees nothing but confusion—a heap of sins, and very little good, mixed up together; and he knows not how to separate them, or how to begin self-examination. But let him persevere in his efforts, and order will arise out of confusion." She mentioned to him a passage in the life of Alleine, which led him to say, "We never confess any faults that we really think disgraceful. We complain of our hardness of heart, stupidity, &c. but we never confess envy, covetousness, and revenge, or any thing that we suppose will lower us in the opinion of others; and this proves that we do not feel ashamed of coldness and stupidity. In short, when young Christians make confessions, unless there is an obvious call for it, it commonly proceeds from one of the following motives: either they wish to be thought very humble, and to possess great knowledge of their own hearts; or they think it is a fault which the other has perceived, and they are willing to have the credit of having discovered, and striven against it; or they confess some fault from which they are remarkably free, in order to elicit a compliment."

His solicitude for the welfare of his people was so great, that though he had given them one solemn address, he was not contented with that, but sent for particular classes of them. On one day, he had the young men of the congregation assembled around him, when he delivered to them a peculiarly solemn, tender, and appropriate exhortation. He also sent an affectionate valedictory address to the Association of ministers with whom he had been connected. The substance of it was, "A hearty assurance of the ardent love with which he remembered them even in death—an exhortation to love one another with a pure heart fervently—to love their work—to be diligent in it—to expect success, and to bear up under discouragements—to be faithful unto death, and to look for their reward in Heaven."

While speaking of the rapturous views which he

had of heaven, he was asked if did not appear like the clear light of vision, rather than that of faith. He said, "I don't know—it is too much for the poor eyes of my soul to bear—they are almost blinded with the excessive brightness. All I want is, to be a mirror, to reflect some of those rays to those around me."— "My soul, instead of growing weaker and more languishing, as my body does, seems to be endued with an angel's energies, and to be ready to break from the body, and join those around the throne." When asked, whether it was now incredible to him, that the martyrs should rejoice in the flames and on the rack, "No," said he, "I can easily believe it. I have suffered twenty times as much as I could in being burnt at the stake, while my joy in God so abounded, as to render my sufferings not only tolerable, but welcome. The sufferings of this present time are not worthy to be compared with the glory which shall be revealed in us." At another time, he said, "God is now literally my all in all. While He is present with me, no event can in the least diminish my happiness; and were the whole world at my feet, trying to minister to my comfort, they could not add one drop to the cup." "It seems as if the promise to wipe away all tears, is already accomplished, as it relates to tears of sorrow. I have no tears to shed now but tears of love, and joy, and thankfulness." Shortly before his decease, he was heard to break forth in a soliloquy, of which the following is a specimen:—"What an assemblage of motives to holiness, does the gospel present? I am a Christian; what then? I am a redeemed sinner —a pardoned rebel—all through grace, and by the most wonderful means which infinite wisdom could devise. I am a Christian; what then? Why I am a temple of God, and surely I ought to be pure and holy. I am a Christian; what then? Why I am a child of God, and ought to be filled with filial love and reverence, joy, and gratitude. I am a Christian; what then? Why I am a disciple of Christ, and must imitate him who was meek and lowly of heart, and pleased not himself. I am a Christian.—What then?

Why I am an heir of heaven, and hastening on to the abodes of the blessed." "It seems as if my soul had found a pair of new wings, and was so eager to try them, that in her fluttering she would rend the fine net-work of the body to pieces." He had the choir to come in and sing for him, and chose the hymn, "*Rise, my soul,*" &c. Soon after which he expired, October 21, 1827.

The Rev. Dr. Samuel Finley, who had been for some time President of New Jersey College, upon being informed by his physicians that his disease was incurable, expressed his entire resignation, and exclaimed, "Welcome, Lord Jesus." On the Sabbath preceding his death, Dr. Clarkson, one of his physicians, told him that he observed a manifest alteration, and that he could not live many days. He said, "may the Lord bring me near himself! I have been waiting with a Canaan hunger for the promised land. I have often wondered that God suffered me to live. I have more wondered that he ever called me to be a minister of his word. He has often afforded me much strength which I have abused. He has returned in mercy. O how faithful are the promises of God! O that I could see him as I have seen him before, in his sanctuary. Although I have as earnestly desired death, as the hireling pants for the evening shade, yet will I wait all the days of my appointed time. I have often struggled with principalities and powers, and have been brought to the borders of despair. Lord, let it suffice." He then closed his eyes and sat up and prayed fervently that God would show him his glory, before he departed hence; that he would enable him to endure patiently to the end—and, particularly, that he might be kept from dishonouring the ministry. He then resumed his discourse, and said, "I can truly say that I have loved the service of God. I know not in what language to speak of my own unworthiness—I have been undutiful—I have honestly endeavoured to act for God, but with much weakness and corruption." Then lying down again, he said, "a Christian's death is the best part of his experience.

The Lord has made provision for the whole way; provision for the soul, and provision for the body. The Lord has given me many souls, as the crown of my rejoicing. Blessed be God—eternal rest is at hand. Eternity is but long enough to enjoy my God. This, this has animated me in my severest studies. I was ashamed to take rest here. O! that I could be filled with the fulness of God! that fulness which fills heaven." Being asked whether he would choose to live or die, he said, "To die, though I cannot but feel the same strait that Paul did when he knew not which to choose. *For me to live is Christ—but to die is gain.*' But should God, by a miracle, prolong my life, I would still continue to serve him. His service has been sweet to me. I have loved it much. I have tried my Master's yoke, and will never shrink my neck from it. *His yoke is easy, and his burden is light!*" One said to him, "You are more cheerful and vigorous, sir." "Yes, I rise or fall, as eternal life seems nearer or further off." It being remarked that he always used the appellation, "dear Lord," in his prayers, he answered, "O! he is very dear! very precious, indeed. How pretty is it for a minister to die on the Sabbath! I expect to spend the remainder of this Sabbath in heaven." One said, "You will soon join the blessed society of heaven—you will for ever hold converse with Abraham, Isaac, and Jacob, and with the spirits of the just made perfect—with old friends, and many old fashioned people." "Yes sir," he replied, with a smile, "but they are a most polite people now." He expressed great gratitude to his friends around him, and said, "may the Lord repay you for your tenderness to me! may he bless you abundantly, not only with temporal, but with spiritual blessings." Turning to his wife, he said, "My dear, I expect to see you shortly in glory." Seeing a member of the Second Presbyterian Church present, he said, "I have often preached and prayed among you, my dear sir, and the doctrines I preached are now my support, and, blessed be God, they are without a flaw. May the Lord bless and preserve your church! He designs good for it yet, I trust." To a person from Princeton he said, "give my love to the people of Princeton, and tell them that I am going to die, and that I am not afraid to die."

He would sometimes cry out, "the Lord Jesus will take care of his cause in the world." Upon waking, next morning, he exclaimed, "O what a disappointment I have met with—I expected this morning to have been in heaven." On account of his extreme weakness, he was unable to speak much during the day, but all that he said was in the language of triumph. Next morning, with a pleasing smile on his countenance, he cried out, "O I shall triumph over every foe—the Lord hath given me the victory. Now I know that it is impossible that faith should not triumph over earth and hell—I exult—I triumph. O that I could see untainted purity! I think I have nothing to do but die—yet, perhaps, I have—Lord, show me my task." He then said, "Lord Jesus, into thy hands I commit my spirit—I do it with confidence —I do it with full assurance. I know that thou wilt keep that which I have committed to thee. I have been dreaming too fast of the time of my departure, for I find it does not yet come—but the Lord is faithful, and will not tarry beyond the appointed time."

In the afternoon, the Rev. Mr. Spencer came to see him, and said, "I have come, dear sir, to see you confirm by facts, the gospel you have been preaching. Pray, sir, how do you feel?" To which he replied, "Full of triumph—I triumph through Christ. Nothing clips my wings but the thoughts of my dissolution being prolonged—O that it were to night! My very soul thirsts for eternal rest." Mr. Spencer asked him what he saw in eternity to excite such vehement desires in his soul. He said, "I see the eternal love and goodness of God. I see the fulness of the Mediator. I see the love of Jesus. O to be dissolved and to be with him! I long to be clothed with the complete righteousness of Christ." He then requested Mr. Spencer to pray with him before they parted, and said, "I have gained the victory over the devil; pray to God to preserve me from evil, to keep me from evil in this critical hour; and to support me with his presence through the valley of the shadow of death."

He spent the remainder of the day, in taking an affectionate and solemn leave of his friends, and exhorting such of his children as were with him.

On the next day, July 16, the conflict was terminated. He was no longer able to speak, but a friend having desired him to give a token by which his friends might know, whether he still continued to triumph, he lifted up his hand, and uttered the word "Yes." About nine o'clock, he fell into a sound sleep, and appeared much more free from pain than he had been for many days before. He continued to sleep, without changing his position, till about one o'clock, when he expired, without a groan or a sigh. During his whole sickness he was never heard to utter a repining word; and in taking leave of his dearest friends, he was never seen to shed a tear, or exhibit any sign of sorrow.

His remains were interred in the Second Presbyterian Church, on the corner of Mulberry or Arch and Third streets; by the side of his dear friend, the Rev. Gilbert Tennent. From this resting place, their dust and bones were removed to the burying ground on Arch street, when the church was removed. Mrs. Finley survived her husband many years, the latter part of which time she was entirely blind; but bore the affliction with meek and cheerful submission.

CHAPTER XX.

Remarks on Death-bed Exercises, with several illustrative examples

THE cases of religious experience, at the close of life which have been presented to the reader, furnish much reason for encouragement and hope to the real Christian. We learn from them, that death, however terrible to nature, may be completely divested of its terrors; that the Christian religion when it has been cordially embraced, has power to sustain the soul in the last conflict; that the supplies of grace may be so rich and abundant, that the bed of death may be the happiest situation which the child of God ever occupied, and his last hours the most comfortable of his whole life; that it is possible for such a flood of divine consolation to be poured into the soul, that the pains of the body are scarcely felt; by which we may understand how it was that the martyrs could rejoice in the midst of flames, and on the rack. We learn, also, that these blessed communications of the joy of the Holy Ghost, are derived to the soul, through the promises of God; and that all that is necessary to fill it with these divine consolations, is a firm and lively faith. There is, in all these extatic and triumphant feelings, nothing miraculous; nothing different from the common mode of God's dealing with his people, except in the degree. The things of eternity are more clearly apprehended; confidence in the promises is more unshaken; submission to the will of God is more unreserved, and gratitude for his goodness more fervent. Another thing suggested by such happy death-bed exercises, is, that the dying saint never entertained a more humble sense of his own unworthiness, than during this season of the anticipation of the joys of heaven. These experiences, therefore, furnish strong evidence of the truth of the doctrines of grace; indeed, free grace is the predominant theme in the minds of these highly favoured servants of God. It is also highly worthy of our marked attention, that the Lord Jesus Christ is precious to the dying believer, in proportion as his consolations abound. He attributes all that he enjoys, or hopes for, to this blessed Redeemer. And He who loved him, and died for him, is most faithful to his gracious promises, at this trying moment. Now, when heart and flesh fail, He will be the strength of their hearts. Now, he enables them to say, with confidence, "Though I walk through the valley and shadow of death, I will fear no evil, for thou art with me; thy rod and staff comfort me." Death is, indeed, a formidable enemy when armed with his envenomed sting; but when this sting is extracted, death is harmless; death comes as a friend to release us from a body of sin and misery. "The sting of death is sin, and the strength of sin is the law;" but when the law has received a full satisfaction, and all sin is pardoned through the blood of Christ, the sting exists no longer. There is no condemnation to them who are in Christ Jesus. It is God that justifieth, who is he that condemneth? It is Christ that died; yea, rather who is risen again. "Precious in the sight of God is the death of his saints." The meek shall sing even on a dying bed. Here, often, the timid grow bold; the feeble strong. Here doubts and fears which harassed the weary pilgrim, all the journey through, are dismissed for ever; and that joyful assurance is realized, which had long been ardently desired and hoped for. Where else, but among real Christians, do we witness such happy scenes, at the near approach of death? Can the infidel point to any of his associates, who could thus exult in the prospect of death? Can the man of the world exhibit any thing like this? Alas! they are driven away from all they love: they may die stupidly; they may be under an awful, blinding delusion; but the positive joys of the believer, they cannot experience. Now, as we must all die, and that soon, ought we not to take all pains, and use all possible diligence, to be ready to die the death of the righteous? When that awful hour shall arrive, worldly honours, and worldly possessions will be nothing to us. Royal sceptres and crowns, and treasures, will be utterly unavailing; but the humble believer, however racked with pain of body, is safe in the hands of a kind Redeemer, who having himself experienced the pangs of death, knows how to sympathize with and succour his beloved disciples, when they are called to this last trial. He will not then forsake those whom he has supported through their whole pilgrimage. His everlasting arms of love and faithfulness will be placed underneath them, and he will bear them as on eagles' wings. Truly, then, for them to die, is gain! They rest from their labours, exchange darkness, sin, and sorrow, for perfect light, perfect purity, and perfect felicity. Lift up your heads, then, ye servants of God, for the day of your redemption draweth nigh. The night is far spent, the day is at hand. With some of us, it must be near the dawn. The darkness will soon be past for ever. Let us then rejoice in the hope of the glory of God, and wait till our salvation cometh. Now is our salvation nearer than when we believed.

But, it may be asked, do all real Christians die in such joy and triumph, as those whose experience has been related? No; this is not pretended. Some, no doubt, die under a cloud, and go out of the world in distressing doubt respecting their eternal destiny. It is to guard against such an event, that we would exhort all professors of religion, and include ourselves in the number, to begin in time to make preparation for death. Dear brethren, let us look well to the foundation of our hope; we cannot bestow too much pains and diligence in making our calling and election sure. We shall never regret, on a death-bed, that we were too much concerned to secure the salvation of our souls; or, that we were too careful in making preparation for another world. Let us remember that our time on earth is short, and that whatever is done, must be done quickly. There will be no opportunity of coming back to rectify what has been done amiss, or to supply what is wanting. "Now is the accepted time, now is the day of salvation." Let us work while it is day, knowing that the dark night cometh when no man can work. Let us then awake to righteousness. Let us watch and be sober. Let us put on the armour of light, and especially let us see to it, that we have on the wedding garment; else we shall never find admittance to the marriage-supper of the Lamb. The only robe which can bear the scrutinizing inspection of the King, is the perfect and spotless robe of Christ's imputed righteousness. This will render us acceptable in the

Beloved. With this, we must put on the robe of inherent righteousness; for "without holiness, no man shall see the Lord;" and these two, though distinct, are never separated. Only, the latter is never perfect until we come to the end of our course; and this single consideration should reconcile us to the thoughts of death; that then we shall be freed from all sin. O how blessed is that state, where we shall see no more darkly through a glass, but face to face; where we shall know no more in part, but as we are known. O bright and delightful vision of the glory of God in the face of Jesus Christ! Surely this is worth dying for.

But it may be asked, Is there not evidence of too much excitement, in the experiences which have been narrated? May not a part at least of the elevated and exhilarated feelings be the effect of an accelerated circulation? People who die of pulmonary consumption are apt to be sanguine, and to indulge buoyant hopes even in regard to recovery. In answer, I would say, that this may be admitted to have some effect in increasing the degree of excitement; but it never can account for the bright views and unspeakable joys which some experience. And the truth is, we are poor judges of the degree of elevated excitement, which the sense of God's love will produce.

It must be confessed, that while we may admire and breathe after such an elevated and triumphant state of mind, as was experienced by those of whom some account has been given; yet we cannot so readily sympathize with such high emotions, as with a more calm and deliberate frame of spirit. Indeed, it is here as in health, when we see persons much excited in regard to religion, or any thing else, we do not place such entire confidence in what they utter, as when the same persons calmly and soberly express their sentiments. The reason is, that in all great excitements the imagination and feelings predominate over the judgment; and experience teaches that in all such cases there is a tendency to exaggeration, and to the use of strong expressions; and it cannot be doubted that, in some cases, the religious exultation experienced is somewhat delirious. The nervous system loses its tone, and although its agitations are violent, they are somewhat irregular and excessive, so as to produce an irrepressible thrilling through the soul. It is not wonderful, that while the mysterious connexion between soul and body is coming to an end, there should be something in the emotions new, and in the looks, tones, and gestures, out of the common way. This does not alter or vitiate the nature of the pious exercises of the soul, though it may modify them, and give them a peculiar aspect and expression. If any person chooses to suppose, that, in some of the cases specified, while faith was triumphant, and hope full of assurance, there might be superadded an exhilaration arising out of the peculiar state of the body, he will not have me objecting. The last exercises of that useful and devoted man, Jeremiah Evarts, were very remarkable for the degree of powerful excitement manifested; and the more remarkable, because his mind was highly intellectual, and very little subject to excitement, in common. Still it was well known to those intimate with him, that when he was aroused, his feelings were very strong.

Often, officious friends and physicians are extremely averse to have any thing said to their friends, on the subject of religion, when they are sick, lest it should disturb their minds, and so increase the violence of the disease. I would not, it is true, admit every loquacious old man or woman, into the chamber of a friend dangerously ill, but a discreet and pious counsellor is of great value at such a time. If the patient is hopefully pious, none can doubt the propriety and comfort of aiding such by holding forth to their view the rich promises of a faithful God. But even when the character of the sick is different, it often gives relief to have an opportunity of conversation with a pious friend or minister. Anxious feelings, pent up in the soul and finding no vent, are far more injurious than a free expression of them; and if the person is in danger of death, will you, can you, be guilty of the cruelty of debarring him from the only opportunity of salvation, which he may ever have? If you do, his blood will be found in your skirts To show how erroneous the opinion is, that religious conversation tends to injure the sick by increasing his disease, I will relate a fact which fell under my own observation.

A young gentleman of fortune and liberal education, had been for some months thinking seriously about his soul's salvation; but the work had not come to any maturity, when by making too great an exertion of his bodily strength, he ruptured a large blood vessel in the lungs, and was brought to death's door; not being able to speak above a low whisper. Having been a pupil of mine, I was permitted to see him, and upon asking the state of his mind, he whispered in my ear, that he was overwhelmed with the most awful darkness and terror—not one ray of light dawned upon his miserable soul. I prayed with him and presented to him a few gospel invitations and promises, and left him, never expecting to see him alive. Next day I called, the physician coming out of his room, informed me, that while they were waiting for his last breath, a favourable change seemed unexpectedly to have taken place, and that he had revived a little. When I approached his bed, he looked joyfully in my face, pressed my hand, and said, "All is well—I have found peace.—This morning, about the dawn, I had the most delightful view of Christ, and of his ability and willingness to save me." And upon inquiry, I found, that that was the moment when the favourable change took place in his symptoms. Faith and joy accomplished what no medicine could, and acted as a reviving cordial to his dying body. He so far recovered as to live a number of years afterwards, though his lungs were never sound; and his consistent walk and conversation attested the reality of his change. He soon joined himself to the communion of the church, and died in her communion.

While spending a summer in Germantown, near

Philadelphia, I was sent for to visit a young man, whom I had often seen. He did not belong to my charge, but two pious ladies who did, were his friends, and had come out of the city to nurse him. He had a hemorrhage of the lungs, which left little room to hope for recovery. As he was a mild and moral man, I did not know, but that he might be a professor of religion; but upon asking him a question respecting his hope, he frankly told me that he had been skeptical for many years, and had no belief that the gospel was divine. I never felt more at a loss. The man was too weak to attend to argument, and if I could by reasoning convince him of his error, it would not be a saving faith, and he must die before this process could be gone through. I found that his infidelity afforded him no comfort in a dying hour, and that he wished he could believe in Christ. It occurred to me that the word of God contained light and energy in itself, and that if he could not attend to the external evidences, the beams of truth might shine in upon his soul, and thus generate a saving faith by the efficient aid of the Spirit. After pointing out the probable sources of his skepticism, I requested the ladies who were attending on him, to read certain portions of the gospel to him, as he could bear it—for he was very low. This was done; and next day, when I came to see him, he declared that his doubts were all scattered, and that he had hope in Christ. Afterwards, he was never able to converse; but as far as is known died in hope.

I never saw any one approach death so deliberately and composedly, as the late Rev. Robert Ray, pastor of the church of Freehold, in New Jersey. He had spent a winter at St. Augustine, with the hope of restoring his health, but came home more diseased than before he went. His lungs were deeply affected, and he foresaw that his end was approaching. But as long as he was able to speak, he caused himself to be carried to the church and to be assisted into the pulpit, where he would preach and exhort until his breath failed, when he would pant as if about to die, and then be conveyed home as he came. This was done not once or twice, but for many weeks; for he said, as he must die, he might as well die preaching; and he felt a strong desire to be the means of saving the people committed to his charge; and he hoped that a voice of affectionate warning from the grave might have the effect of awakening some of them. As he suffered but little acute pain, he appeared until his dying day, as calm and cheerful, as a man long absent from home would, when the time came to return to his friends. He conversed as familiarly and composedly about his approaching change, as if there was nothing formidable in it. Indeed, it had no terrors for him. Even when death was upon him, having observed some of his neighbours coming in, he said, "Well, you have come to see your pastor die." He then remarked, that his feelings were very peculiar, such as he had never experienced before; and without any perturbation of mind or bodily agony, he gently fell asleep.

Wishing in these experiences of dying saints to give as great a variety as is compatible with my limits, I will now extract an account of the last illness of Mrs. Susan Huntington, of Boston, taken down by her pastor, the Rev. Dr. Wisner, after his visits to her sick room.

Tuesday, October 28, 1823. Called on Mrs. Huntington about half-past nine in the morning. Found that she had failed considerably since my last visit. To an inquiry respecting the state of her mind, she said, "I think I have felt more of the presence of Christ, than when I saw you last. I have not had those strong views and joyful feelings, with which I have sometimes been favoured. My mind is weak; I cannot direct and fix my thoughts as I once could. But I think I have fled for refuge to lay hold on the hope set before me in the precious gospel; and He who is the foundation of that hope will never forsake me." Then, with a most interesting expression of countenance, she said, "I trust we shall meet in heaven, and spend an eternity in praising our dear Redeemer." "I feel," said she, "that I have been very,

very unfaithful; but He is merciful—his blood cleanseth from all sin: and I trust he has blotted out my sins from the book of his remembrance. O what should we do without Christ?" "As much debtors to free grace at the end of our course as at the beginning," observed her pastor. "More, far more," she replied, "for we sin against greater light and love, after we are born again. Yes, it is all free grace—if it were not, what would become of me?" It was answered, "You would have perished—justly perished." "Yes," she replied, "what a glorious plan, what a precious Saviour! O that I could love him more! Pray that I may love and glorify him for ever!"

On Friday, October 31, found her more comfortable. She said, "My mind has generally been in a peaceful frame since I saw you; but I want to realize the presence and preciousness of Christ, more distinctly and constantly than my great weakness permits me to do." In answer to some remarks on the covenant of grace, she said, "Glorious covenant! precious promises! I have given myself and body to Him, in whom they are yea and amen, and I do not fear; I desire him to do with me as it shall please him."

Tuesday, November 3. To the usual inquiry, she replied, "Mrs. Graham accurately describes my feelings, when she says, 'Thus far the Lord hath brought me through the wilderness, bearing, chastising, forgiving, restoring. I am near to Jordan's flood. May my blessed High Priest and ark of the covenant, lead on my staggering steps, the little further I have to go.'" And on December 4, she breathed her last, in the faith and hope of the gospel.

As in the preceding account of Mrs. Huntington, mention is made of Mrs. Graham, of New York, it may be in place to give a few particulars of this wise woman, as she may properly be called, during her last illness. Foreseeing that her end was near, she sent for Mrs. Chrystie, a dear friend, between whom and herself an agreement had been made, that whichever was first summoned away, should be attended, in her last moments, by the other. To her son-in-law,

Mr. Bethune, whom she saw standing by, she said, "My dear, dear son, I am going to leave you; I am going to my Saviour." He answered, "I know that when you do go from us, it will be to the Saviour; but, my dear mother, it may not be the Lord's time now to call you to himself." "Yes," said she, "now is the time; and Oh! I could weep for sin." Her words were accompanied with her tears. "Have you any doubts, then, my dear friend," asked Mrs. Chrystie. "O no," replied she, "I have no more doubt of going to my Saviour, than if I were already in his arms. My guilt is all transferred. He has cancelled all my debt; yet I could weep for sins against so good a God. It seems to me there must be weeping even in Heaven." When her dear friend and pastor, Dr. Mason, came to see her, they had a very interesting interview—at the close of which, he inquired if there was any thing, in particular, for which he should pray. She said, "The Lord will direct," and immediately offered up this short prayer: "Lord, direct thy servant in prayer." During her sickness, she was for much of the time lethargic, and it was often difficult to arouse her. But when at any time waked up for a moment, she would utter some sweet word—such as "peace," indicating the happy state of her mind. Dr. Mason, in his funeral sermon, said, "This may truly be called falling asleep in Jesus." All terror seemed to be removed, and her countenance was placid, and looked younger than before her illness. At a quarter past 12 o'clock, on the 27th of July, 1814, without a struggle or a groan, her spirit winged its flight from a mansion of clay to the realms of glory.

CHAPTER XXI.

Death-bed exercises of Mr. Baxter, and the Rev. Thomas Scott, D. D.

Dr. Bates, in his funeral sermon, occasioned by the death of Mr. Baxter, has given us an interesting account of his last days, some part of which I will extract, as furnishing an example, not of a highly excited state of feeling, but of a truly pious, calm, submissive frame of mind. Few persons, who ever lived, have given more convincing evidence of fervent piety, throughout a long life, than this devoted servant of God. His end corresponded with the tenor of his life, and with the religion which he inculcated in his sermons.

"He continued," says Dr. Bates, "to preach so long, notwithstanding his wasted and languishing body, that the last time, he almost died in the pulpit. It would doubtless have been his joy to be transfigured in the mount. Not long after, he felt the approaches of death, and was confined to his sick bed. Death reveals the secrets of the heart: then words are spoken with most feeling and least affectation. This excellent saint was the same in his life and his death: his last hours were spent in preparing others and himself to appear before God. He said to his friends, who came to see him, 'Ye come hither to learn to die. I am not the only person that must go this way. I can assure you, that your whole life, be it ever so long, is little enough to prepare for death. Have a care of this vain, deceitful world, and the lusts of the flesh. Be sure you choose God for your portion, heaven for your home, God's glory for your end, and his word for your rule, and then you need never fear, but we shall meet in comfort.' Never was penitent sinner more humble, never was a sin cere believer more calm and comfortable. He acknowledged himself to be the vilest dunghill-worm (it was his usual expression) that ever went to heaven. He admired the divine condescension to us, often saying, 'Lord, what is man! what am I, a vile worm, to the great God!' Many times he prayed, 'God be merciful to me a sinner,' and thanked God that this was left on record, in the gospel, as an effectual prayer. He said, 'God may justly condemn me for the best duty I ever performed. All my hopes are from the free mercy of God in Christ.' After a slumber, he awaked, and said, 'I shall rest from my labour.' A minister present said, 'And your works shall follow you.' To whom he replied, 'No works—I will leave out works, if God will grant me the other.' When a friend was comforting him with the good which many had received by his preaching and writing, he said, 'I was but a pen in God's hand, and what praise is due to a pen?'

"His resigned submission to the will of God, in his sharp sickness, was eminent. When extremity constrained him earnestly to pray to God for his release, by death, he would check himself, 'It is not fit for me to prescribe—when thou wilt, what thou wilt, and how thou wilt.' Being in great anguish, he said, 'O how unsearchable are his judgments, and his ways past finding out—the reaches of his providence we cannot fathom.' And to his friends, 'Do not think the worse of religion for what you see me suffer.' Being often asked, how it was with the inner man, he replied, 'I have a well-grounded assurance of my eternal happiness, and great peace and comfort within.' He said, 'Flesh must perish, and we must feel the perishing of it,' and that though his judgment submitted, yet sense would still make him groan. He derived great comfort from that description in Heb. xii. 22; that he was going to the innumerable company of angels, and to the general assembly and church of the first-born. whose names are written in heaven; and to God the Judge of all, and to the spirits of just men made perfect, and to Jesus the Mediator of the new covenant, and to the blood of sprinkling, that speaketh better things than the blood of Abel. 'That Scripture,' he said, 'deserved a thousand and a thousand thoughts.'

"At another time, he said he derived great comfort and sweetness, in repeating the Lord's prayer, and was sorry some good people were prejudiced against the use of it, for there were all necessary petitions for the soul and body contained in it. He gave excellent counsels to young ministers, that visited him, and earnestly prayed to God to bless their labours, and make them very successful in turning many souls to Christ; expressed great joy in the hopes that God would do a great deal of good by them, and that their spirits might be moderate and peaceful. He often prayed that God would be merciful to this miserable, distracted world, and that he would preserve his church and interest in it. He advised his friends to beware of self-conceit, as a sin that was likely to ruin the nation.

"I visited him, with a very worthy friend, Mr. Mather, from New England, the day before he died. I said to him, 'You are now approaching your long desired home:' he answered, 'I believe, I believe.' He expressed great willingness to die, and during his sickness, when asked, 'How he did,' his reply was, '*Almost well.*' His joy was most remarkable, when, in his own apprehension, death was nearest; and his spiritual joy was at length consummated in eternal joy. On the day of his death, a great trembling and coldness extorted strong cries from him, for pity and relief from heaven; which cries and agonies continued for some time, till at length he ceased, and lay in patient expectation of his change. The last words he spoke to me, on being informed that I was come to see him, were, 'Oh, I thank him, I thank him,' and turning his eyes to me said, 'The Lord teach you how to die!' To the last I never could perceive his peace and heavenly hopes assaulted or disturbed. I have often heard him greatly lament that he felt no greater liveliness in what appeared so great and clear to him, and so much desired by him

He told me he knew it should be well with him, when he was gone. He wondered to hear others speak of their sensible and passionately strong desires to die, and of their comforts of spirit, when sensible of their approaching death; when, though he thought he knew as much as they, and had as rational satisfaction as they could have, that his soul was safe, he never could feel their sensible consolations. I asked, whether much of this was not to be resolved into bodily constitution: he told me he thought it must be so.

A wicked and groundless report was circulated, that he was greatly troubled with skeptical thoughts before he died. Mr. Sylvester, who was with him during his whole sickness, declares there was not the least foundation whatever, for such a report. But the devil seems to be greatly envious at the comfortable death of God's people, and therefore his agents are busy in circulating slanders against the saints, in regard to this matter. So, although Calvin ended his days in great tranquillity and in the full exercise of faith and enjoyment of reason, his enemies circulated the report, that he died in all the horrors of despair. Thus also, when the Rev. Augustus Toplady was near his end, it was circulated that he had renounced all those doctrines of grace, for which he was so zealous in his life. Happily the report reached him before his decease, which gave him the opportunity of contradicting it, and leaving his dying testimony in favour of those doctrines. His dying experience was of the most joyful and triumphant kind, and would do to be classed with those of John Janeway, Edward Payson, and Dr. Samuel Finley, but we have not room for it, and many others.

The two Henrys, father and son, so eminent for their piety and usefulness, were carried off by sudden and painful diseases, which afforded little opportunity for much conversation. They experienced, however, much of the divine aid and support. John Howe's death was exactly in character with his life and writings.

It may be thought, that all the specimens of the ex

perience of believers, during their last illness, have been of the favourable kind; and far above what is witnessed in the greater number of Christians, on their dying bed. It may be so. But I wish to remark, that in all my life, I have known few persons, who lived like Christians, when in health, who did not in their approach to death, manifest as much hope and fortitude, in that trying hour, as could reasonably have been expected from the character of their piety. In many cases as I have before stated, the comfort and assurance of some timid and desponding believers, have risen far above what any of their friends dared to hope. In general the result of my observation is, that the pious find death less terrible on their near approach to the event, than when it was viewed at a distance. Some persons have naturally a much greater dread of death than others, though their piety may be more lively. Of this class was the late Dr. Thomas Scott, the author of the Commentary on the Bible. Few men of the last age, gave stronger evidence of deep-rooted and constant attachment to the Saviour, than this devoted man. In the service of his Master, he was most laborious and faithful, and it would be difficult to name any man whose evangelical labours have been attended with happier results. He contributed much, in conjunction with such men as Romaine, Newton, Cecil, and others, to extend the influence of vital religion, far and wide, through the established church of England; and his usefulness was not confined to his own country, or to the period of his life; but, in these United States, I know no writings which have been so extensively circulated, and which have so powerful an effect in correcting prevailing errors in religion, and promoting sound, evangelical views of Scriptural truth. I have selected the dying experience of this man, of undoubted and eminent piety, for the reason hinted at in the beginning of this chapter; because his exercises, though deeply serious, were not for the most of the time, remarkably comfortable; and in no part of his illness, did he express much elevated joy. I think it right to view God's people in their various states and frames, as they approach the end of their pilgrimage. A pious clergyman remarked, in relation to the exercises of Dr. Scott, that men of profound thought, and deep reflection, are not commonly so joyful on a dying-bed as Christians of less understanding and less experience, and he referred to Bunyan, as of the same mind, who represents CHRISTIAN, his chief pilgrim, as almost overwhelmed with the waters of Jordan, while the less experienced pilgrim, HOPEFUL, goes over with little difficulty or danger. I cannot say, that I can altogether concur in this remark. It may often happen, that the unlettered Christian has a livelier faith than the profoundly learned theologian, and of course will be likely to have a calmer, happier exit from the world. But if men of talents and learning possess a vigorous, evangelical faith, they are as likely to rejoice on a dying bed as any others, as is evinced by the examples of Rivet, Baxter, Howe, &c. The difference between the comforts of dying saints may be attributed, first to divine sovereignty, which distributes grace and consolation as seemeth good unto him; secondly, to bodily temperament; some persons being more fearful than others, and more prone to suspect their own sincerity; and thirdly, to the nature of the disease by which the body is brought down to the grave. It is the tendency of some diseases, while they do not disturb the intellect, to exhilarate the spirits, and enliven the imagination; while a distressing depression or perturbation is the effect of others; to say nothing of the different degrees of pain experienced by different persons; and we know that some diseases have a deplorable stupefying effect. A fourth and frequent cause of difference in the exercises of dying persons is produced by the medicine which is administered. When physicians can do nothing to cure, they think it right to lull their patients by opiates, or excite them by alcohol. I have, when sick, been more afraid of nothing than these intoxicating and stupefying, or even exhilarating drugs. O let no artificial means be ever used with me, in that dread hour, to interrupt sober and deliberate reflection!

But to return to Dr. Scott; his disease was a violent fever, so that the range of his pulse was from 150 to 175 in a minute. Under such a disease it is not wonderful that he was often restless and uncomfortable in his feelings. The Rev. Daniel Wilson, (now bishop of Calcutta) in his funeral sermon observes, " That for several years preceding the event itself, his bodily infirmities had been increasing. His strength and natural spirits at times sensibly failed. His own impression was, that his departure was approaching, and he contemplated it with calmness and tranquillity." Mr. Wilson with great propriety remarks, " Before I proceed to give some particulars of his most instructive and affecting departure, I must observe, that I lay no stress on them as to the evidence of his state before God. It is the tenor of the life, not that of the few suffering and morbid scenes which precede dissolution, that fixes the character. We are not authorized from Scripture to place any dependence on the last periods of sinking nature, through which the Christian may be called to pass to his eternal reward. But though no importance is to be attached to these hours of fainting mortality, with reference to the acceptance and final triumph of the dying Christian, yet, where it pleases God to afford one of his departing servants, as in the instance before us, such a measure of faith and self-possession, as to close a holy and most consistent life, with a testimony which sealed, amidst the pains of acute disease, and in the most impressive manner, all his doctrines and instructions, during forty-five preceding years, we are called on, as I think, to record with gratitude the divine benefit, and to use it with humility, for the confirmation of our own faith and joy."

His second son, writes from his bed-side, " His gloom, of which I had heard a good deal, in an indistinct manner, by no means relates to the prospects which lie before him. He is perfectly calm and cheerful in the view of dissolution, and seems disappointed at the symptoms of recovery He thought his trials were almost over; and said, that yesterday morning he had hoped to end the sacred services of the day in heaven. Indeed, his wish is, decidedly, *to depart*, in the confidence that he shall *be with Christ, which is far better.* His dejection is manifestly nothing more than the feeling of a mind exhausted by its own exertions. His feelings on Sunday were very distressing both to himself and others, and were clearly aggravated by a degree of delirium arising from fever. Yesterday and to-day he has been quite calm, and though too weak to speak much, is evidently in a tranquil state. I brought my eldest boy with me, that he might once more see his grandfather, and receive his last blessing. He spoke to him this morning for a few minutes in a most affecting manner, and pronounced his blessing upon him, in a way, which I trust, he will never forget. May God grant that he may walk in the steps which are leading his grandfather to glory!" In another letter, a few days afterwards, he says, "Though I can say nothing favourable respecting his health, for he appears approaching very near to his end, yet, thanks be to God, the clouds which overspread his mind are breaking away, and he talks with a placidity and cheerfulness greater than I have before seen, since I came." "Just as we had assembled for family worship, he sent to say, that he wished us to meet in his room, and join in the Lord's supper, as a means of grace through which he might receive that consolation that he was seeking. The whole family—with one exception—was present, and an old parishioner. It is impossible to describe the deeply interesting and affecting scene. The fervour displayed by my dear father, the poor emaciated form, the tears and sobs of all present, were almost more than I could bear with that degree of composure which was requisite to enable me to read the service, so as to make him hear, (Dr. S. had become very deaf.) But it was a delightful feeling, and has done more to cheer our downcast hearts, than can well be conceived. It was, moreover, a cordial to my father's spirits, who adopted the words of the venerable Simeon, in the prospect of dissolution; *Now lettest thou thy servant depart in peace."*

The Rev. D. Wilson, in his funeral sermon, of which a number of editions were published, makes the following just remarks:—" The remarkable sufferings of so eminent a saint, in his last sickness, may, perhaps, at first perplex the mind of a young Christian. But such a person should remember, that the way to Heaven is ordinarily a way of tribulation, and that the greatest honour God puts on his servants, is to call them to such circumstances of affliction as display and manifest his grace. What would have crushed a weak and unstable penitent, with immature knowledge of the promises of salvation, only illustrated the faith of the venerable subject of this discourse. God adapts the burden to the strength. As to the darkness and anguish which at times rested on his mind, they were clearly the combined effects of disease and the temptations of the adversary. The return of comfort as the fever remitted, made this quite certain, and he was himself able, at times, to make the distinction. But even in the midst of his afflictive feelings, it is manifest to every real judge of such a case, that a living and a strong faith was in vigorous activity. For consolation is one thing, faith another. This latter grace often lays hold of the promises made in Christ with the firmest grasp, at the very time when hope and comfort are interrupted by the morbid state of the bodily and mental powers. Our feelings and powers, thank God, are not the foundation on which we build. Never, perhaps, was stronger faith exhibited by our Saviour himself, than when he uttered those piercing words, *" My God, my God, why hast thou forsaken me?"*

His daughter, in giving an account of the condition of her dying father, says, " In the time of his darkness and gloom, he prayed without ceasing, and with inexpressible fervour. He seemed unconscious of any one being near him, and gave vent to the feelings of his mind without restraint. And, Oh! what holy feelings were they! What spirituality; what hatred of sin; what humility; what simple faith in Christ; what zeal for God's glory; what submission! Never could I hear him without being reminded of Him, *who being in an agony, prayed the more earnestly.* 'I think nothing,' said he, 'of my bodily pains —my soul is all. I trust all will end well, but it is a dreadful conflict. I hope—I fear—I tremble—I pray Satan tries to be avenged of me in this awful hour, for all that I have done against his kingdom through life He longs to pluck me out of Christ's hand. Subdue the enemy, O Lord! Silence the accuser. Bruise Satan under my feet shortly.—

> 'Hide me, O my Saviour hide,
> Till the storm of life is past
> Safe into the haven guide,
> O receive my soul at last.—
> Other refuge have I none.'

O to enter eternity with one doubt on the mind—O eternity—eternity—eternity! O what a thing sin is! *Who knoweth the power of his wrath?* If this be the way to heaven, what must be the way to hell? *If the righteous scarcely be saved, where shall the ungodly and sinner appear?"*

He mentioned the wonderful way in which his prayers for others had been answered, and seemed to derive some comfort from it. He rejected every attempt to comfort him by reminding him of the way in which he had served and glorified God. "Christ is all," he said, "He is my only hope." His wonderful knowledge of Scripture was a source of great comfort; and the exactness with which he repeated passage after passage, was amazing. The manner in which also he connected one with another, was admirable. His first clear consolation was after receiving the Lord's Supper, of which an account has been given. He had previously observed, "An undue stress is, by some, laid on this ordinance, as administered to the sick; and others, I think, are in danger of undervaluing it. It is *a means of grace;* and may prove God's instrument of conveying to me the comfort I am seeking." After he had partaken of this divine ordinance, he said to his son-in-law, " It was beneficial to me; I received Christ and he received me. I feel a composure which I did not expect last night. I have not a *triumphant* assurance, but something which is more calm and satisfactory. I bless God for it." And then he repeated, in the most emphatic manner, the 12th chapter of Isaiah, *" O Lord, I will praise thee: though thou wast angry with me,"* &c. O to realize the fulness of joy—O to have done with temptation! " They shall hunger no more, nor thirst any more; neither shall the sun light on them nor any heat; for the Lamb which is in the midst of the throne shall feed them, and shall lead them unto living fountains of waters, and God shall wipe away all tears from their eyes."— "They are come out of great tribulation, and have washed their robes and made them white in the blood of the Lamb; therefore are they before the throne of God."— " We know not what we shall be, but we know that when He shall appear, we shall be like him; for we shall see him as he is."—" The righteous hath hope in his death; not driven away—no, no, not driven away!"

" There is one feeling," said he, " which I cannot have if I would. Those that oppose my doctrine have slandered me sadly, but I cannot feel any *resentment.* I can only love and pity them, and pray for their salvation. I never did feel any resentment against them. I only regret that I did not more ardently long and pray for the salvation of their souls. I feel most earnest in prayer for the promotion of Christ's kingdom all over the earth. There are two causes in the world, the cause of God and the cause of the devil; the cause of our Lord Jesus Christ and the cause of the devil. The cause of God will prevail all over the world, among all kindreds, and people, and tongues. It shall fill the whole earth. *' Hallowed be thy name,'* &c."

Waking, after a short sleep, in great calmness, he said, " This is heaven begun; I have done with dark ness *for ever—for ever.* Satan is vanquished. Nothing now remains but salvation, with eternal glory— ETERNAL GLORY." But the conflict was not yet over, for another paroxysm came on with great violence; his sufferings were extreme, and confusion and gloom prevailed. He cried earnestly to God, and said, "All my calm and comfort are gone; nothing remains of them but a faint recollection. Well, after all, God is greater than Satan. Is not Christ all sufficient? Can he not save to the uttermost? Has he not promised to save? Lord, deliver me—suffer not Satan to prevail Pity, pity, Lord, pity me!" But during all his severe sufferings of mind and body, not a word of repining or murmuring ever escaped his lips. He said, with reference to his dying in this gloom, "I cannot help it. *Thou art righteous! Father, glorify thy name.*" And then he repeated those affecting lines of Watts's paraphrase of the fifty-first psalm,

> "And if my soul were sent to Hell,
> Thy righteous law approves it well.
> Yet save a trembling sinner, Lord,
> Whose hope still hovering round thy word,
> Would light on some sweet promise there,
> Some sure support against despair."

To his wife, he said, "God be your father and your husband. I trust all mine will be kind to you. You have been a great blessing to me We shall, I trust, meet in heaven. I have less doubt of you, than of myself."

A message was received from the Rev. D. Wilson, his highly esteemed friend, expressing among other things the great benefit he had been to the church "Now this," said he, "is doing me harm. '*God be merciful to me a sinner*,' is the only ground on which I can rest. If I am saved, God shall have all the glory." Having talked too much, he was again distressed, but having obtained some rest, he awoke in the night, and said to his youngest son, who sat up with him, "What is the world and the glory of it? I would not change my hope, lean and meagre as it is, for all the kingdoms of the world and the glory of them, were I sure of living a thousand years longer, to enjoy them."

His daughter asked him on Sunday, if she should stay from church and attend on him, "O no," he replied, "nothing gives me pleasure but what is for your good, and the thought that you pray for me."

On Monday, he said to the servant who attended him, "I thank you for all your kindness. You have been a faithful domestic, and I hope a conscientious one. If at any time I have been hasty and sharp, forgive me, and pray to God to forgive, but lay the blame upon me, not on religion." A similar address and request he made to his curate. Thus his feelings continued to alternate for several days, until death closed the scene. But whatever were his pains, his prayers were unceasing and most earnest. During the whole scene, his patience, his kindness, his submission, his humility, and his faith, were most manifest.

CHAPTER XXII.

Preparation for Death—The state of the Soul after Death.

It was intended to have added the death-bed experience of the Rev. Dr. Andrew Fuller, and of some others, but it seemed that this part of the subject had been extended far enough. Indeed, some may be ready to inquire, why so much is said respecting the thoughts and speeches of dying persons? To which we would reply, that there is no subject in the world which ought to be more interesting to all men, since all men are appointed to die. Whatever other evils we may escape, "in this war there is no discharge." It is a scene of which we can have no previous experience; and therefore, it is prudent to learn what we can from the experience of those who have gone before us. It is an important and an awful scene, and should therefore occupy many of our thoughts. If due preparation has been neglected in life and health, there is small probability that it will be made on a dying bed. If I had set down all that I have witnessed and read of the dying exercises of unconverted sinners, it would have presented an appalling object for our contemplation. Such scenes have often been exhibited in print, and are not without their use, but such narratives did not fall in with the scope of these essays. But however insipid, or even disgusting these accounts of the dying exercises of believers may be to some readers, there is a class, and a large one too, who will take a deep interest in these things, because they are now waiting till their change come, and are looking forward with intense interest to that inevitable event of which we have been writing so much. These are the persons whom the author has had principally in view, in selecting these experiences of departing saints; and as the hopes and comforts of the children of God in life are very various, so he has endeavoured to show, that a like variety is found in their views and exercises, at the time of their departure out of the world. The writer confesses also, that in dwelling so long on this subject, he had some regard to his own edification, and preparation for death. As he knows from infallible evidence, that he will soon be required to put off this tabernacle, and to emigrate from this lower world, he was solicitous to acquire as much information as he was able from those who have gone before, what were the difficulties, sufferings, and encouragements, of pilgrims in this last stage of their journey. And, however it may be with others, he has derived instruction and encouragement, from the contemplation of such scenes as are here described. It appears to him supremely reasonable, that during the short time which remains of his life, he should be chiefly concerned in the meditation of the things of another world, and in making actual preparation for his own departure. He once supposed that the near approach of death would of itself be sufficient to arouse the mind, and impress upon it the reality and awful importance of eternal things; but he finds by sad experience, that however his judgment is convinced of the certainty of death, and its consequences, nothing will bring these things to bear on the heart, but the illumination of the Holy Spirit. He wishes, therefore, to engage in such reading, meditation, and writing, as may have a tendency to fix his thoughts on the solemn scene before him, when he must close his eyes on the light of this world, and bid adieu to all friends and objects with which he has been conversant here. He is not of opinion, however, that the best way to make preparation for death, is to sit down and pore over the condition of our own souls, or to confine our exertions to those things which are directly connected with our own salvation. We are kept here to do our Master's work, and that relates to others as well as ourselves. We have a stewardship, of which we must give an account; and the faithful and wise steward is careful and diligent in dispensing the blessings committed to him, to others; this is especially the case in regard to ministers of the gospel. We have a responsible office, and our account before the tribunal of Jesus Christ must be solemn and awful; and it will not do to relinquish the proper work of our calling, upon the pretext of seeking our own salvation. Our own seeking will be entirely unavailing, without the aid and blessing of God, and this we may expect most confidently, when we are diligently engaged in doing his work, which is always the duties of our station and calling. Active duty must be performed as long as we have strength for the work; and like the Levites, we must attend around the tabernacle and altar, when we are too old for more laborious services. Many of the faithful servants of God have expressed a strong desire not to outlive their usefulness; and some have wished that their departure might occur in the very act of preaching. These things we may better leave to the wisdom of God, who directs all the circumstances of the death of his people, as well as of their lives. Even when by bodily infirmities, the servants of God are obliged to desist from public labours, they do not cease from serving their Master; their lives are not useless. His name is as much honoured by patient submission and cheerful resignation, as by zealous public exertion; and the greatest and most effectual work which can be performed by any on earth, they can perform—I mean the offering of prayers and intercessions, day and night, at the throne of grace. Let not the infirm and aged say, that they can now do nothing for God. They can do much; and for ought they can tell, more than they ever did in the days of their vigour. It is a beautiful sight to see men laden with fruit, even in old age. Such fruits are generally more mature than those of earlier days; and the aged saint often enjoys a tranquillity and repose of spirit, which is almost peculiar to that age. David, or whoever is the author of the 71st Psalm, prays most earnestly a prayer which should be daily on the lips of the aged, "Cast me not off in the time of old age; forsake me not when my strength faileth." And again, "Now when I am old and grey-headed, forsake me not, until I have showed thy strength to this generation, and thy power to all that are to come." Let the aged then tell to those that come after them, the works of divine grace which they have witnessed or which their fathers have told them. Let them be active as long as they can, and when bodily strength faileth, let them wield the pen; or if unable to write for the edification of the church, let them exhibit a consistent and shining example of the Christian temper, in kindness and good will to all; in uncomplaining patience; in contented poverty; in cheerful submission to painful providences; and in mute resignation to the bereavement of their dearest friends. And when death comes, let them not be afraid or dismayed; then will be the time to honour God by implicitly and confidently trusting in his promises. Let them "against hope believe in hope." It is by faith that the last enemy must be conquered. He that believeth shall not be confounded, in this trying hour. The great Shepherd will not forsake his redeemed flock, for whom he has shed his blood; and though the adversary may rage and violently assault dying saints, he shall not overcome them. Each one of them may say with humble confidence, " Though I walk through the valley and shadow of death, I will fear no evil, for thou art with me, thy rod and thy staff they comfort me."

Let us not desire to make a parade and ostentatious display on a dying bed. Death has been called the *honest hour*, but hypocrisy may be practised even on a dying bed. Although this event often reveals secrets, and brings deceived souls to a conviction of the sandy foundation on which they have built their hopes; yet some keep on the mask to the last moment. More, however, suppress the expression of their fears and distress of mind. So much is said often about the manner in which persons meet death, that some good men have wished and requested to be left very much alone: they have feared lest they should be tempted to vain-glory, even on a dying bed; or they have feared lest their courage should fail them in the last struggle, and they should, through pain and imbecility of mind, be left to bring dishonour on their profession. The late excellent and evangelical Simeon of Cambridge, seems to have been under the influence of a feeling of this kind. But the best and safest way is submissively to commit all the circumstances of our death unto God.

We have no conception of the soul, but as a thinking, active being. The body is merely an organ, or instrument by which the soul acts while connected with it; indeed, it cannot be demonstrated that the soul performs all its acts here by the use of this organ. But whether or not, is of little consequence. We know that activity belongs to the soul, not to the body; and it would be a strange conclusion, that that which is essentially active, should cease to act, because it had been deprived of one set of organs. The only legitimate inference is that when separated from the body, the mode of action is different from what it was before. As we learn the various operations of the soul, only by experience, it is plain, that we cannot fully understand or explain the precise mode of its action after it is separated from the body. Paul teaches us, that the soul may exist and have conscious exercises of a very exalted kind; for he says, speaking of his rapture into heaven, "Whether in the body or out of the body, I cannot tell." Now, if the soul could not act without the body, he could have told certainly that he was in the body, when he witnessed, in the third heavens, things which it is not lawful for a man to utter. But this truth is taught more clearly and directly by Christ himself, when he said to the penitent thief, on the cross, "This day shalt thou be with me in Paradise." This testimony is of itself abundantly sufficient, and there is no evasion of its force, but by an interpretation so frigid and far-fetched, that it only serves to betray the weakness of the cause which it is brought to support. Paul, in another passage, speaks clearly and explicitly on this point: "Therefore, we are always confident, knowing that whilst we are at home in the body, we are absent from the Lord. We are confident, I say, and willing rather to be absent from the body, and to be present with the Lord." In the previous context this apostle intimates that when the clay tabernacle is dissolved, the soul will not be found naked, but that there will be another house ready to receive it; so that it will not be *unclothed,* but *clothed upon.* "For," says he, "in this we groan, earnestly desiring to be clothed upon with our house, which is from heaven; if so be that being clothed, we shall not be found naked. For we that are in this tabernacle do groan, being burdened, not that we would be unclothed but clothed upon, that mortality might be swallowed up of life." It would seem, then, that the soul is never without a suitable dwelling; it will not be unclothed; it only passes from one house to another — from an earthly to a heavenly habitation. But what this celestial clothing will be, of course we cannot now tell. When Stephen was dying, he cried " Lord Jesus, receive my spirit." The Lord Jesus is every where near to his saints; and as he watches over his sheep during their whole passage through the wilderness, so He is especially near to them, when they come to the "valley and shadow of Death," so that they may then sing with the sweet psalmist of Israel, "When I walk through the valley and shadow of death, I will fear no evil, for thou art with me, thy rod and thy staff they comfort me." But as Jesus the Lord has his residence in heaven, where he occupies a place on the throne of God, at the right hand of the Father, and is surrounded by an innumerable host ready to execute all his commandments; so he commissions messengers to attend at the dying bed of believers, and receive the spirits of the just and conduct them to his presence. It is evident that the departing soul will need a guide and convoy, for utterly ignorant of the glorious world into which it has entered, it would not know which way to direct its course, or where to find its allotted mansion. For heaven is a wide domain—the house of the Father of our Lord Jesus Christ, has MANY MANSIONS, and every redeemed soul has provided for it, an appropriate residence, for Christ says, "I go to prepare a place for you." And that guardian angels are sent to perform these kind offices for departed saints, we are not left to conjecture, for we read, that as soon as Lazarus died, he "was carried by the angels into Abraham's bosom." There is no reason for supposing that the privilege now conferred on the beggar, was peculiar to him; every saint needs the guidance and guardianship of angels as well as Lazarus; and we may conclude, therefore, that angels will attend on every departing saint.

Although we cannot now understand, how the soul will act in the future world, when divested of the body of clay; we cannot doubt that its consciousness of its identity will go with it. The memory of the past, instead of being obliterated, will, in all probability, be much more perfect, than while the person lived upon earth. It is by no means incredible, that memory, in the future world, will present to men, every thing which they have ever known, and every transaction in which they were ever engaged. The susceptibility of joyful emotions will also accompany the soul into the invisible world; and one of the first feelings of the departed saint, will be a lively sense of complete deliverance from all evil, natural and moral. The pains of death will be the last pangs ever experienced. When these are over, the soul will enjoy the feelings of complete salvation from every distress. What a new and delightful sensation will it be, to feel safe from every future danger, as well as saved from all past trouble. But the most important change experienced at this time, will be a perfect purification of the soul from sin. The soul, heretofore struggling with inbred corruption, which damped its ardour, darkened its views, and stupefied its feelings, now can act without any moral obstruction. Who that has often complained, like Paul, "O wretched man that I am, who shall deliver me from the body of this death?" but will feel this to be indeed heaven begun, when there will no more be felt any secret working of pride, or envy, or selfishness; but when it shall be pure, and sweetly conscious of its own purity? As perfection in holiness supposes a clear knowledge of spiritual objects; so we know, that we shall no more see the divine glory, as it were, by reflection from a glass, but directly, or "face to face." The soul of man, though probably greatly enlarged in its powers, may have new faculties developed, for which there was no use here, and of which it had no consciousness; yet the field of knowledge being boundless, and our minds being capable of attending only to one thing at a time, our knowledge of celestial things will be gradually acquired, and not perfected at once. Indeed, there can be no limit set to the progression in knowledge; it will be endless And no doubt the unalloyed pleasures of the future state, will be intimately connected with this continual increase of divine knowledge. And as here, knowledge is acquired by the aid of instructors, why may not the same be the fact in heaven? What a delightful employment to the saints who have been drinking in the knowledge of God and his works for thousands of years, to communicate instruction to the saint just arrived! How delightful to conduct the pilgrim who has just finished his race, through the ever blooming bowers of paradise, and to introduce him to this and the other ancient believer, and to assist him to find out and recognize, among so great a multitude, old friends and earthly relatives. There need be no dispute about our knowing, in heaven, those whom we knew and loved here; for if there should be no faculty by which they could at once be recognized, yet by extended and familiar intercourse with the celestial inhabitants, it cannot be otherwise but that interesting discoveries will be made continually; and the unexpected recognition of old friends may be one of the sources of pleasure which will render heaven so pleasant. But as the fleshly bond of relationship is dissolved, at death, it seems reasonable to think, that the only bond of union and kindred in heaven, will be the spiritual bond, which unites all believers in one body, and to Christ their living head; therefore, we may presume, that there will be felt an ardent desire to form an acquaintance with the most remarkable personages, who have lived from Adam downward. Who, if admitted into paradise, could repress his curiosity to see, and if possible, to converse with the progenitor of our race? Doubtless, he could tell us some things which we do not fully understand. And who would not wish to see the first person who ever entered those blessed abodes from our earth? Aye, and Enoch too, who never tasted death, and who still possesses his original body, changed and glorified, it is true, but still substantially the same? We might expect to find him in the company of Elijah, who is similarly circumstanced; and some think that the body of Moses, though it was dead and buried, was raised again, as he seems to have appeared in his own proper body on the mount of Transfiguration. And where is Abraham, that venerable saint, who in faith and obedience exceeded all other men, and obtained from God the honourable appellation of "the Father of the Faithful," and the friend of God? And who would be in heaven ever so short a time, without desiring to see Paul, the apostle of the Gentiles; and not him only, but Peter, and John, and all the college of the apostles? But methinks we are in danger of indulging our imaginations too far, and of transferring to a heavenly state, too many of the feelings and associations of our earthly condition. And I am reminded also, that as the twinkling stars are lost in the blaze of the rising sun, so there is one Person in the highest heavens, visible to all who enter that place, whose glory irradiates all the celestial mansions; whose love and smiles diffuse ineffable joy through all the heavenly hosts, and in whom every believer has an absorbing interest with which no other can be compared. On his head he wears many crowns, and in his hand he holds a sceptre by which he governs the universe; but yet he exhibits, visibly, the marks of a violent death, which, for us, he once endured. His name is, THE WORD OF GOD, KING OF KINGS, AND LORD OF LORDS, The ALPHA AND OMEGA, The ALMIGHTY. And behold, all the angels of God worship Him. And the host of the redeemed, which no man can number, sing a song of praise to the LAMB, which no man can learn, except those that are redeemed from among men; for the burden of their song is, "To Him that loved us, and washed us from our sins in his own blood. These are they that have washed their robes, and made them white in the blood of the Lamb." Every redeemed soul, upon being admitted into heaven, will, for a while, be so completely absorbed in the contemplation of that DIVINE PERSON, that he will be incapable of paying much attention to any others. Like that Armenian princess, of whom Xenophon gives an account, who, after all the rest of the company had been expressing their admiration of Cyrus, one praising one thing and one another, upon being asked what about this royal personage she admired most, answered, that she did not even look at him, because her whole attention had been absorbed in admiring him (her young husband) who had offered to die fo. her. But the saved sinner may say, that his attention was completely absorbed in gazing upon Him, who not only said that He would die for him, but who actually did die in his place, and by this sacrifice redeemed him from the curse of the law, and from all iniquity. The sweet and intimate intercourse which the redeemed soul will have with his Saviour cannot now be conceived: it will far transcend all the ideas which we now can form; and will be a perfection of bliss so great that nothing can be added to it in any other way, than by an increase of the capacity of the soul. But still, all that is enjoyed in this intermediate state between death and judgment, is but a part of that felicity to which the redeemed of the Lord are destined hereafter. It is only the enjoyment of a separate soul; but "the exceeding great and eternal weight of glory" laid up in heaven for the children of God is for the whole man, made up of soul and body; and as even in this world many pleasures are enjoyed by means of bodily organs, who can tell what new and ever varying delights may be let into the soul by means of bodies of a celestial mould, bodies fashioned after the model of the glorious body of Jesus Christ! If our senses now bring to our view so many glorious objects both in the heavens and the earth, how rich and delightful will be the vision of the upper heavens by the eyes of the resurrection body? Then shall we see Jesus with our bodily eyes—then shall we behold what now no tongue can describe, nor even heart conceive. The departed saints, therefore, though blessed to the full amount of their present capacity, yet are living in joyful expectation of a more glorious state. We should not think that the redemption and resuscitation of the body is a small matter. The body is an essential part of human nature, and the glorified body will add to the felicity of the redeemed in a degree which we have no means of calculating. The inspired writers, therefore, when they speak of the blessedness of Heaven, speak sparingly of the state of the separate soul; but when they describe the resurrection, they seem to be enraptured. Hear Paul, drawing a comparison between this mortal, corrupt, and earthly body, and that immortal, pure, and spiritual body, which will be possessed by every saint "It is sown in corruption; it is raised in incorruption It is sown in dishonour; it is raised in glory. It is sown in weakness; it is raised in power. It is sown a natural body; it is raised a spiritual body. As we have borne the image of the earthy, so shall we bear the image of the heavenly. For this corruptible must put on incorruption, and this mortal must put on immortality." No sooner shall these resuscitated bodies open their immortal eyes, than they shall behold the *Son of Man* coming in the clouds of Heaven And no sooner is the judgment set, than all these shall be caught up to meet the Lord in the air, and shall be so highly honoured as to have a place, as assessors, on the judgment seat with Him. And when the awful transactions of that day are ended, the redeemed shall accompany their Lord and Saviour to Heaven, where they shall be put in full and eternal possession of that felicity and glory which Christ has purchased for them by his precious blood. In this sublime temple, their songs shall mingle with those of the holy angels, for ever and ever. It need not be supposed that saints in Heaven will be continually employed in nothing but praise. This, indeed, will be their noblest employment; and the anthems of praise to God and the Lamb will never cease; but may we not reasonably suppose that the exercises and pursuits of the saints will be various? The wonderful works of God will open to their contemplation. They may be employed, as angels are now, as messengers to distant worlds, either as instruments of justice or mercy: for we find that the angels are employed in both these ways. While, then, one choir surrounds the throne, and elevates the celestial song of praise for redemption, others may be employed in executing the commands of their Lord; and then, in their turn, these last may keep up the unceasing praise, while the first go forth on errands of mercy or wrath.

Some have divided the angels into *assisting* and *ministering :* the first are supposed to be always engaged in acts of worship, while the last are always employed in other services. But it would be much more reasonable to suppose, that they all, in turn, take their part in both these services. Here, however, it becomes us to pause, and in deep humility, on account of our ignorance and unworthiness, to put our hands on our mouths, and our mouths in the dust. We are slow to learn earthly things; how then can we comprehend those which are heavenly? But if we are the children of God, we shall have experience of these celestial employments and never ending joys. Soon, very soon, these things which are now dimly discerned by means of faith, will be realized, when every humble saint shall appear with Christ in glory, and shall never be exposed any more to danger or suffering. Let us, then, now begin the song which shall never cease to Him that loved us and washed us from our sins in his own precious blood.

PRAYER

FOR ONE WHO FEELS THAT HE IS APPROACHING THE BORDERS OF ANOTHER WORLD.

O MOST merciful God! I rejoice that thou dost reign over the universe with a sovereign sway, so that thou dost according to thy will, in the armies of heaven and among the inhabitants of the earth. Thou art the maker of my body, and Father of my spirit, and thou hast a perfect right to dispose of me, in that manner which will most effectually promote thy glory: and I know that whatsoever thou dost, is right, and wise, and just, and good. And whatever may be my eternal destiny, I rejoice in the assurance that thy great name will be glorified in me. But as thou hast been pleased to reveal thy mercy and thy grace, to our fallen miserable world; and as the word of this salvation has been preached unto me, inviting me to accept of eternal life, upon the gracious terms of the gospel, I do cordially receive the Lord Jesus Christ as my Saviour and only Redeemer, believing sincerely the whole testimony which thou hast given respecting his divine character, his real incarnation, his unspotted and holy life, his numerous and beneficent miracles, his expiatory and meritorious death, and his glorious resurrection and ascension. I believe, also, in his supreme exaltation, in his prevalent intercession for his chosen people, in his affectionate care and aid afforded to his suffering members here below, and in his second coming to receive his humble followers to dwell with himself in heaven; and to take vengeance on his obstinate enemies. My only hope and confidence of being saved, rests simply on the mediatorial work and prevailing intercession of the Lord Jesus Christ; in consequence of which the Holy Spirit is graciously sent to make application of Christ's redemption, by working faith in us, and repentance unto life; and **rendering us meet for the heavenly inheritance, by sanctifying us in the whole man, soul, body, and spirit.** Grant, gracious God! that the rich blessings of the new covenant may be freely bestowed on thy unworthy servant. I acknowledge that I have no claim to thy favour, on account of any goodness in me by nature; for alas! there dwelleth in me, that is in my flesh, no good thing; nor on account of any works of righteousness done by me; for all our righteousnesses are as filthy rags. Neither am I able to make atonement for any one of my innumerable transgressions; which I confess before thee, are not only many in number, but heinous in their nature, justly deserving thy displeasure and wrath; so that if I were immediately sent to hell, thou wouldst be altogether just in my condemnation. Although I trust, that I have endeavoured to serve thee with some degree of sincerity; yet whatever good thing I have ever done, or even thought, I ascribe entirely to thy grace, without which I can do nothing acceptable in thy sight. And I am deeply convinced, that my best duties have fallen far short of the perfection of thy law, and have been so mingled with sin in the performance, that I might justly be condemned for the most fervent prayer I ever made. And I would confess with shame and contrition, that I am not only chargeable with sin in the act, but that there is a law in my members, warring against the law of my mind, aiming to bring me into captivity to the law of sin and death. This corrupt nature is the source of innumerable evil thoughts and desires, and damps the exercise of faith and love, and stands in the way of well-doing, so that when I would do good, evil is present with me. And so deep and powerful is this remaining depravity, that all efforts to eradicate or subdue it, are vain without the aid of divine grace. And when at any time I obtain a glimpse of the depth and turpitude of the sin of my nature, I am overwhelmed, and constrained to exclaim with Job, "I abhor myself and repent in dust and ashes." And now, RIGHTEOUS LORD GOD ALMIGHTY, I would not attempt to conceal any of my actual transgressions, however vile and shameful they are. But would penitently confess them before thee; and would plead in my defence, nothing but the perfect righteousness of the Lord Jesus Christ, who died, the just for the unjust, to bring us near to God. For his sake alone, do I ask or expect the rich blessings necessary to my salvation. For although I am unworthy, he is most worthy; though I have no righteousness, he has provided by his expiatory death, and by his holy life, a complete justifying righteousness, in which spotless robe I pray that I may be clothed; so that thou my righteous Judge, wilt see no sin in me, but wilt acquit me from every accusation, and justify me freely by thy grace, through the righteousness of my Lord and Saviour, with whom thou art ever well pleased. And my earnest prayer is, that Jesus may save me from my sins, as well as from their punishment; that I may be redeemed from all iniquity, as well as from the condemnation of the law; that the work of sanctification may be carried on in my soul by thy word and Spirit, until it be perfected at thine appointed time. And grant, O Lord! that as long as I am in the body, I may make it my constant study and chief aim to glorify thy name, both with soul and body, which are no longer mine, but thine; for I am "bought with a price"—not with silver and gold, but with the precious blood of Christ, as of a lamb without blemish and without spot. Enable me to let my light so shine, that others, seeing my good works, may be led to glorify thy name. O! make use of me as an humble instrument of advancing thy kingdom on earth, and promoting the salvation of immortal souls. If thou hast appointed sufferings for me, here below, I beseech thee to consider my weakness, and let thy chastisements be those of a loving father, that I may be made partaker of thy holiness. And let me not be tempted above what I am able to bear, but with the temptation make a way for escape.

O most merciful God! cast me not off in the time of old age; forsake me not when my strength declineth. Now, when I am old and grey-headed, forsake me not; but let thy grace be sufficient for me; and enable me to bring forth fruit, even in old age. May my hoary head be found in the ways of righteousness! Preserve my mind from dotage and imbecility, and my body from protracted disease and excruciating pain. Deliver me from despondency and discouragement, in my declining years, and enable me to bear affliction with patience, fortitude, and perfect submission to thy holy will. Lift upon me perpetually the light of thy reconciled countenance, and cause me to rejoice in thy salvation, and in the hope of thy glory. May the peace that passeth all understanding be constantly diffused through my soul, so that my mind may remain calm through all the storms and vicissitudes of life."

As, in the course of nature, I must be drawing near to my end, and as I know I must soon put off this tabernacle, I do humbly and earnestly beseech thee, O Father of mercies, to prepare me for this inevitable and solemn event. Fortify my mind against the terrors of death. Give me, if it please thee, an easy passage through the gate of death. Dissipate the dark clouds and mists which naturally hang over the grave, and lead me gently down into the gloomy valley. O my kind Shepherd, who hast tasted the bitterness of death for me, and who knowest how to sympathize with and succour the sheep of thy pasture, be thou present to guide, to support, and to comfort me. Illumine with beams of heavenly light the valley and shadow of death, so that I may fear no evil. When heart and flesh fail, be thou the strength of my heart, and my portion for ever. Let not my courage fail in the trying hour. Permit not the great adversary to harass my soul, in the last struggle, but make me a conqueror and more than a conqueror in this fearful conflict. I humbly ask that my reason may be continued to the last, and if it be thy will, that I may be so comforted and supported, that I may leave a testimony in favour of the reality of religion, and thy faithfulness in fulfilling thy gracious promises; and that others of thy servants who may follow after, may be encouraged by my example, to commit themselves boldly to the guidance and keeping of the Shepherd of Israel.

And when my spirit leaves this clay tenement, Lord Jesus, receive it. Send some of the blessed angels to convoy my inexperienced soul to the mansion which thy love has prepared. And O! let me be so situated, though in the lowest rank, that I may behold thy glory. May I have an abundant entrance administered unto me into the kingdom of our Lord and Saviour Jesus Christ; for whose sake, and in whose name, I ask all these things. Amen.

LETTERS TO THE AGED.

LETTER I.

The autumn of our life has actually arrived. The scenes of our youth have fled forever; and the feelings and hopes of that period have passed away also, or are greatly changed. When we take a retrospect of the past, several weighty reflections cannot but press upon our minds and sadden our hearts. How true do we now find that trite remark, that the longest life in the retrospect appears exceedingly short, though in prospect, the same period appeared almost interminable! Old age has come upon us, (though its approaches were very gradual,) by surprise; and even now, except when feeling something of the infirmities of age, or when viewing our altered image in the mirror, we are prone to forget that we are old; and often are impelled to undertake labours to which our strength is no longer competent. Truly our life of three-score, or more, appears like a dream, when we awake from sleep. And as the past years have passed so quickly, the few that remain will not be less rapid in their flight. Indeed, to the aged, except when they are suffering protracted pain, time appears shorter than it did when they were young. Thus at least it seems to the writer: the year, when its days and weeks and months are numbered, is as long as ever, but to our *sense*, it seems to grow shorter. We are less absorbed and interested in passing scenes than the young. Life has with us become a sober reality. The enchanting visions of a youthful imagination have now entirely vanished. But it brings a solemn and tenderly melancholy feeling over the minds of the aged to inquire for the friends and companions of their youth. How few of these can we now find upon earth? The ministers whose labours were made useful to us, and the very sound of whose voice was sweeter than the richest music, are now lying beneath the cods of the valley. The beloved friends with whom we were wont to take sweet counsel, and to whom we could confidingly open our whole hearts, have been torn from our side. Many dear relatives, loved it may be as our own life, have slept the sleep of death. Time may have healed the painful wounds made by such bereavements, but their loss often leaves a chasm which can never be supplied; and, at any rate, a scar which we shall carry to the grave. There is one reflection connected with this subject still more sad; it is, that some in whom we once delighted, and in whom we reposed strong confidence, have turned aside from the ways of truth and righteousness in which they appeared to be walking, and though they may be still walking up and down upon the earth, are dead to us, and to all those interests, which once seemed to be common to them and us. And as to those who remain steadfast, and have continued their pilgrimage without turning aside into crooked ways, what a sad change has time made upon their persons! Where is the bloom of youth, the robust strength of manhood, the eye sparkling with intelligence, and the countenance beaming with animation? Alas! they are fled; and in their place we see the decrepid body, the sunken eye, the withered countenance, and the tottering gait. All are not equally changed by the ravages of time. Indeed, to some the access of gray hairs and old age brings an addition of comeliness. There is something peculiarly lovely, as well as venerable, in the silvery locks and placid countenance of a good old man. There is in his countenance a chastened expression of benignity and sobriety, which long experience alone can produce.

But the bitterest of all reflections to the aged is that of sins committed, duties omitted, time wasted, and opportunities of doing good neglected.—Reflections of this kind, at certain times, become insufferably painful.

And although we could not wish to go a second time through such a pilgrimage; yet we cannot but wish often that with our present views, and with the aids of experience, we could enjoy again the opportunities of usefulness which were suffered to pass without improvement. But even in these painful regrets and this bitter repentance our deceitful hearts often impose upon us; and we give ourselves more credit for present good feelings than we deserve. For let us only ask ourselves, whether we now avail ourselves of all the advantages of our situation to do good. Are we not now guilty of as gross neglects, as when younger? The probability is, therefore, yea, the certainty, that if left to ourselves as much as we were, we should do no better, if we were permitted to live over our unprofitable lives a second time. But while we should lay aside all fruitless wishes, we ought certainly to reflect upon our sins and short-comings, until our godly sorrow is so enkindled within us, as to work a repentance not to be repented of. We cannot atone for our sins by tears of penitence; for this we must have recourse to another fountain, even the blood of Christ, which cleanseth from all unrighteousness; but the flow of ingenuous, godly sorrow has a tendency to soften and purify the heart; and our iniquities are rendered by this means odious; so that while we are penetrated with unfeigned gratitude to God for pardoning mercy, we are rendered more watchful against our besetting sins, and made to walk more tenderly and circumspectly; and more humbly too; for I have thought, that the reason why a covenant-keeping God sometimes permits his children to fall into shameful acts of transgression, is because nothing else but such a sight of themselves as these falls exhibit, would sufficiently humble their proud hearts. The recollection of such sins serves all their life long to convince them that they ought to place themselves among the "chief of sinners" and "the least of saints." And this view of our exceeding depravity of heart, serves to show us the faithfulness and loving kindness of God in the strongest light. According to that which he speaks in Ezek. ch. xvi. 62, 63, "And I will establish my covenant with thee; and thou shalt know that I am the Lord: that thou mayest remember and be confounded, and never open thy mouth any more, because of thy shame, when I am pacified toward thee for all that thou hast done, saith the Lord God."

My aged friends, permit me to counsel you not to give way to despondency, and unprofitable repining at the course of past events. Trust in the Lord, and encourage your hearts to hope in his mercy and faithfulness. Your afflictions may have been many and sore, and your present circumstances may be embarrassing, and your prospects for the future, gloomy. Providence may seem to have set you up as a mark for the arrows of adversity. Stroke upon stroke has been experienced. Billow after billow has gone over you, and almost overwhelmed you. Truly the time has come, when you can say, "My joys are gone." But though friends have been snatched from you, or have proved unfaithful—though children, once your hope and joy are numbered with the dead, or what is far worse, profligate or ungrateful; though your property has wasted away, or your riches suddenly taken wings and flown like the eagle to heaven; though bodily diseases and pain distress you; still trust in the divine promise, "I will never leave thee, nor forsake thee." Though friends die, God forever liveth. Though your earthly comforts and supports are gone, you are heir to an inheritance "incorruptible, undefiled, and that never fadeth away." Take for your example the prophet Habakkuk, who triumphantly declares, "Although the fig tree shall not blossom, neither shall fruit be in the vines; the labour of the olive shall fail, and the fields shall yield no meat; the flock shall be cut off from the fold, and there shall be no herd in the stalls; yet I will rejoice in the Lord, I will joy in the God of my salvation." Learn to live by faith: no class of people need the supports of faith and hope more than the aged.— And not only believe, but act. "Work while it is called to-day." "To do good, and communicate, forget not, for with such sacrifices, God is well pleased." Your work is never ended while you are in the body. It is a sad mistake for aged persons to relinquish their usual pursuits, and resign every thing into the hands of their children. Many have dated their distressing melancholy from such a false step. The mind long accustomed to activity is miserable in a state of stagnation; or rather having lost its usual nutriment, it turns and preys upon itself. Lighten your burdens, but do not give up business or study, or whatever you have been accustomed to pursue. Imbecility and dotage are also prevented or postponed, or mitigated, by constant exercise of the mind. Keep also as much of your property if you have any, in your own hand, as is necessary for your own support, and make not yourselves dependent on the most affectionate and obedient children. They will be more affectionate and more respectful when you are not dependent. Dismiss corroding cares and anxieties about what you shall do to get a living. How strange it is, that the nearer men come to the end of their journey, the greater concern they feel as to the means of future subsistence. God's hand will provide. His command to us is, " Be careful for nothing; but in every thing by prayer and supplication with thanksgiving let your requests be made known unto God."

"And the peace of God, which passeth all understanding, shall keep your hearts and minds through Christ Jesus."

LETTER II.

As an aged man, I would say to my fellow-pilgrims who are also in this advanced stage of the journey of life, ENDEAVOUR TO BE USEFUL, as long as you are continued upon earth. We are, it is true, subject to many peculiar infirmities, both of body and mind, to bear up under which requires much exertion, and no small share of divine assistance; but still we have some advantages not possessed by the young. We have received important lessons from experience, which if they have been rightly improved, are of inestimable value. The book of divine providence, which is in a great measure sealed to them, has been unfolded to us. We can look back and contemplate all the way along which the Lord has led us.—We can now see the wise design of our Father, in many events, which, at the time, were dark and mysterious. The knowledge to be derived from studying the book of God's providence, cannot be communicated to another; the lessons are like the name upon the white stone, which none can read but he that has it. The successive events of our lives we can make known, but the connexion which these events have with our character, our sins, and our prayers, can be fully understood only by ourselves. He who neglects to study the pages of this book, deprives himself of one most important means of improvement; yet many professors of religion appear to pay little or no attention to the providence of God, in relation to themselves. If they meet with some severe judgment, or some great deliverance, their attention is arrested, and they acknowledge the hand of God in the dispensation; but as to the succession of ordinary events, they seem to have no practical belief that they are ordered by divine providence, or have any important relation to their duty or interest. I would affectionately entreat my aged brethren to make the dealings of God's providence towards themselves, a subject of careful study. There is within our reach, except in the Bible, no source of instruction more important. And to aid you in this business, permit me to recommend to your careful perusal, two little volumes on Providence, which I have found useful and comfortable to myself. The first is, Flavel's "Mystery of Providence Opened"; and the other is, Boston's "Crook in the Lot." These excellent treatises may be read over and over again with profit. Perhaps, the best method of studying such books is, not to read the whole at once, or in a short time, but to peruse a few paragraphs at a time, and then reflect upon the subject, and make application of what we read to our own case. And while I am recommending works on this subject, I ought not to omit mentioning Charnock's treatise on "Providence." I confess I am not so familiar with this as the treatises before mentioned, but I have found his other writings, especially those on the Divine Attributes, so surpassing in excellence, that I feel willing to recommend any thing which ever proceeded from his pen.

I began this letter with an exhortation, to endeavour to be useful, while you live. To comply with this, you should, in the first place, guard vigilantly against those faults and foibles, into which old people are apt to fall. We must be careful not to mistake moroseness for seriousness, austerity for gravity, or discontent with our condition, for deadness to the world.

Why should the aged be more peevish and morose than others? If they are pious, there can be no good reason for it; but it is not difficult to account for the *fact*. In the decline of life a gradual change takes place in our physical system, by which the mind is considerably affected; and often positive disease is added to this natural change. The nervous system is debilitated and shattered; and in consequence, the spirits are apt to sink, or to become irregular. To these may be added, the afflictions and disappointments which most experience in the course of a long life, by which the temper is apt to be soured. And when men, by reason of the decay of mind and body, become disqualified for the same active services which they were long accustomed to perform, and these fall into the hands of juniors, whom they knew when children, it is very natural to feel, as if the world was turning round—as if every thing was going wrong. Old men have always been wont to laud the times long past, when they were young, and to censure all the innovations which have come in since. Sometimes, also, the aged experience a neglect from the young, and even a want of respect from their own children, which is exceedingly mortifying, and tends much to foster that acerbity of temper so frequently found in the aged. But although these and other similar things may be truly pleaded in extenuation of the fault under consideration; yet they do by no means amount to an apology which exculpates us from blame. And that old age is not necessarily accompanied by these unamiable traits of character is proved by many happy examples. Some aged persons exhibit an uniform cheerfulness and serenity of mind; and the remarkable fact has been recorded in regard to a few, that a naturally irritable temper has been softened and mellowed, instead of being exacerbated by old age. If I recollect rightly, this is mentioned as true in relation to the Rev. Dr. Rodgers of New York, by his biographer, my respected colleague, the Rev. Dr. Miller. The late venerable Dr. Livingston of the Dutch Reformed Church, President of their College and Seminary, was distinguished by uniform cheerfulness to a very advanced age; and his cordial and affectionate manners were remarked and felt by all who approached him. The Rev. John Newton, of London, seems to have possessed, with large measures of divine grace, a very happy physical temperament. It is delightful to contemplate the old age of such a man. And while I am mentioning recorded examples of a temper in old age deserving of imitation, I would recall to the remembrance of my readers the case of the Rev. Dr. Thomas Scott, who, at a period of life when most men relinquish all severe labour, actually undertook to learn the Arabic language, that he might be able to give instruction to the missionaries going to the East. It has often been noticed, that piety is apt to decline with the decline of manly vigour. If this be really a common event, it is exceedingly to be deplored. But, perhaps, it is more in appearance than reality. It requires much stronger faith, and feelings of warmer piety to enable an old man to go forward in his course with zeal and alacrity, than for a young man, who is buoyed up and borne along by the vigour of youthful passions, to do the same. But I rejoice to know, that piety does not always even appear to grow cold, by the descent into the vale of years. In some Christians it evidently goes on advancing; and their growth in grace is much more rapid in this period of life, than any other. As they approach nearer to heaven, their hearts and their conversation are more in heaven. O that it might be thus with us all! As these letters are intended also for my aged friends of the female sex, I would recommend to their notice and imitation the old age of Mrs. Hannah More. From her first appearance as a Christian, she seems to have gone on advancing in evangelical knowledge, and ardent piety, until she was completely superannuated. And even then, she lost nothing of the respect and affection, which by her pious and benevolent labours she had gained; for still, when her memory was so impaired that she did not remember the books she had written, the elevation of her piety and the enlargement of her benevolence remained unimpaired. And it is truly a delightful thought that when in the wreck of mind, the whole cargo of knowledge seems to be lost, and parents no longer recognize their own children, religion, where it was possessed, still remains. JESUS CHRIST IS NEVER FORGOTTEN. Pious sentiments are never obliterated. Cicero in his beautiful little treatise on Old Age, in which many judicious and pleasing sentiments are expressed, when speaking of the decay of the memory, says, that he never heard of a miser forgetting the place where he had buried his treasure. What the mind prizes most is longest retained in memory. It is often remarked, and justly, 'how beautiful does unaffected piety appear in youth!' But it may as truly be said, 'how amiable and venerable is exalted piety in old age!'

It has been said that avarice is peculiarly the sin of age: we often hear of an old, but scarcely ever of a young miser. This may be true in regard to those who have cherished the love of the world all their lives. They will hug their treasures with a closer grasp, and their affections will be more concentrated on them, when other objects are removed; but this vice does not originate in old age, it is only the mature fruit of the seed planted in early life; and though it becomes deeply radicated in old age, it is not now so much the desire of acquiring wealth, as of holding fast what they have got: The folly of the miser who hoards his money without a thought of using it, is easily shown, and has often been ridiculed. But the truth is, that all ardent pursuit of worldly objects beyond what is necessary for the real wants of nature, might be demonstrated to be equally absurd. But whatever men of the world may do, let not Christians dishonour their holy profession by an inordinate love of the world Especially, let not the aged professor bring into doubt the sincerity of his religion, by manifesting a covetous disposition. "Take heed," said the Great Teacher, "and beware of covetousness; for a man's life consisteth not in the abundance of the things which he possesseth." Many begin the world with little, and the claims of an increasing family render it necessary to exercise much diligence and economy to make a living; but thus it often happens that an avaricious disposition under the semblance of necessity, and even of duty, strikes its roots deep into the soul, ere the man is aware of any danger. Indeed, it is almost impossible to convince a man of the sin of covetousness, while he avoids open acts of injustice or fraud. Dear friends, it is time for many of you to give up the further pursuit of wealth; unless your object is to acquire the means of doing good. But beware of the deceitfulness of the heart. Covetousness will allow you to *promise* such an appropriation of your gains. But put yourselves to the test by a simple experiment. Ask yourselves whether you are now willing to make that use of the property which God has given you, that his honour and the advancement of Christ's kingdom require. If you indeed find in yourself that disposition to consecrate all that you have to the glory of God, then it may be lawful to go on to acquire further means of usefulness. But whatever you now possess, or may hereafter acquire of this world's goods, for your soul's sake, set not your affections on these perishable things. Be not proud of your wealth. Neglect not while you live, to do good and communicate. Remember that you are but the stewards of the wealth which you possess, and therefore it is required of you to be faithful in the distribution of what is put into your hands. If you have tried the plan of parsimony, lest you should lessen your estate, now try the plan of wise liberality, and see whether that saying of Christ is not verified by experience, that "It is more blessed to give than to receive."

Whether in the former periods of our lives, we have had prosperity or have passed through the deep waters of affliction, it is nearly certain that in our old age we shall feel the strokes of adversity. If our friends have been preserved in life thus far, yet we know they must all die. If hitherto we have enjoyed uninterrupted health, yet now we must expect to encounter pain and disease.—Old age itself may be called the common disease of our nature, which can only be escaped by death. Mr. Newton, in one of his last letters, says that he had but one disease, but that was incurable, which was old age. Then, my dear friends, let us set an example of patience and cheerful resignation under the afflictions which may be laid upon us. The passive virtues are more difficult to be exercised than the active; and God is perhaps more honoured by quiet submission to his will under sufferings, than by the greatest achievements of zeal and exertion. But let us never forget that we have not the least strength in ourselves. We are dependent on the grace of God for every good thought and desire. But if we trust in Him we shall never be ashamed.

LETTER III.

I HAVE no doubt that you have remarked with surprise, that the impression of the reality and importance of eternal things is not increased by the nearness of your approach to the end of your course. Time glides insensibly away, and it is with us in this respect, as in relation to the globe on which we reside. While other things appear to be in motion, our feeling is that we are stationary. The mere circumstance of being old seems to affect no one with a more lively concern about the salvation of the soul.—None appear to be more blind and stupid in regard to religious matters, than many who are tottering on the brink of the grave. This, indeed, is so commonly the fact, with those who have grown old without religion, that very little hope is entertained of the conversion of the aged, who have from their youth enjoyed the means of grace. And it is also a fact, that real Christians are not rendered more deeply sensible of the awful importance of eternal things, by becoming old and infirm. The truth is, that nothing but an increase of faith by the operation of the Holy Spirit, will be effectual to prepare us for that change which we know is rapidly approaching. Counsels and exhortations, however, are not to be neglected, as God is pleased to work by means. I have, therefore, undertaken to address to you such considerations as occur to me. Having already spoken of the infirmities and sins which are apt to cleave to us in advanced years, I propose in this letter, to inquire what are the peculiar duties incumbent on the aged. What would the Lord have us to do?—for undoubtedly, we are not privileged to fold our hands, and sit down in idleness, as if our work was ended. Indeed, it would be no privilege to be exempt from all occupation. Such a life to the aged or the young, must be a life of misery; for man never was made to be idle, and his happiness is intimately connected with activity. We may be no longer qualified for those labours which require much bodily strength—we may, indeed, be so debilitated or crippled by disease, that we can scarcely move our crazy frame —and some among us may be vexed with excruciating pain—yet still we have a work to perform for God, and for our generation. If we cannot use our hands and feet, so as to be useful in the labours which we were wont to perform, yet we may employ our tongues to speak the praises of our God and Saviour. We may drop a word of counsel to those around us; and especially, the aged owe a duty to the young, to whom they may have access, and who are related to them. Every aged Christian must have acquired much knowledge from experience, which he should be ready to communicate as far as it is practicable. Why is it, my dear friends, that we suffer so many opportunities of usefulness to pass without improvement? Why are we so often silent, when the suggestions of our own conscience urge us to speak something for God? How is it, that we consume hours in unprofitable talk, and seldom attempt to say any thing which can profit the hearers? We may plead inability—we may excuse ourselves, because we are unlearned and not able to speak eloquently and correctly—but let us be honest; is not the true reason because our own hearts are so little affected with these things? We cannot consent to play the hypocrite, by uttering sentiments which we do not feel; and we have often been disgusted with the attempts of others, who, in a cold and constrained manner, have introduced religious conversation. It is easy to see where the fault lies; it is in the state of our own hearts. Let us never rest, then, until we find ourselves in a better state of mind. Let us get our hearts habitually under the influence of divine things, and then conversation on this subject, will be as easy as on any other. "Out of the abundance of the heart, the mouth speaketh." There are companies and occasions, when to obtrude remarks on religion, would be unseasonable and imprudent; for we must not cast our pearls before swine: but, in most cases, an aged person may give utterance to seasonable and solemn truths, without offence—and very often a word spoken in season, has been the means of saving a soul; and the advice and exhortation of parents and pious friends, are remembered and prove salutary, after their heads are laid low under the clods of the valley.

I have often heard aged persons, incapable any longer of active service, express surprise that their unprofitable lives were so long protracted; while the young and laborious servants of God were cut off in the midst of their years. The dispensations of God are indeed inscrutable—"his ways are past finding out"—and we are too little acquainted with his counsels, to sit in judgment on them. But I would say to those who think that they can be of no further use in the world, that they do not form a just estimate of the nature of the service which God requires, and by which he is glorified by his creatures upon earth. All true obedience originates in the heart, and consists essentially of the affections of the heart: external duties are to be performed, but are only holy as connected with holy motives. The aged man may serve God, therefore, as sincerely and fervently as any others, if only the heart be right in the sight of God. He can glorify God in his spirit, by thinking affectionately of his glorious name, by contemplating his divine attributes, and by exercising love and gratitude towards him.—His devotion might thus approach more nearly to our conceptions of the services and exercises of the saints in heaven. But it may be that the lives of some are lengthened out, that they may offer up many prayers for the church and for the world; for, after all the activity and bustle and zeal apparent, there is no service which can be performed by mortals, so effectual as prayer.—Here there is a work to which the aged may be devoted. While Joshua and the men of war contend with the Amalekites in the battle, Moses assists by lifting up his hands in prayer; and when he is, through fatigue, no longer able to hold them up, he is assisted by Aaron on one side, and Hur on the other. If you cannot preach, you can, by prayer, hold up the hands of those who do. You can follow the missionary, who leaves all to go and labour in heathen lands, with your daily and fervent prayers. It is not in vain for you to live, while you have access to a throne of grace. Before the advent of Christ, there were some aged persons who seem to have been preserved in life, that they might pray for this event, and that they might enjoy the pleasure of seeing the answer of their prayers, and embracing Him in their arms, whom they had so often embraced by faith. While all around was spiritual death and desolation, and corruption and error had infected all classes, from the priesthood downward, there was a little band who had taken up their residence in the temple, or often frequented this holy place, who were waiting for the consolation of Israel. Two of these were Simeon and Anna; but there were others of the same character; for we read that this very aged and pious widow, who departed not from the temple, but served God with fasting and prayers, night and day, "spake of Christ after she had seen him, *to all them who looked for redemption in Israel.*" The darker the times, the more closely do the truly pious adhere to each other. This little knot of praying people knew each other, and no doubt spake often one to another; and in this case, the Lord hearkened and heard; for the object of their desires and prayers was given to them. Was the life of Anna an unprofitable life, although she never left the temple, and did nothing but fast and pray? Was Simeon a useless member of the church, because he was probably too old for labour? The truth was—and the same is often verified—that the true church of God was at this time confined to a few pious souls; while the priests and the scribes and the rulers, had neither part nor lot in the matter. As God preserved Simeon, according to a promise made to him, until he saw the Lord's Christ, so he may be lengthening out the lives of some of you, my aged brethren, until you may have the opportunity of seeing the salvation of Israel come out of Zion. Do you not wish to be witnesses of the rise and glory of the church? Pray then incessantly for the peace and prosperity of Jerusalem. Consider it as your chief business, to pray that the kingdom of God may come.—What though the signs of the times be discouraging—what though you live in troublous times—what though the church may be shaken, and the prospects of her increase be dark, yet remember that she is founded on a rock, and the gates of hell cannot prevail against her. The vessel which carries Christ, though it be buffeted by storms, is in no danger of being wrecked. But to govern and direct does not belong to you; your duty is to pray —to pray without ceasing—to wrestle with the ange' of the covenant, and not to let him go until he bless you. Give him no rest until he establish and make Jerusalem a praise in all the earth. You cannot offend by importunity, but by this you will be sure to prevail; for " will not God hear his own elect, who cry day and night unto him?"—Therefore, never hold your peace, but as long as you live intercede with him to fulfil his gracious promises, and to cause the earth to be filled with the knowledge of himself as the waters cover the sea, when his people shall be all righteous, and there shall be no need any longer for any one to say to his neighbour, Know the Lord, for all shall know him from the least to the greatest.

Thanksgiving is also a duty peculiarly incumbent on the aged. In the providence of God you are spared, whilst most of your coevals have been cut off in the midst of their career. Some of you have enjoyed almost uninterrupted prosperity. When you consider the dispensations of God's providence towards you, in the time and place and circumstances of your birth, in giving you pious and intelligent parents, who took care of your health and education, and in following you with goodness and mercy all the days of your life; giving you kind friends, faithful teachers, health and reason, together with abundant religious privileges, how thankful ought you to be! But that which above all other things enhances your obligations to gratitude is, that in his own good time He effectually called you from the devious paths of iniquity, and adopted you as a child into his own household and family, and perhaps has made you the instrument of much good to others; if not on a large scale, yet in your own family, and in the church of which you are a member. If now, to all these blessings, he has given you pious children, who promise, when you are gone, more than to supply your place in society; or even if they have been preserved from infidelity and disgraceful immoralities, and are disposed to pay a serious attention to the preaching of the gospel, no words can express your obligations to give thanks unto the Lord, and continually to praise his name, whose mercy endureth forever and ever. "Let us, therefore, offer the sacrifice of praise to God continually—that is, the fruit of our lips, giving thanks to his name."

LETTER IV.

There is one remaining subject, my dear friends, to which I wish to call your attention. I refer to the solemn event of our departure out of life. Whatever may be uncertain in the future, concerning this there cannot exist the shadow of a doubt,—"It is appointed unto men once to die." "I know that thou wilt bring me to the house appointed for all living." "The grave is mine house." But we do not need the voice of revelation to assure us of our mortality: the evidence is daily before our eyes. Hundreds of our race close their eyes in death every day. The grave is never satisfied; nor says, It is enough. Of the thousands of millions who have inhabited this globe, no more than two have escaped the dissolution of the body. And we are as certain as we can be of any thing, that all future generations shall go the same way, until Christ shall suddenly make his glorious appearance, coming in the clouds of heaven, with all his mighty angels. The men who shall then be found upon the earth shall not die, but they shall undergo a transformation equivalent to the death and resurrection of the body. "Behold," says Paul, "I shew you a mystery; we shall not all sleep, but we shall all be changed in a moment, in the twinkling of an eye, at the last trump, for the trumpet shall sound." If then the second coming of Christ should occur, before our departure from life, we should, indeed, escape a literal death; but we can scarcely cherish the faintest hope of this kind. Prophecy leads us to believe, that many ages of the world are still future, and that the most glorious period of the church is to come; when the gospel shall not only be preached to all nations, but shall be embraced by all; "when the earth shall be full of the knowledge of God, as the waters cover the sea."

Death, when viewed merely by the light of nature, is truly an appalling event. It is commonly preceded by disease, or the decrepitude of old age. The separation between the soul and body is usually accompanied with a convulsive struggle, and the appearance of extreme agony; so that "the pangs of death," and "the agonies of death," are familiar phrases among all people. It is manifestly an unnatural event; that is, these constituent parts of human nature do not seem willing to part, but the severance of the one from the other is brought about by the operation of some violent cause. That the soul instinctively and strongly cleaves to its tenement as long as it can, and by every possible means resists the separation, requires no proof. That in some instances this adherence to life is counteracted, so that persons voluntarily put an end to this union of soul and body, or desire to leave the body, furnishes no evidence to the contrary: it only shows that it is possible for causes to be put into operation which are even stronger than our attachment to this life. Besides the pains and agonies of dissolution, there are other circumstances which render death an object abhorrent to human feelings. It is a forcible and everlasting separation from all persons and things with which we have been conversant on earth. In it, we take a final leave of our dearest friends and beloved relatives, dear to our hearts as our own lives. Husbands are divorced from their wives; parents separated from their children; brothers and sisters must part; friends—who often stick closer than brothers—here have the tenderest bonds sundered. The scenes to which we have long been accustomed; the houses in which we have long dwelt; the churches where we have met the solemn assembly of God's people, must all be left behind. The old man's arm-chair is left vacant; his place in the house of God is empty; the social circle of which he formed a part is broken; and the work which he was accustomed to perform stands still, or falls into other hands. And he who departs, leaving behind him numerous attached friends, cannot avoid the foresight of the deep affliction. Already, before his eyes are closed, he sees the mournful group crowding around his dying bed, to catch the last look of affection,—to hear the last broken tones of a voice soon to be silent in death. The heart-breaking and tears of affectionate relatives often form one of the most painful circumstances attending the death of a good man. He might well express his feelings in the language of Paul, on another occasion: "What mean ye to weep and to break my heart?" But if the dearest friends which the dying man has, attempt to save themselves and him from the almost intolerable pang of separation, by withdrawing from the mournful scene; this, in a very small degree, if at all, mitigates the dreaded pang. The imagination often paints the scene in more vivid colours than the reality. When the husband gasping for his last breath, observes the absence of the beloved partner of his joys and sorrows, he knows that she is gone into some secret chamber " to weep there." And she cannot withdraw into any recess so secluded, as not to seem to hear the deep-drawn sighs and heavy groans, to see the ghastly looks and contortions of him on whom all her earthly reliance has been long placed. I would say then, take her not away from the bed-side of the dying husband. Let her hold his trembling, cold hand to the last. Let him have the comfort of casting his last look on the object of his tenderest affections. The Rev. Samuel Davies—a name so deservedly loved and revered in Virginia—has a poem, in which he describes the feelings of a husband and wife, tenderly attached, in the prospect of the dissolution of either first. But there is not much to choose between the two cases, as far as relates to the parting scene. Those, however, who are left behind are most deserving of compassion. They *who die in the Lord* are at once blessed, because they rest from their labours; but they who survive are often burdened with sorrow, and with a desolate heart go mourning all the day, enveloped in the sombre weeds of grief, and their heads hang down as the bulrush. It seems to me, however, that the mourning on account of the decease of pious friends, ought to be very moderate, and our tears soon dried up. What better can we ask for our friends, than that they might be safely lodged in the bosom of Abraham; where they will enjoy to the full such "good things" as they could never hope to enjoy in this world? There is, however, one case of the death of dear relatives, to which the aged especially are liable, in which there is but one topic of consolation; that is, the departure from life of those in whose end there is no ground for scriptural hope. At the prospect of this judgment my soul has often trembled. May a merciful God avert it from every pious parent! If we were persuaded that we had uniformly done our duty towards our deceased friends, the stroke would not be so heavy; but when remorse for unfaithfulness mingles its bitter streams with the sorrow occasioned by bereavement, the cup must be bitter beyond conception. On this subject, however, I have met, among professing Christians, with what I consider a fault on both extremes. A venerable clergyman, who had lost a beloved son, who never gave, as far as known, any evidence of genuine repentance or faith in the Lord Jesus Christ, was unable to bear up under the reflection that his dear child was in a state of hopeless misery; he therefore sought relief to his agonized mind, by cherishing an error contrary to the analogy of his whole system of theology. He said to me, I cannot bring myself to think that a moral and amiable person, brought up under the gospel, and assenting to its doctrines, will, by a gracious God, be made eternally miserable in hell, although he may not have experienced a change of heart. O sad necessity, which drives a good man to such a resource for support and comfort! But this is the practical belief of multitudes of professors. They hold the doctrine of regeneration and its necessity as a matter of creed and theory, but in fact, they believe otherwise. A gay and blooming young

.ady, who probably had never spent one half hour in serious thought, was suddenly carried off by an acute disease, which was so rapid and violent in its progress, that little or no opportunity was afforded for conversation with the pastor or pious friends.—When some serious person lamented the unprepared state of the deceased, the suggestion was received in a Christian congregation and by nominal Christians with a sort of indignation; as though it was an evidence of uncharitable bigotry, to believe one of the plainest doctrines of the Bible.—The other extreme is—peremptorily deciding upon the case of those who die without having given evidence of a change of heart. This case I will also illustrate by an anecdote which I know to be true. The brother of a zealous preacher of the gospel came to his end suddenly by the starting of his horse, by which his brains were knocked out against a tree; and it was conjectured that the young man had been indulging too freely in the use of intoxicating liquor. When the brother above mentioned came to the house, where the corpse was laid out, he raised the covering from the face, and, after a solemn pause, said, with an audible voice, "There lies the senseless body, but the soul is burning in hell:" And this, too, when the room was full of people. The true doctrine on this subject is, that friends may indulge hope in relation to these deceased friends, as far as they can consistently with the truth of God; but let no one seek healing for his wounded spirit, by "denying the faith." Even when there is no positive evidence of a change, we may resort to the possibility that it might have taken place in the last moments; for who has a right to set limits to the mercy of God, when he has not limited himself? There is great danger, however, of expressing opinions or hopes, which may lead careless sinners to indulge in carnal security. It is much better, in such cases, to be silent. Some ministers, whom I have known, have been so solicitous to keep sinners from delaying repentance, that they have inculcated the opinion, that a death-bed repentance is not only uncertain, but absolutely ineffectual, and that no hope can be justly entertained for those who never repented until the last hour. It is true, that many who on a sick-bed appear penitent, when they recover, soon lose all their serious impressions, and return with renewed avidity to the pursuits of the world. Their repentance is thus proved to have been spurious. But every fit of fear, produced by the near prospect of death, ought not to be called repentance; or at any rate, *that* repentance which, in scripture, is connected with the pardon of sin—which is a real change of the views and tempers of the mind—by which a man becomes a new creature, old things having passed away, and all things having become new. All repentance on a deathbed is not, however, by these instances proved to be spurious, any more than all conversions of people in health are proved to be counterfeit—because a great many such are to be met with. I have seen cases of repentance on a death-bed, as satisfactory, and in which I had as much confidence as in any that I have known among those in health, prior to the evidence of a good life. And why should it be supposed that a gracious God will never manifest his power and grace in the conversion of a sinner on a sick-bed? If this should once be admitted as a principle, it would be worse than useless for a minister of the gospel, or any other pious person, to visit an unconverted sinner when on a sick-bed; or to give any answer to his most anxious inquiry, "What shall I do to be saved?" I recollect to have heard a preacher from the pulpit, solemnly aver that there was no instance in the Bible of the conversion of an aged sinner. This is another *ultraism*, which has no good foundation. One of the most remarkable cases of the conversion of an exceeding great sinner, recorded in the sacred Scriptures, is of an aged man. I refer to the late repentance of king Manasseh. There is no man, of whom mention is made in the sacred volume, to whom a worse character is given, as one that exceeded the worst of the heathen in his abominable idolatries:—"Moreover, Manasseh shed innocent blood very much, till he had filled Jerusalem from one end to the other." It is true, it is not expressly said, that his repentance occurred in his old age, but it may, with strong probability, be inferred from the history. (2 Chron. xxxiii.)

If, among my readers, there should be any aged persons who are still impenitent, I would earnestly and affectionately exhort them, not to despair of God's mercy; there still may be hope in their case. My dear fellow-sinners, there is nothing in God's word, which excludes you from salvation, unless you voluntarily and obstinately exclude yourselves, by a rejection of the overture of reconciliation. Christ says to you, as much as to others, "Ye will not come unto me that ye may have life."

I find that I shall be under the necessity of claiming the old man's privilege of rambling from one subject to another: and, in writing to the aged, I hope I shall be excused for my prolixity in this letter. I have not fulfilled my own purpose, either as to the subject matter or length; and the consequence will be the *infliction* of another epistle. But before I conclude this, I wish to say that death, viewed in the light of Scripture, exhibits a very different aspect from what it does when viewed by the light of nature; both as it relates to the sinner and the saint. In regard to the former, we are taught in the volume of truth, "that death was introduced by the transgression of man." The penalty of the original law given to man was, "In the day thou eatest thereof (that is, of the forbidden fruit) thou shalt surely die." And when man became guilty, the sentence was denounced, "Dust thou art, and unto dust thou shalt return"—the execution of which penalty has been going on from that day to this, sweeping off generation after generation, until almost every part of the earth is filled with dust which once constituted the bodies of men. Even reason, when soberly consulted, would indicate that death comes as the punishment of sin; for otherwise, the transition from one state of existence to another, would not, under the government of a good God, be attended with so much pain and fear. But, what reason discovers only in dim perspective, revelation writes as with a sunbeam

"THE WAGES OF SIN IS DEATH." "AS BY ONE MAN SIN ENTERED INTO THE WORLD, AND DEATH BY SIN SO DEATH HATH PASSED ON ALL MEN, FOR THAT ALL HAVE SINNED."

On the other hand, true believers are now delivered from the curse of the law, and consequently from death, as it is a curse. We may say, therefore, that the righteous shall never taste death; for Christ, the Lord, hath solemnly averred, "If a man keep my sayings, he shall never see death." Accordingly, the inspired writers of the New Testament, commonly speak of the decease of Christians as a "sleep." "Them that sleep in Jesus will God bring with him." "We shall not all sleep, but we shall all be changed." And of Stephen, it is said, when he "kneeled down, and said with a loud voice, Lord, lay not this sin to their charge, HE FELL ASLEEP." But when the word *death* is retained, it must be understood to have a new sense in relation to the children of God. It is death despoiled of his sting. It is the outward appearance of death, while its nature is entirely changed—so changed, that the curse is converted into a blessing. That which is a rich gain cannot be a curse; but to the sincere follower of Christ, "TO DIE IS GAIN." That which may be lawfully an object of ardent desire, cannot be of the nature of a penalty or curse; but Paul had a desire to depart and be with Christ, and the same desire has been felt by thousands since. But to cut the matter short, death is placed in the category of the richest blessings. "For all things are yours, whether Paul, or Apollos, or Cephas, or the world, or life, or DEATH, or things present, or things to come, all are yours." The true Christian, then, has no reason to be appalled at the necessity of entering this darkly shaded valley. Dear friends, if we only approach, holding up the torch of revelation by faith, the dismal gloom which has gathered over the tomb will be immediately dissipated. Faith looks beyond this darkness and across this valley, and beholds a celestial city, the new Jerusalem. Though much indebted to John Bunyan,—one of the most fertile geniuses the world ever produced—I cannot easily forgive him for making the passage over Jordan to Canaan so very difficult for Christian. If he had carried out the allegory, he would have turned the swelling waves backward, and have shewn a dry path across the stream; for no sooner had the priests, who carried the ark of the testimony, dipped their feet in the brim of the river than—"all the Israelites passed over on dry ground." But, after all, perhaps, the honest tinker drew his picture from the fact; for as Christians seldom enjoy in life the comfort provided for them, so it is analogous, that in death they should want that comfort to which in Christ they are entitled.

LETTER V.

CAN we do any thing to render our death—which cannot be far off—both safe and comfortable? No doubt, by God's assistance, we can do much to accomplish these desirable ends, if we will set about the work in good earnest. I know that there is a feeling of despondency habitually existing in the minds of some aged persons of serious disposition, which leads them to conclude, that if they are not now prepared to die, they never will be. And from all the acquaintance which I have had with professors of religion, I am constrained to think that, as their near approach to the grave does not increase their impressions of the importance of eternal realities, so old age has no tendency to render the evidences of their union with Christ more clear and satisfactory. You may frequently inquire of a dozen such professors in succession, whether they have obtained a comfortable assurance of the goodness of their spiritual condition, and the probability is, that four out of five, if not nine out of ten, will answer in the negative, and will express serious doubts whether they were ever the subjects of regenerating grace. It was not, I believe, always so with those who cordially received the doctrines of grace, and rested their souls upon them. To say nothing about the joyful confidence and assured hope of the apostles and primitive Christians, the members of the first reformed churches seem to have derived from the pure doctrines of the Bible a high degree of peace and joy. The same was the fact among the pious Puritans of Old and New England; and the Presbyterians of Scotland, in the best and purest days of the Scottish church. The question has often occurred, why does the belief of these doctrines afford less comfort now, than in former times. It is not my purpose, at present, to attempt to account for this fact. I adduce it merely to show, that most professors among us, are not *actually* prepared for death. Even if their state should be one of safety, they cannot view their approaching end with confidence and comfort. And whilst their evidences of genuine piety are so dubious, they of course cannot know that they are in a safe condition. It is, then, of the utmost importance that all professors of the above description, and especially the aged, should be importunately urged " to give diligence to make their calling and election sure." I am aware that some Christians, who enjoy very comfortable evidences of being the adopted children of God, are not willing to profess that they have arrived at full assurance. They suppose that they who have attained to this high privilege are in a state of uninterrupted joy, and that no shadow of doubt ever passes over their minds. The truth is, they do possess a solid assurance, although their frames of mind are not always equally comfortable, and although the evidence is not so great that it cannot be increased. I recollect, when very young, to have heard a judicious minister conversing with an eminently pious old lady, who had belonged to the church under the care of the Rev. Samuel Davies, in the county of Hanover. In answer to some inquiry respecting the comfort which she enjoyed in the service of her Divine Master, she said, after expressing lively feelings of faith, penitence and gratitude, "but, my dear friend, I have never yet attained to the faith of assurance; all I can say is, that I have the faith of reliance." "Well," said the minister, "if you know that you have the faith of reliance, that is assurance." The degrees of evidence possessed by different Christians, are various, from the feeblest hope up to strong confidence, and the clearness of the evidence to the same person varies exceedingly; but in general, there seems to be in our church a sad falling below *par* in respect to this matter. It has, however, often been correctly observed, that we are not to expect *dying grace*, before the dying hour arrives. God gives strength as we need it; and when the believer is called to severe trials, or to difficult duties, he commonly receives aid proportioned to the urgency of his wants, and is surprised to find himself held up by a power not his own. Thus we have often seen the sincere humble Christian, who, during life, was subject to bondage through fear of death, triumphing in the dying hour. This expectation of special aid ought to be encouraged. It is, indeed, a part of that preparation which we should make; and if we confidently rely on the great Shepherd to meet us, and comfort us, while walking through the valley and shadow of death, he will not disappoint us.

But, in dealing with professors troubled with doubts, we are too apt to proceed on the assumed principle, that notwithstanding their sad misgivings and fears, they are at bottom sincere Christians, and have the root of the matter in them; while in regard to many, this may be an entire mistake, and we are in danger of cherishing in them a fatal delusion. Here the skill and fidelity of the spiritual watchmen are put to the test; and while they should not deviate a hair's-breadth from the rule of the divine word, it is better that the pious Christian should suffer some unnecessary pain, than that the false professor should be bolstered up with delusive hopes. I must say, therefore, that the true reason why many professors have no comfortable evidence of their religion, is because they have none. They have never experienced the new birth; and being still dead in trespasses and sins, it is no wonder that that they cannot find in themselves what does not exist

I abhor a censorious spirit, which, upon slight grounds, judges this and that professor to be graceless; but all my experience and observation lead me to believe that, in our day as well as in former times, the "foolish virgins" constitute a full moiety of the visible church. What I would urge, therefore, on you, my aged friends, and on myself, is a more serious, impartial, and thorough examination into the foundation of our hope of heaven, than perhaps we have ever yet made.—Let us go back to the commencement of our religious course, and see whether, in our present more mature judgment, we can conclude that we were then the subjects of a saving change. I do not ask you whether you had an increase of serious feelings, or whether your sympathies were strongly excited and experienced some change from a state of terror or distress to comfort; for all these things may be experienced, and have been experienced by unregenerate persons. Let us carefully inquire whether the habitual tenor of our lives has been such as to satisfy us that a new nature was received. If we have fallen into sin, have we deeply and sincerely repented of it? Have we wept bitterly for our sin, like Peter? or have we mourned in deep sorrow, like David? Not such repentance as some experience, who, after all their convictions and confessions, return again to the same course of iniquity. But, after all examinations of past experience, the main point is, what is the present, habitual state of our hearts? Do we now love God as his character is exhibited in his word? Do we hunger and thirst after holiness, or a complete conformity to the law of God? Would we be willing that that law should be relaxed in its demands to afford us some indulgence? Do we seek our chief happiness in the favour of God, and in communion with him in his word and ordinances? Is his glory uppermost in our desires, and do we sincerely wish and determine to do all that we can to promote the kingdom of the Redeemer? Do we sincerely love the people of God, of every sect and name, because they bear his image, and are the redeemed children of God? Again: what is the ground on which we expect the pardon of sin and the favour of God? Is it because we are better than many others? Is it because we have had what we esteem great experiences? Is it on account of our moral demeanour, or charitable benefactions? Dare we trust in any measure to our own goodness and righteousness? If we build on any of these, or on any similar grounds, then are we on a sandy foundation, and all our towering hopes must fall. But, methinks, I hear the humble penitent saying, "all these things I count loss for Christ —I feel that I deserve to die—I never was more convinced of any thing, than that it would have been perfectly just for God to send me to hell. And now, all my trust and all my hope, if I know my own heart, is in the Lord Jesus Christ, and in his perfect righteousness and intercession; and all my confidence of being able to serve God hereafter, or to persevere for a single day, is in the grace of the Holy Spirit. The whole evidence of Christian character may be reduced to two particulars—entire trust in Christ for justification, and a sincere and universal love of holiness, with a dependence on the Holy Spirit for its existence, continuance and increase. If, my friend, you have these evidences *now*, you need not perplex yourself by a multitude of scruples. You may dismiss your doubts. God's word will never deceive any who rely upon its guidance. You may not know the day nor even the year, when spiritual life commenced in your soul; and yet, if you now feel its warm pulsations—if you breathe its genuine aspirations—if your heart's treasures are in heaven, and if the cause of God is dearer to you than any other interest—if his people are dearer to you than any other people—if your most constant and supreme desire is to glorify God your Redeemer, whether by living or dying—then may you welcome death. He is no king of terrors to you. You may say, "Come, Lord Jesus, come quickly!"

Perhaps some of you are afraid of the pangs of death. You have heard of the convulsive struggle—the dying groans—the difficult breathing—and the ghastly countenance! Well, it must be confessed, the scene is appalling; but it is soon over, forever. I am of opinion, however, that often, there is the appearance of dreadful suffering where the patient is unconscious of any very acute pain; and very frequently, the departure of the immortal spirit is, at the last, like falling into a gentle sleep. And not unfrequently, while the body is racked with pain, or with what would produce pain in other circumstances, the soul is so supported and comforted by the sweet peace of God poured into it, that the disorders and convulsions of the body are scarcely thought of. And in many instances, God takes his people away by a sudden stroke;—they know nothing about it, until they awake in heaven. O! what a transition! Or, if it be necessary to let in the light of glory gradually, God, who knows our constitution, will order all things well. But I would advise you to meditate much on death. Collect, and have in memory, a number of precious promises for the occasion. Put up many prayers for grace and strength for a dying hour. Beg an interest in the intercessions of your Christian friends. Keep your minds calm, and yield not to perturbing cares. Be found at your post, when the summons comes, with your loins girded and lights burning. Settle beforehand all your worldly affairs.

COUNSELS OF THE AGED TO THE YOUNG

IT is a matter of serious regret, that young persons are commonly so little disposed to listen to the advice of the aged. This prejudice seems to have its origin in an apprehension, that austerity and rigour naturally belong to advanced years; and that the loss of all susceptibility of pleasure from those scenes and objects which afford delight to the young produces something of an ill-natured or envious feeling towards them. Now, it cannot be denied, that some of the aged are chargeable with the fault of being too rigid in exacting from youth the same steady gravity, which is becoming in those who have lived long, and have had much experience in the world: not remembering, that the constitutional temperament of these two periods of human life is very different. In youth, the spirits are buoyant, the susceptibilities lively, the affections ardent, and the hopes sanguine. To the young, every thing in the world wears the garb of freshness; and the novelty and variety of the scenes presented keep up a constant excitement. These traits of youthful character, as long as irregularity and excess are avoided, are not only allowable, but amiable; and would in that age be badly exchanged for the more sedate and grave emotions which are the natural effects of increasing years, and of long and painful experience. But it is greatly to be desired, that the lessons of wisdom taught by the experience of one set of men should be made available to the instruction of those who come after them. We have, therefore, determined to address a few short hints of advice to the rising generation, on subjects of deep and acknowledged importance to all; but previously to commencing, we would assure them, that it is no part of our object to interfere with their innocent enjoyments, or to deprive them of one pleasure which cannot be shown to be injurious to their best interests. We wish to approach you, dear youth, in the character of affectionate friends, rather than in that of dogmatical teachers or stern reprovers. We would therefore, solicit your patient, candid and impartial attention to the following counsels:

I. RESOLVE to form your lives upon some certain principles, and to regulate your actions by fixed rules. Man was made to be governed by reason, and not by mere accident or caprice. It is important, therefore, that you begin early to consider and inquire, what is the proper course of human conduct, and to form some plan for your future lives. The want of such consideration is manifest in the conduct of multitudes. They are governed by the impulse of the moment, reckless of consequences. They have fixed no steady aim, and have adopted no certain principles of action. Living thus at random, it would be a miracle if they went uniformly right. In order to your pursuing a right path, you must know what it is, and to acquire this knowledge, you must divest yourselves of thoughtless giddiness, you must take time for serious reflection. It will not answer, to adopt without consideration the opinions of those who may be about you; for they may have some sinister design in regard to you; or they may themselves be misled by error or prejudice. Persons already involved in dissipation or entangled in error, naturally desire to keep themselves in countenance, by the number of followers whom they can seduce into the paths of vice. As reasonable creatures, therefore, judge for yourselves what course it is right and fitting that you should pursue. Exercise your own reason independently and impartially, and give not yourselves up to be governed by mere caprice and fashion, or by the opinions of others.

II. WHILE you are young, avail yourselves of every opportunity of acquiring useful knowledge.—Reason should guide us; but without correct knowledge reason is useless; just as the most perfectly formed eye would be useless, without light. There is in every man a natural thirst for knowledge, which needs only to be cultivated and rightly directed. All have not equal opportunities of obtaining important knowledge: but all have more advantages for this object than they improve. The sources of information are innumerable: the principal, however, are books and living men. In regard to the former, no age of the world which has passed, was so favoured with a multiplicity of books as our own. Indeed, the very number, and diversity of character and tendency of authors now create one of the most obvious difficulties to those who are destitute of wise advisers. It would be an unwise counsel, to tell you to read indiscriminately whatever comes to hand. The press gives circulation not only to useful knowledge, but to error dressed up plausibly in the garb of truth. Many books are useless, others are on the whole injurious, and some are impregnated with a deadly poison. Waste not your time in works of idle fiction. Touch not the book which exhibits vice in an alluring form. Seek the advice of judicious friends in the choice of books.

But you may also learn much from listening to the conversation of the wise and good. There is scarcely a person so ignorant, who has lived any time in the world, that cannot communicate some profitable hint to the young. Avail yourselves, then, of every opportunity of learning what you do not know; and let not pride prevent you from seeking instruction, lest by this means you should betray your ignorance. Cherish the desire of knowledge, and keep your mind constantly awake, and open to instruction, from every quarter.

But, especially, I would recommend to you the acquisition of self-knowledge. "KNOW THYSELF" was a precept held in such high esteem among the ancients, that the honour of inventing it was claimed for several of their wisest men; and not only so, but on account of its superlative excellence, it was believed by many to have been uttered by the oracle of Apollo, at Delphos; at which place, as Pliny informs us, it was conspicuously written in letters of gold, over the door of the temple.

And this species of knowledge is also inculcated i

the Christian Scriptures, as most useful and necessary. "Examine yourselves," says Paul, "whether ye be in the faith; prove your own selves; know ye not your own selves?" And in the Old Testament, the value of this knowledge is also fully recognized, where we are exhorted "to commune with our own hearts,"—and "to keep our hearts with all diligence." And the possession of it is made an object of fervent prayer: "search me, O God, and know my heart, try me, and know my thoughts,"—"examine me, O Lord, and prove me, try my reins and my heart."

As this knowledge is necessary to all, so it is placed within the reach of all. But it cannot be acquired without diligent self-examination. To this duty there exists, in human nature a strong repugnance; partly from natural, and partly from moral causes; so that, by most, it is entirely neglected, to their exceeding great detriment. But, when it is attempted, we are in great danger of being misled by self-love and prejudice. To acquire any true knowledge of ourselves, some good degree of honesty and impartiality is essentially requisite. But an honest desire to arrive at the truth is not the only prerequisite to self-knowledge. The mind must be enlightened in regard to the standard of rectitude, to which we ought to be conformed. "The entrance of thy word giveth light." The word of God should dwell richly in us, and by the rules and principles of the sacred volume, we should form all our sentiments respecting ourselves. This is the candle of the Lord which searcheth the inward parts of man; and without such a lamp it would be as impossible to obtain any considerable degree of self-knowledge, as to distinguish the objects in a dark room, without a light. Self-examination, accompanied with a careful perusal of the Holy Scriptures, will lead us daily to a more thorough knowledge of our own character.

Beware of the common illusion of forming your estimate of yourselves, from the favourable opinions of those around you. They cannot know the secret principles from which you act; and flattery may have much influence in leading them to speak in your praise

Seize favourable opportunities of judging of the latent strength of your passions. The fact is, that until some new conjuncture or occasion elicits our feelings, we are as ignorant of what is within us, as other persons.

Study also your constitutional temperament, and consider attentively the power which particular objects and circumstances have over you. You may often learn even from your enemies and calumniators what are the weak points in your character.—They are sagacious in detecting faults; and, generally, have some shadow of pretext for what they allege against us. We may, therefore, derive more benefit from the sarcasms of our foes than from the flattery of our friends.

Learn, moreover, to form a correct estimate of your own abilities, as this is necessary to guide you in your undertakings.

III. BE careful to form good habits. Almost all permanent habits are contracted in youth; and these do in fact form the character of the man through life. It is Paley, I believe, who remarks, that we act from habit nine times, where we do once from deliberation. Little do young persons apprehend the momentous consequences of many of their most frequently repeated actions. Some habits are merely inconvenient, but have no moral quality; others affect the principles of our conduct; and become sources of good or evil, to an incalculable degree. As to the former, they should be avoided, as detracting from our comfort, and ultimately interfering with our usefulness; but the latter should be deprecated, as laying the foundation of a wicked character, and as standing in the way of all mental and moral improvement.

IV. BE particular and select in the company which you keep, and the friendships which you form. 'Tell me,' says the proverb, ' what company you keep, and I will tell you what you are.' 'Evil communications corrupt good manners.' Vice is more easily and extensively diffused by improper companions, than by all other means. As one infected sheep communicates disease to a whole flock; so one sinner often destroys much good, by corrupting all the youth who fall under his influence. When vicious men are possessed of wit and fascinating manners, their conversation is most dangerous to the young. We would entreat you, dear young friends, to form an intimacy with no one whose principles are suspicious. The friendship of profligate men is exceedingly dangerous. Listen not to their fair speeches, and warm professions of attachment. Fly from contact with them, as from one infected with the plague. Form no close alliance with such. No more think of taking them to your bosom, than you would a viper.—Gaze not on their beauty, nor suffer yourselves to be charmed with their fascination of manners. Under these specious appearances, a deleterious poison lurks.

'Be not unequally yoked together with unbelievers,' is the exhortation of scripture. And what can be more unseemly and incongruous, than for an amiable and virtuous woman to be indissolubly united to an unprincipled debauchee? Or, for a good man to be connected with a woman destitute of piety and virtue? Be especially careful, therefore, in forming alliances for life. Seek a connexion with the wise and good, and you will become wiser and better by converse with such.

V. ENDEAVOUR to acquire and maintain a good reputation. 'A good name is rather to be chosen than great riches.' A ruined fortune may be recovered, a lost reputation never. Young men are often laying the foundation of an unenviable reputation, while they are thinking of no such thing. They never dream that the character which they attain at school or college, will probably be as lasting as life. The youth who is known to be addicted to falsehood, knavery, treachery, &c., when arrived at the age of man, will be viewed by those who know him with distrust. A stain on the character is not easily washed out; at a distant period the faults and follies of youth may be revived to a man's confusion and injury. But especially is the female character exquisitely delicate. A small degree of imprudence will often fix a stigma on the gay young lady, which no subsequent sobriety can completely erase.

We do not mean, that the young should cherish a false sense of honour, which would lead them to fight and contend for reputation. No man ever secured or increased a good name, by shedding the vital blood of a human being. The reputation which we recommend must arise from a life of consistent and uniform well-doing. Prize such a character, as of inestimable value to your own peace, and as a most powerful means of usefulness. The most potent human engine of utility is influence; and this depends entirely on reputation.

VI. Manage your worldly concerns with economy and discretion. Avoid the inconvenience, embarrassment, and vexation of being in debt. Conduct your business with attention and diligence; and have your accounts in such a condition, that you will be at no loss to ascertain the true state of your affairs. Men often become unjust, and injurious to others, without having intended any such thing, merely by a confused and careless manner of transacting their business. Such a man, after a while, feels an unconquerable aversion to a scrutiny into his affairs. He shuts his eyes against the ruin which he is bringing on himself, and heedlessly rushes forward in the path which habit or fashion has rendered agreeable. When, at length, an exigence arrives, which constrains him to adopt some measure to extricate himself from his difficulties, he is placed under strong temptation to resort to a course which is not strictly honourable. He persuades himself, that if he can save his credit for the present, he will be able to rectify every thing, by diligence and good fortune, and to preserve his friends from suffering on his account. But these efforts to recover lost ground commonly prove ineffectual, and render the situation of the person more involved than before. He finds, at length, that he is sinking; and this discovery often produces a desperate recklessness. He plunges deeper and deeper into debt; and often drags to ruin, not only his own family, but some of his friends who confided too implicitly in his truth and integrity. It is also too common for men who have failed in trade, to resort to means for the support of a helpless family, which a sound moral faculty never can approve. The tempta tion arising from the tender love of wife and children is indeed very strong, but not invincible. In the commercial world, there are many illustrious examples of merit, honour, and the strictest probity, in men who had it in their power to defraud their creditors, or to deeply involve their confiding friends, but who chose rather to look haggard poverty in the face, and to see their beloved families descending from affluence into the vale of obscurity, than to be guilty of a dishonourable act. And in the long run this turns out more to the benefit of those persons, than any advantage obtained by a resort to shifts and evasions not entirely consistent with the highest integrity. He who sacrifices reputation for present comfort, buys it at too dear a rate. The merchant, who, when he fails, loses his reputation for truth and integrity, will meet with but little favour from the world, and will have very little chance of rising again. But he who has been unfortunate, and yet maintains his integrity, and preserves his character unsullied, is often able to enter again into business under favourable auspices; and is encouraged and aided in his attempts to gain a living, by men of wealth and standing; so, that such a man is often successful to such a degree, that he has it in his power to compensate those from whom benefit was derived in the day of his calamity. Beware of being governed by ambition in your commercial enterprises. The pride of doing a large business, and of being considered as at the head of the profession, seduces many aspiring young merchants: and greediness of gain tempts still more to engage in hazardous speculations, and to trade to an extent not authorized by the capital which they have at command. In this way bankruptcies become so common that the event ceases to excite much surprise. Families delicately educated, and long accustomed to the luxuries as well as the comforts of life, are reduced to poverty. Multitudes of such fa milies are found in our large commercial cities, who are really more properly the objects of benevolence, than the common beggar who clamorously solicits your charity. The real privations and sufferings of such are not fully known; for, from the desire of avoiding the contempt and the pity of vulgar minds, such persons spread a decent veil over their indigence, and prefer to pine secretly in want rather than to seek relief by a public disclosure of their necessities. The Christian philanthropist will, however, seek out such sufferers, and will contrive methods of bestowing relief upon them in a way consistent with the delicacy of their feelings.

The above remarks are particularly adapted to those who engage in commerce; but they are not inapplicable to others. It is true, integrity is the soul of a merchant; but it is a sterling quality which every man ought to possess; and all men are liable to be reduced to a state of indigence by a long series of untoward events. My counsel then is, that you commence and pursue business with prudence; and when unfortunate, that you so act as to preserve your integrity and your reputation, by resorting to no equivocal means of relief; but resolve to act in conformity with the strictest rules of justice and honour.

VII. Aim at consistency in your Christian character. There is a beauty in moral consistency which resembles the symmetry of a well proportioned building, where nothing is deficient, nothing redundant. Consistency can only be acquired and maintained by cultivating every part of the Christian character. The circle of virtues must be complete, without chasms or obliquities. A character well proportioned and nicely balanced in all its parts, we are not very frequently permitted to witness; for, while in one branch there is vigour, and even exuberance, in another there may be the appearance of feebleness and sterility. The man who is distinguished for virtues of a particular class is apt to be deficient in those which belong to a different class. This is so commonly the fact, that many entertain the opinion that the same person cannot excel in every virtue. Thus, it is not expected that the man of remarkable firmness and intrepidity, should at the same time be distinguished for meekness and gentleness. But after making due allowances for a difference of constitutional temperament, we must maintain, that there is not, nor can there be, any incompatibility between the several virtues of the Christian life. They are all branches of the same root, and the principle which affords nourishment to one, communicates its virtue to all. As all truth is harmonious, however it may, on a superficial and partial view, seem to be contradictory; so all the exercises of moral goodness are not only consistent, but assist and adorn each other. This is so much the case, that symmetry of Christian character has, by some distinguished casuistical writers, been laid down as a necessary evidence of genuineness; and it has been insisted on, as probable, that where one virtue seems to exist in great strength, while others are remarkably wanting, it is a mark of spuriousness. There is much reason in this view of the subject; for men are frequently found whose zeal blazes out ardently and conspicuously, so as to leave most others far back in the shade, while they are totally destitute of that humility, meekness, and brotherly kindness, which form an essential part of the Christian character. Some men are conscientious and punctilious in the performance of all the rites and external duties connected with the worship of God, who are inattentive to the obligations of strict justice and veracity in their intercourse with men: and on the other hand, many boast of their morality, and yet are notoriously inattentive to the duties of religion. Real Christians too, are often chargeable with inconsistency, which arises from a want of clear discernment of the rule of moral conduct, in its application to particular cases; for while the general principles of duty are plain, and easily understood by all, the ability to discriminate between right and wrong, in many complicated cases, is extremely rare. This delicate and correct perception of moral relations, can only be acquired by the divine blessing on our assiduous exertions. It is too commonly taken for granted, that Christian morals are a subject so easy, that all close study of it is unnecessary. This is an injurious mistake. Many of the deficiencies and inconsistencies of Christians, are owing to a want of clear and correct knowledge of the exact rule of moral conduct. On no subject will you find a greater diversity of opinion, than in regard to the lawfulness or unlawfulness of particular practices: and even good men are often thrown into difficulty and doubt, respecting the proper course to be pursued. But while many cases of inconsistency arise from ignorance of the exact standard of rectitude, more must be attributed to heedlessness and forgetfulness. Men do not act sufficiently from principle, but too much from custom, from fashion, and from habit. Thus many actions are performed without any inquiry into their moral character. There is an obtuseness in the moral sensibility which permits evils to pass without animadversion. Another cause of the inconsistency so commonly observed, is the prevalence which certain passions or appetites may obtain, in the time of temptation. The force of the internal principles of evil is not perceived, when the objects and circumstances favourable to their exercise, are absent. As the venomous adder seems to be harmless while chilled with cold, but soon manifests his malignity when brought near the fire; so sin often lies hid in the bosom, as though it were dead, until some exciting cause draws it forth into exercise; and then the person himself is surprised to find the strength of his own passions, above any thing which he had before conceived. Thus men often act, in certain circumstances, in a way altogether contrary to the general tenor of their conduct. It is by no means a fair inference from a single act of irregularity, that the person who is guilty of it has acted hypocritically in all the apparent good actions of his former life. The true explanation is, that principles of action which he has commonly been able to govern and restrain, acquire, in some unguarded moment, or under the power of some strong temptation, a force which his good principles are not at that moment strong enough to oppose. The man who is usually correct and orderly may thus be overtaken in a fault; and as all are liable to the same frailties, there should exist a disposition to receive and restore an offending brother, when he gives sufficient evidence of penitence. Man, at his best estate in this world, is an inconsistent creature. The only persons in whom this defect is not observed are the men who by grace live near to God, and exercise a constant jealousy and vigilance over themselves. But when faith is weak and inconstant, great inconsistencies will mar the beauty of the Christian character. Young persons ought, therefore, to begin early to exercise this vigilance, and to keep their hearts with all diligence, lest they be ensnared by their own passions, and overcome by the power of temptation. I counsel you then, my young friends, to aim at consistency. Cultivate assiduously every part of the Christian character; so that there may appear a beautiful proportion in your virtue.

The reflections to which I have been led in speaking of consistency of Christian character, suggest the importance of urging upon you the government of your passions. A man who has no control over his passions, is justly compared to a ship at sea, which is driven by fierce winds, while she neither is governed by the rudder nor steered by the compass. By indulgence, the passions gain strength very rapidly; and when once the habit of indulgence is fixed, the moral condition of the sinner is most deplorable, and almost desperate. To preserve consistency, it is necessary to be well acquainted with the weak points in our own character, to know something of the strength of our own passions, and to guard beforehand against the occasions and temptations which would be likely to cause us to act inconsistently with our Christian profession. Many men have successfully contended with their own passions, and although naturally of a hasty and irritable temper, have, by constant discipline, brought themselves into a habitual state of equanimity; so that however they may be conscious of the strugglings of the natural passions, they are kept so completely under restraint, that to others they do not seem to exist.—The anecdote which is related of Socrates and the physiognomist, is instructive on this point. When the latter, upon examining the lines of the philosopher's face, pronounced that he was a man of bad temper, and exceedingly irascible, the disciples of Socrates laughed him to scorn, as having betrayed the weakness of his art, by so totally mistaking the true disposition of their master; but he checked their ridicule, by acknowledging that his natural temper had been truly represented by the physiognomist, but that by the discipline of philosophy, he had been able to acquire such a mastery over his passions, that their existence was not apparent. To achieve a victory of this kind, is more honourable than to conquer in the field of battle; according to that of the wise man, "He that is slow to anger is better than the mighty; and he that ruleth his spirit, than he that taketh a city." And again, "He that hath no rule over his own spirit, is like a city that is broken down, and without walls." Learn then, my young friends, to bridle your passions, and govern your temper, from your earliest days.

VIII. BE contented with the station and circumstances in which Providence has placed you. Never repine at God's dealings towards you, nor envy those who are above you in worldly advantages. Consider not so much what you want, as what you have; and look less at those above you, than at those in inferior circumstances. Accustom yourselves to look on the bright, rather than the dark side of the picture. Indulge not in unreasonable fears, nor give way to feelings of despondency. Exercise fortitude, and maintain tranquillity of mind. Be not ruffled and disconcerted by every little cross event which may occur. Place not your happiness at the disposal of every one who may be disposed to speak an unkind word, or to do an unhandsome thing. Learn to possess your souls in patience, believing that when appearances are darkest, the dawn of a more comfortable day is near.

IX. LET your intercourse with men be marked by a strict and conscientious regard to truth, honour, justice, kindness and courtesy. We should certainly have recommended politeness, as a happy means of polishing social intercourse, and affording pleasure to those with whom you are conversant; but many are accustomed to connect an unpleasant idea with this word. But, surely, genuine politeness, if not itself a virtue, spreads a charm and a beauty over that which is virtuous. And, certainly, there is no merit in awkwardness and clownishness. But our chief object under this particular is to urge upon you a constant and punctilious regard to the social virtues. Be honest, be upright, sincere, men of your word, faithful to every trust, kind to every body, respectful where respect is due, generous according to your ability, grateful for benefits received, and delicate in the mode of conferring favours. Let your integrity be unsuspected. Never resort to any mean or underhand measure: but let your conduct and conversation be characterized by frankness and candour, by forbearance, and a spirit of indulgence and forgiveness. In short, "do unto others as you would have them do unto you."

X. LIVE not merely for yourselves, but also for the good of others. Selfishness contracts the soul, and hardens the heart. The man absorbed in selfish pursuits is incapable of the sweetest, noblest joys of which our nature is susceptible. The author of our being has ordained laws, according to which the most exquisite pleasure is connected, not with the direct pursuit of our own happiness, but with the exercise of benevolence. On this principle it is, that he who labours wholly for the benefit of others, and as it were forgets himself, is far happier than the man who makes himself the centre of all his affections, the sole object of all his exertions. On this principle it was, that our Saviour said, "It is more blessed to give, than to receive." Resolve, therefore, to lead lives of usefulness. Be indifferent to nothing which has any relation to the welfare of men. Be not afraid of diminishing your own happiness, by seeking that of others. Devise liberal things, and let not avarice shut up your hand from giving to him that needeth, and to promote the cause of piety and humanity.

XI. BE faithful and conscientious in the discharge

of all duties which arise out of the relations which you sustain to others. Relative duties are far more numerous than all others; because the occasions requiring their performance are constantly occurring. The duties of parents, of children, of brothers and sisters, of neighbours, of masters and servants, of teachers and pupils, of magistrates and citizens, of the learned professions, of trade, of the rich and the poor, occupy a very large portion of the time and attention of every man. And these furnish the proper test of character. 'He who is faithful in little, is faithful also in much.' And he who is not attentive to the daily recurring duties of his station, in vain claims the reputation of virtue or piety, by splendid acts of public beneficence. 'Though I give all my goods to feed the poor, and have not charity, it profiteth me nothing.'

XII. EXERCISE incessant vigilance against the dangers and temptations by which you are surrounded, and by which you will certainly be assailed. These dangers are too numerous to be specified in detail; but I will mention a few. Guard solicitously against all approaches towards infidelity. Reject unbelieving thoughts and skeptical doubts from the beginning. Even if the system of infidelity were true, it promises no comfort, and cannot possibly be serviceable to you. But the best security will be to study diligently the evidences of religion, and be ready to meet the cavils of infidelity at all points. Make yourselves well acquainted with the best authors on this subject, and let your faith rest on the firm ground of evidence.

Another danger against which you must be watchful, is pleasure—sensual pleasure. Worldly amusements, however innocent they may appear, are replete with hidden dangers. These scenes exhilarate the spirits, and excite the imagination, until reason and conscience are hushed, and the real end of living is forgotten. For the sake of pleasure, every thing important and sacred is neglected, and the most valuable part of human life wasted in unprofitable engagements. Beware then of the vortex of dissipation, and especially of the least approach towards the gulf of intem perance. On that slippery ground, many strong men have fallen, never to rise. The trophies of this insidious and destructive vice are widely spread on every side, and the wise and the good have come to the conclusion, that there is no effectual security against this enemy, but in a resolute and persevering abstinence from inebriating drink. Seek your happiness, dear youth, in the pursuit of useful objects, and in the performance of duty, and then you will be safe, and will have no reason to envy the votaries of sensual pleasure.

XIII. A COUNSEL, near akin to that which has been just given, is, "GOVERN YOUR TONGUE." More sin, it is probable, is committed, and more mischief done, by this small member, than in all other ways. The faculty of speech is one of our most useful endowments, but it is exceedingly liable to abuse. He who knows how to bridle his tongue, is, therefore, in Scripture, denominated "a perfect man;" and again, of him "who seemeth to be religious and bridleth not his tongue," it is declared that "that man's religion is vain." The words which we utter are a fair index of the moral state of the mind. "By thy words," saith our Lord, "shalt thou be justified, and by thy words shalt thou be condemned." Not only are sins of the tongue more numerous than others, but some of them are the most heinous of which man can be guilty—even that one sin which has no forgiveness, is a sin of the tongue.

Not only should all profaneness, obscenity, and falsehood, be put far away, but you should continually endeavour to render your conversation useful.—Be ever ready to communicate knowledge, to suggest profitable ideas, to recommend virtue and religion, to rebuke sin, and to give glory to God. Beware of evil-speaking. A habit of detraction is one of the worst which you can contract, and is always indicative of an envious and malignant heart. Instead of prostituting this active and useful member to the purposes of slander, employ it in defending the innocent and the injured.

Permit me to suggest the following brief rules for the government of the tongue. Avoid loquacity. "In the multitude of words there wanteth not sin." If you have nothing to communicate which can be useful, be silent. Think before you speak. How many painful anxieties would be prevented by obeying this simple, common-sense precept. Especially, be cautious about uttering any thing in the form of a promise, without consideration. Be conscientiously regardful of truth, even to a tittle, in all that you say. Never speak what will be likely to excite bad feelings, of any kind, in the minds of others. Be ready, on all suitable occasions, to give utterance to good sentiments, especially such as may be useful to the young. Listen respectfully to the opinions of others, but never fail to give your testimony modestly, but firmly, against error. "Let your speech be always with grace, seasoned with salt. Let no corrupt communication proceed out of your mouth, but that which is good to the use of edifying, that it may minister grace unto the hearers."

XIV. KEEP a good conscience. If wickedness had no other punishment than the stings of conscience which follow evil actions, it would be reason enough to induce every considerate man to avoid that which is productive of so much pain. No misery of which the human mind is susceptible is so intolerable and so irremediable as remorse of conscience. And it is liable to be renewed as often as the guilty action is distinctly recollected. It is true, the conscience, by means of error and repeated resistance to its dictates, may become callous—"seared as with a hot iron;" but this apparent death of moral sensibility, is no more than a sleep. At an unexpected time, and in circumstances the most inconvenient, conscience may be aroused, and may exert a more tremendous power than was ever before experienced. The long arrearages of sins committed, while no notice seemed to be taken of them, now demand and enforce consideration. Joseph's brethren seem to have almost forgotten their unnatural and cruel conduct in selling him as a slave into a foreign country; but when many years had elapsed, and they found themselves environed with difficulties and dangers in that very land, the remembrance of their crime painfully rushed upon their minds, and extorted from them mutual confessions of their guilt. "God," said they, "hath found out the iniquity of thy servants." "And they said one to another, we are verily guilty concerning our brother, in that we saw the anguish of his soul, when he besought us, and we would not hear; therefore is this distress come upon us." Men often endeavour to escape from the stings of a guilty conscience by a change of place; but the remedy is ineffectual. The transgressor may traverse the widest ocean, and transcend the loftiest mountains, and may bury himself in the dark recesses of the desert, but he cannot fly so far, nor conceal himself so effectually, as to escape from his tormentor. In some cases, the agonies of remorse have been so intolerable, that the guilty perpetrator of great wickedness has preferred 'strangling and death' to a miserable life, and has rushed uncalled into the presence of his Judge. And in other cases, men guilty of bloody crimes have found the pangs of remorse so intolerable that they have voluntarily given themselves up to justice; and by a voluntary confession, have convicted themselves, when no human witnesses were competent to prove their guilt. But what man is there who has not committed sins, the recollection of which gives him sensible pain? And such acts often stand out in strong relief in the retrospect of the past. No effort can obliterate such things from the memory. We may turn away our eyes from the disagreeable object; but the painful idea will return again; and thus men whose consciences are not seared, are haunted by guilt as by a troublesome ghost; and often their sins find them out, and stare them in the face, when danger threatens, or when calamity has overtaken them. Why moral sensibility should be so much more exquisite at some times than others, cannot be easily explained; but the fact is certain, and is probably familiar to the consciousness of all. There may indeed exist a morbid susceptibility, an unreasonable scrupulousness and terror of conscience, which is a real and distressing disease, and which yields only to physical remedies judiciously applied. Melancholy is not the effect of religious impressions; but is a state of mind of a most unhappy kind, produced by a derangement of the physical system, and which leads the subject of it to fix his thoughts on those things which are most awful and gloomy. The same is true in regard to insanity. Many people entertain strong prejudices against experimental religion, because they apprehend that it endangers the reason, and drives the timid and weak-minded into mania.

Now it is no doubt true, that any strong emotion or passion may, when there exists a predisposition to the disease, disturb the regular exercise of reason; but that this danger is greater to persons deeply exercised about religion than to others, is utterly without foundation. Fanaticism, it may be conceded, has a tendency to insanity. Indeed, it has long appeared to me, that fanaticism, especially in its mildest forms, is nothing else than a species of insanity. I have upon no other hypothesis been able to account for the opinions and conduct of some persons who have been led away into the excesses of enthusiasm. But what is the most effectual preservative from this kind of mental derangement? Is it irreligion, vice, and infidelity? By no means. Persons who take refuge in such things, find them to be " refuges of lies." The only effectual remedy against the misery of a disturbed mind and a guilty conscience, is true religion. For this wound the balm of Gilead is the only medicine which is proved by experience to be efficacious. He who is able to cherish a lively hope of happiness beyond the grave, who can look up to God as a reconciled Father, and who feels good will to all men, has surely within him the ingredients of a settled peace of mind. When I counsel you, my young friends, to keep a good conscience, I mean, that you should, in the first place, endeavour to obtain this inestimable blessing. by an application to " the blood of sprinkling." Until the soul is justified and sin pardoned, there can be no true peace of conscience. While the law remains unsatisfied for us, and denounces vengeance against us for our sins, what in the universe can give us peace? But when by faith the soul apprehends the atonement, and sees that it is commensurate to all the demands of the law, and that in the cross, justice is not only satisfied, but gloriously illustrated, it is at once relieved from the agony of guilt, and the peace of God which passeth understanding pervades the soul. The great secret of genuine peace is, therefore, living faith in the blood of Christ. But if you would preserve your conscience pure and enjoy peace, you must not only obtain forgiveness for the past, but must be very careful to sin no more in future. The law of God is exceeding broad, and if we would preserve peace of conscience, we must conform our actions to its precepts with assiduous and holy diligence.

A good conscience is always an enlightened conscience. Through error, a man may believe that he is doing God service, when he is persecuting his people; but such a conscience is not good. Men may act conscientiously, and yet act very wickedly. I suppose that all the devotees of the most absurd and impious superstition, act according to the dictates of conscience, even when they sacrifice human beings, and expose to death their own offspring, or themselves; but who would say that such a conscience was good? The correct knowledge of truth, therefore, lies at the foundation of a good conscience. Nothing is more important to man than the truth; therefore "buy the truth and sell it not." But too often conscience is not regarded when it correctly dictates what should be done or avoided. Amidst the cravings of appetite, the storm of the passions, and the incessant bustle of the world, the whispers of conscience are not heeded. In multitudes of instances, where persons do wrong, they have a premonition of the evil; or, at least, a suggestion, that it is proper to inquire and consider what duty is Some persons are conscientious in great matters, who, in comparatively small concerns, seem to have no moral discernment. The habit of consulting the moral sense in all things is of great importance. Before you act, consider; and beware of the false colouring which passion and self-interest throw around the subjects of duty. Lean to the safe side Where an action is of dubious character, do not venture upon it. Be fully persuaded in your own mind, " for whatsoever is not of faith is sin." Some persons are conscientious and punctilious about little things, but careless about the weightier matters of the law. This is the conscience of a hypocrite. Others have a mind ill at ease, because the festering wound of guilt has never been thoroughly probed and cleansed, but merely externally healed. Their repentance has not been deep enough, nor universal enough: some secret sin is still too much indulged. Now, while these are the facts, a good conscience is an impossible thing. Sincere penitence, humiliation and confession, are God's prescribed remedy, and where these are wanting the conscience will not be at peace.

Now whatever may be the infirmity or moral defect which cleaves to us, it is odious in the sight of God, and tends to grieve the Holy Spirit. In just judgment, we are left to darkness, barrenness, and misery, because we have not sufficiently desired deliverance from sin, but have made vain excuses for our own faults. I would then counsel you, especially, to cherish the motions of the Holy Comforter. By his divine influences alone, a good conscience can be maintained. And if you are sensible that you have grieved the Spirit, so that you are left comfortless, never rest until you again experience the peace and joy, which is the fruit of his indwelling.

XV. CULTIVATE peace. Next to the blessing of peace with God and in our own conscience, is that of peace with our fellow men. "As much as lieth in you, live peaceably with all men." And again, "Follow peace with all men." The true source of all the wars, contentions, and disturbances which are in the world, is the pride, the envy, the covetousness, and other evil passions of our nature. Eradicate these, and in their place introduce pure and kind affections, and you will experience a double peace—peace within, and peace without. Every Christian temper is friendly to peace. I know, indeed, that Christ says, that he came not to bring peace but a sword: but he refers not to the nature of his religion, but to the event which he foresaw would occur, from the perverse opposition of men, to that which is good. The genuine spirit and tendency of the gospel is beautifully and emphatically expressed in the angelic anthem, sung by the celestial choir at the nativity of our Saviour—" Glory to God in the highest, and on earth PEACE; good will to men." All the adopted sons of God are sons of peace; and are peace-makers. " Live in peace," says Paul, "and the God of peace shall be with you." Humility, meekness, and benevolence, must, from the nature of the case, have a mighty influence in producing and maintaining peace. For, as the apostle Peter argues, " who will harm you, if ye be followers of that which is good." No system was ever so well adapted to produce universal peace as Christianity; and the only reason why this effect has not followed its reception everywhere, is, that its true spirit has not been imbibed. Just so far as this blessed system is cordially embraced, it cuts up by the roots all causes of contention; except that which has for its subjects sin and error. It teaches us not only to love our friends and brethren but also our bitterest enemies; to return blessing for cursing, and kindness for ill treatment. Endeavour then, to cherish habitually those kind affections which lead to peace; and while you seek peace in your own souls, make it an object to promote peace in the world, and covet the blessedness which is pronounced to belong to peace-makers. Their high honour it is to be denominated "THE SONS OF GOD."

XVI. As "man is born to sorrow as the sparks fly upwards;" as no situation is exempt from the arrows of adversity, I would give it as a necessary counsel, to learn to bear affliction with fortitude and resignation. To dream of escaping what is appointed unto all, would be to fall wilfully into a dangerous delusion. Every man is vulnerable in so many points, that nothing short of a perpetual miracle could shield any one from the strokes of adversity. Indeed, piety of the most exalted kind does not secure its possessor from affliction and persecution. Christ himself suffered while in the world, and has left his followers a perfect example of holy fortitude, and filial submission to the will of God. When sorely pressed with the inconceivable load of our sins, so that his human soul could not have sustained it unless supported by the divine nature, his language was, "Not my will but thine be done." Those afflictions which are allotted to the people of God, are necessary parts of salutary discipline, intended to purify them from the dross of sin, and to prepare them for the service of God here, and his enjoyment in the world to come. They are, therefore, to them, not penal judgments, but fatherly chastisements, which, though "not joyous but grievous" for the present, "afterwards work for them the peaceable fruits of righteousness." But whatever may be our moral and spiritual condition, whether we are friends or enemies to God, we must be subject to various afflictions. This is a dying world. The nearest and dearest friends must part. Death sunders the tenderest ties, and often pierces the susceptible heart with a keener anguish, by directing the mortal stroke to a dear companion, or child, than if it had fallen on our own head. When I see youth rejoicing in the sanguine hopes and brilliant prospects which the deceitful world spreads out before them, I am prevented from sympathizing with their happy feelings, by the foresight of a speedy end to all their earthly pleasures. Their laughter will be converted into mourning. Their day of bright sunshine will soon be overcast with dark clouds; and all their brilliant prospects will be obscured, and the overwhelming gloom of sorrow will envelope them.

It is indeed, no part of wisdom to torment our minds with vain terrors of evils which are merely possible. Many persons suffer more in the apprehension of calamities, than they would if they were present. The imagination represents scenes of adversity in a hue darker than the reality. In regard to such evils, our Saviour has taught us not to yield to useless anxieties about the future, but to trust to Providence. "Let the morrow take care of itself." But that to which I would bring my youthful readers is a state of mind prepared for adversity, of whatever kind it may be; that they may not be taken by surprise when calamity falls upon them. And when the dark day of adversity arrives, be not dismayed, but put your trust in the Lord, and look to Him for strength to endure whatever may be laid upon you. Never permit yourselves to entertain hard thoughts of God, on account of any of his dispensations. They may be dark and mysterious, but they are all wise and good. What we cannot understand now, we shall be privileged to know hereafter. Exercise an uncomplaining submission to the will of God, as developed in the events of Providence. Believe steadfastly that all things are under the government of wisdom and goodness. Remember that whatever sufferings you may be called to endure, they are always less than your sins deserve: and consider, that these afflictive dispensations are fraught with rich, spiritual blessings. They are not only useful, but necessary. We should perish with a wicked world, if a kind Father did not make use of the rod to reclaim us from our wanderings. Besides, there is no situation in which we can more glorify God, than when in the furnace of affliction. The exercise of faith, and humble resignation, with patience and fortitude, under the pressure of heavy calamity, is most pleasing to God, and illustrates clearly the excellency of religion which is able to bear up the mind, and even render it cheerful, in the midst of scenes of trouble. Bear then, with cheerful submission, the load which may be laid upon you; and learn from Paul to rejoice even in the midst of tribulation. And not only bear your cross with cheerful resignation, but endeavor to extract from sorrow a rich spiritual blessing. While enjoying such an effectual means of grace, improve it to the utmost, to promote growth in the divine life. Be willing to suffer any pain which will render you more holy. Although we naturally desire uninterrupted prosperity, yet if the desire of our hearts was always given to us, it would prove ruinous.

And when schooled in adversity, you will be better qualified to sympathize with the children of sorrow, and better skilled in affording them comfort, than if you had no experience of trouble.

XVII. My next counsel is, that you set a high value upon your time. Time is short; and its flight is rapid. The swiftness of the lapse of time is proverbial in all languages. In Scripture, the life of man is compared to a multitude of things which quickly pass away, after making their appearance; as to a post, a weaver's shuttle, a vapour, a shadow, &c. All the works of man must be performed in time; and whatever acquisition is made of any good, it must be obtained in time. Time, therefore, is not only short, but precious. Every thing is suspended on its improvement, and it can only be improved when present; and it is no sooner present, than it is gone: so that whatever we do must be done quickly. The precious gift is sparingly parcelled out, by moments, but the succession of these is rapid and uninterrupted. Nothing can impede or retard the current of this stream. Whether we are awake or asleep, whether occupied or idle, whether we attend to the fact or not, we are borne along by a silent, but irresistible force. Our progressive motion in time, may be compared to the motion of the planet on which we dwell, of which we are entirely insensible; or, to that of a swift-sailing ship, which produces the illusion that all other objects are in motion, while we seem to be stationary. So in the journey of life, we pass from stage to stage, from infancy to childhood, from childhood to youth, from youth to mature age, and finally, ere we are aware of it, we find ourselves declining towards the last stage of earthly existence. The freshness and buoyancy of youth soon pass away: the autumn of life, with its "sere leaf," soon arrives; and next, and last, if disease or accident do not cut short our days, old age with its gray hairs, its wrinkles, its debility and pains, comes on apace. This period is described by the wise man, as one in which men are commonly disposed to be querulous, and to acknowledge that the days draw nigh in which they have no pleasure. "The keepers of the house tremble, and the strong men bow themselves, and the grinders cease because they are few, and those that look out of the windows are darkened. When men rise up at the noise of the bird—when all the daughters of music are brought low, and there shall be fears. And the almond tree shall flourish, and the grasshopper be a burden."

Time wasted can never be recovered. No man ever possessed the same moment twice. We are, indeed, exhorted "to redeem our time," but this relates to a right improvement of that which is to come; for this is the only possible way by which we can redeem what is irrevocably past. The counsels which I would offer to the young on this subject are: Think frequently and seriously on the inestimable value of time. Never forget that all that is dear and worthy of pursuit must be accomplished in the short span of time allotted to us here. Meditate also profoundly, and often, on the celerity of the flight of time. Now you are in the midst of youthful bloom, but soon this season will only exist in the dim shades of recollection, and unless it has been well improved, of bitter regret.

If you will make a wise improvement of your time, you must be prompt. Seize the fugitive moments as they fly; for, otherwise, they will pass away before you have commenced the work which is appropriated to them.

Diligence and constancy are essential to the right improvement of time. "Whatsoever thy hand findeth to do, do it with thy might." "Work while it is called to-day." Walk while you have the light; for the dark night rapidly approaches, when no work can be done.

Let every thing be done in its season. There is a time for all things; and let all things be done in order. The true order of things may be determined by their relative importance, and by the urgency of the case, or the loss which would probably be sustained by neglect.

If you would make the most of your time, learn to do one thing at once, and endeavour so to perform every work, as to accomplish it in the best possible manner. As you receive but one moment at once, it is a vain thing to think of doing more than one thing at one time; and if any work deserves your attention at all, it deserves to be well done. Confusion, hurry, and heedlessness, often so mar a business, that it would have been better to omit it altogether.

Beware of devolving the duty of to-day on to-morrow. This is called procrastination, which is said, justly, to be "the thief of time." Remember, that every day, and every hour, has its own appropriate work; but if that which should be done this day, is deferred until a future time, to say the least, there must be an inconvenient accumulation of duties in future. But as to-morrow is to every body uncertain, to suspend the acquisition of an important object on such a contingency, may be the occasion of losing forever the opportunity of receiving it. The rule of sound discretion is, never to put off till to-morrow, what ought to be done to-day.

XVIII. CHERISH and diligently cultivate genuine piety. "The fear of the Lord is the beginning of wisdom."

Early piety is the most beautiful spectacle in the world. Without piety all your morality, however useful to men, is but a shadow. It is a branch without a root. Religion, above every other acquisition, enriches and adorns the mind of man; and it is especially congenial with the natural susceptibilities of the youthful mind. The vivacity and versatility of youth, the tenderness and ardour of the affections in this age, exhibit piety to the best advantage. How delightful is it, to see the bosoms of the young swelling with the lively emotions of pure devotion! How beautiful is the tear of penitence or of holy joy, which glistens in the eye of tender youth! Think not, dear young people, that true religion will detract from your happiness. It is a reproach cast upon your Maker, to indulge such a thought. It cannot be. A God of goodness never required any thing of his creatures, which did not tend to their true felicity. Piety may indeed lead you to exchange the pleasures of the theatre and ball-room, for the purer joys of the church and prayer-meeting. It may turn your attention from books of mere idle fancy and fiction, to the word of God, which to a regenerated soul, is found to be sweeter than honey, and more excellent than the choicest gold; but this will add to your happiness, rather than diminish it. We would then affectionately and earnestly exhort and entreat you, to "remember now your Creator in the days of your youth." This will be your best security against all the dangers and temptations to which you are exposed; this will secure to you "the favour of God which is life, and his loving kindness which is better than life." Delay not your conversion; every day is lost time, which is not spent in the service of God. Besides, procrastination has proved ruinous to many. Eternity is at hand; the judgment day must be met, and how can we appear there, without piety? This is our only preparation and passport for heaven. Dear youth, be wise, and secure an inheritance among the saints in light. God invites you to be reconciled. Christ extends his arms of mercy to secure you. Angels are waiting to rejoice at your conversion, and to become your daily and nightly guardians. The doors of the church will be opened to receive you. The ministers of the gospel, and all the company of believers, will hail your entrance and will welcome you to the precious ordinances of God's house. And, finally, remember, that "now is the accepted time and the day of salvation."

XIX. SEEK divine direction and aid, by incessant, fervent prayer. You need grace to help you every day. Your own wisdom is folly, your own strength weakness, and your own righteousness altogether insufficient. "It is not in man that walketh to direct his steps." But if you lack wisdom, you are permitted to ask; and you have a gracious promise, that you shall receive. Whatever we need will be granted, if we humbly and believingly ask for it. "Ask and ye shall receive, seek and ye shall find, knock and it shall be opened unto you." "Be careful for nothing, but in every thing with prayer and supplication, with thanksgiving, let your requests be made known unto God."

Faith and prayer are our chief resource under all the various and heavy afflictions of this life. When a other refuges fail, God will hide his people who seek Him in his secret pavilion, and shelter them under the shadow of his wings. Prayer is essential to the existence and growth of the spiritual life. It is the breath of the new man. By this means he obtains quick relief from innumerable evils; and draws down from heaven blessings of the richest and sweetest kind. Possess your minds fully of the persuasion, that prayer is efficacious, when offered in faith and with importunity, to obtain the blessings which we need. God has made himself known as a hearer of prayer: yea, he has promised that we shall have, as far as may be for his glory and our good, whatever we ask. The most important events may be brought about by prayer. One righteous man, by fervent and effectual prayer, has been able to shut heaven and open it again. How often did Moses by his prayers avert the divine wrath from the people of Israel! That man who has access to a throne of grace will never want any thing which is really needful. " God will give grace and glory, and no good thing will he withhold from them that walk uprightly." "But He will be inquired of by the house of Israel for this thing that he may do it for them." Banish, as most unreasonable, the idea that prayer is a dull or melancholy business. Such a sentiment must have been invented by Satan; for it never could have been suggested by reason, or taught by experience. Intercourse with the greatest and best of all Beings must be a source of exalted pleasure; and surely, man can have no greater honour and privilege conferred upon him, than to be admitted to converse intimately and confidentially with the God whom angels adore. The experience of every saint attests, that " it is good to draw near to God;" and that " one day in his courts is better than a thousand." I need not be afraid, therefore, to counsel the young to cultivate the spirit of prayer, and to be constant in its exercise. "Pray without ceasing." " Be instant in prayer." It will not spoil your pleasures, but will open for you new sources of enjoyment, far more refined and satisfactory, than any which prayerless persons can possess. Prayer is the only method by which intercourse between heaven and earth can be kept open. Often, too, in the performance of this duty, a taste of heaven is brought down to earth; and the pious worshipper anticipates, in some degree, those joys which are ineffable and eternal.—Prayer will, moreover, be your most effectual guard against sin and the power of temptation:

> " For Satan trembles, when he sees
> The weakest saint upon his knees."

XX. I conclude my counsels to the young, by a serious and affectionate recommendation to every one who reads these pages, to make immediate preparation for death. I know that gay youth are unwilling to hear this subject mentioned. There is nothing which casts a greater damp upon their spirits, than the solemn fact that death must be encountered; and that no earthly possessions or circumstances can secure us from becoming his victims, on any day. But if it is acknowledged that this formidable evil is inevitable, and that the tenure by which we hold our grasp of life is very fragile, why should we act so unreasonably, and I may say, madly, as to shut our eyes against the danger? If, indeed, there was no way of preparing to meet this event, there might be some reason for turning away our thoughts from immediate destruction: but if by attention and exertion, it is possible to make preparation for death, then nothing can be conceived more insane, than to refuse to consider our latter end.—How often are we called to witness the decease of blooming youth, in the midst of all their pleasures and prospects! Such scenes have been exhibited within the observation of all of you. Dear friends and companions have been snatched away from the side of some of you. The grave has closed upon many whose prospects of long life were as favourable as those of their survivors. Now, my dear young friends, what has so frequently happened in relation to so many others, may take place with regard to some of you. This year you may be called to bid farewell to all your earthly prospects, and all your beloved relatives. The bare possibility of such an event ought to have the effect of engaging your most serious attention, and of leading you to immediate preparation. Do you ask what preparation is necessary? I answer, reconciliation with God, and a meetness for the employments and enjoyments of the heavenly state. Preparation for death includes repentance towards God for all our sins, trust in the Lord Jesus Christ and reliance on his atoning sacrifice, regeneration of heart, and reformation of life; and, finally, a lively exercise of piety, accompanied with a comfortable assurance of the divine favour. In short, genuine and lively piety forms the essence of the needed preparation. With this your death will be safe, and your happiness after death secure; but to render a death-bed not only safe but comfortable, you must have a strong faith, and clear evidence that your sins are forgiven, and that you have passed from death unto life. Be persuaded, then, before you give sleep to your eyes, to commence your return unto God, from whom like lost sheep you have strayed. "Prepare to meet your God." "Be ye also ready, for in such an hour as ye think not, the Son of man cometh."

Seek deliverance from the fear of death by a believing application to Him who came on purpose to deliver us from this bondage. With his presence and guidance we need fear no evil, even while passing through the gloomy valley and shadow of death. He is able by his rod and his staff to comfort us, and to make us conquerors over this last enemy.

COUNSELS TO CHRISTIAN MOTHERS.

WHEN I address myself to Christian Mothers, I do not mean to intimate that those who cannot with propriety be thus addressed, stand in no need of admonition. Alas! that in a Christian country there should be mothers who have nothing of the spirit of Christ. Young persons often promise themselves that they will attend to religion after they are married and settled in the world. How preposterous is this! It ought rather to be their resolution not to think of entering into a state involving such weighty responsibilities, and the exercise of so many virtues, until they have become the possessors of true religion. Without piety how is it possible for any woman rightly to fulfil the duties of a wife, and especially of a mother? Some correct views on this subject probably led the legislators of one of the provinces of Holland, as I have read some where, to enact a law, that whenever any persons applied to be united in marriage, they should produce evidence that they were in the full communion of the church. But this was a dangerous misapplication of a sound principle. Just as in the case of civil rulers, it is exceedingly important that they who are appointed to rule over men should be truly pious; but it is a sad mistake in legislation, to make the profession of religion a qualification for office. But while I would not have a law requiring piety as a qualification for entering into the band of matrimony, I would still insist upon it, that no woman, destitute of religion, is fit to become a wife and mother. Only think of it—an irreligious mother! If it were not so common, the very expression would excite emotions similar to those which we experience, when we hear of an irreligious minister of the gospel. I address Christian mothers, because from them only can I expect a patient hearing. I address Christian mothers, because all mothers ought to be sincere Christians. Is there a person on earth, whose mind is so perverted by prejudice, as not to perceive a congruity between piety and this tender relation? It was formerly a current opinion, even among infidels, in Virginia, that religion was an ornament and safeguard to a woman. I knew one distinguished man who had renounced all belief in the Christian religion himself, who encouraged it in his wife, and furnished her with all the necessary means of attending church; and when one of his friends complained to him, that his wife was becoming religious, which gave him great concern, he told him that he was a fool, for that nothing was more suitable and desirable, than that a wife should be pious. Even infidels are constrained, like the demons of old, to give their testimony in favour of Christ. Many irreligious men desire to obtain wives of genuine piety; and few intelligent men in our country would be pleased with a female infidel. Such a character was so rare in Virginia forty years ago, when infidelity abounded among the higher classes of men, that when a certain lady was pointed out as the advocate of deistical opinions, it created a revulsion of feeling in almost every mind. Here I take pleasure in saying, that in no class of society any where, have I found examples of more pure and elevated piety than among the ladies of Virginia. And I have reason to believe that these examples have rather been increased than diminished since I left my native State. It may, in an important sense, be said that the Commonwealth has been preserved from utter destruction by the prudence, purity and piety of Virginia mothers. They have been the salt which has arrested the progress of moral corruption in the mass of society. Accordingly, there is no country in the world, perhaps, where mothers are so much respected by their children, and have so great an influence over them. Ask almost any young Virginian, where he will look for the brightest examples of moral excellence, and his thoughts will turn at once to the character of pious females, and perhaps to his own mother, if she happens to be pious. I recollect a young gentleman, who, although he had an uncommonly pious mother, broke over all the restraints of his education, and became a professed infidel, and the advocate of licentiousness in its vilest forms; but a gracious God heard the unceasing prayers of his mother, and by means somewhat unusual, he was converted from the error of his ways. In speaking of his former career—which he evidently did with shame and humility—he said, "I could get over all arguments in defence of religion but one, and that I never could obviate, which was the pious example and conversation of my mother. When I had fortified myself against the truth, by the aid of Bolingbroke, Hume, and Voltaire; yet, whenever I thought of my mother, I had the secret conviction which nothing could remove, that there was a reality in religion."

I could soon fill my paper with salutary precepts for mothers; but this is not exactly what is wanted. Knowledge as to maternal duty, is widely diffused. The theory of education, as it falls under the direction of mothers, is perhaps sufficiently understood by most. What I aim at, is "to stir up their pure minds by way of remembrance," or in other words, to arouse them to the consideration of the importance of the station which they occupy, and to persuade them to exert that influence which they possess. I have often heard pious females complain that they had little or nothing in their power, and they felt as if they were almost useless members of society. This is an egregious miscalculation. Their influence is silent and spreads imperceptibly, but it is real and effective. Piety is like light, which cannot be hid. The more it seeks concealment, and retires from public notice, the more brightly it shines. Female influence only ceases, or operates unfavourably, when women depart from their own proper sphere; or when they endeavour to obtrude themselves upon the notice and admiration of the pub tic. As we are shocked with infidelity in a female, so female ambition is odious. Let the devoted mother exert herself in her own proper sphere, which is in the retirement of the domestic circle, and in constant and devout attendance on the worship of God. Let her look well to the affairs of her household. Let her manifest her benignity and forbearance in the steady government of her children and servants. Let her set an example of order, neatness, industry, and hospitality, and she will have enough to do. Every hour, and almost every minute, will furnish opportunity for the exercise of some virtue; and that Eye which goes every where, will graciously notice and bring to light too, those acts which are cheerfully and conscientiously performed. A mother cannot be placed in a more interesting field of labour, than in the midst of a large circle of children. Here is her appropriate sphere of action. Here she has work enough to occupy her heart and hands.

But some will be ready to think this is a narrow field in which to labour. They wish to act on a larger scale, and do something which will *tell* on the destinies of men—something more intimately connected with the conversion of the world. Some few women, by the possession of peculiar talents, and by being placed in peculiar circumstances, have been able to accomplish so much that the world has been filled with their fame. Such was the brilliant course of Mrs. Hannah More, who by her benevolent exertions, and by her writings, became the benefactress of the human race. And such is now the luminous orbit in which Mrs. Fry moves. But it falls to the lot of very few of either sex to do good on what may be called a national scale. And if all should aim at such achievements, very little would be done. Much the larger part of the female sex must be contented to cultivate the small garden which providence has committed to them. But as the mothers in ancient Israel were solicitous to bear sons, in hope that they might enjoy the honour and unspeakable pleasure of giving birth to the promised Messiah, so mothers *now* may cherish the pleasing hope that of the first fruit of their womb, God will raise up men of renown, eminent ministers, devoted missionaries, distinguished philanthropists, wise statesmen, or even men of humble, exemplary piety in retired life. Hannah waited with God for her Samuel; and no doubt before the child was born, she consecrated him to God, from whom she received him; and when she embraced him in her arms, and nursed him at her breast, she continually darted up petitions for God's blessing upon his own precious gift. And O! how richly was she rewarded. I have read or heard that some one asked an uncommonly devout woman, how it happened that all her children became pious at an age so early. The good woman modestly disclaimed all merit or agency in the affair; but said she, "as many children as I have nursed, I never took one of them to my breast, to afford it the necessary nourishment, but at the same time I lifted up my heart in prayer to God for his blessing on the dear little infant." Would not this be a good rule for mothers universally to observe? Who can tell what the effect would be on the next generation? The question is often asked, "By whom shall Jacob arise?" One answers one thing, and one another; but if I may be permitted to give a partial answer, though I believe a true one, I would say, BY PIOUS MOTHERS. Yes, as a woman had the unspeakable blessing of being the mother of our LORD AND SAVIOUR; so woman, collectively, shall be the mother of the church. Ten thousand Loises and Eunices will, at the same time, be training their little Timothys on the knee, and with sweet and persuasive speech, instilling into their opening minds, the words of those "HOLY SCRIPTURES, which are able to make them wise unto salvation, through faith which is in Christ Jesus." A genuine and thorough reformation must commence in the family, which is the foundation of all social institutions, civil and religious. Here is the root, whence springs the whole tree with all its spreading and towering branches. And if true religion, to be general, must begin in the domestic circle, to whom will belong the chief agency and the most distinguished honour? Undoubtedly to pious mothers. Theirs must be the hands which plant the precious seed—theirs the prayers and tears which water the growing plant—theirs the kind, seasonable, and well adapted instructions, which distil into the tender, susceptible mind like the gentle rain on the tender grass, or the more imperceptible dew upon the thirsty plant. Those are not the most important lectures which are, with solemn pomp, delivered in the schools; but those which flow sweetly from the affectionate lips of mothers to their docile and interested group of little ones, gathered around their knees. No eloquence equals that of a sensible and pious mother, because no impressions made by human speech are so deep and indelible. These lessons, whether she knows it or not, she is engraving on fleshly tablets, from which the inscription can never wholly be obliterated. Impression after impression may be made on the same, but these have the advantage of being first and deepest; and when all the others are gone, these will be left. In visiting a family, belonging to my charge in Philadelphia, I observed a very brisk but old woman bringing chips into the house in her apron. I asked the lady of the house who it was. "It is my mother," said she, "but she no longer knows me." Upon inquiry, I found that she had forgotten every thing except what had occurred in her early life. And though she had left Switzerland when a girl of fourteen, and had not spoken the German language since that time, yet she now repeats her German prayers aloud every night.

It would be difficult to draw a definite line of distinction between a good mother and a good wife. The character of the latter must have an important bearing on that of the former. For a woman to perform her part well when united with a worthy and affectionate husband is comparatively easy; but when a pious woman of refined and susceptible feelings is connected with a man, whose true character and temper have been destroyed by habits of intoxication—when she is treated with brutal tyranny, and even cruelty, to preserve equanimity, and to perform the duties of an obedient, respectful wife, requires the exercise of much self-denial; and such a situation is one peculiarly painful and trying to a pious mother; but it is one to which many excellent women, in our day, have been subjected. But the greater the trial, the more grace is wanted; and the brighter the character, which is enabled with meekness and fortitude, to bear up under such a burden. If such a calamity should come on a woman of refined feelings at once, it would be overwhelming; but she is gradually prepared for the worst, and learns to discipline her passions, so as to exhibit no temper unsuitable to her station, and the tender relation of a wife. She avoids reproaches, and in her mouth there are no reproofs. Some change in her appearance, and occasional spells of bitter weeping, when alone, will not escape the jealous eye of a drunkard; and it is not improbable that such symptoms of deep distress as these, will only serve to provoke his ire, and cause him to rage more furiously, when under the influence of his inebriating cups. And what can she say to her children as they become capable of observation? She never mentions the subject to them, if it can be avoided; and when necessary, with no remarks which would tend to lessen their respect for an unworthy parent. She conceals from his children the faults and ill-treatment of the father as much as possible. And to all other persons, however intimate their mutual friendship, her lips are sealed. This is the difficulty of patiently bearing this heavy burden, that it must be borne alone, in silence, without the usual relief derived from venting our sorrows into the bosom of a faithful, sympathizing friend. I know of no condition in human life, free from guilt, which is more deplorable than that of a lady of education, piety, and sensibility, tied to a brutal husband, who is seldom in his right mind; or who, though for a season he may refrain, yet has his paroxysms of the worst species of insanity, to which our race is subject. This leads me to remark, that the very best view which a wife can take of such a case, is to consider it a real madness, and to feel and act just as if it was the effect of some physical cause. However difficult the practice of duty may be in such circumstances, I have observed not a few examples of such consummate prudence, Christian fortitude, and meek forbearance, as excited my admiration. As gold is purified by the fire of the furnace, so it is probable that some women, under the pressure of such afflictions rise to an eminence of piety, to which in other circum stances they never could have attained.

But I must not indulge myself in speaking in a strain too laudatory of Christian mothers. Some have great weaknesses, the effects of which upon the character and destinies of their children are very unhappy. I recollect to have once been acquainted with a Virginia planter, of the best old stamp. He was rich, hospitable, kind hearted, and better than all, truly pious. When he heard the gospel, his whole soul seemed to be laid open to the impression of the truth; and so susceptible was he, that often while the man of God described the love of a Saviour, the large, and not unmanly tear, would trickle down his cheek. He was a man without guile; and you always might know where to find him. But I was grieved and surprised to find that his sons were all profligates. By drinking and gambling and other vices, they soon ruined their reputation, wasted their estates, injured their health, and shortened their lives. In searching for the cause of this wide departure from the example of a good and affectionate father, I traced it to the injudicious indulgence of a fond mother. Not that she wished her sons to become dissipated; but when they did wrong, she carefully concealed their conduct from their father, connived at their vices, and afforded them facilities of gratifying their corrupt propensities, by plentifully supplying them with money. And with such care were their vices concealed from the unsuspecting father, that the first knowledge which he obtained was, when his sons' ruin was completed, and their habits so fixed, that all regard to decorum was laid aside, and even the displeasure of a father could be braved.

Another class of mothers, happily not numerous, injure their children by a discipline too rigorous. They expect by external restraints and confinements to preserve them from temptation. The general principle is good, but may be pushed too far. A gradual exposure to such temptations as must be encountered in the world, is safer than for a son to be suddenly subjected to the whole influence of the world at once. If children dislike the severity of the discipline under which they are placed, they will be ingenious in finding opportunities of evading a yoke which they do not like to bear. And when they get free from parental restraint, they will be apt to run to greater excess than others.

While sober, consistent piety in mothers has a powerful and lasting effect on children, fanaticism has a contrary tendency. The children of parents who indulge in extravagant expressions of religious feeling, and whose religion comes on in violent paroxysms, are, in most cases, devoid of reverence for sacred things, and often show a disregard of moral principle. It is exceedingly important in the education and discipline of children, not to confound their notions of right and wrong by treating little matters with the same seriousness and severity as great. Our instructions and conduct towards children, should be such as to present to their minds, virtues and vices, according to a just graduation. If we pursue a peccadillo with as much severity as a great crime, the danger is, that a great crime will be committed with as little sense of its evil as a fault of the minor class. It is also dangerous to proclaim a crusade against some one vice, and magnify its evil beyond all comparison, while other vices equally or more malignant, pass unnoticed. So one virtue or duty may be held up so continually, and placed in such bold relief, that other virtues, equally important and valuable, are left concealed in the back ground. As in the Christian character, symmetry or a due proportion of every grace, is essential to perfection; so in teaching morality, a strict regard should be had to the magnitude and proportion of every part of the system

Let all vice be treated as vice; but let not all vices be treated as equal; so let every virtue occupy its proper place, and fill its due space.

It is a good rule, even in the government of children, not to legislate too much. Vex them not with trivial and unnecessary rules. Train them to govern themselves as much as possible. That child who is obedient only when the eye of the parent is on it, has not been properly managed. Allow children liberty in such things as are innocent, and to which they are inclined by the instinct of nature. It is a poor, short-sighted plan to keep children moping all day over their books; they learn far more that is valuable while sporting in the fields, than we can teach them by such a process in the house. It is wonderful how much they learn without effort, both of words and things.

We may even exceed the mark by inculcating religion upon their tender minds too incessantly. Mothers should watch the favourable moment for instilling religious instruction. One sentence at the favourable moment is better than a long lecture at an unseasonable time. Holiness cannot be rendered pleasing to the natural heart, but religious instruction may be made interesting. Indirect methods of reaching the conscience are often better than the more direct. Occasional remarks not seeming to be intended for them, are often noticed and remembered; especially conversation with respectable strangers in their presence, has a wonderful effect. Let your children come early into company, that they may hear—that is, if the conversation be edifying. By eliciting remarks on certain subjects from ministers and other respectable persons in the hearing of children, you will be likely to produce greater effect, than if the same things were addressed directly to them by their parents.

Family slander is an evil against which mothers cannot too sedulously guard. There are some families who are extremely cautious about speaking evil of their neighbours out of their own houses; but there they feel privileged; and in the presence of their children, allow themselves great liberties in traducing the characters of those with whom they are living, ostensibly, in the habits of friendly intercourse. This is not only an evil habit, and readily contracted by children, but it is the most effectual method of teaching them to play the hypocrite, by constantly assuming the appearance of friendship, and using the language of kindness, when a contrary feeling is habitually cherished. It is impossible to entertain sentiments of true friendship towards those whom we are in the practice of maligning every day. O mothers, guard your children against this common vice; so freely indulged, and so little criminated by many.

Akin to this, but less malignant, is the practice of ridiculing the foibles, and caricaturing the imperfections or personal defects of our friends. In some whole families there exists a talent for mimicry: they can so exactly imitate the tones, gestures, attitudes and manners of others, that the exercise of this faculty becomes a source of much amusement at the expense of their neighbours; especially when the quality or action imitated is a little exaggerated or distorted. This propensity should be carefully and resolutely repressed in young persons. It is very apt to occasion a separation or alienation of affection among friends: for who among us is willing to be laughed at for the entertainment of others?

There is no one thing on which mothers should insist more uniformly and peremptorily, than that their children should tell the truth, the whole truth, and nothing but the truth. Lying above all other things may be said to be the vice of children. "We go astray from the womb, speaking lies." Children soon learn that others cannot look into their hearts: they will often therefore say what they know is not true, from the confidence that they cannot be detected. Keep a vigilant eye on this matter, and pass not slightly over an offence of this kind. Many worthy parents, I have observed, seem to know little, or care little about the habit of fibbing, in their children. Manifest by every proper means your utter detestation of lying, in all its kinds and degrees.

I would also caution mothers against the foolish ambition of trying to make prodigies of their children; and against the vanity of so exaggerating their smart speeches and exploits as to make them appear to be prodigies. I would not be so rigid as to prohibit mothers from speaking of their own dear offspring; for out of the abundance of the heart the mouth will speak; but I may advise you not to make your children the everlasting theme of your conversation, morning, noon, and night. Rest assured, that other people do not take as much interest in the subject as you do. And while I would commend those mothers who are diligent in the instruction of their children, I would respectfully say, be thankful that they are not idiots, nor deformed, nor destitute of the common senses of human nature; but be not anxious that they should be thought prodigies. Children may be so trained as to perform wonders, but what good can come of it? Do we not see pigs trained in the same way? Exercise a salutary discipline towards your children, even with the rod, when it is necessary; but let this species of discipline be the last resort, and used rather seldom. It is far better than a dark room, or starvation, or any thing which keeps the child a long time in a bad humour. But carefully avoid chastisement in the heat of passion, for this will do your children more harm than good. Keep your children as long as you can in your own house. Domestic feeling is a sacred tie, which should be preserved fresh and strong, as long as possible. Often, mothers lose all their influence over sons by their being sent abroad to school. Have as much of your children's education, therefore, conducted at home, as is practicable. Be assured, that no place is so favourable to the good feelings and morals of the young, as the family circle, unless the family be destitute of religion and virtue; and for such I do not now write. Boarding schools, for girls, may be useful,— but I would advise you to keep your daughters at home, under your own eye,—and when they go to school in the day, let them come home at night. You may possibly find a better school by sending them abroad, but the sacrifice is too great; and the risk of evil habits and evil sentiments is not small. And as to your sons, if they must go abroad, place them in the family of some pious man, and under the maternal care of some pious woman, where they may find a substitute for parental attention. While absent, let them return home as frequently as may be, that what I have called the 'domestic' feeling may be preserved. If your sons must be put to a trade, or become clerks in a store or counting-house, be very particular as to the character and conscientious fidelity of their master. It is lamentable to see, how youth in these circumstances are neglected; and how they are exposed to temptations, from which it is hardly possible they should escape without guilt and contamination.

I would earnestly recommend it to mothers to keep up a correspondence, by letter, with their children when removed from the domestic roof: a single word of admonition and warning, from a mother, might be the means of reclaiming a beloved son from the verge of a precipice. But whatever else you neglect, omit not to follow your children, when absent, with your daily prayers. Very often, this is the only thing which is left to mothers. Their children are either removed far from them; or, if near, they have lost their influence over them. But there is ONE, who is near to them, and who can influence them. O mothers! plead for your dear offspring at the throne of grace, travail in birth for them, a second time. God is gracious. God will regard the fervent, importunate cry of Christian mothers. Bespeak also the prayers of friends. Get them to unite with you in social prayer. This leads me to speak of those societies, called "Maternal Associations." If prudently and humbly conducted, they are calculated to be eminently useful. Let all parade and ostentation be avoided, and mothers may meet and pray for their dear children, as often as they are disposed.

LETTER TO A MOURNING, AFFLICTED WIDOW.

My Dear Friend,—What a change in your circumstances and worldly prospects within a short time! A few months since, you appeared to be carried along in the full tide of prosperity. Every thing seemed to smile around you, and probably you had no anticipation of the sad reverse which has occurred. Blessed with health and abundance; happy in the possession and regard of an excellent husband, and in seeing around you lovely and promising children, who were the joy of your heart. But now, alas! you are a bereaved, desolate widow;—you have experienced the greatest loss which you could experience of any earthly possession;—and, to increase the calamity, (for afflictions are apt to come in clusters,) another stroke has fallen on you, so that you have sorrow upon sorrow. Under such afflicting circumstances, what can I say to alleviate your distress? I am afraid that I can do no more than to express my tender sympathy. Though far off from the scene of your suffering, I feel for you—I could weep with you. Officious efforts to check the swelling torrent of grief, on such occasions, are injudicious, and rather tend to aggravate than relieve our misery. Nature must have its course. Tears, if deep-rooted grief does not prevent, furnish almost the only mitigation of which the mourner is susceptible: and what nature demands, God does not forbid. There is no sin in the feelings of lively sorrow, which such bereavements produce. The blessed Saviour did indeed forbid the daughters of Jerusalem to weep for him, because he had undertaken to bear the curse of God for us, without alleviation; but he tells them to weep for themselves and their children. He did also exhort the bereaved widow of Nain not to weep; but the reason of this was, that he intended immediately to restore to life her only son, then lying dead before her. When our blessed Lord came to Bethany, and found the two sisters, Martha and Mary, in a state of deep distress, on account of the recent death of their only brother (the support and protector of the family), does he forbid their tears? No: the compassionate Jesus weeps with them! How interesting, how amiable, does the kind condescension and tender sympathy of the Son of God towards this afflicted family appear! They had reason to be surprised at his conduct beforehand, because, when they sent for him, he delayed coming until their brother was dead. His motive for this delay, they understood not; but, when he came, they both remarked with sorrowful regret, "Lord, if thou hadst been here, my brother had not died." And when he answered, "Thy brother shall rise again," they still had no other apprehension of his meaning, than that he should arise at the last day. But his benevolent purpose was to restore to them their beloved brother, by raising him from the grave, where he had lain four days. But so deeply was his compassionate heart affected by the sight of the tears and distress of his beloved friends, that he not only wept with them, but groaned in his spirit, and was troubled, and said, "where have you laid him?" And before he would enter the house to rest himself after his journey, he must visit the grave of his friend, that he might at once relieve the aching hearts of these pious women. But no such relief can now be expected. Jesus, the almighty Saviour, who is "the resurrection and the life," no longer sojourns among men. But it should still be a consolation to mourners, that, though exalted at the right hand of God, the compassionate Redeemer is accessible, and that his tender sympathy is still retained; "for we have not an High Priest who cannot be touched with a feeling of our infirmities." He knows as well what his disciples suffer, as if he were upon earth; and is as able to aid them and to comfort them in all their sorrows. I cannot, then, give you better advice, than to "look unto Jesus"—"who, for the joy set before him, endured the cross, despising the shame, and is now set down at the right hand of God." I know of no consideration which is more effectual to reconcile us to bear with submission our heaviest afflictions, than the contemplation of our divine Redeemer wading through floods of sorrow for our sake; yea, overwhelmed with a weight of distress which pressed him to the ground in a bloody agony, and caused him to cry out with an exceeding bitter cry, "My soul is exceeding sorrowful, even unto death;" and on the cross to exclaim, "My God, my God, why hast thou forsaken me?" "Did Jesus thus suffer, and shall I repine?" He was the Son of God: he was holy, harmless, undefiled, and separate from sinners; and yet for our sake, he bore this infinite pressure of grief. This suggests another consideration, which I have always found, when I could feel its force, to have a powerful effect in repressing a murmuring and repining disposition. It is, that we suffer less than we deserve. God afflicts us, it may be, severely; but his strokes are lighter than our sins. If it were not for his unmerited mercy, we should now be in hell.

Add to this, that God does not willingly afflict: he takes no pleasure in the sufferings of any of his creatures, much less in the sorrows of his children; but he chastises them for their real good. Why some are so much more afflicted than others, we do not know; but we do know, "that all things work together for good to them that love God;" and that, although "no chastening for the present is joyous, but grievous, yet afterwards it yieldeth the peaceable fruit of righteousness unto them who are exercised thereby." The afflicted mourner finds it hard to believe this promise, and cannot see how it is possible that such a calamity should be of any benefit. But God's word is to be credited in opposition to our own feelings, and to all appearances. He has ways of working which we do not now understand, but shall know hereafter. He can make our bitterest anguish a salutary medicine for our diseased souls. Our whole course througn this world is intended to be a state of trial and discipline; and therefore it is ordained, that " through much tribulation, we must enter the kingdom." And all who are seen standing on Mount Zion, clothed in white robes and palms in their hands, had "come out of great tribulation."

Another consideration of great weight in reconciling us to our lot is, the shortness of time, and our nearness to the joys of heaven. When, by faith, we can form some just estimate of this matter, the keenest sufferings and most distressing bereavements, sink into insignificance. Who in our times suffer as did the primitive Christians? and yet Paul calls their afflictions light and momentary. And well may we be satisfied to bear them; "for they work out for us a far more exceeding and eternal weight of glory." And again, he says, " the sufferings of this present time are not worthy to be compared with the glory which shall be revealed in us." And it is reasonable to think that "the rest that remaineth for the people of God," will be enjoyed with a higher zest, by those who pass into heaven from a state of affliction, than by others.

I know, indeed, that by this visitation of God, your worldly prospects are sadly clouded; and you may feel yourself to be in a deplorably helpless condition. Unaccustomed to manage or preside, you are thrown into distressing perplexity whenever you reflect upon your condition. But I entreat you not to indulge these gloomy forebodings. God has a way by which you and your little family can be supported. He will guide, protect, and bless you, if you confide in Him. You are, indeed, in an unfriendly world, and will frequently meet with selfish and unfeeling men, who will not scruple to take advantage of your ignorance of the affairs of the world; but a "judge of the fatherless and widow is God;" and he invites you in a peculiar manner to make him your refuge. "Leave," says he, "thy fatherless children, and I will preserve them, AND LET YOUR WIDOWS TRUST IN ME." Take shelter under the covert of his wings, and commit yourself entirely into his hand, and he will never leave nor forsake you. The more you get into the habit of seeing to your own affairs, and transacting your own business, the better it will be for you. Nothing will preserve you more effectually from melancholy and dejection, than constant occupation. Females are often found to possess a talent for business, which neither they nor others ever suspected. Accept the kind aid of friends, but do not depend upon it. If necessary, engage in some business that will help to support you. Teaching children is a peculiarly suitable employment for a widow who has children of her own to be educated. Widows who reside in towns and cities are often enabled to obtain the means of subsistence by taking genteel boarders. Know exactly what your income is, and be sure to keep within it in your expenses. Debt is ruinous to all, and especially to widows. Take counsel from judicious friends; but seek, in all cases, direction from the Lord. Be strict in the government of your children. Make them obey you implicitly, while they are young, and do not spoil them by indulgence. But I do not recommend severity. Of this, however, you will be in no danger. Inculcate religion upon their minds, and pray much for them. Teach them, when old enough, the loss they have sustained, and impress upon their minds the necessity of sobriety and frugality. "Bring them up in the nurture and admonition of the Lord."

LETTER TO A BEREAVED WIDOWER.

My Dear Afflicted Friend—Since I heard of your bereavement, by which "the desire of your eyes" has been taken away from you by a sudden stroke, I have thought often of you, and resolved to write you a letter of condolence; but perhaps, every effort to soothe your sorrow, at present, will prove ineffectual. It is not improbable, that the only relief which I can afford you under the heavy calamity which a mysterious providence has laid upon you, will arise from the mere expression of my affectionate sympathy. I know that your loss is great; and that your heart is more rent and broken than I, who have never experienced a similar bereavement, can conceive. I admit that your loss is irreparable. The beloved wife of your youth, and the object of your earliest affection, whose chaste and reciprocal affection cemented an union which nothing but death could dissolve, and which made her as necessary to your comfort as your own heart, is gone. Her worth as an affectionate companion and most intimate friend, could only be fully known to yourself. She was, indeed, like a guardian angel, who was ever present to aid you; and although she was careful never to leave her own proper sphere, to obtrude her opinion in matters of which she was no competent judge; yet, in innumerable cases, when your spirit was too much excited, or even exasperated, by the rude collisions with the world, she has gently and almost imperceptibly kept you back from rash expressions and precipitate acts, to which your disposition is, in such circumstances, somewhat inclined. Even when she did not speak a word, the example of her meekness and gentleness has been the means of restraining you, or recalling you to a sense of your Christian duty. If I should attempt to lessen your feeling of the greatness of your loss, I should but mock your sincere and deep-rooted grief. No; the chasm made in your earthly enjoyments can never, in any event, be completely filled. That this is indeed the true state of the case, I cannot but feel, when I think of your dear little motherless children. Their loss surely cannot be made up. They can never have a second mother. God has implanted the genuine maternal feeling in no heart, but that of the real mother. I can imagine the desolate feeling of helplessness and wretchedness which spreads over your soul with an overwhelming weight, whenever you look on these beloved babes, who are too young to be fully sensible of the greatness of their bereavement; and especially when you gaze upon the little stranger, of whom it can scarcely be said, that she ever saw her mother. No one feels more dependent and helpless, in such circumstances, than a father, much occupied with the important concerns of the public. And did not kind female friends come to his assistance, he would be almost ready to despair. But these are the occasions in which the interpositions of Providence are most remarkable. Help comes seasonably, when no helpers seem to be near; and it comes often from unexpected quarters. I have often wondered at the tenderness and assiduity of female nurses, and their cheerful performance of painful services, when their prospect of remuneration was small. I have little doubt, but that already, although your affliction is so recent, you have had much cause to adore the kind workings of a benignant Providence in your behalf. Your cup is not one of unmixed misery. In the midst of judgment there is mercy. God hitherto has provided for your necessities, and will still provide. Let your trust in Him be constant and unwavering. Although the stroke which has laid you low, and clothed you, as it were, with sackcloth and ashes, must be attended, upon every reflection, with piercing anguish; yet let one idea be ever prominent in your mind, while thinking on this mournful subject: "it is my Father's hand which has inflicted this wound, and caused this pain; and He doth not afflict willingly, nor grieve the children of men." The uninterrupted and uncommon prosperity which has hitherto attended you, makes this stroke doubly distressing. From your youth, you seem to have enjoyed the peculiar care of Providence. Though early deprived of the watchful care of an excellent father, you found friends who almost supplied the place of a father; who not only provided for your bodily wants, but took care of your education; and I do not know that your advantages could have been greater, had your good father continued to live. And since you have become a man, and entered into that course of life which you were permitted to choose for yourself, I know of no one, in the same line, who has been more successful in his pursuits, or who has been able to conciliate more effectually the public favour. Indeed, until this sad event, in a moment, dashed the cup of worldly prosperity, you might be said to have been like a favourite child, dandled on the knee, and exposed to no rude blasts of adversity. But however pleasing such scenes of prosperity, and however ardently we cling to worldly comforts, it is a fact confirmed by general experience, that a long continuance of such a state is not favourable to the growth of piety. The heart hardens in this continual sunshine. Imperceptibly we lose the abiding, practical sense of our entire dependence and weakness, and are prone to say, like the royal psalmist, "My mountain stands strong, I shall never be moved." And in such a state, we not only have a weak impression of our feebleness and dependence, but a greatly diminished sense of our own sinfulness. And we know that a deep feeling of our wretched depravity lies at the foundation of "repentance towards God, and faith in our Lord Jesus Christ," and of every lively exercise of piety. It is then good—it is necessary, to have the blindness of our minds and the hardness of our hearts removed by some means. Our love of ease would have it done in some less painful manner. We are willing to obtain the blessing, but not to endure the chastisement connected with it. We love health, but utterly dislike the medicine suited to restore it. But could not God carry on his people's sanctification without inflicting upon them wounds so deep and painful? What he can do is not the question. He is a sovereign, and doth what he will, and requires submission on our part. "Be still and know that I am God." "Hear the rod, and him that hath appointed it." It is enough for us to be assured, that this is God's usual and appointed method of leading his chosen people to the heavenly Canaan. They must first pass through the briers and thorns of the wilderness. Through much tribulation they must enter the kingdom. Although severe afflictions are sometimes sent principally as a trial of faith, patience and submission, as we learn from the example of Job, yet most men, who know themselves, will not be at a loss for reasons to consider their own afflictions as chastisements. One of the first salutary effects of the rod, is to stir up to thorough self-examination. It leads to "great searchings of heart," awakens the sleeping conscience, and dispels the illusion which worldly prosperity had imperceptibly spread over the mind. The wounded soul starts and trembles, and takes a retrospect of the course which has been pursued. If pride, or avarice, or luxury has been too much indulged, and has led to unchristian behaviour, those indulgences and those actions (the turpitude of which was concealed,) now stand forth in bold relief, in the view of the awakened mind; and the penitent backslider falls prostrate, confesses the enormity and ingratitude of his sins, and earnestly cries to God for mercy and for healing. Alas! when we are at ease, and living in prosperity, how cold and careless are we in our devotional exercises! Engrossed with worldly business, and too well satisfied with creature comforts, we forget God, and lose sight of heaven. From this state of alienation we are seldom reclaimed by the word alone. Indeed, in such a frame, the truth can scarcely be said to have access to our minds. But when the severe stroke of our Father's rod is experienced, we begin to feel with keen sensibility, and to pray with unwonted fervency and importunity. And the afflicted child of God thus arrested, convinced and humbled, cannot rest until he obtains some new evidence of reconciliation—some manifestation of the love and favour of his offended Father

My dear sir, this affliction, severe as it is, may here after appear to have been in its consequences, a most important blessing. In the view of it you may cry out, "It was good for me to be afflicted; for before I was afflicted, I went astray, but now I keep thy statutes." This dispensation may be not only useful but necessary. It is not extravagant, nor inconsistent with the unchangeableness of God's purpose of mercy to his people to say, that severe chastisements may be indispensably necessary to their salvation. His promise of eternal life to believers is not irrespective of the appropriate means. The apostle Peter speaks of a *need be*, that some should "be in heaviness through manifold temptation;" "that the trial of your faith," says he, "being much more precious than of gold that perisheth, though it be tried by fire, might be found unto praise and honour and glory, at the appearing of Jesus Christ." And Paul exalts the value and efficacy of afflictions above all comparison, when he says, "These light afflictions, which are but for a moment, work out for us a far more exceeding and eternal weight of glory." But observe, he calls them all light and momentary—that is, in comparison with eternal blessedness. As he says, in another place, "For I reckon that the sufferings of this present time, are not worthy to be compared with the glory which shall be revealed in us." Is not the fact, that we are so cast down and overwhelmed with afflictions, an evidence of the weakness of our faith? If eternity was in full view, should we be so deeply affected with our bereavements; especially, when we have good reason to hope that our departed friends are happy in heaven? They are only gone before to the place whither we hope soon to follow them. I would say then, "gird up the loins of your mind." You are in the vigour of life, and in the midst of your days, and your Lord has much work for you to do. The talents which he has committed to you, should be most diligently improved. The best cure for grief is, unceasing activity in the cause of the Redeemer. I seem to feel assured that this will be a new era in your life; and although you have not been idle, nor unconcerned for the glory of your Master, yet methinks the remainder of your days will be far more fruitful than the past. I do trust that your light will burn with a more bright and steady flame. Henceforth you will not be liable to look for a paradise on this side heaven. And you will be more disposed than ever before, to concentrate your affections on those things which are above. And as God's people are a poor and afflicted people, for the most part, he may be preparing you to be a comforter of the mourners in Zion; for none are qualified for this office, but such as, having tasted the bitter cup of sorrow, have been made partakers also of divine consolation,—as Paul says to the Corinthians, "Blessed be God, even the Father of our Lord Jesus Christ, the Father of mercies and God of all comfort; who comforteth us in all our tribulations, that we may be able to comfort them which are in any trouble, by the comfort wherewith we ourselves are comforted of God."

It would be utterly superfluous to dissuade you from thinking soon of a second marriage. Your own feelings render every such idea abhorrent to your mind. Perhaps it is indelicate and unkind to mention the subject at all; but, as human feelings undergo a great change in the lapse of a few months, and I may not have the opportunity of speaking to you again, I would say, be not hasty in this matter. Consider long, and pray much over the subject, before you determine to place a step-mother over your children. I do not wish to lay any heavy burthen on your shoulders. I do not mean to say that it may not be a duty in due time to seek another companion; but I do say, proceed cautiously and conscientiously in this business. I do believe that many make a sad mistake in entering a second time into the bonds of wedlock. As a prudent wife comes from the Lord, ask counsel of Him.

THE END.

www.ingramcontent.com/pod-product-compliance
Lightning Source LLC
Chambersburg PA
CBHW020105020526
44112CB00033B/922